LAUGH AGAIN

HOPE AGAIN

TWO BOOKS *to* INSPIRE
A JOY-FILLED LIFE

CHARLES R. SWINDOLL

THOMAS NELSON
Since 1798

NASHVILLE   DALLAS   MEXICO CITY   RIO DE JANEIRO

Published in Nashville, Tennessee, by Thomas Nelson. Thomas Nelson is a registered trademark of Thomas Nelson, Inc.

Thomas Nelson, Inc., titles may be purchased in bulk for educational, business, fund-raising, or sales promotional use. For information, please e-mail SpecialMarkets@ThomasNelson.com.

Unless otherwise noted, Scripture quotations are taken from the NEW AMERICAN STANDARD BIBLE®. © The Lockman Foundation 1960, 1962, 1963, 1968, 1971, 1972, 1973, 1975, 1977. Used by permission.

Scripture quotations marked NIV are from the HOLY BIBLE: NEW INTERNATIONAL VERSION®. © 1973, 1978, 1984 by International Bible Society. Used by permission of Zondervan Publishing House. All rights reserved.

Scripture quotations marked PHILLIPS are from J. B. Phillips: THE NEW TESTAMENT IN MODERN ENGLISH, Revised Edition. © J. B. Phillips 1958, 1960, 1972. Used by permission of Macmillan Publishing Co., Inc.

Scripture quotations marked TEV are from Today's English Version. © American Bible Society 1966, 1971, 1976, 1992.

Scripture quotations marked TLB are from *The Living Bible.* © 1971. Used by permission of Tyndale House Publishers, Inc., Wheaton, Illinois 60189. All rights reserved.

Scripture quotations marked KJV are from The King James Version of the Bible. Public Domain.

Scripture quotations marked MSG are from *The Message* by Eugene H. Peterson. © 1993, 1994, 1995, 1996, 2000. Used by permission of NavPress Publishing Group. All rights reserved.

ISBN: 978-1-4002-8061-2
ISBN: 978-1-4002-0271-3 (tp)

Printed in the United States of America

11 12 13 RRD 6 5 4 3 2

LAUGH AGAIN

This book is affectionately dedicated to
Al and Margaret Sanders
and
Jon and Peggy Campbell
with gratitude for their unselfish devotion
to the radio ministry of
Insight for Living.
It was the Sanderses' vision that launched the broadcasts and
the Campbells' commitment that sustained it during its infancy.
Because of their tireless involvement in and appreciation for the
ministry, I find myself encouraged and invigorated.
And because of their spirit of outrageous joy,
our times together are often punctuated
with fun and laughter.

Ken Davis
Super Sheep

Contents

Acknowledgments

The closest a man can come to understanding childbirth is by writing a book. Passing a kidney stone ranks right up there. I've had four of those, but that's another story.

The process of this particular bookbirth has been unusually delightful and relatively free of pain. Maybe after my many literary "kids," I'm getting the hang of it.

Those who have served as midwives are among the best in the business. Byron Williamson, Kip Jordan, Ernie Owen, and David Moberg not only rejoiced to know I was "expecting," but they also helped name the baby and provided a colorful jacket for it to wear. In fact the whole atmosphere they brought to the delivery center was so pleasant, I found myself forgetting that it was supposed to be a difficult process.

Once again I want to express my gratitude to Helen Peters, who cleaned the baby up after it was born. Thanks also to Judith Markham and Ed Curtis, who again gave me wise editorial counsel and helpful ideas that would keep this newborn healthy and strong. As all my immediate family members either came by to visit or phoned to see how I was feeling as I was moving closer to the delivery date, my spirits were lifted. And, as always, Cynthia was especially encouraging, knowing how concerned I was that this be a happy baby and free of needless complications. Her supportive presence proved crucial.

Finally, I want to declare my gratitude to my Great Physician who allowed me to meet with Him regularly without a scheduled appointment, provided excellent checkups, demonstrated compassionate care, and assisted me in the birth with gentleness and joy. I knew that everything was going to be all right because immediately after it was born, something most unusual happened. Unlike all the others I have had, when this one finally came, it laughed.

ACKNOWLEDGMENTS

I am grateful for you too. As you hold it close and enjoy its company, may its happy disposition bring you hours of delight. All I ask is that when it smiles at you, smile back. If you do, you will soon discover a bond forming between the two of you that will lighten your load and help you relax. It is a funny thing about babies—the way they curl up in our arms and become a part of our lives the longer we spend time with them. Who knows? At some unguarded moment when you two are all alone and no one else is watching, you might even break down and laugh again. Feel free. As a proud parent, I can't think of anything that would please me more.

Introduction

This is a book about joy.

It's about relaxing more, releasing the tension, and refusing to let circumstances dominate our attitudes.

It's about looking at life from a perspective other than today's traffic report or the evening news.

It's about giving the child within us permission to look at life and laugh again.

Can you remember when life was joyful? I certainly can. Without any knowledge of the Dow index or the drop in the gross national product or the accelerating crime rate in twenty-five of America's largest cities or the decreasing healthcare benefits in our country's major companies, I was happy as a clam. I neither expected much nor needed much. Life was meant to be enjoyed, not endured, and therefore every day I found something—anything—to laugh about.

Through my childlike eyes people were funny. (When did they stop being funny?) When school was out and those lazy, hazy months of summer were mine to enjoy, there was usually enough water somewhere to swim in or a basketball to dribble and shoot hoops with or old roller skates to make a sidewalk scooter from or a crazy joke to laugh at. (When did everything get so serious?)

Our family of five had no wealth whatsoever. My dad was a machinist, often holding down more than one job to make ends meet. My mom stayed home and did all the stuff moms do at home with three strong-willed, very normal kids. Since there was a war raging on both sides of our nation, we had a truckload of reasons not to laugh . . . but I never got that message back then. I was a child and I did what children did. We made music in our family, another relaxing pastime. Some of it was pretty scary music, but we laughed that off too. And why not? I mean, it wasn't like we were rehearsing for Carnegie Hall or hoping to get a scholarship to the Juilliard School of Music. We were just having fun . . . and music was the creative avenue we chose to enjoy. Boy, did we ever! (Why have families stopped making music together?)

While flying back from Germany in the fall of 1990, I met a delightful man with an infectious laugh. It was fascinating talking with him, and as we talked, I learned that he speaks all around the world and brings joy to thousands, from prisoners to presidents. As you can imagine, he had one great story after another, most of them true and each one absolutely hilarious. Our multiple-hour flight passed all too quickly.

One of my favorites makes me smile every time I recall it. This incident actually happened to the woman who passed the story on to my fellow passenger.

Grandmother and granddaughter, a very precocious ten-year-old, were spending the evening together when the little girl suddenly looked up and asked, "How old are you, Grandma?"

The woman was a bit startled at the question, but knowing her granddaughter's quick little mind, she wasn't completely shocked.

"Well, honey, when you're my age you don't share your age with anybody."

"Aw, go ahead, Grandma . . . you can trust me."

"No, dear, I never tell anyone my age."

Grandmother got busy fixing supper and then she suddenly realized the little darling had been absent for about twenty minutes—much too long! She checked around upstairs in her bedroom and found that her granddaughter had dumped the contents of her grandmother's purse on top of her bed and was sitting in the midst of the mess, holding her grandmother's driver's license.

When their eyes met, the child announced: "Grandma, you're seventy-six."

"Why, yes, I am. How did you know that?"

"I found the date of your birthday here on your driver's license and subtracted that year from this year . . . so you're seventy-six!"

"That's right, sweetheart. Your grandmother is seventy-six."

The little girl continued staring at the driver's license and added, "You also made an F in sex, Grandma."[1]

Sometime between that age of childhood innocence and right now, life has become a grim marathon of frowns—a major downer for far too many adults. I suppose some would justify the change by saying, "When you become an adult, you need to be responsible." I couldn't agree more.

I had that drilled into my cranium. (Remember, my middle name starts with an R!) Furthermore, the same ones would say, "Being responsible includes living in a world of reality, and not everything in the real world is funny. Some things are extremely difficult." Again, you're speaking my language. Having been engaged in real-world responsibilities for well over thirty of my adult years, I am painfully aware that this old earth is not a giant bowl of cherries. They continue, "So then, since adulthood is a synonym for responsibility, and since reality certainly includes difficulties, we have no business laughing and enjoying life." It's at that point of the logic I balk. I simply do not accept the notion that responsible people in touch with the real world must wear a perpetually serious countenance and adopt a grim-reaper mind-set.

My question is this: When did a healthy, well-exercised sense of humor get sacrificed on the altar of adulthood? Who says becoming a responsible adult means a long face and an all-serious attitude toward life?

My vocation is among the most serious of all professions. As a minister of the gospel and as the senior pastor of a church, the concerns I deal with are eternal in dimension. A week doesn't pass without my hearing of or dealing with life in the raw. Marriages are breaking, homes are splitting, people are hurting, jobs are dissolving, addictions of every description are rampant. Needs are enormous, endless, and heartrending.

The most natural thing for me to do would be to allow all of that to rob me of my joy and to change me from a person who has always found humor in life—as well as laughed loudly and often—into a stoic, frowning clergyman. No thanks.

Matter of fact, that was my number-one fear many years ago. Thinking that I must look somber and be ultraserious twenty-four hours a day resulted in my resisting a call into the ministry for several years. Most of the men of the cloth I had seen looked like they held down a night job at the local mortuary. I distinctly remember wrestling with the Lord over all this before He pinned me to the mat and whispered a promise in my ear that forced me to surrender: "You can faithfully serve Me, but you can still be yourself. Being My servant doesn't require you to stop laughing." That did it. That one statement won me over. I finally decided I could be one of God's spokesmen and still enjoy life.

Not too many years ago when I started the radio program, "Insight for Living," I flashed back to that original call, and I decided to be myself, no matter what. Whether the broadcasts succeeded or fizzled, I wasn't about to come across as some superpious religious fanatic, intense about everything. When things struck me funny, I would laugh.

One of the listeners wrote in and commented: "I appreciate your program. The teaching has helped a lot . . . but I have one major request: Don't stop laughing! You can stop teaching and you can make whatever other changes you wish on your broadcasts, but *don't stop laughing!*" And then she added: "Yours is the only laughter that comes into our home."

Her ten concluding words have been ringing in my ears for years. What a sad commentary on our times! In many homes—dare I say most?—laughter has left. Joy that was once a vital ingredient in family life has departed, leaving hearts that seldom sing, lips that rarely smile, eyes that no longer dance, and faces that say no. Tragically, this is true in Christian homes as well as non-Christian . . . maybe more so.

It is my firm conviction that a change is urgently needed—which is precisely why I have taken up my pen to write again. A couple of years ago I warned of grace killers and urged my readers to be courageous as they joined the ranks of the grace-awakening movement. Many have done so. Later, I became concerned about all the complicated busywork many were adding to the life of faith, so I exposed the faith crushers as I encouraged folks to cultivate a simple-faith lifestyle. Many have done that as well. Maybe you are one of them. Now, within the last few months, I have felt an urgent need to take on the joy stealers who have been growing in number, especially since recessionary times have hit. Bad news has become the only news.

Tough times are upon us, no question. The issues we all face are both serious and real. But are they so intense, so all-important, so serious and all-consuming that every expression of joy should be eclipsed? Sorry, I can't buy that.

This book will tell you why. Hopefully, as a result of traveling through its pages with me, you will gain a new perspective on how to view these harsh days. Best of all, many of your childlike qualities will emerge and soften the blows of your intensity. Your attitude will change. You will find yourself changing. How will you know? There is one telltale sign. You'll begin to laugh again.

Chuck Swindoll
Fullerton, California

Where there is no belief in the soul, there is very little drama. . . .
Either one is serious about salvation or one is not. And it is well to
realize that the maximum amount of seriousness admits the
maximum amount of comedy. Only if we are secure in our beliefs
can we see the comical side of the universe.

Flannery O'Connor

1

Your Smile Increases Your Face Value

I know of no greater need today than the need for joy. Unexplainable, contagious joy. Outrageous joy.

When that kind of joy comes aboard our ship of life, it brings good things with it—like enthusiasm for life, determination to hang in there, and a strong desire to be of encouragement to others. Such qualities make our voyage bearable when we hit the open seas and encounter high waves of hardship that tend to demoralize and paralyze. There is nothing better than a joyful attitude when we face the challenges life throws at us.

Someone once asked Mother Teresa what the job description was for anyone who might wish to work alongside her in the grimy streets and narrow alleys of Calcutta. Without hesitation she mentioned only two things: the desire to work hard and a joyful attitude. It has been my observation that both of those qualities are rare. But the second is much rarer than the first. Diligence may be difficult to find, but compared to an attitude of genuine joy, hard work is commonplace.

Unfortunately, our country seems to have lost its spirit of fun and laughter. Recently, a Brazilian student studying at a nearby university told me that what amazes him the most about Americans is their lack of laughter. I found myself unable to refute his criticism.

Just look around. Bad news, long faces, and heavy hearts are everywhere—even in houses of worship (especially in houses of worship!). Much of today's popular music, which many consider a voice for the nation's conscience, promotes misery, sorrow, and despair. If sex and violence are not the pulsating themes of a new film, some expression of unhappiness is. Newspapers thrive on tragedies and calamities, lost jobs and horrible accidents. The same can be said of televised newscasts. Even the weather reports give their primary attention to storms, droughts, and blizzards. Tomorrow is usually "partly cloudy with a 20 percent chance of rain," never "mostly clear with an 80 percent chance of sunshine." If you do find laughter on the tube, either it is a recorded laugh track on some stupid sitcom or a stand-up comedian telling filthy jokes.

This long-faced, heavy-hearted attitude has now invaded the ranks of Christianity. Visit most congregations today and search for signs of happiness and sounds of laughter and you often come away disappointed. Joy, "the gigantic secret of the Christian,"[1] is conspicuous by its absence. I find that *inexcusable*. The one place on earth where life's burdens should be lighter, where faces should reflect genuine enthusiasm, and where attitudes should be uplifting and positive is the place this is least likely to be true.

When I was a teenager, the most popular business advertisements in magazines read: SEND ME A MAN WHO READS. As much as I value reading and applaud the resourcefulness of those who pore over the pages of good books, I think today's slogan should be: SEND ME ONE WHOSE ATTITUDE IS POSITIVE, WHOSE HEART IS FULL OF CHEER, WHOSE FACE SHOUTS YES!

Some critics would be quick to point out that our times do not lend themselves to such an easygoing philosophy. They would ask, "Under these circumstances how could I be anything but grim?" To which I reply, "What are you doing *under* the circumstances?" Correct me if I'm wrong, but isn't the Christian life to be lived *above* the circumstances?

A good sense of humor enlivens our discernment and guards us from taking everything that comes down the pike too seriously. By remaining lighthearted, by refusing to allow our intensity to gain the mastery of our minds, we remain much more objective. Ogden Nash believed this so strongly that he claimed that if the German people had had a sense of humor, they would never have let Adolf Hitler deceive them. Instead, the first time they saw some fellow goose-stepping and raising a stiff arm to shout, "Heil Hitler," they'd have keeled over in side-splitting laughter.[2]

People who live above their circumstances usually possess a well-developed sense of humor, because in the final analysis that's what gets them through. I met such a person at a conference in Chicago several years ago. We shared a few laughs following a session at which I had spoken. Later she wrote to thank me for adding a little joy to an otherwise ultra-serious conference. (Why are most Christian conferences ultraserious?)

Her note was a delightfully creative expression of one who had learned to balance the dark side of life with the bright glow of laughter. Among other things she wrote:

> Humor has done a lot to help me in my spiritual life. How could I have reared twelve children, starting at age 32, and not have had a sense of humor?
>
> After your talk last night I was enjoying some relaxed moments with friends I met here. I told them I got married at age 31. I didn't worry about getting married; I left my future in God's hands. But I must tell you, every night I hung a pair of men's pants on my bed and knelt down to pray this prayer:
>
>> Father in heaven, hear my prayer,
>> And grant it if you can;
>> I've hung a pair of trousers here,
>> Please fill them with a man.

The following Sunday I read that humorous letter to our congregation, and they enjoyed it immensely. I happened to notice the different reactions of a father and his teenaged son. The dad laughed out loud, but the son seemed preoccupied. On that particular Sunday the mother of this family had stayed home with their sick daughter. Obviously neither father nor son mentioned the story, because a couple of weeks later I received a note from the mother:

> Dear Chuck:
>
> I am wondering if I should be worried about something. It has to do with our son. For the last two weeks I have noticed that before our son turns the light out and goes to sleep at night, he hangs a woman's bikini over the foot of his bed. . . . Should I be concerned about this?

I assured her there was nothing to worry about. And I am pleased to announce that the young man recently married, so maybe the swimsuit idea works.

Perhaps you find yourself among those in the if-only group. You say you would laugh *if only* you had more money . . . *if only* you had more talent or were more beautiful . . . *if only* you could find a more fulfilling job? I challenge those excuses. Just as more money never made anyone generous and more talent never made anyone grateful, more of *anything* never made anyone joyful.

The happiest people are rarely the richest, or the most beautiful, or even the most talented. Happy people do not depend on excitement and 'fun' supplied by externals. They enjoy the fundamental, often very simple, things of life. They waste no time thinking other pastures are greener; they do not yearn for yesterday or tomorrow. They savor the moment, glad to be alive, enjoying their work, their families, the good things around them. They are adaptable; they can bend with the wind, adjust to the changes in their times, enjoy the contests of life, and feel themselves in harmony with the world. Their eyes are turned outward; they are aware, compassionate. They have the capacity to love.[3]

Without exception, people who consistently laugh do so *in spite of*, seldom *because of* anything. They pursue fun rather than wait for it to knock on their door in the middle of the day. Such infectiously joyful believers have no trouble convincing people around them that Christianity is real and that Christ can transform a life. Joy is the flag that flies above the castle of their hearts, announcing that the King is in residence.

MEET A MAN WHO SMILED IN SPITE OF . . .

There once lived a man who became a Christian as an adult and left the security and popularity of his former career as an official religious leader to follow Christ. The persecution that became his companion throughout the remaining years of his life was just the beginning of his woes. Misunderstood, misrepresented, and maligned though he was, he pressed on joyfully. On top of all that, he suffered from a physical ailment so severe he called it a "thorn in my flesh"—possibly an intense form of migraine that revisited him on a regular basis.

By now you know I am referring to Saul of Tarsus, later called Paul. Though not one to dwell on his own difficulties or ailments, the apostle did take the time to record a partial list of them in his second letter to his friends in Corinth. Compared to his first-century contemporaries, he was—

. . . in far more imprisonments, beaten times without number, often in danger of death. Five times I received from the Jews thirty-nine lashes. Three times I was beaten with rods, once I was stoned, three times I was shipwrecked, a night and a day I have spent in the deep. I have been on frequent journeys, in dangers from rivers, dangers from robbers, dangers from my countrymen, dangers from the Gentiles, dangers in the city, dangers in the wilderness, dangers on the sea, dangers among false brethren; I have been in labor and hardship, through many sleepless nights, in hunger and thirst, often without food, in cold and exposure. Apart from such external things, there is the daily pressure upon me of concern for all the churches.

2 Corinthians 11:23–28

Although that was enough hardship for several people, Paul's journey got even more rugged as time passed. Finally he was arrested and placed under the constant guard of Roman soldiers to whom he was chained for two years. While he was allowed to remain "in his own rented quarters" (Acts 28:30), the restrictions must have been irksome to a man who had grown accustomed to traveling and to the freedom of setting his own agenda. Yet not once do we read of his losing patience and throwing a fit. On the contrary, he saw his circumstances as an opportunity to make Christ known as he made the best of his situation.

READ A LETTER WITH A SURPRISING THEME

Interestingly, Paul wrote several letters during those years of house arrest, one of which was addressed to a group of Christians living in Philippi. It is an amazing letter, made even more remarkable by its recurring theme—joy. Think of it! Written by a man who had known excruciating hardship and pain, living in a restricted setting chained to a Roman soldier, the letter to the Philippians resounds with joy! Attitudes of joy and contentment are woven through the tapestry of these 104 verses like threads of silver. Rather than wallowing in self-pity or calling on his friends to help him escape or at least find relief from these restrictions, Paul sent a surprisingly lighthearted message. And on top of all that, time and again he urges the Philippians (and his readers) to be people of joy.

Let me show you how that same theme resurfaces in each of the four chapters.

- When Paul prayed for the Philippians, he smiled!

    I thank my God in all my remembrance of you, always offering prayer *with joy* in my every prayer for you all.

    Philippians 1:3–4

- When he compared staying on earth to leaving and going to be with Jesus, he was joyful.

> For to me, to live is Christ, and to die is gain. But if I am to live on in the flesh, this will mean fruitful labor for me; and I do not know which to choose. But I am hard-pressed from both directions, having the desire to depart and be with Christ, for that is very much better; yet to remain on in the flesh is more necessary for your sake. And convinced of this, I know that I shall remain and continue with you all for your progress and *joy in the faith.*

> *Philippians 1:21–25*

- When he encouraged them to work together in harmony, his own joy intensified as he envisioned that happening.

> If therefore there is any encouragement in Christ, if there is any consolation of love, if there is any fellowship of the Spirit, if any affection and compassion, *make my joy complete* by being of the same mind, maintaining the same love, united in spirit, intent on one purpose.

> *Philippians 2:1–2*

- When he mentioned sending a friend to them, he urged them to receive the man joyfully.

> But I thought it necessary to send to you Epaphroditus, my brother and fellow worker and fellow soldier, who is also your messenger and minister to my need; because he was longing for you all and was distressed because you had heard that he was sick. For indeed he was sick to the point of death, but God had mercy on him, and not on him only but also on me, lest I should have sorrow upon sorrow. Therefore I have sent him all the more eagerly in order that when you see him again you may *rejoice* and I may be less concerned about you. Therefore *receive him in the Lord with all joy,* and hold men like him in high regard.

> *Philippians 2:25–29*

- When he communicated the "core" of what he wanted them to hear from him, he was full of joy.

> Finally, my brethren, *rejoice in the Lord.* To write the same things again is no trouble to me, and it is a safeguard for you.

> *Philippians 3:1*

- When he was drawing his letter to a close, he returned to the same message of joy:

  Rejoice in the Lord always; again I will say, rejoice!

  Philippians 4:4

- Finally, when Paul called to mind their concern for his welfare, the joy about which he writes is (in my opinion) one of the most upbeat passages found in Scripture.

  But I *rejoiced* in the Lord greatly, that now at last you have revived your concern for me; indeed, you were concerned before, but you lacked opportunity. Not that I speak from want; for I have learned to be content in whatever circumstances I am. I know how to get along with humble means, and I also know how to live in prosperity; in any and every circumstance I have learned the secret of being filled and going hungry, both of having abundance and suffering need. I can do all things through Him who strengthens me. Nevertheless, you have done well to share with me in my affliction. And you yourselves also know, Philippians, that at the first preaching of the gospel, after I departed from Macedonia, no church shared with me in the matter of giving and receiving but you alone; for even in Thessalonica you sent a gift more than once for my needs. Not that I seek the gift itself, but I seek for the profit which increases to your account. But I have received everything in full, and have an abundance; I am amply supplied, having received from Epaphroditus what you have sent, a fragrant aroma, an acceptable sacrifice, well-pleasing to God. And my God shall supply all your needs according to His riches in glory in Christ Jesus.

  Philippians 4:10–19

NEEDED: A JOY TRANSFUSION

I strongly suspect that after the Philippians received this delightful little letter from Paul, their joy increased to an all-time high. They had received a joy transfusion from someone they dearly loved, which must have been all the more appreciated as they remembered Paul's circumstance. If he, in that irritating, confining situation, could be so positive, so full of encouragement, so affirming, certainly those living in freedom could be joyful.

Life's joy stealers are many, and you will need to get rid of them if you hope to attain the kind of happiness described by Paul's pen. If you don't, all attempts to receive (or give) a joy transfusion will be blocked. One of the ringleaders you'll need to do battle with sooner rather than later is that sneaky thief who slides into your thoughts and reminds you of something from the past that demoralizes you (even though it is over and done with and fully forgiven) or conjures up fears regarding something in the future (even though that frightening something may never happen). Joyful people stay riveted to the present—the here and now, not the then and never.

Helen Mallicoat made a real contribution to your life and mine when she wrote:

> I was regretting the past
> And fearing the future . . .
> Suddenly my Lord was speaking:
> "MY NAME IS I AM." He paused.
> I waited. He continued,
>
> "WHEN YOU LIVE IN THE PAST,
>   WITH ITS MISTAKES AND REGRETS,
>   IT IS HARD. I AM NOT THERE.
>   MY NAME IS NOT *I WAS*.
>
> "WHEN YOU LIVE IN THE FUTURE,
>   WITH ITS PROBLEMS AND FEARS,
>   IT IS HARD. I AM NOT THERE.
>   MY NAME IS NOT *I WILL BE*.
>
> "WHEN YOU LIVE IN THIS MOMENT,
>   IT IS NOT HARD.
>   I AM HERE.
>   MY NAME IS *I AM*."[4]

IF GOD IS GOD . . . THEN LAUGHTER FITS LIFE

As I attempt to probe the mind of Paul, trying to find some common denominator, some secret clue to his joy, I have to conclude that it was his confidence in God. To Paul, God was in full control of everything. Everything! If hardship came, God permitted it. If pain dogged his steps, it was only because God allowed it. If he was under arrest, God still remained the sovereign director of his life. If there seemed to be no way out, God knew he was pressed. If things broke open and all pressure was relieved, God was responsible.

My point? God is no distant deity but a constant reality, a very present help whenever needs occur. So? So live like it. And laugh like it! Paul did. While he lived, he drained every drop of joy out of every day that passed. How do I know? This little letter to the Philippians says so—as we shall see in the following chapters.

- In the first chapter of Philippians we learn *there is laughter in living*—whether or not we get what we want, in spite of difficult circumstances, and even when there are conflicts.

- In the second chapter we learn *there is laughter in serving*. It starts with the right attitude (humility), it is maintained through right theology (God is God), and it is encouraged by right models and mentors (friends like Timothy and Epaphroditus).

- In the third chapter, we learn *there is laughter in sharing* as Paul shares three happy things: his testimony, his goal of living, and his reason for encouragement.

- Finally, in the fourth chapter we learn *there is laughter in resting*. These have to be some of the finest lines ever written on the principle of personal contentment.

What a treasure house of joy! Frankly, I'm excited—and I know you will be too. Before we are very far along, you will begin to realize that joy is a choice. You will discover that each person must choose joy if he or she hopes to laugh again.

Jesus gave us His truth so that His joy might be in us. And when that happens, our joy is full (John 15:11). The tragedy is that so few choose to live joyfully.

Will you? If you will, I can make you a promise: laughter and enthusiasm will follow.

I came across a story in one of Tim Hansel's books that points this out in an unforgettable way. It's the true account of an eighty-two-year-old man who had served as a pastor for over fifty of those years. In his later years he struggled with skin cancer. It was so bad that he had already had fifteen skin operations. Tim writes:

Besides suffering from the pain, he was so embarrassed about how the cancer had scarred his appearance, that he wouldn't go out. Then one day he was given *You Gotta Keep Dancin'* in which I tell of my long struggle with the chronic, intense pain from a near-fatal climbing accident. In that book, I told of the day when I realized that the pain would be with me forever. At that moment, I made a pivotal decision. I knew that it was up to me to choose how I responded to it. So I chose joy. . . .

After reading awhile, the elderly pastor said he put the book down, thinking, "He's crazy. I can't choose joy."

So he gave up on the idea. Then later he read in John 15:11 that joy is a gift. Jesus says, "I want to give you my joy so that your joy may be complete."

A *gift!* he thought. He didn't know what to do, so he got down on his knees. Then he didn't know what to say, so he said, "Well, then, Lord, *give it to me.*"

And suddenly, as he described it, this incredible hunk of joy came from heaven and landed on him.

"I was overwhelmed," he wrote. "It was like the joy talked about in Peter, a 'joy unspeakable and full of glory.' I didn't know what to say, so I said, 'Turn it on, Lord, turn it on!'" And before he knew it, he was dancing around the house. He felt so joyful that he actually felt born again—again. And this astonishing change happened at the age of 82.

He just had to get out. So much joy couldn't stay cooped up. So he went out to the local fastfood restaurant and got a burger. A lady saw how happy he was, and asked, "How are you doing?"

He said, "Oh, I'm wonderful!"

"Is it your birthday?" she asked.

"No, honey, it's better than that!"

"Your anniversary?"

"Better than that!"

"Well, what is it?" she asked excitedly.

"It's the joy of Jesus. Do you know what I'm talking about?"

The lady shrugged and answered, "No, I have to work on Sundays."[5]

Every time I read Tim's story, I shake my head. What a ridiculous response! But not unusual. Basically there are two kinds of people: people who choose joy and people who don't. People who choose joy pay no attention to what day of the week it is . . . or how old they are . . . or what level of pain they are in. They have deliberately decided to laugh again because they have chosen joy. People who do not choose joy miss the relief laughter can bring. And because they do not, they cannot. And because they can't, they won't.

Which one are you?

2

Set Your Sails for Joy

*T*his year I turn fifty-eight. Thought I might as well let the whole world know.

When you're my age you discover that your closest friends are the most unmerciful in the cards they send you. Last year, at fifty-seven, it was one insult after another! Like, "Confound your enemies. Amaze your friends. Blow out *all* your candles!"

Another said on the front: "Wish I could be there to help you light your birthday candles . . . ," and on the inside, "but I'll be watching the glow in the sky and thinking of you."

That one was from Helen Peters, my longtime executive assistant who has typed every book I have written . . . someone you would expect to be compassionate and caring toward a guy my age, right? Wrong.

Several more mentioned the cake and candles, one warning me of two dangers: the candles would melt the frosting in fifteen seconds, so blow them out as fast as possible. Once that happens, however, the smoke alarm is likely to go off.

Garfield, the ornery cat, appears on the front of another. He is lying down (naturally) and thinking (with one eye open), "You can tell you're getting older when you wake up with that awful 'morning after' feeling . . . and you didn't do anything the night before!"

When you are this age—matter of fact, when you are *any* age—a sense of humor is essential. I once heard a great talk from a veteran missionary who spoke on "What I Would Pack in My Suitcase If I Were to Return to the Mission Field." The first item he named? A sense of humor. A friend of mine who once served the Lord for several years on foreign soil has a similar saying: "You need two things if you want to be happy in God's work overseas: a good sense of humor and no sense of smell!"

I have discovered that a joyful countenance has nothing to do with one's age or one's occupation (or lack of it) or one's geography or education or marital status or good looks or circumstances. As I wrote earlier—and will continue to write throughout this book—joy is a choice. It is a matter of attitude that stems from one's confidence in God—that He is at work, that He is in full control, that He is in the midst of whatever has happened, is happening, and will happen. Either we fix our minds on that and determine to laugh again, or we wail and whine our way through life, complaining that we never got a fair shake. We are the ones who consciously determine which way we shall go. To paraphrase the poet:

> One ship sails east
> One ship sails west
> Regardless of how the winds blow.
> It is the set of the sail
> And not the gale
> That determines the way we go.[1]

Laughing one's way through life depends on nothing external. Regardless of how severely the winds of adversity may blow, we set our sails toward joy.

I witnessed a beautiful example of this several months ago. Being one of the members of Dallas Seminary's Board of Regents, I have the privilege of interviewing new faculty members. At that particular time we were meeting with four of their newest faculty members, one of whom was a woman. Not just any woman, but the *first* woman ever invited to join the distinguished ranks of the faculty of Dallas Theological Seminary.

Lucy Mabery is her name, and several of us on the board flashed back as she told us of her pilgrimage. We have known Lucy for years.

This delightful, intelligent woman was rearing a family, teaching Bible classes, and busily engaged in a dozen other involvements while happily married to Dr. Trevor Mabery, a successful physician who was at the zenith of his career. Then her whole world caved in.

Trevor was flying back to Dallas with three other men from a Montana retreat, where they had been with Dr. James Dobson, discussing and praying about the Focus on the Family ministry. Their plane crashed, and all four of the men perished in the accident.

18

Shock waves stunned the city of Dallas. All four men were public figures and highly respected. Their widows were left to pick up the pieces of their own lives and begin again.

Lucy chose to do it with joy. Without a moment's warning, her beloved Trevor was gone. Grief, one of the most vicious of all the joy stealers, tore into the Mabery family like a tornado at full force. But, determined not to be bound by the cords of perpetual grief, Lucy remained positive, keen thinking, and joyful.

As we interviewed Lucy that day, her eyes sparkled with a delightful sense of humor, and her smile was contagious.

We asked what it was like to be the first woman serving on the faculty. With a smile she answered, "I have had great warmth and reception from the faculty members. Now the student body," she added, "is another story." We asked how she handled the more conservative male students who didn't agree with her being in that position. She said, "Oh, I take them to lunch and we talk about things. They soften a bit." After a brief pause, she added, "It's been a joyous experience. As a matter of fact, I was given an award from the student body recently for being the best-dressed woman faculty member!"

How can a person in Lucy's situation recover, pick up the pieces, and go on? How does anyone press on beyond grief? How do you still laugh at life? How do you put your arms around your children as a new single parent and help them laugh at the future? It comes from deep within— because people like Lucy Mabery set their sails for joy regardless of how the wind blows.

Lucy has a quiet confidence. Not in the long life of a husband and not in the fact that external circumstances always will be placid, peaceful, and easy, but in God, who is at work, who is in control, and who is causing all things to result in His greater glory. When you and I focus on that, we too discover we can laugh again, even after the horror of an airplane crash and the loss of our life's partner. Everything, I repeat, is determined by how we set our sails.

A SMALL BUT POWERFUL LETTER

All of this leads us quite naturally into the magnificent though brief letter to the Philippians. Although it contains only 104 verses, this delightful piece of inspired mail brings a smile to the faces of all who read it. Why? Because of the one who wrote it! In customary first-century

manner he signs his name at the beginning rather than at the end—
Paul. What memories must have swirled in the minds of his friends in
Philippi when they read that name. Ten years ago this man had been
in their midst, founding their church. Ten years ago he had been tossed
into jail, though he had committed no crime. Ten years ago they had
seen God work in pulling together a small group of young Christians
in this unique Roman colony. And now, a decade later, they read the
name again. It must have thrilled them just to see that name resurface.
Like art-loving Italians . . . thrilled by the works of Michelangelo,
like sixteenth-century German believers who were inspired by a spokesman named Martin Luther, like nineteenth-century black Americans
who grasped at every word from Abraham Lincoln, like twentieth-
century patriotic Britons who needed a Winston Churchill to help them
hold fast, the people of the church at Philippi respected and needed Paul.
He was their founder and friend. He was their teacher, their able and
much-admired leader.

But Paul doesn't simply sign his name to this letter. He also mentions Timothy, a name that means "he who honors God." Timothy is
mentioned alongside Paul, not because he wrote the letter, but because
he was known to the Philippians, loved by them, and would soon visit
them. The first-century dynamic duo: Paul and Timothy! I would imagine the Philippians could not wait to hear what Paul had to say.

From Servants to Saints

Instead of introducing themselves as "Paul and Timothy, hotshot
celebrities," or "Paul and Timothy, superleaders," or "Paul and Timothy,
men whom you must respect," the apostle writes, "Paul and Timothy,
servants." Don't you like that? That's why Paul was great. He didn't act
like a prima donna who had to be worshiped, or a fragile hero who had
to be treated with kid gloves. He saw himself as a servant.

The Greek term translated *servant* means many things: One bound
to another . . . by the bands of constraining love . . . one in such close
relationship to another that only death could break the bond . . . one
whose will is swallowed up in the sweet will of God . . . one who serves
another [Christ] . . . with reckless abandon, not regarding his or her
own interests.[2] Those words defined Paul and Timothy.

Interestingly, this is a letter from servants to saints. "Paul and
Timothy . . . to all the saints in Christ Jesus in Philippi, including

overseers and deacons"(1:1). Today we might say, "to pastors and deacons" or to "elders and deacons."

Saints is a very interesting term. If you've traveled in Europe, you have seen a lot of stone saints in and around huge cathedrals. If you worship in a liturgical church, you have seen them in icons—plaster or marble statues representing people whose lives have become famous in the long and colorful history of the church.

In my reading I came across a fascinating article entitled "On Making Saints." It was not referring to the manufacture of oversize statues, but of the process whereby people today are "sainted."

"Pope John Paul II has been sainting more men and women than all of his predecessors in the 20th century taken together,"[3] writes the author, who goes on to explain the lengthy process behind naming someone as an official saint. You have to know who to contact and what steps to take. I should also add, you need a pretty good slug of money to saint people.

But the saints Paul was writing to were not those kinds of saints. The saints in Philippi were ordinary people. They were everyday, normal folks like you and me. We seldom put common names in that light, but we could! Saint Chuck. Saint Frank. Saint Shirley. Saint Cynthia. Saint Sylvester. Saint Margaret. Saint Bob. Saint You. That's right—you!

The Greek term translated *saint* is from a word that means "set apart and consecrated for the purpose of God's service." Isn't that a great idea? That's why you are a saint. When you were born into God's family by faith in the Lord Jesus Christ, you got that title. You were set apart for God's special purpose. Consecration is at the core of the word.

"Paul and Timothy, servants of the living Christ, to all those set apart for the purpose of serving God, who live in the city of Philippi"; that's the idea.

Both Grace and Peace

And what does Paul offer these saints? "Grace and peace." (I love that.) Grace is something that comes to us which we don't deserve. Peace is something that happens within us which is not in any way affected by our external circumstances. With grace from above and peace within, who wouldn't have cause for rejoicing?

In its earliest form the word *peace* meant "to bind together" and came to include the whole idea of being bound so closely together with something or someone that a harmony resulted. The right woman who is joined in harmony with the right man in marriage begins a "peaceful" companionship. One friend who is joined in heart and soul to another friend sustains a "peaceful" relationship where harmony exists. When there is such grace-and-peace harmony, choosing joy flows naturally. And that certainly explains why Paul remained joyful. He had every reason not to. But he deliberately chose joy. Paul set his sails on the very things he offered his friends in Philippi, grace and peace.

JOYFUL THANKSGIVING

What was it about those folks in Philippi that brought Paul so much joy?

First, *he had happy memories of the people.*

I thank my God in all my remembrance of you, always offering prayer with joy in my every prayer for you all, in view of your participation in the gospel from the first day until now.

Philippians 1:3–5

His memory of them made him smile. Meaning what? What were Paul's happy memories? He had no regrets, he nursed no ill feelings, he struggled through no unresolved conflicts. When he looked back over a full decade and thought of the Philippians, he laughed!

I wonder how many pastors can say that about former churches they have served? Could you say that about former friends you have had? Or places where you have worked? Are yours happy memories? Unfortunately, the memory of certain people makes us churn. When we call them to mind, they bring sad or disappointing mental images. Paul knew no such memories from his days in Philippi. Amazingly, he could not remember one whom he would accuse or feel ill toward, not even those who threw him in prison or those who stood in a courtroom and made accusations against him. He entertained only good memories of Philippi. Positive memories make life so much lighter.

Another reason he was joyful? *He had firm confidence in God.*

For I am confident of this very thing, that He who began a good work in you will perfect it until the day of Christ Jesus. For it is only right for me to feel this way about you all, because I have you in my heart, since both in my imprisonment and in the defense and confirmation of the gospel, you all are partakers of grace with me.

Philippians 1:6–7

Paul's confidence in God was a settled fact. He knew that God was at work and in control. He was confident that God was bringing about whatever was happening for His greater glory. When we possess that kind of confidence, we have a solid platform built within us—a solid platform upon which joy can rest.

Look back at the words *began* and *perfect.* They represent opposite ends or, if you will, the *bookends* of life. The One who *started* (began) a good work in your life will *complete* (perfect) it.

> The work You have in me begun
> Will by Your grace be fully done.[4]

That's what gives us confidence. That's what helps us laugh again.

Focus on the word *perfect.* I doubt that we have imagined the true meaning of it. Travel back in your mind to the cross where Christ was crucified. See the Savior lifted up, paying for the sins of the world. Listen to His words. There were seven sayings that Christ uttered from the cross, commonly called the seven last words of Christ. One of them our Lord cried out was a single word, *Tetelestai!* Translated, it means, "It is finished!" *Telos* is the root Greek term, the same root of the word translated *perfect.* Paul was saying, "He who began a good work in you when you were converted ten years ago, Philippians, will bring it to completion. It will be finished! Jesus will see to it. And that gives me joy."

You want a fresh burst of encouragement? You may have a good friend who is not walking as close to the Lord as he or she once was. Here is fresh hope. Rest in the confidence that God has neither lost interest nor lost control. The Lord has not folded His arms and looked the other way. That person you are concerned about may be your son or daughter. Find encouragement in this firm confidence: The One who began a good work in your boy or in your girl will bring it to completion; He will finish the task. I repeat, that firm confidence in God's finishing what He started will bring back your joy.

I have mentioned joy stealers several times already. Perhaps this is a good place for me to identify three of these most notorious thieves at work today. All three, by the way, can be resisted by firm confidence, the kind of confidence we've been thinking about.

The first joy stealer is *worry.* The second is *stress.* And the third is *fear.* They may seem alike, but there is a distinct difference.

Worry is an inordinate anxiety about something that may or may not occur. It has been my observation that what is being worried about usually does not occur. But worry eats away at joy like slow-working acid while we are waiting for the outcome. I'll say much more about this thief in chapter 12.

Stress is a little more acute than worry. Stress is intense strain over a situation we cannot change or control—something out of our control. (Occasionally the safest place for something to be is out of *our* control.) And instead of releasing it to God, we churn over it. It is in that restless churning stage that our stress is intensified. Usually the thing that plagues us is not as severe as we make it out to be.

Fear, on the other hand, is different from worry and stress. It is dreadful uneasiness over the presence of danger, evil, or pain. As with the other two, however, fear usually makes things appear worse than they really are.

How do we live with worry and stress and fear? How do we withstand these joy stealers? Go back to Paul's words:

> For I am confident of this very thing, that He who began a good work in you will perfect it until the day of Christ Jesus.
>
> *Philippians 1:6*

Let me be downright practical and tell you what I do. First I remind myself early in the morning and on several occasions during the day, "God, You are at work, and You are in control. And, Lord God, You know this is happening. You were there at the beginning, and You will bring everything that occurs to a conclusion that results in Your greater glory in the end." And then? Then (and *only* then!) I relax. From that point on, it really doesn't matter all that much what happens. It is in God's hands.

I love the story of the man who had fretted for fifteen years over his work. He had built his business from nothing into a rather sizable operation. In fact, he had a large plant that covered several acres. With growth and success, however, came ever-increasing demands. Each new day brought a whole new list of responsibilities. Weary of the worry, the stress, and the fear, he finally decided to give it *all* over to God. With a smile of quiet contentment, he prayed, "Lord God, the business is Yours. All the worry, the stress, and the fears I release to You and Your sovereign will. From this day forward, Lord, You own this business." That night he went to bed earlier than he had since he started the business. Finally . . . peace.

In the middle of the night the shrill ring of the phone awoke the man. The caller, in a panicked voice, yelled, "Fire! The entire place is going up in smoke!" The man calmly dressed, got into his car and drove to the plant. With his hands in his pockets he stood there and watched, smiling slightly. One of his employees hurried to his side and said, "What in the world are you smiling about? How can you be so calm? Everything's on fire!" The man answered, "Yesterday afternoon I gave this business to God. I told Him it was His. If He wants to burn it up, that's His business."

Some of you read that and think, *That's insane!* No, that is one of the greatest pieces of sound theology you can embrace. Firm confidence in God means that it is in His hands. He who started something will bear the pressure of it and will bring the results exactly as He planned for His greater glory. How could a business burned to the ground be of glory to God? you may ask. Well, sometimes the loss of something very significant—perhaps something we are a slave to—is the only way God can get our attention and bring us back to full sanity. The happiest people I know are the ones who have learned how to hold everything loosely and have given the worrisome, stress-filled, fearful details of their lives into God's keeping.

We have seen that Paul remained joyful because he had great memories and because he lived with firm confidence.

Third, *he felt a warm affection toward his fellow believers.*

> For it is only right for me to feel this way about you all, because I have you in my heart, since both in my imprisonment and in the defense and confirmation of the gospel, you all are partakers of grace with me. For God is my witness, how I long for you all with the affection of Christ Jesus.
>
> *Philippians 1:7–8*

The term Paul uses for affection is, literally, the Greek word for "bowels." In the first century it was believed that the intestines, the stomach, the liver, even the lungs, held the most tender parts of human emotions. That explains why this joyful man would use "bowels" in reference to "affection." He says, in effect, "As I share with you my feelings, I open my whole inner being to you and tell you that the level of my affection is deep and tender." Too many people live with the inaccurate impression that Paul was somewhat cold and uncaring. Not according to this statement; in fact, quite the contrary! When he was with those he loved, Paul went to the warmest depths in conversation and affection.

If you have not yet read John Powell's *Why Am I Afraid to Tell You Who I Am?* you are missing a great experience. There is a section in the book that is worth a great deal of your time and attention. It is where the author presents the five levels of communication, which, he says, are like concentric circles—from the most shallow and superficial level (outer circle) to the deepest, most intimate level (smallest circle at the core).

Level five, the outer circle of superficiality, is the level he calls "cliché conversation."

> On this level, we talk in clichés, such as: "How are you? . . . How is your family? . . . Where have you been?" We say things like: "I like your dress very much." "I hope we can get together real soon." "It's really good to see you." [Which might really mean, "We may not see each other for a year, and I'm not going to sweat it."] . . . If the other party were to begin answering our question, "How are you?" in detail, we would be astounded. Usually and fortunately the other party senses the superficiality and conventionality of our concern and question, and obliges by simply giving the standard answer, "Just fine, thank you."[5]

That's cliché communication. Tragically, that is the deepest many people choose to go.

Level four is where we "report facts" about each other.

> We remain contented to tell others what so-and-so has said or done. We offer no personal, self-revelatory commentary on these facts, but simply report them.[6]

This is the realm of gossip and petty, meaningless little tales about others.

Level three leads us into the area of ideas and judgments. Rarely do people communicate at this deeper level. They are able, but they're not willing.

As I communicate my ideas, etc., I will be watching you carefully. I want to test the temperature of the water before I leap in. I want to be sure that you accept me with my ideas, judgments, and decisions. If you raise your eyebrows or narrow your eyes, if you yawn or look at your watch, I will probably retreat to safer ground. I will run for the cover of silence, or change the subject of conversation.[7]

Because this begins to get below the "skating" level, those who go to the depths of ideas and judgments are quite courageous.

Level two moves into "feelings."

If I really want you to know who I am, I must tell you about my stomach (gut-level) as well as my head. My ideas, judgments, and decisions are quite conventional. If I am a Republican or a Democrat by persuasion, I have a lot of company. If I am for or against space exploration, there will be others who will support me in my conviction. But the *feelings* that lie under my ideas, judgments and convictions are uniquely mine. . . .

It is these feelings, on this level of communication, which I must share with you, if I am to tell you who I really am.[8]

I would hazard a guess that less than 10 percent of us ever communicate on that "feeling" level. To my disappointment, I have discovered that husbands and wives can live for years under the same roof without reaching this level.

Level one is the most personal, intimate form of communication.

All deep and authentic friendships, and especially the union of those who are married, must be based on absolute openness and honesty. . . .

Among close friends or between partners in marriage there will come from time to time a complete emotional and personal communion.[9]

Such depth of communication, which Paul seems to have practiced on a regular basis, brings a satisfaction—and joy—like few things on earth. And when we are free to express our feelings this deeply, we have little difficulty offering up prayers that are meaningful and specific. Which is precisely what Paul mentions next.

SPECIFIC PRAYING

He names two things that are of equal importance: abounding love and keen discernment. Verse 9 says, "I pray that your love may abound." Verse 10, "I pray that you may approve things that are excellent."

To begin with, love—abounding love—needs to flow freely, somewhat like a river. But that river must be kept within its banks or it swells and overflows. And when that happens, disaster! If you have ever been in a region that has been flooded, you know the calamity floodwaters can create.

When love floods indiscriminately, we love everything, even the wrong things. Paul said it well. It is knowledge—*real* knowledge—and discernment—*keen* discernment—that keep love within its banks.

He concludes this opening paragraph on a high note when he writes of . . .

> . . . having been filled with the fruit of righteousness which comes through Jesus Christ, to the glory and praise of God.
>
> *Philippians 1:11*

What a prayer! I realize how much he loved those folks at Philippi when I read words like this.

When was the last time you wrote somebody and mentioned what you were praying for on their behalf? You and I may frequently pray for individuals, but seldom do we sit down and write a note, "Dear So-and-So, I want you to know I'm praying for these three things to take place in your life: one . . . two . . . three. . . ." Paul's model is worth duplicating. You quickly move beyond level five when you begin to communicate like that, and I challenge you to do it.

PRACTICAL APPLICATION

We begin to laugh again when we rest our full confidence in God. More specifically, according to what we have just read in Philippians 1:

- Confidence brings joy when we fix our attention on the things for which we are thankful.
- Confidence brings joy when we let God be God.
- Confidence brings joy when we keep our love within proper limits.

Even though we are just getting started, we have covered a lot of important territory. As I think about the practical side of all this, it occurs to me that joy is ours to claim. In fact, no one on earth can invade and redirect our life of joy unless we permit them to do so.

Hudson Taylor put it like this:

> It doesn't matter, really, how great the pressure is; it only matters *where the pressure lies*. See that it never comes *between* you and the Lord— then, the greater the pressure, the more it presses you to His breast.[10]

The pressure on you may be intense. A half-dozen joy stealers may be waiting outside your door, ready to pounce at the first opportunity. However, nothing can rob you of your hold on grace, your claim to peace, or your confidence in God without your permission. Choose joy. Never release your grip!

I have lived almost fifty-eight years on this old earth, and I am more convinced than ever that the single most important choice a follower of Christ can make is his or her choice of attitude. Only you can determine that. Choose wisely . . . choose carefully . . . choose confidently.

Earlier I paraphrased a poem by Ella Wheeler Wilcox. I want to close this chapter by quoting it as she wrote it.

The Winds of Fate

One ship drives east and another drives west
　With the selfsame winds that blow.
　　'Tis the set of the sails
　　And not the gales
　Which tells us the way to go.

Like the winds of the sea are the ways of fate,
　As we voyage along through life:
　　'Tis the set of a soul
　　That decides its goal,
　And not the calm or the strife.[11]

My advice? Set your sails for joy! You will never regret it.

3

What a Way to Live!

*A*s a boy I spent my leisure hours in the evening listening to various radio shows. In those days before television, action-packed dramas, murder mysteries, and comedy programs—all on radio in the evening hours—were the ticket to adventure and imagination.

There were many to choose from in the 1940s: "The Green Hornet," "Captain Midnight," "Lum 'n' Abner," "The Lone Ranger," "Gang Busters," "Inner Sanctum," "Jack Armstrong (the All-American Boy)," "Fibber McGee and Molly," "Edgar Bergen and Charlie McCarthy," and my all-time favorite, "Mr. District Attorney." I listened to that program so often I memorized the announcer's words of introduction, which always concluded with "defender of our right to life, liberty, and the pursuit of happiness." I used to strut around the house mouthing those lines.

I didn't know it at the time but that part of the announcer's script was borrowed from Thomas Jefferson's immortal words in our nation's Declaration of Independence:

> We hold these Truths to be self-evident; that all Men are created equal, that they are endowed by their Creator with certain unalienable Rights; that among these are Life, Liberty, and the Pursuit of Happiness.

Those final words still intrigue me. One of our unalienable rights is to pursue happiness—to seek out a life of joy and to find peaceful satisfaction. For many, however, happiness is a forgotten pursuit. A dream that has died.

For the longest time I wondered why. Why has a joyful life, an attitude of happiness, eluded so many? Within the past few years I have come to realize why. It's because most people think that happiness is something that happens to them rather than something they deliberately and

33

diligently pursue. Circumstances seldom generate smiles and laughter. Joy comes to those who determine to pursue it in spite of their circumstances.

A good reminder of this is the short story by G. W. Target entitled "The Window," which tells of two men, both seriously ill, who occupied the same small hospital room. One man was allowed to sit up in his bed for an hour each afternoon to help drain the fluid from his lungs. His bed was next to the room's only window. The other man had to spend all his time flat on his back.

The men talked for hours on end. They spoke of their wives and families, their homes, their jobs, their involvement in the military service, where they had been on vacation. And every afternoon when the man in the bed by the window could sit up, he would pass the time by describing to his roommate all the things he could see outside the window. The man in the other bed began to live for those one-hour periods where his world would be broadened and enlivened by all the activity and color of the outside world.

The window overlooked a park with a lovely lake, the man said. Ducks and swans played on the water while children sailed their model boats. Lovers walked arm in arm amid flowers of every color of the rainbow. Grand old trees graced the landscape, and a fine view of the city skyline could be seen in the distance. As the man by the window described all this in exquisite detail, the man on the other side of the room would close his eyes and imagine the picturesque scene.

One warm afternoon the man by the window described a parade passing by. Although the other man couldn't hear the band, he could see it in his mind's eye as the gentleman by the window portrayed it with descriptive words. Unexpectedly, an alien thought entered his head: *Why should he have all the pleasure of seeing everything while I never get to see anything?* It didn't seem fair.

As the thought fermented the man felt ashamed at first. But as the days passed and he missed seeing more sights, his envy eroded into resentment and soon turned him sour. He began to brood and he found himself unable to sleep. *He* should be by that window—that thought now controlled his life.

Late one night as he lay staring at the ceiling, the man by the window began to cough. He was choking on the fluid in his lungs. The other man watched in the dimly lit room as the struggling man by the window groped for the button to call for help. Listening from across the room, he never moved, never pushed his own button which would have brought the nurse running. In less than five minutes the coughing and choking stopped, along with the sound of breathing. Now there was only silence—deathly silence.

The following morning the day nurse arrived to bring water for their baths. When she found the lifeless body of the man by the window, she was saddened and called the hospital attendants to take it away—no words, no fuss. As soon as it seemed appropriate, the other man asked if he could be moved next to the window. The nurse was happy to make the switch, and after making sure he was comfortable, she left him alone.

Slowly, painfully, he propped himself up on one elbow to take his first look. Finally, he would have the joy of seeing it all himself. He strained to look out the window beside the bed.

It faced a blank wall.[1]

The pursuit of happiness is a matter of choice . . . it is a positive attitude we choose to express. It is not a gift delivered to our door each morning, nor does it come through the window. And it is certain that our circumstances are not the things that make us joyful. If we wait for them to get just right, we will never laugh again.

NEEDED: A POSITIVE MIND-SET

Since the pursuit of happiness is an inward journey, it might be helpful to see the two options available to us. Maybe if I put them into opposing columns, the contrast will leave a lasting impression.

Negative Mind-set	Positive Mind-set
• The need for certain things before there can be joy	• The need for virtually nothing tangible to be joyful
• A strong dependence on others to provide joy	• The ability to create one's own reasons for joy
• Focusing on joy as being "out there," always in the future . . . waiting for something to happen and thereby bring happiness	• Choosing joy now, making it a present pursuit . . . never waiting for everything to fall into place or for some "ship" to come in

These minds of ours are like bank vaults awaiting our deposits. If we regularly deposit positive, encouraging, and uplifting thoughts, what we withdraw will be the same. And the interest paid will be joy.

One day I came across a fat little book on a friend's desk, and the title grabbed my attention: *14,000 Things to Be Happy About.* As I thumbed through the contents, I realized that each of those 14,000 things was a happy thought, and each one could make the reader happy. However, there isn't one of those 14,000 things that will make us laugh again unless we give ourselves permission to do so. The secret lies in our mind-set—in the things we fix our minds on. As Paul wrote to the Philippians:

> And now, brothers . . . let me say this one more thing: Fix your thoughts on what is true and good and right. Think about things that are pure and lovely, and dwell on the fine, good things in others. Think about all you can praise God for and be glad about.
>
> *Philippians 4:8* TLB

PAUL: A CLASSIC EXAMPLE OF HOW TO LIVE

Speaking of Paul, let me reintroduce you. This is the man who wanted to go to Rome as a preacher in order to testify of his faith before the emperor, Nero. Instead, he wound up in Rome as a prisoner. He was a Roman citizen with every right to appeal to Caesar and await an audience before him. Instead, he was illegally arrested in Jerusalem, misrepresented before the court, incorrectly identified as an Egyptian renegade, entangled in the red tape of political machinery, and finally granted a trip across the Mediterranean, only to encounter a storm and be shipwrecked. When he finally arrived in Rome, he was incarcerated and virtually forgotten for two years. If we looked up *victim* in the dictionary, Paul's picture should appear beside the word!

And yet he is the man who wrote his friends the most joyous letter in the entire New Testament.

Confident, Even Though a Victim

Read his words slowly and see if you find even a hint of resentment or negativism:

> Now I want you to know, brethren, that my circumstances have turned out for the greater progress of the gospel, so that my imprisonment in the cause of Christ has become well known throughout the whole

praetorian guard and to everyone else, and that most of the brethren, trusting in the Lord because of my imprisonment, have far more courage to speak the word of God without fear.

Philippians 1:12–14

Doesn't sound to me like a guy licking his wounds or attending a pity party in honor of himself. On the contrary, he reminds me of the man by the window in that hospital room, looking at a bleak, blank wall but determined to see the unseen. Sitting there with an iron cuff and chain on one arm, bound to a Roman soldier, Paul wrote of his circumstances as having turned out "for the greater *progress* of the gospel."

What a grand, positive statement! After all the man had been through, he considered the things most people would call setbacks as progress. The Greek term Paul selected is colorful. It was used in ancient times to describe a group of pioneer woodcutters who preceded an advancing army, clearing the way through an otherwise impenetrable forest of trees and underbrush. Paul viewed his circumstances as having cleared the way "for the greater progress of the gospel" of Christ to be released.

Instead of seeing the soldier on duty next to him as a galling restriction to the gospel, Paul saw him as a captive audience. What an opportunity to share Christ with one soldier after another, who would, in turn, take the same message back to the barracks so others in the elite praetorian guard might hear and believe. Instead of feeling frustrated and victimized, Paul laughed at the open window of unique opportunity offering numerous possibilities. Paul's joy was outrageous!

How can a person think like that? The answer is neither difficult nor complicated—but it all depends on the question we ask ourselves. Either we ask the negative: Why did this have to happen to me? Or we choose the positive: How has this resulted for some benefit God had in mind?

Like Joseph said many years earlier to his brothers who had ripped him off, "You meant evil against me, but God meant it for good" (Gen. 50:20). With that same positive mind-set, Paul chose to count his blessings rather than list his disappointments. Looking at everything from that perspective, he realized that what seemed a waste or a detour was, in fact, God's divine alchemy. What seemed like a delay had proven to be a divinely appointed opportunity for the message of Christ.

Joyful in Spite of Others

Some, to be sure, are preaching Christ even from envy and strife, but some also from good will; the latter do it out of love, knowing that I am appointed for the defense of the gospel; the former proclaim Christ out of selfish ambition, rather than from pure motives, thinking to cause me distress in my imprisonment. What then? Only that in every way, whether in pretense or in truth, Christ is proclaimed; and in this I rejoice, yes, and I will rejoice.

Philippians 1:15–18

Even back in that first-century era, in the earliest, dynamic days of the church, not everyone who spoke for God was a vessel of pure motive and guileless proclamation. Some deliberately tried to cause Paul distress. Spiritual dynamo though he was, Paul was not perpetually above pain or personal hurt. The man must have had a few dog days like the rest of us. In fact, I like the way Stuart Briscoe describes Paul:

Whatever we may think of Paul, he was no alabaster saint on a pedestal. The statue and the pedestal are the products of our own lack of reality. The real Paul had a temper that got heated and feelings that got hurt. He was no computerized theological machine churning out inspired writings, but a very warm human individual who needed as much love as the next man, and then some.

You can't hurt a computer's feelings or grieve a theological concept, but you can destroy a man. Paul was destructible, but he wasn't destroyed. And it wasn't for lack of somebody trying! The perspective that he had discovered allowed him to say that he didn't really mind what happened to him so long as nothing happened to stop the gospel, because in his understanding the message preached mattered more than the man preaching.[2]

A large part of learning how to laugh again is being broad-shouldered enough to let things be . . . to leave room for differences . . . to applaud good results even if the way others arrive at them may not be our preferred method. It takes a lot of grace not to be petty, but, oh, the benefits!

Let's see if I can paraphrase what the apostle is communicating here:

So what if some preach with wrong motives? Furthermore, some may be overly impressed with themselves . . . and take unfair shots at me.

Who cares? What really matters is this: *Christ is being proclaimed* . . . and that thought alone intensifies my joy! All the other stuff, I leave to God to handle.

To do otherwise is to clutter our minds with judgmental and bor-derline legalistic thoughts which become joy stealers. They rob us of a positive mind-set. And what happens then? We become petty, cranky, grim people who must have everyone poured into our mold before we are able to relax.

It is important that we understand what is worth our passionate concern and what is not. Most things are not worth the trouble. But some things are. For example, when Paul wrote to the Galatians, he was so concerned about what was happening there that he exclaimed:

> But even though we, or an angel from heaven, should preach to you a gospel contrary to that which we have preached to you, *let him be accursed*. As we have said before so I say again now, if any man is preaching to you a gospel contrary to that which you received, *let him be accursed*.
>
> *Galatians 1:8–9 (italics mine)*

I don't think there is any disagreement . . . the man was hot! But here in Philippians Paul looked at what was going on around him and said, "So what?" The difference is that in Galatia the gospel was being tampered with—some people were preaching a false message of salvation. But in Philippi the truth was being proclaimed even though Paul, personally, was being attacked. When people mess with the message, they need to be rebuked, exposed, and corrected. But when they mess with the messenger, they need to be ignored. No big deal. Not even Paul wasted his time or burnt up a lot of energy nitpicking his way through all that. He was just thrilled that the gospel was being declared.

I have learned over the years that only a few things are worth going to the mat for, and those things always center on the clear gospel message and its surrounding truths. They do not have to do with defending one-self or trying to straighten out other preachers' motives or changing their style. Grace says to let them be. If Paul could shrug it off and say, "So what?" so should we. We will live a lot longer, and we'll start to laugh again.

Hopeful, Regardless of Uncertainties

> For I know that this shall turn out for my deliverance through your prayers and the provision of the Spirit of Jesus Christ, according to my earnest expectation and hope, that I shall not be put to shame in anything, but that with all boldness, Christ shall even now, as always, be exalted in my body, whether by life or by death.
>
> *Philippians 1:19–20*

Those are the words of a man whose image was secure and whose reputation was not in need of being protected, massaged, or defended. His mind was firmly fixed on essentials, so much so that nothing brought him anxiety. "Whether by life or by death," his focus was concentrated. He concerned himself only with things that mattered. For all he knew, death might be right around the corner.

That thought alone provides an excellent filtering system, enabling us to separate what is essential from what is not. As dear old Samuel Johnson once stated, "When a man knows he is to be hanged in a fortnight, it concentrates his mind wonderfully."[3]

Paul was hopeful, regardless of the uncertainties he faced. His quiet confidence is revealed in such phrases as "this shall turn out" and "my earnest expectation." In other words, what he was experiencing was not the end—things would turn out exactly as God directed. That brought the man a rush of mind-calming *peace*. And what may have temporarily brought him pain and discomfort would ultimately result in "Christ . . . exalted in my body." That gave him *hope*. Sandwiched between those two statements was his determination not to feel uneasy or ashamed: "I shall not be put to shame in anything." That brought him *confidence*.

Refusing to be crippled by other people's words, refusing to submerge himself in self-pity, and refusing to take criticism and attacks personally, Paul remained strong, positive, and sure. How could he be so strong? No question about that answer. The man was—

Contented Because Christ Was Central

> For to me, to live is Christ, and to die is gain.
>
> *Philippians 1:21*

This is a well-known statement in Christian circles. We have heard it frequently and quoted it often. Since it is so familiar, perhaps if we try to reword the verse we will discover how any other statement lacks the significance of the authentic words of Paul.

- For me to live is *money* . . . and to die is to leave it all behind.
- For me to live is *fame* . . . and to die is to be quickly forgotten.
- For me to live is *power and influence* . . . and to die is to lose both.
- For me to live is *possessions* . . . and to die is to depart with nothing in my hands.

Somehow, they all fall flat, don't they? When money is our objective, we must live in fear of losing it, which makes us paranoid and suspicious. When fame is our aim, we become competitive lest others upstage us, which makes us envious. When power and influence drive us, we become self-serving and strong-willed, which makes us arrogant. And when possessions become our god, we become materialistic, thinking enough is never enough, which makes us greedy. All these pursuits fly in the face of contentment . . . and joy.

Only *Christ* can satisfy, whether we have or don't have, whether we are known or unknown, whether we live or die. And the good news is this: Death only sweetens the pie! That alone is enough to make you laugh again!

The Living Bible states: "For to me, living means opportunities for Christ, and dying—well, that's better yet!" The New Testament in Modern English, J. B. Phillips's paraphrase, reads: "For living to me means simply 'Christ,' and if I die I should merely gain more of Him." The Good News Bible asks: "For what is life? To me, it is Christ. Death, then, will bring more."

What is the sum and substance of all this? The secret of living is the same as the secret of joy: Both revolve around the centrality of Jesus Christ. In other words, the pursuit of happiness is the cultivation of a Christ-centered, Christ-controlled life.

THREE THINGS TO REMEMBER

When Christ becomes our central focus—our reason for existence—contentment replaces our anxiety as well as our fears and insecurities. This cannot help but impact three of the most prevalent joy stealers in all of life.

1. He broadens the dimensions of our circumstances. This gives us new confidence. Chains that once bound and irritated us no longer seem so irksome. Our limitations become a challenge rather than a chore.

2. He delivers us from preoccupation with others. This causes our contentment level to rise. Other people's opinions, motives, and criticisms no longer seem all that important. What a wonderful deliverance!

3. He calms our fears regarding ourselves and our future. This provides a burst of fresh hope on a daily basis. Once fear is removed, it is remarkable how quickly peace fills the vacuum. And when we get those three ducks in a row, it isn't long before we begin to laugh again. What a way to live! Let me urge you not to let anything keep you from it.

Since it is your unalienable right to pursue happiness, I suggest that you *get with it* right away. For some, it is like breaking the spell you have been under for half your life, maybe longer. Won't that take a little extra energy? Probably. You're too tired to exert yourself . . . too tired to pursue *anything* more? Maybe this anonymous piece will help change your mind.

I'm Tired

Yes, I'm tired. For several years I've been blaming it on middle-age, iron poor blood, lack of vitamins, air pollution, water pollution, saccharin, obesity, dieting, underarm odor, yellow wax build-up, and a dozen other maladies that make you wonder if life is really worth living.

But now I find out, tain't that.
I'm tired because I'm overworked.

The population of this country is 200 million. Eighty-four million are retired. That leaves 116 million to do the work. There are 75 million in school, which leaves 41 million to do the work. Of this total, there are 22 million employed by the government.

That leaves 19 million to do the work. Four million are in the armed forces, which leaves 15 million to do the work. Take from that total the 14,800,000 people who work for the state and city governments and that leaves 200,000 to do the work. There are 188,000 in hospitals, so that leaves 12,000 to do the work. Now, there are 11,998 people in prisons. That leaves just 2 people to do the work. You and me. And you're standing there reading this. No wonder I'm tired.[4]

To you I say, *let go*. Let go of your habit of always looking at the negative. Let go of your need to fix everybody else's unhappiness. Let go of your drive to compete or compare. Let go of your adult children, especially your attempts to straighten out their lives. (I read recently that parents are never happier than their least-happy child. What a joy stealer!) Let go of all your excuses. And may I add one more? Let go of so many needless inhibitions that keep you from celebrating life. Quit being so protective . . . so predictable . . . so proper.

Far too many adults I know are as serious as a heart attack. They live with their fists tightened, and they die with deep frowns. They cannot remember when they last took a chance or risked trying something new. The last time they tried something really wild they were nine years old. I ask you, where's the fun? Let's face it, you and I are getting older—it's high time we stop acting like it!

Sooner than we realize, all of us will be looking out that window at a blank wall.

4

Laughing Through Life's Dilemmas

Life gets complicated.

I can't speak for you, but for me dilemmas are a regular occurrence. Some folks—at least from all outward appearances—seem to deal with life on a black-and-white basis. Stuff they encounter is either right or wrong. Not for me. Somehow I wind up in the gray area more often than not. Perhaps that's been your experience too.

If so, folks like us can appreciate the frustrations Charlie Brown frequently has, as portrayed in Charles Schulz's famous "Peanuts" cartoons. Like the one where Lucy is philosophizing and Charlie is listening. As usual, Lucy has the floor, delivering one of her dogmatic lectures.

"Charlie Brown," she begins, "life is a lot like a deck chair. Some place it so they can see where they're going. Others place it to see where they've been. And some so they can see where they are at the present."

Charlie sighs, "I can't even get mine unfolded!"

More than a few of us identify with Charlie. Life's dilemmas leave us unsettled and unsure. We find ourselves, like the old saying, between a rock and a hard place.

FAMILIAR DILEMMAS

Dilemmas have the potential of being some of life's most demanding joy stealers. Being stuck between two possibilities where a case could be made for going either way . . . ah, that's a tough call. We've all been there. I think they fall into at least three categories.

Volitional Dilemmas

A volitional dilemma occurs when we want to do two different things at the same time.

Young couples who have been married for two or three years, sometimes less, are often trying to finish their schooling, yet they are anxious to start a family. Which should they do? To start having children means extra financial pressure and an even greater struggle with time and energy drain. Yet to wait several years means that they may be in their thirties, and they would much rather begin parenting earlier than that. Which do they do?

Another volitional dilemma occurs when we find ourselves unhappy in our church. The problem is exacerbated by the fact that we have been members for many years and have our closest friends there. Do we stick it out and try to help bring about needed changes, which may not be too promising and could create ill feelings, or do we graciously declare our disagreement and leave?

Emotional Dilemmas

Emotional dilemmas are even more intense. They occur when we entertain contrary feelings about the same event.

Not too many months ago our younger son, Chuck, discovered that his longtime pet had a dreadful skin disease. Sasha, a beautiful white Samoyed, had been his dog for many years. To say they were close is to understate the inseparable bond between them. No matter what Chuck tried—and believe me, he tried everything—nothing helped. The dog became increasingly miserable. You have already guessed the dilemma. To provide Sasha relief meant putting her to sleep . . . an option so painful to Chuck he could scarcely discuss it.

If you think that one is difficult, how about dealing with a rebellious adult son or daughter? He or she has moved out of the home but is living a lifestyle that is both personally destructive and disappointing to you. It's obvious that some financial assistance could be put to good use. In fact, a request is made. Do you help or do you resist? Seems so objective, so simple on paper, but few dilemmas are more heartrending.

Geographical Dilemmas

Geographical dilemmas occur when we desire to be in two places at the same time. We love living where we have been for years, but moving would bring an encouraging financial advancement, not to mention the opportunity to cultivate new friendships and enjoy some much-needed changes. To leave, however, would be difficult because of the ages of the kids (two are older teenagers) and the longstanding relationships we have enjoyed at our church, in our neighborhood, and especially with our friends. We weigh both sides. Neither is ideal, yet both have their benefits—a classic geographical dilemma.

I am aware that there are some crossovers within these three categories, but by separating them we are able to see that each pulls at us and introduces numerous and deep feelings of strain, which can quickly drain our reservoir of joy. I might also add that being older and wiser does not mean we are immune to the problem. As Charlie Brown admitted, even seasoned veterans of life can find it difficult to get their deck chairs unfolded.

PAUL'S PERSONAL DILEMMA

All this brings us back to the man we have been getting to know better, Paul, a prisoner of Rome in his own house. We have watched him react positively to his circumstances, and we have cheered him on as he wrote words of encouragement to his friends in Philippi. Now we find ourselves identifying with his own personal dilemma to which he admits in the familiar words:

> For to me, to live is Christ, and to die is gain. But if I am to live on in the flesh, this will mean fruitful labor for me; and I do not know which to choose. But I am hard-pressed from both directions, having the desire to depart and be with Christ, for that is very much better; yet to remain on in the flesh is more necessary for your sake.
>
> *Philippians 1:21–24*

There can be no doubt: Paul's dearest friend, in fact his most intimate relationship on earth, was Christ. No one else meant more to him; therefore, the thought of being with Him brought Paul great joy.

His feelings could be those so beautifully summed up in an old gospel song:

> Jesus is all the world to me,
> My life, my joy, my all;
> He is my strength from day to day,
> Without Him I would fall. . . .

Jesus is all the world to me,
I want no better friend;
I trust Him now, I'll trust Him when
Life's fleeting days shall end.

Beautiful life with such a Friend;
Beautiful life that has no end;
Eternal life, eternal joy,
He's my Friend.[1]

When someone who is eternal and lives in heaven means that much to you, an inescapable dilemma is created: You want to be with Him! Now!! That explains why Paul did not hesitate to write "to die is *gain*." However, his work on earth was unfinished. God had more He wanted to do through His servant who was then under house arrest in Rome. Paul knew that, which was what caused the dilemma. He was between a rock and a hard place, or as he put it, "hard-pressed from both directions." And what were they?

1. "Having the desire to depart and be with Christ" (which he called "very much better"), and

2. "To remain on in the flesh . . . for your sake" (which he admitted, "is more necessary").

Let me spell all that out in even greater detail. To do so we need to analyze the benefits and the liabilities on both sides.

To Depart

The benefits? He would be with Christ instantly. He would be free of all earth's hassles and limitations, pain and frustrations. He would immediately experience uninterrupted peace and the joy of unending pleasure in the most perfect of all places.

The liabilities? He would be absent from those who needed him, which would seriously affect their spiritual growth. He would no longer be a witness to the Roman guards assigned to watch him or an encouragement to those who came to visit him. In addition, his missionary outreach to those who had not heard of Christ would instantly cease. Furthermore, all those whose cause he championed would be without a voice of authority and affirmation. As relieving as death may have seemed, it was not without its liabilities.

My mind rushes back to 1865 when our country was torn asunder by the Civil War. Abraham Lincoln stood in the gap as a source of strength when many grieving families were doubting and when helpless slaves were despairing. We can only imagine the pressure of that awful position. The photographs taken of the man before the war and during the conflict tell their silent story of a battle-weary warrior who must have longed for relief. Suddenly a shot was fired in Ford's Theater and everything changed. Our sixteenth president finally knew peace as he had never known it before. Were there benefits? Yes! For him they were immediate and eternal. But the liabilities cannot be ignored: political chaos and rivalry among those in authority, heartbreaking sorrow added to an already grieving nation, and the voice of the African-American's most eloquent and powerful advocate forever silenced.

To Remain

If the apostle Paul remained on and continued his ministry, the benefits were obvious. He would have a hand in the spiritual growth of many, his role as mentor to the Philippians (and many others) would be sustained, and his vision for reaching a world without Christ would continue to rekindle the fires of evangelism everywhere he went. And we cannot forget the man's writing ministry. By remaining, his inspired pen would go on flowing.

The liabilities? He would remain absent from his heavenly home. The bonds of his imprisonment would not be broken, his pain would only increase, and his threatened future would intensify. And after all he had been through, who needed more? Bring on the relief!

You and I might think that the man was mature enough to hammer out this decision without too much of a struggle. After all, he was a strong and faithful soldier of the Christian faith, a wise counselor, and a spiritually minded man of God. Surely he could decide on his own. Yet, according to his own testimony, he admitted, "I do not know which to choose" (v. 22). Both made logical sense. Neither would be wrong . . . a real tossup. The Lord must lead, no question.

Horatius Bonar put his finger on the best solution to such a dilemma when he wrote:

> Thy way, not mine, O Lord,
> However dark it be!
> Lead me by Thine own hand,
> Choose out the path for me.

51

Smooth let it be or rough,
   It will be still the best;
Winding or straight, it leads
   Right onward to Thy rest.

I dare not choose my lot;
   I would not, if I might;
Choose Thou for me, my God;
   So shall I walk aright.

The kingdom that I seek
   Is Thine; so let the way
That leads to it be Thine;
   Else I must surely stray.

Take Thou my cup, and it
   With joy or sorrow fill,
As best to Thee may seem;
   Choose Thou my good and ill;

Choose Thou for me my friends,
   My sickness or my health;
Choose Thou my cares for me,
   My poverty or wealth.

Not mine, not mine the choice,
   In things or great or small;
Be Thou my guide my strength,
   My wisdom, and my all![2]

This is a timely moment for me to return to the greater theme of this book—joy. When we arrive at such dilemmas in life and are unable to decipher the right direction to go, if we hope to maintain our joy in the process, we must (repeat *must*) allow the Lord to be our Guide, our Strength, our Wisdom—our all! It is easy to read those words, but so tough to carry through on them. When we do, however, it is nothing short of remarkable how peaceful and happy we can remain. The pressure is on His shoulders, the responsibility is on Him, the ball is in His court, and an unexplainable joy envelops us. As viewed by others, it may even be considered outrageous joy.

To be sure, such an unusual method of dealing with dilemmas is rare—there aren't many folks willing to turn the reins over to God—and calls for humility, another rare trait among capable people. But it works!

The Lord is a Master at taking our turmoil and revealing the best possible solution to us.

As Peter once wrote:

> Humble yourselves, therefore, under the mighty hand of God, that He may exalt you at the proper time, casting all your anxiety upon Him because He cares for you.
>
> *1 Peter 5:6–7*

When we do that, He trades us His joy for our anxiety. *Such a deal!* As He then works things out and makes it clear to us which step to take next, we can relax, release the tension, and laugh again.

This is extremely hard for Type A personalities. If you happen to be more intelligent than the average person, it's even more difficult. And if you are the super-responsible, I-can-handle-it individual who tends to be intense and impatient, letting go and letting God take charge will be one of life's most incredible challenges. But I urge you, do it! Force yourself to trust Another who is far more capable and intelligent and responsible than you (or a thousand like you) ever could be. And in the meantime, enjoy!

Because I used to be much more driven and demanding (especially of myself), I would often search for things to read that would help me cool my jets. One excellent piece, written by a friar in a Nebraska monastery, has contributed more to my less-intense lifestyle than the author will ever know. I hope it will bring similar benefits your way.

> If I had my life to live over again, I'd try to make more
> mistakes next time.
> I would relax, I would limber up, I would be sillier than
> I have been this trip.
> I know of very few things I would take seriously.
> I would take more trips. I would be crazier.
> I would climb more mountains, swim more rivers, and
> watch more sunsets.
> I would do more walking and looking.
> I would eat more ice cream and less beans.
> I would have more actual troubles, and fewer imaginary
> ones.
> You see, I'm one of those people who lives life
> prophylactically and sensibly hour after hour, day

after day. Oh, I've had my moments, and if I had
to do it over again I'd have more of them.
In fact, I'd try to have nothing else, just moments, one
after another, instead of living so many years ahead
each day. I've been one of those people who never
go anywhere without a thermometer, a hot-water
bottle, a gargle, a raincoat, aspirin, and a
parachute.
If I had to do it over again I would go places, do things,
and travel lighter than I have.
If I had my life to live over I would start barefooted
earlier in the spring and stay that way later in the
fall.
I would play hookey more.
I wouldn't make such good grades, except by accident.
I would ride on more merry-go-rounds.
I'd pick more daisies.[3]

I know, I know. Just tolerating the idea of making mistakes and playing hookey and taking the time to pick daisies is tough for a lot of us. And
admittedly some have gone too far in this direction. It's one thing to err,
but when you wear out the eraser before the pencil, you're overdoing it.

Nevertheless, many need the reminder that life is more than hard
work and serious decisions and ultra-intense issues. I have often been
comforted with the thought that "He gives to His beloved even in his
sleep" (Ps. 127:2). How easy to forget that "God is for us" (Rom. 8:31)
and "richly supplies us with all things to enjoy" (1 Tim. 6:17). Some of us
need to read those statements every day until we really begin to believe
them.

Well, did Paul experience God's leading? Was he ever removed from
the horns of his dilemma? Did he get his deck chair unfolded? You bet.
Read it for yourself.

> And convinced of this, I know that I shall remain and continue with
> you all for your progress and joy in the faith, so that your proud confidence
> in me may abound in Christ Jesus through my coming to you again.
>
> *Philippians 1:25–26*

Somehow the Lord made it clear to Paul that His plan was to have
him remain and continue doing what he was doing. Though departing

would have brought the man instant relief and rewards for a job well done, he accepted God's decision and unselfishly pressed on.

A Spiritual Challenge

The closing words of Paul's opening chapter to his friends in Philippi are words of challenge—to them and to us.

> Only conduct yourselves in a manner worthy of the gospel of Christ; so that whether I come and see you or remain absent, I may hear of you that you are standing firm in one spirit, with one mind striving together for the faith of the gospel; in no way alarmed by your opponents—which is a sign of destruction for them, but of salvation for you, and that too, from God. For to you it has been granted for Christ's sake, not only to believe in Him, but also to suffer for His sake, experiencing the same conflict which you saw in me, and now hear to be in me.
>
> *Philippians 1:27–30*

What stands out to me is Paul's initial reminder that others are not responsible for our happiness. We are. "Whether I come and see you or remain absent," he expects to hear that they are together. What an important reminder!

So many live their lives too dependent on others. Such clinging vines draw most, if not all, of their energy from another. Not only is this unhealthy for the clinger, but it also drains too much energy from the clingee!

Paul would have none of that, and neither should we. Maturity is accelerated when we learn to stand firm on our own. There may be occasions when others play helpful roles during needy episodes of our lives, but those should be the exception rather than the rule. Codependent people are not joyful people.

Does this discount the need for close and harmonious relationships? Hardly. In fact, after encouraging a healthy independence, Paul turns the coin to the other side and suggests a need for balance: "with one mind striving together." Why? Because life includes tests, and some of those tests involve "opponents" who are not to alarm us. By striving together, we keep from being intimidated and frightened.

Great comfort comes when we realize that our striving is not an isolated series of battles fought one-on-one, but that we are fighting together against a common foe. There is a sense of camaraderie and support when we realize we are in the ranks of the faithful, a "mighty army" of those set apart by Christ, a force to reckon with.

After speaking at a church recently, I noticed an interesting sign as we were leaving the parking lot. It read:

YOU ARE NOW ENTERING

THE MISSION FIELD

Nice reminder. And even more encouraging, we enter it together. So we need to remember:

1. We are not alone.

2. We are promised the victory.

3. We are called (among other things) to suffer.

4. We are in good company when conflicts arise.

Paul reminds his friends at Philippi that their conflicts are the same as his conflicts. The Greek word translated *conflicts* here is the term from which we get our word *agony*. We agonize together just as we stand and strive for the gospel together. I gain strength from the thought that our sufferings and conflicts are on a par with Paul's. Agony is agony, pure and simple. It makes mature believers out of all of us. It also develops our spiritual muscles and gives us fresh courage to face whatever foe we may encounter. And let us never forget . . . our side ultimately wins!

In the early days of Christianity, a scoffer once inquired, "What is your Carpenter doing now?" And the answer of the unperturbed Christian was bold: "Making a coffin for your Emperor!"[4]

Never, ever forget that our role is twofold: not only "to believe in Him" (that's the delightful part), but also "to suffer for His sake" (the difficult part). That poses yet another dilemma, which would perhaps fall under a fourth category—the *practical* dilemma. We who love the Lord and faithfully serve Him, doing our best to live for His glory, occasionally find ourselves suffering for the cause rather than being rewarded for our walk. The dilemma: Do we run toward it or run from it?

Most in our day would consider anyone a fool who pursued anything but comfort and ease. But since when did the majority ever vote in favor of Christ? If this happens to be your current way of life, if suffering and difficulty have come your way because of your walk with Him, take heart. You are in good company. And some glorious day in the not-too-distant future, God will reward you for your faithfulness. You will have forgotten the pain of pressing on. And, like never before, you will laugh again.

OUR PERSONAL RESPONSE

Two final principles emerge from the things we have been thinking about in this chapter.

• Making right decisions amidst dilemmas forces us to rethink our priorities.

There is nothing quite like a dilemma to bring us back to the bedrock of what we consider essential. Happy is the one who sets aside selfish ambition and personal preference for God's will and way.

• Choosing right priorities forces us to reconsider the importance of Christ in our lives.

There are many voices these days. Some are loud, many are persuasive, and a few are downright convincing. It can be confusing. If you listen long enough you will be tempted to throw your faith to the winds, look out for number one, let your glands be your guide, and choose what is best for you. Initially you will get a rush of pleasure and satisfaction, no question. But ultimately you will wind up disappointed and disillusioned.

Malcolm Muggeridge died in the fall of 1990. He had been a foreign correspondent, newspaper editor, editor of *Punch* magazine, and a well-known television personality in Great Britain. As an adult, he finally turned to Christ and wrote of his own dilemmas as a journalist-turned-believer. Among his works are *Jesus Rediscovered, Christ and the Media, Something Beautiful for God,* and his multivolume autobiography, *Chronicles of Wasted Time.* He frequently spoke and wrote of "feeling like a stranger" in the world.

In an interview a few years before his death, Muggeridge was asked if he would be willing to explain that feeling. His answer is worth repeating.

I'd very gladly do so, because I've thought about it often. In the war, when I was in North Africa, I heard some lieutenant colonel first use the phrase "displaced person." That phrase was very poignant to me. But it's also a very good definition of a person who's come to see that life is not about carnal things, or success, but is about eternity rather than time. . . . I don't really belong here, I'm simply staying here.[5]

Since I am committed to what is best for you, I am not going to suggest, "Oh, well, do whatever." I am going to challenge you to keep an eternal perspective, even though you are in the minority, even though you are surrounded by a host of success-oriented individuals who are urging you to ignore your conscience and grab all you can now. You want joy? You really want what is best? Simply consider yourself a displaced person and go God's way. His is the most reliable route to follow when life gets complicated. It will have its tough moments, but you will never regret it.

Some glorious day, trust me, you will look back on the dilemma that now has you so stressed out . . . and you will finally get your deck chair unfolded. You will then sit down on it and laugh out loud.

5

The Hidden Secret of a Happy Life

I have been writing a lot about choosing joy and about cultivating a good sense of humor. On several occasions I have mentioned the value of one's attitude, which is the secret behind learning how to laugh again. Cultivating the right attitude, in my opinion, is absolutely crucial. Now let's take a deeper look at the subject of our attitude.

The dictionary on my desk defines attitude as "a manner of acting, feeling, or thinking that shows one's disposition . . . opinion, mental set." That means that how we think determines how we respond to others. As a matter of fact, I have found that my view of others is a direct reflection of my own "mental set."

> Our attitude toward the world around us depends upon what we are ourselves. If we are selfish, we will be suspicious of others. If we are of a generous nature, we will be likely to be more trustful. If we are quite honest with ourselves, we won't always be anticipating deceit in others. If we are inclined to be fair, we won't feel that we are being cheated. In a sense, looking at the people around you is like looking in a mirror. You see a reflection of yourself.[1]

Since I am a minister of the gospel, much of my time is spent studying the Bible and then sharing the things I have discovered. Lately my study has led me into the Gospel written by an ancient physician named Luke. As he began to do his research on the most incredible individual who ever lived on our planet, Dr. Luke was led to portray Jesus as a man. This portrayal provides fascinating information for anyone interested in Jesus' interpersonal relationships.

As I have pored over Luke's descriptions and observations, looking for insights into the Savior's life, I have been intrigued by His responses to others. How could any man be as patient as He was? How could He keep His cool under constant fire? How could He demonstrate so much grace, so much compassion, and at the same time so much determination? And when faced with the Pharisees' continued badgering and baiting, how could He restrain Himself from punching their lights out? As a man, He had all the emotions we have as human beings. What was it that gave Him the edge we so often lack? *It was His attitude.* To return to Webster's words, He acted and felt as He did because of His "disposition," His "mental set."

All this brings up a question: What is the most Christlike attitude on earth? Think before you answer too quickly. I am certain many would answer *love*. That is understandable, for He did indeed love to the uttermost. Others might say *patience*. Again, not a bad choice. I find no evidence of impatience or anxious irritability as I study His life. *Grace* would also be a possibility. No man or woman ever modeled or exhibited the grace that He demonstrated right up to the moment He breathed His last.

As important as those traits may be, however, they are not the ones Jesus Himself referred to when He described Himself for the only time in Scripture. I am thinking of those familiar words:

> Come to Me, all who are weary and heavy-laden, and I will give you rest. Take My yoke upon you, and learn from Me, for I am gentle and humble in heart; and you shall find rest for your souls. For My yoke is easy, and My load is light.
>
> *Matthew 11:28–30*

Did you catch the key words? "I am gentle and humble in heart," which might best be summed up in the one word *unselfish*. According to Jesus' testimony, that is the most Christlike attitude we can demonstrate. Because He was so humble—so unselfish—the last person He thought of was Himself.

ANALYZING UNSELFISHNESS

To be "humble in heart" is to be submissive to the core. It involves being more interested in serving the needs of others than in having one's own needs met.

Someone who is truly unselfish is generous with his or her time and possessions, energy and money. As that works its way out, it is demonstrated in various ways, such as thoughtfulness and gentleness, an unpretentious spirit, and servant-hearted leadership.

- When a husband is unselfish, he subjugates his own wants and desires to the needs of his wife and family.
- When a mother is unselfish, she isn't irked by having to give up her agenda or plans for the sake of her children.
- When an athlete is unselfish, it is the team that matters, not winning the top honors personally.
- When a Christian is unselfish, others mean more than self. Pride is given no place to operate.

As Isaac Watts wrote early in the eighteenth century:

> When I survey the wondrous cross
> On which the Prince of glory died,
> My richest gain I count but loss,
> And pour contempt on all my pride.[2]

What strange-sounding words! Not because they are archaic but because everyone today is so selfish—and we are never told by our peers to be otherwise. Ours is a day of self-promotion, defending our own rights, taking care of ourselves first, winning by intimidation, pushing for first place, and a dozen other self-serving agendas. That one attitude does more to squelch our joy than any other. So busy defending and protecting and manipulating, we set ourselves up for a grim, intense existence—and it is not a modern problem.

> Greece said, "Be wise, know yourself."
> Rome said, "Be strong, discipline yourself."
> Religion says, "Be good, conform yourself."
> Epicureanism says, "Be sensuous, satisfy yourself."
> Education says, "Be resourceful, expand yourself."
> Psychology says, "Be confident, assert yourself."
> Materialism says, "Be possessive, please yourself."

Ascetism say, "Be lowly, suppress yourself."

Humanism says, "Be capable, believe in yourself."

Pride says, "Be superior, promote yourself."

Christ says, "Be unselfish, humble yourself."

When I write that last line, I find myself shaking my head and smiling. In our selfish, grab-all-you-can-get society, the concept of cultivating an unselfish, servant-hearted attitude is almost a joke to the majority. But, happily, there are a few (I hope you are one of them) who genuinely desire to develop such an attitude. I can assure you, if you carry out that desire, you will begin to laugh again—and I mean really laugh. It is the hidden secret of a happy life.

At our church in Fullerton, California, we are always looking for better ways to communicate with one another. It is easy for those of us in leadership to think everyone in the congregation is in the know when, in fact, they may be in the dark. We who stand up front and do the teaching and preaching can think everything we say is clear when it may not be. One method that has helped the congregation respond is the use of a tear-off section on our Sunday bulletins. Frequently folks will ask questions on these stubs or make a statement that helps them get a more realistic or complete view of something I have said from the pulpit.

Several Sundays ago someone wrote: "Chuck, I understand what you said today. I appreciate your commitment, and I believe every word of it. My problem is knowing how to do it!" I call that an extremely honest and humble response.

You may feel the same way about the things I have been saying regarding the value of maintaining an unselfish attitude. Perhaps you would even agree that unselfishness is the stuff of which Christlikeness is made . . . but how do we pull it off? You need to have it spelled out in more explicit, practical ways? Fair enough.

EXAMINING CHRISTLIKENESS

Let's go back to the little letter Paul wrote to his friends in Philippi. I think what he says regarding the attitude of unselfishness will help lift the fog of indefiniteness and enable us to get down to the nubbies of how to make it happen.

He begins this section with a plea:

> If therefore there is any encouragement in Christ, if there is any consolation of love, if there is any fellowship of the Spirit, if any affection and compassion, make my joy complete by being of the same mind, maintaining the same love, united in spirit, intent on one purpose. Do nothing from selfishness or empty conceit, but with humility of mind let each of you regard one another as more important than himself; do not merely look out for your own personal interests, but also for the interests of others.
>
> *Philippians 2:1–4*

These opening lines conclude with the theme of what is on his mind—"others." As we read Paul's initial plea, it is obvious that his major concern is that there not be disunity or conflict among his friends. It is as if he is pleading: Whatever else may happen, my friends, don't let a selfish attitude sneak in like a thief and steal your joy or interrupt your closeness.

What Is Needed?

Most of all, harmony is needed . . . a like-minded spirit with one another. I like the way The Living Bible renders the opening lines of this paragraph:

> Is there any such thing as Christians cheering each other up? Do you love me enough to want to help me? Does it mean anything to you that we are brothers in the Lord, sharing the same Spirit? Are your hearts tender and sympathetic at all? Then make me truly happy by loving each other and agreeing wholeheartedly with each other, working together with one heart and mind and purpose.
>
> *Philippians 2:1–2* TLB

What a wonderful way to live one's life! That "one heart and mind and purpose" suggests unity, a genuine Spirit-filled unselfishness that breeds strength and spreads cheer.

Is this suggesting uniformity? Does it mean we always have to agree on everything? Is that what harmony is all about? No. There is a difference between unity and uniformity. Uniformity is gained by pressure from without. The English word *uniformity* has within it the word *uniform*. We dress alike, look alike, sound alike, think alike, act alike. But that is neither healthy nor biblical. Unity comes from deep within. It is the inner desire to conduct oneself in a cooperative manner . . . to be on the same team, to go for the same objectives, for the benefit of one another.

As Harry A. Ironside said,

> It is very evident that Christians will never see eye to eye on all points. We are so largely influenced by habits, by environment, by education, by the measure of intellectual and spiritual apprehension to which we have attained, that it is an impossibility to find any number of people who look at everything from the same standpoint. How then can such be of one mind? The apostle himself explains it elsewhere when he says, "I think also that I have the mind of Christ." The "mind of Christ" is the lowly mind. And, if we are all of *this* mind, we shall walk together in love, considering one another, and seeking rather to be helpers of one another's faith, than challenging each other's convictions.[3]

Interestingly, Paul admits that their maintaining such a spirit of harmony would "make my joy complete." Harmony promotes happiness. If you question that, you've not worked at a place where disharmony reigns or lived in a home fractured by disunity. Joy cannot survive such settings. If we hope to laugh again, harmony needs to be restored.

How Is It Accomplished?

The question, I repeat, is how? How is it possible to pull off such an unselfish attitude when we find ourselves surrounded by quite the opposite? Let's look a little closer at what Paul wrote:

> Do nothing from selfishness or empty conceit, but with humility of mind let each of you regard one another as more important than himself; do not merely look out for your own personal interests, but also for the interests of others.
>
> *Philippians 2:3–4*

As I consider his counsel, three practical ideas emerge that may help us cultivate an unselfish attitude.

First, never let selfishness or conceit be your motive. That's right, *never.* That is Paul's advice, isn't it? "Do *nothing* from selfishness or empty conceit" (emphasis mine).

Second, always regard others as more important than yourself. Though this is not a natural trait, it can become a habit—and what an important one!

Third, don't limit your attention to your own personal interests— include others. I think it was Andrew Murray who said: "The humble person is not one who thinks meanly of himself; he simply does not think of himself at all."

Some may try to dissuade you from what may appear to be an unbalanced, extremist position. They may tell you that anyone who adopts this sort of attitude is getting dangerously near self-flagellation and a loss of healthy self-esteem. Nonsense! The goal is that we become so interested in others and in helping them reach their highest good that we become self-forgetful in the process.

Go back momentarily to Paul's choice of words, "humility of mind." As we pursue this attitude (exalting Christ) and get involved in the same objective (being of help and encouragement to others), we set aside our differences (harmony) and lose interest in pleasing ourselves (unselfishness). Perhaps the closest we come to that is when we are forced to mutually endure hard times.

Martyn Lloyd-Jones, writing in England shortly after World War II, recalled the terror of the blitzkrieg bombing attacks of Hitler's Luftwaffe:

> How often during that last war were we told of the extraordinary scenes in air-raid shelters; how different people belonging to different classes, there, in the common need to shelter from the bombs and death, forgot all the differences between them and became one. This was because in the common interest they forgot the divisions and the distinctions. That is why you always tend to have a coalition government during a war; in periods of crises and common need all distinctions are forgotten and we suddenly become united.[4]

I have seen similar scenes out here in California in the midst of an awful fire that sweeps across thousands of acres, until finally those flaming fingers reach into a residential section. What happens? Immediately people pull together. They pay no attention to who makes what salary, which kind of car a person drives, or how much they might receive from their neighbor by helping out. Totally disregarding any benefit they personally might derive from their acts of heroism (usually nothing) and with no thought of personal danger, they "regard one another as more important" than their own possessions or safety. When we are forced to focus only on the help we can be to others in a time of crisis, we begin to demonstrate this Christlike attitude.

To be truthful about it, it does not always require a crisis. I have found that just having a large family—say, four or five kids—is enough to teach us how selfishness fouls up the works. I recall when Cynthia and I began to have children, I thought two would be perfect. "Alpha and Omega" . . . *ideal!* Along came our third . . . and not too many years later a fourth.

Now, you need to understand the kind of guy I am. I like my shoes spit-shined rather than stepped on and scuffed up. And I like my clothes hanging in the closet in an orderly and neat manner rather than drooled on and wrinkled up. And I really like milk in a glass on the table and not on the floor. I especially like a clean car with no fingerprints on the windows and no leftover school assignments spread across the floorboards.

So what does the Lord do to help broaden my horizons and assist me in seeing how selfish I am? Very simple: He gives me four busy kids who step on shoes, wrinkle clothes, spill milk, lick car windows, and drop sticky candy on the carpet. You haven't lived until you've walked barefoot across the floor in the middle of the night and stomped down full force on a jack . . . or a couple of those little Lego landmines. I'll tell you, you learn real quick about your own level of selfishness.

You see, this is not some deep, ethereal, or theological subject we're thinking about. Being unselfish in attitude strikes at the very core of our being. It means we are willing to forego our own comfort, our own preferences, our own schedule, our own desires for another's benefit. And that brings us back to Christ. Perhaps you never realized that it was His attitude of unselfishness that launched Him from the splendor of heaven to a humble manger in Bethlehem . . . and later to the cross at Calvary. How did He accept all that? Willingly.

CHRIST'S LIFE . . . BEFORE AND AFTER

A significant transitional statement appears at this juncture in Paul's words to the Philippians.

Have this attitude in yourselves which was also in Christ Jesus. . . .

Philippians 2:5

Christ Jesus, what a perfect example of an unselfish attitude! What Paul has been pleading for among his friends at Philippi, he illustrates in the person of Jesus Christ. In effect, he is saying, "You want to know what I'm getting at? You would like a 'for instance' to help you better understand what I mean by 'looking out for . . . the interest of others'? I call before you the perfect example: Christ Jesus."

Take a look at how He modeled this attitude:

> Have this attitude in yourselves which was also in Christ Jesus, who, although He existed in the form of God, did not regard equality with God a thing to be grasped, but emptied Himself, taking the form of a bond-servant, and being made in the likeness of men. And being found in appearance as a man, He humbled Himself by becoming obedient to the point of death, even death on a cross.
>
> *Philippians 2:5–8*

Everything that was involved in Jesus' becoming human began with an attitude of submission . . . a willingness to cooperate with God's plan for salvation. Rather than lobbying for His right to remain in heaven and continuing to enjoy all the benefits of that exalted role as the second member of the Godhead and Lord of the created world, He willingly said yes. He agreed to cooperate with a plan that would require His releasing ecstasy and accepting agony. In a state of absolute perfection and undiminished deity, He willingly came to earth. Leaving the angelic hosts who flooded His presence with adoring praise, He unselfishly accepted a role that would require His being misunderstood, abused, cursed, and crucified. He unhesitatingly surrendered the fellowship and protection of the Father's glory for the lonely path of obedience and torturous death.

Don't miss the steps downward:

1. He emptied Himself.
2. He took the form of a servant.
3. He was made in the likeness of humanity.
4. He humbled Himself by becoming obedient unto death.
5. He accepted the most painful and humiliating way to die—crucifixion.

Did He realize all this ahead of time? Of course. Was He aware that it would require such an extensive sacrifice? Without question. Did He do it all with a grim face and tight lips? Not at all. How do we know? You will find the answer to that tucked away in Hebrews 12:2,

> Fixing our eyes on Jesus, the author and perfecter of faith, who for the joy set before Him endured the cross, despising the shame, and has sat down at the right hand of the throne of God.
>
> *Hebrews 12:2*

Look at that! He saw those of us who would benefit from His sacrifice as "the joy set before Him." We're back to our theme—joy! He did not come to us grudgingly or nursing a bitter spirit. He came free of all that. While it was certainly not a pleasurable experience, He accepted His coming among us and His dying for us willingly and unselfishly.

And what ultimately happened? Read and rejoice!

> Therefore also God highly exalted Him, and bestowed on Him the name which is above every name, that at the name of Jesus every knee should bow, of those who are in heaven, and on earth, and under the earth, and that every tongue should confess that Jesus Christ is Lord, to the glory of God the Father.
>
> *Philippians 2:9–11*

Paul seems especially fond of compound superlatives. "God supremely exalted Him!" He was welcomed back with open arms. Heaven's applause was the supreme reward for His earthly sacrifice. Once again submission paid a rich dividend. We are told that two things occurred after the price for sin was paid:

1. God highly exalted Jesus Christ to the pinnacle of authority.
2. God bestowed on Him a name of highest significance: *Kurios Iesous Christos* . . . "Jesus Christ—Lord!"

No one else deserves that title. Only one is LORD. All knees will ultimately bow before Him. Above the earth? All angels will bow . . .

and all who have gone on before us. On the earth? Every living human being . . . those who love and worship Him and, yes, even those who deny and despise Him. One day in the future, all on earth will bow. Under the earth? The devil and his demonic forces along with those who have died without faith, unbelieving and lost.

> The lost will never be reconciled. Heaven and earth will eventually be filled with happy beings who have been redeemed to God by the precious blood of Christ. . . .
> But "under the earth" will be those who "have their part" in the outer darkness, the lake of fire. They flaunted Christ's authority on earth. They will have to own it in hell! They refused to heed the call of grace and be reconciled to God in the day when they might have been saved.[5]

A Concluding Encouragement and Example

My emphasis in this chapter has been on the attitude that releases joy and launches it from our lips, the hidden secret of a happy life on earth—an attitude of unselfishness. My encouragement to you is that you not put it off until it is a little more convenient. Many will tell you that you will be taken advantage of if you begin to live for others or if you don't defend your rights and "get even." I offer the opposite counsel: God will honor your decision to demonstrate an attitude of humility. You will find that feelings of hate will be replaced with a relieving flood of peace and happiness. As Solomon has written, "When a man's ways are pleasing to the Lord, He makes even his enemies to be at peace with him" (Prov. 16:7).

Actually, it all begins with your knowing Jesus Christ in a personal way . . . and your allowing Him to take the blows of life for you. If you willingly do His will, you will find He gives you joy that even the angels of heaven cannot experience. Someday our voices will join the angelic host and together we will make great music! But our joy will outdo theirs.

There is an old gospel song I seldom hear anymore. Its chorus states what I'm trying to communicate:

> Holy, holy, is what the angels sing,
> And I expect to help them make the courts of heaven
> ring;

But when I sing redemption's story, they will fold their
  wings,
For angels never felt the joys that our salvation
  brings.[6]

When we acknowledge that Jesus Christ is Lord and begin to release
our cares, our disappointments, and our heartaches to Him, we not only
keep our equilibrium, we also keep our sense of humor. Joys multiply
when we have Someone to bear our burdens.

I mentioned earlier that I serve on the board of my alma mater. That
assignment carries with it many serious responsibilities but also several
joyous benefits. One of those has been the privilege of getting better acquainted with a fine group of Christian gentlemen who serve as colleagues
on the same leadership team. One of them is a man I have admired from
a distance for many years—Tom Landry. As head coach of the Dallas
Cowboys for twenty-nine years and a member of the National Football
League Hall of Fame, his record speaks for itself. But what I find even
more admirable are his character, his integrity, and his humility. Now that
I have gotten to know the man "up close and personal," my appreciation
for him has only increased.

Most of us were surprised and disappointed at the way a new
owner of the Cowboys released Coach Landry from his position. I had
the privilege of watching and listening to him during that time . . . even
having a few personal conversations without microphones or television
cameras or news reporters nearby. He had ample opportunities to blast
the new management by criticizing their methods and defending himself. Not once—not a single time—following his forced resignation did
I hear an ugly remark or a blaming comment cross Tom Landry's lips.
The only response was something like, "You know, Chuck, a fellow in
my position has to realize it's going to be taken from him whether or not
he is ready for it to happen. It's just a matter of being willing to accept
that." Those are the unselfish words of a man who was told rather hur-
riedly to clean out his desk and be on his way . . . after giving almost
three decades of his life to something he loved. Most others in his place
would have held a news conference within hours and blasted the new
management unmercifully.

I have been with Coach Landry on numerous occasions since then.
We have had him at our church to speak to a gymnasium full of men
with their sons and friends. It has been delightful to observe a total

absence of bitterness in the man and, at the same time, the continued presence of a sense of humor and the joy of Christ. Personally, I am convinced his current attitude is a greater message to those to whom he speaks than all those years of success and championship seasons. It is reassuring to know that joy can endure hardship as long as that Christlike attitude of unselfishness is in place.

6

While Laughing, Keep Your Balance!

*D*ied, age thirty. buried, age sixty.

That's an appropriate epitaph for too many Americans. Mummification sets in on a host of young men and women at an age when they should be tearing up the track. All of us have so much more to offer for so much longer than we realize; it would boggle our minds if we could envision our full potential.

I came across an article way back in 1967 that I still return to on occasion. Entitled "Advice to a (Bored) Young Man," it communicates how much one person can contribute, if only—

Many people reading this page are doing so with the aid of bifocals. Inventor? *B. Franklin*, age 79.

The presses that printed this page were powered by electricity. One of the first harnessers? *B. Franklin*, age 40.

Some are reading this on the campus of one of the Ivy League universities. Founder? *B. Franklin*, age 45.

Some got their copy through the U.S. Mail. Its father? *B. Franklin*, age 31.

Now, think fire. Who started the first fire department, invented the lightning rod, designed a heating stove still in use today? *B. Franklin*, ages 31, 43, 36.

Wit. Conversationalist. Economist. Philosopher. Diplomat. Printer. Publisher. Linguist (spoke and wrote five languages). Advocate of paratroopers (from balloons) a century before the airplane was invented. All this until age 84.

And he had exactly two years of formal schooling. It's a good bet that you already have more sheer knowledge than Franklin had when he was your age.

Perhaps you think there's no use trying to think of anything new, that everything's been done. Wrong. The simple, agrarian America of Franklin's day didn't begin to need the answers we need today.
Go do something about it.[1]

After digesting a list like that, my immediate response is *Wow!* Who wouldn't be impressed? Examples like Benjamin Franklin are nothing short of fantastic. But they can also be frustrating.

I'm trying to put myself into the house slippers of a mother of four or five young children who does well to get dressed by eleven o'clock in the morning . . . or the recently unemployed forty-five-year-old husband and father who is spending his day on a job search, caught somewhere between pressure and panic. Furthermore, a lot of us do well just finding time to read about such inventions, to say nothing of spending the time it takes to discover them.

To keep things in balance it is helpful to remember the words of humorist Mark Twain: "Few things are harder to put up with than the annoyance of a good example."[2]

Admiration for a great person may inspire us, but it cannot enable us. Great potential notwithstanding, it is easy to feel overwhelmed.

WRONG RESPONSES TO RIGHT EXAMPLES

So what are the options frustrated folks take when exposed to great examples? To be sure, some *fake it.* Just polish the image and make a good appearance. Many make a career of doing that and never get caught. Others try to once and it backfires in spades. Back in 1990 a scandal hit the music industry. Milli Vanilli, who had won a Grammy Award for the album "Girl You Know It's True," finally had to confess it wasn't. They had lip-synced the entire recording, which resulted in the disgrace of having to return the Grammy.

To all that, Jimmy Bowen, president of Capitol Records, replied:

> Ya have to remember that music is a mirror of the times. And when the mirror is close to what's happening, that's what sells. The times we live in are very plastic. There are a lot of phony things happening in people's daily lives. So Milli Vanilli is just playing the game.[3]

Another spokesperson in the same newspaper article added,

As technology allows music producers to use increasingly sophisticated electronic trickery to make albums and videos, the Milli Vanilli scandal will only repeat itself—unless audiences stop valuing image more than content.[4]

Another common technique when facing a great example is to *hurry the process.* I find that our generation, more than any in the past, wants more, *quicker.* "Don't slow me down by making me pay a price or go through some long and painful process. I don't want to wait until I'm in my fifties, sixties, or seventies. I want it now."

Regardless of your opinion of him, you have to agree that Liberace was one of the most popular entertainers of the latter half of the twentieth century. Recently I was interested to discover these comments on his style from the late pianist himself:

"My whole trick," he says, "is to keep the tune well out in front. If I play Tschaikovsky, I play his melodies and skip his spiritual struggles. Naturally, I condense. I have to know just how many notes my audience will stand for. If there's time left over, I fill in with a lot of runs up and down the keyboard."[5]

There is another option, quite common in Christian circles. When faced with an example to whom we feel we cannot measure up, we *strive harder.* The old familiar song states this philosophy: "Striving to please Him in all that I do."

I ask you, is that the Christian life? If the answer is not faking it and if it is not hurrying things, is it striving hard for it? You want to live the rest of your life striving to please Him in all that you do? Some who are painfully honest will admit, "I'm doing my best. I'm trying. But I'm exhausted." Surely that's not God's plan.

CHRIST, OUR EXAMPLE

What may be true of other examples is not true of Jesus. Whether they be president or statesman, inventor or novelist, athlete or artist, all other great examples may inspire, but they cannot enable. They may motivate us, but they have no power to change us. There is nothing of Ben Franklin left over that can make you or me the inventor he was. But when it comes to Christ, things are different. He says, in effect, "You want to live My life? Here is My power." Lo and behold, He strengthens us within. "You want to please My heavenly Father? Here's My enablement." And He enables us by His Spirit.

Having failed far more than I have succeeded at many of my dreams, I find that very encouraging. And perhaps you would have to say the same thing. Having been swamped by sin all our lives, struggling to find our way to the top of the water to breathe, we can find great hope in the ability He gives us not only to breathe but to swim freely. You see, Christ not only lived an exemplary life, He also makes it possible for us to do the same. He gives us His pattern to follow *without* while at the same time providing the needed power *within*. And guess what that makes us able to do? Laugh again!

I mean it in the right sense when I say that for years Jesus has made me laugh. Because we have His example to follow and His power to pull it off, you and I no longer have to fake it or hurry it or strive for it. Once He gets control of our minds, the right attitudes bring about the right actions.

LIFE, OUR CHALLENGE

Having established the preeminent role Christ plays in our minds, we need to see how all that works its way out in our lives. Which brings us back to the little letter Paul wrote his friends in Philippi. In this choice missive promoting outrageous joy, he spells out the importance of keeping ourselves balanced as we take on the challenges of life. In doing this he specifies three of the most significant areas we must deal with:

- Balancing purpose and power (2:12–13)
- Balancing attitude and action (2:14–16)
- Balancing seriousness and joy (2:17–18)

Let's take them in that order.

Balancing Purpose and Power

So then, my beloved, just as you have always obeyed, not as in my presence only, but now much more in my absence, work out your salvation with fear and trembling; for it is God who is at work in you, both to will and to work for His good pleasure.

Philippians 2:12–13

80

We need to keep in mind that Paul is writing to Christians ("my beloved"), so obviously these words have nothing to do with his readers' becoming Christians—they already are. Therefore, the idea of working out one's salvation must be referring to living out one's faith—carrying it out correctly. In other words, we, as God's people, are charged with the importance of obedience. Just as Christ, our example, was "obedient to the point of death" (2:8), so we are to carry out our purpose with equal diligence.

Interestingly, the word translated "work out" was the same Greek term popularly used for "working a mine" or "working a field." In each case there were benefits that followed such diligence. The mine would yield valuable elements or ore . . . the field would yield crops. Paul's point is clear: By working out our salvation, we bring the whole purpose to completion . . . we carry out our reason for existence. So let's not stop short!

When a musician has a fine composition placed before her, that music is not the musician's masterpiece; it is the composer's gift to the musician. But it then becomes the task of the musician to work it out, to give it sound and expression and beauty as she applies her skills to the composition. When she does, the composition reaches its completed purpose and thrills the hearts of her listeners.

When we become ill, we go to a physician. He diagnoses our ailment and prescribes the proper treatment. He hands us a small slip of paper upon which he has written the correct prescription, and we take it to the pharmacist who fills that prescription and gives us the medication. So far, everything has been done for us—diagnosis, prescription, medication. It now becomes our responsibility to follow the doctor's orders exactly as stated. By working out the process we enjoy the benefits of the physician's and pharmacist's contributions to our health. We recover.

Spiritually speaking, the ultimate goal or purpose of our lives is "His good pleasure." Our lives are to be lived for God's greater glory—not our own selfish desires.

Are we left to do so all alone? Is it our task to gut it out, grit our teeth, and do His will? Not at all. Here's the balance: *God is at work in us!* He is the one who gives us strength and empowers our diligence. As He pours His power into us, we do the things that bring Him pleasure. Take special note that His pleasure (not ours), His will (not ours), His glory (not ours) are what make life meaningful. And therein lies a potential conflict, since most of us prefer to have things go our way. All this brings us back to that famous A-word—attitude.

Balancing Attitude and Action

Do all things without grumbling or disputing; that you may prove yourselves to be blameless and innocent, children of God above reproach in the midst of a crooked and perverse generation, among whom you appear as lights in the world, holding fast the word of life, so that in the day of Christ I may have cause to glory because I did not run in vain nor toil in vain.

Philippians 2:14–16

The first part of Paul's counsel here represents the negative side and the last part, the positive. The two provide another needed balance.

Negatively, watch your attitude! A bad attitude reveals itself from two sides: something we do alone—"grumbling"—and something we do when we are with others—"disputing." Both of these joy stealers need to be exposed.

What exactly is grumbling? It is not loud, boisterous grousing but rather low-toned, discontented muttering. It is negative, muted comments, complaining and whining. Disputing, however, is vocal, ill-natured argumentation . . . verbal expressions of disagreement that stir up suspicion and distrust, doubt and other disturbing feelings in others.

Some folks, like the British novelist J. B. Priestly (by his own admission), spread negative germs by their bad attitudes and acrid tongues. He once declared:

I have always been a grumbler. I am designed for the part—sagging face, weighty underlip, rumbling, resonant voice. Money couldn't buy a better grumbling outfit.[6]

Ever been around a sourpuss like that? We all have. And even when we try to resist being influenced by such negativism, we find some of it rubbing off. How unfair to pass around the poison of pessimism! But it happens every day, and it steals our joy. It creates an atmosphere of wholesale negativism where nothing but the bad side of everything is emphasized. It is enough to make you scream!

I couldn't help but smile when I read Barry Siegel's satirical article "World May End with a Splash" in the *Los Angeles Times*. In a lighthearted way it shows how ridiculous it is to let negativism take charge:

> Alarmists, worrying about such matters as nuclear holocaust and pesticide poisoning, may be overlooking much more dire catastrophes. Consider what some scientists predict: If everyone keeps stacking *National Geographics* in garages and attics instead of throwing them away, the magazine's weight will sink the continent 100 feet some time soon and we will all be inundated by the oceans.
>
> If the number of microscope specimen slides submitted to one St. Louis Hospital laboratory continues to increase at its current rate, that metropolis will be buried under 3 feet of glass by the year 2024. If beachgoers keep returning home with as much sand clinging to them as they do now, 80 percent of the country's coastline will disappear in 10 years. . . .
>
> [It has also been reported] that pickles cause cancer, communism, airline tragedies, auto accidents and crime waves. About 99.9% of cancer victims had eaten pickles some time in their lives. . . . So have 100% of all soldiers, 96.8% of Communist sympathizers and 99.7% of those involved in car and air accidents. Moreover those born in 1839 who ate pickles have suffered 100% mortality rate and rats force-fed 20 pounds of pickles a day for a month ended up with bulging abdomens and loss of appetite.[7]

Crazy stuff, but isn't that the way it is when grumbling and complaining are allowed to run wild? Those who hope to laugh again—those who genuinely wish to get beyond the doomsday mentality that pervades so much of today's newscasts, shop talk, and run-of-the-mill conversations among Christians and non-Christians alike—must learn to "do all things without grumbling or disputing." Verbal pollution takes a heavy toll on everyone. Furthermore, who gave anyone the right to pollute the air with such pessimism? I agree with the person who said:

> We have no more right to put our discordant states of mind into the lives of those around us and rob them of their sunshine and brightness than we have to enter their houses and steal their silverware.[8]

I would love to hurry on past this subject, but I'd be less than honest if I left the impression that this is never my problem. I must confess that

I, too, occasionally battle with negativism. When I do, it is usually my wife Cynthia who suffers the brunt of it. She has been pretty patient to endure it for more than thirty-seven years. I'm not as bad as I used to be, but every once in a while it surfaces.

Some of my readers know the ongoing debate that Cynthia and I have about bougainvillea. Years ago she really wanted us to plant several containers of bright red bougainvillea. It is a wonderful plant if you look at just the blossoms. But hidden within the plant are thorns . . . I mean those suckers are wicked! When Cynthia looks at bougainvillea, she sees only blossoms. When I look at the plant, I see only thorns. Unfortunately, there is a house not far from our home with a spectacular blooming bougainvillea climbing off the roof out front. Whenever we pass that house, Cynthia likes to drive a little slower and enjoy the blossoms. At certain times of the year she will point out, "Look how beautifully that bougainvillea is blooming." I will usually respond, without looking, "Do you realize the size of its thorns? I mean they are big . . . and they grow all over that plant. You may not see them, but if you walk close enough, you may never get free. It could catch you and hold you for half a morning."

Cynthia isn't convinced. She even said to me on one occasion, "Do you realize, honey, that every time—I mean *every time*—I mention bougainvillea, you grouse about the thorns?" (I might add that that conversation led to a dispute between us.)

In a lighthearted moment several years ago, I revealed our ongoing disagreement from the pulpit of our church, and much to my chagrin some anonymous soul sent us ten five-gallon containers of bougainvillea. I never told my wife, however, and we still have not planted bougainvillea. It is not God's will that we have bougainvillea. Too many thorns. Cynthia says she is confident that heaven will be full of bougainvillea. Since heaven is a perfect place, I maintain they would have to be a thornless species.

Positively, *prove that you are different!*

. . . prove yourselves to be blameless and innocent, children of God above reproach in the midst of a crooked and perverse generation, among whom you appear as lights in the world, holding fast the word of life, so that in the day of Christ I may have cause to glory because I did not run in vain nor toil in vain.

Philippians 2:15–16

Ours is a world of crooks and perverts, says my friend Ray Stedman, when he teaches this passage of Scripture. He is right. And since that is true, we need to model lives that are not like the majority. A positive attitude makes a major statement in our "crooked and perverse generation." We don't need to shout it out or make a superpious appearance; just don't grumble or dispute.

Paul goes further as he identifies four startling differences between those who know Christ and those who don't. These four descriptive words make all the difference in the world. Unlike our unbelieving friends, we are to be:

1. *Blameless.* This suggests a purity of life that is both undeniable and unhypocritical . . . free of defect.

2. *Innocent.* This means unmixed and unadulterated . . . inexperienced in evil . . . untainted in motive . . . possessing integrity.

3. *Above reproach.* This description is used of sacrificial lambs offered on altars and means free of blemish.

4. *Lights.* Actually the term used here means "luminaries," meaning we are to shine like stars surrounded by darkness.

In fact, Paul goes on to say that as we shine like stars, we are "holding fast the word of life."

Where did we pick up the mistaken idea of "This little light of mine, I'm gonna let it shine"? We are never called "little lights" in the Bible . . . we are *stars.* Bold, blazing, light-giving stars! This aching, hurting, confused world of lost humanity exists in dark rooms without light. Let it shine, fellow star! Why? Jesus answers that question in the sermon He delivered on the mountain:

> Let your light shine before men in such a way that they may see your good works, and glorify your Father who is in heaven.
>
> *Matthew 5:16*

No need to shout, scream, or make a scene. Just shine. Just live a life free of grumbling and disputing. The difference will jolt them awake. Furthermore, we will not live our lives "in vain." And speaking of that, Paul declares that he "did not run in vain nor toil in vain." What a claim to make as one begins to get up in years: No wasted effort!

My good friend David Roper, a pastor in Boise, Idaho, was, for a number of years, associate pastor alongside Ray Stedman at Peninsula Bible Church. You may know and appreciate Dave's ministry and writings, as I certainly do. Many years ago while Dave was ministering in Palo Alto on the campus of Stanford University, he arrived early one morning before the Bible study group had gathered. He was standing near an open courtyard and noticed an overgrown area where some kind of stonework was buried beneath vines and overgrowth. Dave's curiosity led him to go over and pull the vines away and tear back some of the overgrowth. When he did, he uncovered an ornate, hand-sculptured, stone birdbath. Though beautiful and unique, it was no longer being used. All the work the sculptor had put into that birdbath was wasted. When he saw this, Dave said he was moved to pray, "Lord, keep me from wasted effort. Don't let me build birdbaths with my life."

You and I can "run in vain and toil in vain" so easily. And afterward, looking back on that life, we will have to live with those vivid memories and feelings, "in vain . . . all wasted effort." We may not be in the category of a Ben Franklin, but we have the power of Jesus Christ working within us to give us all that is needed to make whatever impact He would have us make.

Balancing Seriousness and Joy

Not allowing our lives to become useless birdbaths—that is an extremely serious thought. But Paul gets even more serious:

> But even if I am being poured out as a drink offering upon the sacrifice and service of your faith, I rejoice and share my joy with you all. And you too, I urge you, rejoice in the same way and share your joy with me.
>
> *Philippians 2:17–18*

I find another word picture worth analyzing here. Paul speaks of the possibility of his "being poured out as a drink offering." This picture is drawn from a practice the pagans had of pouring out a chalice of wine before or after their meals in honor of the gods they worshiped. It was called a libation and was poured out either to gain the favor of or soften the anger of their gods.

Paul's thought is a serious analogy: I may never get out of this situation alive. It may be God's will that my life be poured out as a libation.

Even if that is so, even if it means the end of my life, this pouring out of my days on your behalf is worth every moment. Even if this imprisonment is my last, I rejoice!

I want to underscore something about Paul here: *There lived a balanced man.* While imagining that he might be living his final days, the single most serious thought a person could have, he was still able to rejoice. He refused to focus only on the dark side. He refused to let even the possibility of immediate and sure death steal his joy. In fact, he urged his friends to "rejoice in the same way."

Amazing! We cannot get through any major section of this letter without returning to Paul's themes of joy, rejoicing, and laughter. What a balanced man! A seasoned and scarred veteran missionary, yet all the while possessing a keen sense of humor. I have known a few men and women like that in my lifetime, and they never fail to bring refreshment and new hope. To remain superserious all the time and fill one's mind with only the harsh and painful realities of life keeps the radius of our perspective too tight and the tunnel of our hope too long. Paul refused to do that, and he wanted to make sure his Philippian friends followed suit.

Virtually every day I can find at least one thing to laugh about. There may be a few exceptions, but those days are rare indeed. Even though pain or difficult circumstances (Paul had both on a daily basis) may be our faithful companions, we encounter something each day that can prompt a chuckle or, for that matter, a hearty burst of laughter. And besides, it's healthy!

Experts tell us that laughter not only makes our serious lives lighter, but laughter also helps control pain in at least four ways: (1) by distracting our attention, (2) by reducing the tension we are living with, (3) by changing our expectations, and (4) by increasing the production of endorphins, the body's natural painkillers.[9] Laughter, strange as it may seem, turns our minds from our seriousness and pain and actually creates a degree of anesthesia. By diverting our attention from our situation, laughter enables us to take a brief excursion away from the pain.

Sometimes it is not literal pain but a too-serious mind-set. When our world begins to get too serious, we need momentary interruptions of just plain fun. A surprising day off, a long walk in the woods, a movie, an enjoyable evening relaxing with a friend over a bowl of popcorn, a game of racquetball or golf—these diversions can make all the difference in our ability to cope with life's crushing demands. We need to give ourselves permission to enjoy various moments in life even though all of life is not in perfect order. This takes practice, but it's worth the effort. It helps break guilt's stranglehold on us.

Some saints can't enjoy a meal because the world is starving. They can't joyfully thank God for their clothing and shelter because the world is naked and homeless. They are afraid to smile because of the world's sadness. They're afraid to enjoy salvation because of the world's lost ones. They can't enjoy an evening at home with their families because they feel they ought to be out 'saving souls'. They can't spend an hour with an unforgiven one without feeling guilty if they haven't preached a sermon or manifested a 'sober Christian spirit'. They know nothing of balance. And they're miserable because of it. They have no inner incentive to bring people into a relationship with Christ which would make them feel as miserable as they themselves feel. They think the Gospel is 'good news' until you obey it and then it becomes an endless guilt-trip.

There are leisure centres, sports centres, sewing centres, diet centres, entertainment centres and guilt centres. This last group is usually called 'Churches'. The endless harping on the string of guilt is part of the reason for all this gloom and uncertainty.[10]

SELF, OUR BATTLE

I want to close this chapter on balance with a warning. Old habits are terribly hard to break. Down inside of you is a voice that continues to nag you as you read these pages. It is saying, "No, no, no, No, NO!" As soon as you attempt to bring some necessary balance into your life, you are going to have a fight on your hands. After all, self has had its way for years. Giving you the freedom to laugh again and bring some needed joy into your life is not on self's agenda.

No matter. This invisible master needs to be brought back under the authority of Christ if you ever hope to laugh again. A life lived under the dominion of self is both unsatisfying and unproductive.

Here are a couple of suggestions for getting started:

1. Control self's urges to take the credit. When self reigns supreme, it lives for moments of personal gratification. Wean it away. Once you are able to see how out of balance you have become, you will have fresh strength to control its urges. Self needs to be bucked off its high horse.

John Wooden, former coach of the UCLA Bruins basketball team for so many national championship seasons, gives this helpful advice:

Talent is God-given, be humble;
Fame is man-given, be thankful;
Conceit is self-given, be careful.[11]

2. Conquer self's tendency to take charge. The longer you live the more you will realize the value of having Christ call the shots in your life. Not self, Christ. But that age-old battle will continue. Self wants to gain the mastery and convince you that it is a reusable source of energy. It is not. Self cannot be trusted. Any day you forget that and turn the controls over to self will be another day you will operate on strictly human energy, and you will lack the Spirit's power.

Back in the fall of 1990, I had an opportunity to minister to the military servicemen and women in Mannheim, Germany, along with two colleagues, Paul Sailhamer and Howie Stevenson. Since that area of Europe is Martin Luther Country, during our off-hours we visited the reformer's old haunts, the places he lived and wrote and served his Lord. There is something deeply invigorating about looking at a historic wall black with age or walking through a stone courtyard or standing in an ancient cathedral where a great man or woman once made history. It is as if that voice still speaks from the woodwork or that inimitable shadow still darkens the wall.

We stood where Luther stood at Worms when he defended himself before the Roman Church, a history-making moment known today as the Diet of Worms. There the most significant officials of the church had gathered to hear the German monk's declaration of the doctrine of salvation by grace alone—*Sola Fide.* In that emotion-charged moment he stood alone, unintimidated and resolute.

Just before Luther's audience with the pope, the prelates, the cardinals, and the emperor, a friend moved alongside the maverick monk and asked, "Brother Martin, are you afraid?" Luther responded with a marvelous answer: "Greater than the pope and all his cardinals, I fear most that great pope, self."[12]

And so should we. But if we hope to bring things back into balance—if we hope to change our habits of negative thinking, which leads to grumbling and a too-serious mentality—we'll have to dethrone this master and give the right Master His rightful place over our lives. Not until we do, I remind you, will we begin to laugh again.

7

Friends Make Life More Fun

*I*f I have learned anything during my journey on Planet Earth, it is that people need one another. The presence of other people is essential—caring people, helpful people, interesting people, friendly people, thoughtful people. These folks take the grind out of life. About the time we are tempted to think we can handle things all alone—boom! We run into some obstacle and need assistance. We discover all over again that we are not nearly as self-sufficient as we thought.

In spite of our high-tech world and efficient procedures, people remain the essential ingredient of life. When we forget that, a strange thing happens: We start treating people like inconveniences instead of assets.

This is precisely what humorist Robert Henry, a professional speaker, encountered one evening when he went to a large discount department store in search of a pair of binoculars.

As he walked up to the appropriate counter he noticed that he was the only customer in the store. Behind the counter were two salespersons. One was so preoccupied talking to "Mama" on the telephone that she refused to acknowledge that Robert was there. At the other end of the counter, a second salesperson was unloading inventory from a box onto the shelves. Growing impatient, Robert walked down to her end of the counter and just stood there. Finally, she looked up at Robert and said, "You got a number?"

"I got a what?" asked Robert, trying to control his astonishment at such an absurdity.

"You got a number? You gotta have a number."

Robert replied, "Lady, I'm the only customer in the store! I don't need a number. Can't you see how ridiculous this is?" But she failed to see the absurdity and insisted that Robert take a number before agreeing to wait on him. By now, it was obvious to Robert that she was more interested in following procedures than helping the customer. So, he went to the take-a-number machine, pulled number 37 and walked back to the salesperson. With that, she promptly went to her number counter, which revealed that the last customer waited on had been holding number 34. So she screamed out, "35! . . . 35! . . . 36! . . . 36! . . . 37!"

"I'm number 37," said Robert.

"May I help you?" she asked, without cracking a smile.

"No," replied Robert, and he turned around and walked out.[1]

Now, there's a lady who's lost sight of the objective. I might question whether something like that ever happened if I had not experienced similar incidents in my own life. How easily some get caught up in procedures and lose sight of the major reason those procedures were established in the first place. Without people there would be no need for a store. Without people, who cares how efficient a particular airline may be? Without people a school serves no purpose, a row of houses no longer represents a neighborhood, a stadium is a cold concrete structure, and even a church building is an empty shell. I say again: We need each other.

A while back I came across the following piece that addresses this very subject with remarkable insight:

How Important Are You?

More than
you think.
A rooster
minus a hen
equals
no baby chicks.
Kellogg minus
a farmer
equals
no corn flakes.
If the nail
factory closes,
what good is the
hammer factory?
Paderewski's
genius wouldn't have
amounted to much
if the

```
piano tuner
hadn't shown up.
A cracker maker
will do better
if there's a
cheesemaker.
The most skillful
surgeon needs
the ambulance driver
who delivers the
patient.
Just as Rodgers
needed Hammerstein
you need someone
and someone
needs you.[2]
```

Since none of us is a whole, independent, self-sufficient, super-capable, all-powerful hotshot, let's quit acting like we are. Life's lonely enough without our playing that silly role.

The game's over. Let's link up.

People are important to each other. Above all, people are important to God. Which does not diminish His authority and self-sufficiency at all. The creation of humanity on the sixth day was the crowning accomplishment of the Lord's Creation handiwork. Furthermore, He put into mankind His very image, which He did not do for plant life or animals, birds, or fish. It was for the salvation of humanity, not brute beasts, that Christ came and died, and it will be for us that He will someday return. The major reason I am involved in a writing ministry and a broadcasting ministry and a church ministry is that people need to be reached and nurtured in the faith. This could be said of anyone serving the Lord Christ.

Couldn't God do it all? Of course, He is God—all-powerful and all-knowing and all-sufficient. That makes it all the more significant that He prefers to use us in His work. Even though He could operate completely alone on this earth, He seldom does. Almost without exception, He uses people in the process. His favorite plan is a combined effort: God plus people equals accomplishment.

I often recall the story of the preacher who saved up enough money to buy a few inexpensive acres of land. A little run-down, weather-beaten farmhouse sat on the acreage, a sad picture of years of neglect. The land had not been kept up either, so there were old tree stumps, rusted pieces of machinery, and all sorts of debris strewn here and there, not to mention a fence greatly in need of repair. The whole scene was a mess.

During his spare time and his vacations, the preacher rolled up his sleeves and got to work. He hauled off the junk, repaired the fence, pulled away the stumps, and replanted new trees. Then he refurbished the old house into a quaint cottage with a new roof, new windows, new stone walkway, new paint job, and finally a few colorful flower boxes. It took several years to accomplish all this, but finally, when the last job had been completed and he was washing up after applying a fresh coat of paint to the mailbox, his neighbor (who had watched all this from a distance) walked over and said, "Well, preacher—looks like you and the Lord have done a pretty fine job on your place here."

Wiping the sweat from his face, the minister replied, "Yeah, I sup-pose so . . . but you should have seen it when the Lord had it all to Himself."

God has not only created each one of us as distinct individuals, He also uses us in significant ways. Just stop and think: Chances are you are where you are today because of the words or the writings or the personal influence of certain people. I love to ask people how they became who they are. When I do, they invariably speak of the influence or the encour-agement of key people in their past.

I would be the first to affirm that fact. When I look back across the landscape of my life, I am able to connect specific individuals to each crossroad and every milestone. Some of them are people the world will never know, for they are relatively unknown to the general public. But to me personally? Absolutely vital. And a few of them have remained my friends to this very day. Each one has helped me clear a hurdle or handle a struggle, accomplish an objective or endure a trial—and ultimately laugh again. I cannot even imagine where I would be today were it not for that handful of friends who have given me a heart full of joy. Let's face it, friends make life a lot more fun.

SPECIAL FRIENDS IN PAUL'S LIFE

It is easy to forget that the late, great apostle Paul needed friends too. Being ill on occasion, he needed Dr. Luke. Being limited in strength and unable to handle the rigors of extensive travel alone, he needed Barnabas and Silas. Being restricted in freedom, he needed other hands to carry his letters to their prescribed destinations. And on several occasions he needed someone to actually write out his letters. But isn't it interesting that though we know quite a bit about Paul, we know very little about his circle of friends? Yet in reality, they were part of the reason he was able to move through life as well as he did.

Returning to the letter he wrote to the Philippians, we come upon the mention of two names—a man Paul calls "my son" in another of his writings and a man he calls here "my brother." Since these two men played such significant roles in Paul's life that they deserved honorable mention, let's spend the balance of this chapter getting better acquainted with both. They were friends who made Paul's life richer and more enjoyable.

A "Son" Named Timothy

Being held under Roman guard in his house arrest, Paul found himself unable to travel back to Philippi, so he decided to send his young friend Timothy. More than any other individual, Timothy is mentioned by Paul in his writings. We saw his name earlier, in fact, in the opening line of this very letter: "Paul and Timothy, bond-servants of Christ Jesus."

Who was Timothy?

- He was a native of either Lystra or Derbe, cities in southern Asia Minor . . . today called Turkey.

- He was the child of a mixed marriage: Jewish mother (Eunice) and Greek father (never named).

- Since he remained uncircumcised until he was a young adult, Timothy's childhood upbringing was obviously more strongly influenced by the Greek than the Jewish parentage.

- However, his spiritual interest came from the maternal side of his family. Both Eunice and her mother Lois reared him to be tender toward the things of the Lord. We learn this from two comments Paul makes later in life in his second letter to his young friend.

> For I am mindful of the sincere faith within you, which first dwelt in your grandmother Lois, and your mother Eunice, and I am sure that it is in you as well.
>
> *2 Timothy 1:5*

> You, however, continue in the things you have learned and become convinced of, knowing from whom you have learned them; and that from childhood you have known the sacred writings which are able to give you the wisdom that leads to salvation through faith which is in Christ Jesus.
>
> *2 Timothy 3:14–15*

- Paul, no doubt, led Timothy into a personal relationship with the Lord Jesus Christ. This explains why the older referred to the younger as "my beloved and faithful child in the Lord" (1 Cor. 4:17).

- Once Timothy joined Paul (and Luke) as a traveling companion, the two remained close for the rest of Paul's life. We read of the beginning of their friendship in the early part of Acts 16.

> And he [Paul] came also to Derbe and to Lystra. And behold, a certain disciple was there, named Timothy, the son of a Jewish woman who was a believer, but his father was a Greek, and he was well spoken of by the brethren who were in Lystra and Iconium. Paul wanted this man to go with him; and he took him and circumcised him because of the Jews who were in those parts, for they all knew that his father was a Greek.
>
> *Acts 16:1–3*

So much for a quick survey of Timothy's background. What is of interest to us is how Paul wrote of him to the people of Philippi.

> But I hope in the Lord Jesus to send Timothy to you shortly, so that I also may be encouraged when I learn of your condition. For I have no one else of kindred spirit who will genuinely be concerned for your welfare. For they all seek after their own interests, not those of Christ Jesus. But you know of his proven worth that he served with me in the furtherance of the gospel like a child serving his father. Therefore I hope to send him immediately, as soon as I see how things go with me; and I trust in the Lord that I myself also shall be coming shortly.
>
> *Philippians 2:19–24*

As I ponder those words, three things jump out at me. All three have to do with how Paul viewed his friend.

First, *Timothy had a unique "kindred spirit" with Paul.* The single

Greek term Paul used for "kindred spirit" is a combination of two words, actually: "same souled." This is the only time in all of the New Testament the term is used. We might say Paul and Timothy possessed an "equal spirit," or that they were "like-minded." Mathematically speaking, their triangles were congruent. Just think of the implications of the comment Paul makes: "I have no one else of kindred spirit."

They thought alike. Their perspectives were in line with each other. Timothy would interpret situations much like Paul, had the latter been there. In today's slang, they hit it off. When the older sent the younger on a fact-finding mission, he could rely on the report as being similar to one he himself would have brought back. Being of kindred spirit in no way suggests they had the same temperament or even that they always agreed. What it does mean, however, is that being alongside each other, neither had to work hard at the relationship; things flowed smoothly between them. I would imagine that it was not unlike the closeness David enjoyed with Jonathan, about which we read "the soul of Jonathan was knit to the soul of David, and Jonathan loved him as himself." And a little later, "he loved him as he loved his own life" (1 Sam. 18:1; 20:17).

Coming across a person with a kindred spirit is a rare find. We may have numerous casual acquaintances and several good friends in life, but finding someone who is like-souled is a most unusual (and delightful) discovery. And when it happens, both parties sense it. Neither has to convince the other that there is a oneness of spirit. It is like being with someone who lives in your own head—and vice versa—someone who reads your motives and understands your needs without either having to be stated. No need for explanations, excuses, or defenses. Paul enjoyed all these relational delights with Timothy, along with a spiritual dimension as well.

Second, *Timothy had a genuine concern for others.* That statement opens a window for us into the young man's makeup. When Timothy was with others, his heart was touched over their needs. Compassionate individuals are hard to find these days, but they were hard to find back in those days too. Remember what Paul wrote?

> For they all seek after their own interests, not those of Christ Jesus.
>
> *Philippians 2:21*

Not Timothy. Timothy modeled what Paul wrote earlier concerning an unselfish attitude.

Do nothing from selfishness or empty conceit, but with humility of mind let each of you regard one another as more important than himself; do not merely look out for your own personal interests, but also for the interests of others.

Philippians 2:3–4

That was Timothy. No wonder Paul felt so close to him. Friends like that remind us of the importance of helping others without saying a word. One man writes with understanding:

> A few years ago I stood on the banks of a river in South America and watched a young man in western clothes climb out of a primitive canoe. The veteran missionary with whom I was traveling beamed at the young man and whispered to me, "The first time I saw him he was a naked Indian kid standing right on this bank, and he pulled in my canoe for me. God gave me a real concern for him, and eventually he came to Christ, committed himself to the Lord's work and is just returning home after graduating from seminary in Costa Rica." I could understand the beam on the missionary's face, and I think Paul beamed when he talked of his men. And he had good cause to be thrilled with them.[3]

Third, *Timothy had a servant's heart.* Paul also mentioned Timothy's "proven worth," meaning "caliber"; he was that caliber of man. And what was that? He served like a child serving his father.

Question: How can one grown man serve on behalf of another grown man "like a child serving his father"?

Answer in one word: Servanthood.

In the world of leadership we are overrun with hard-charging, tough-minded, power-loving people who equate position with power. But people can wield power in any position, just as long as they maintain control over something others want.

Which reminds me of a homey little story that illustrates positional power. A new factory owner went to a nearby restaurant for a quick lunch. The menu featured a blue plate special and made it clear—absolutely no substitutions or additions. The meal was tasty, but the man needed more butter. When he asked for a second pat of butter, the waitress refused. He was so irritated he called for the manager . . . who also refused him and walked away (much to the waitress's delight). "Do you people know who I am?" he asked indignantly. "I am the owner of that factory across the street!" The waitress smiled sarcastically and whined,

"Do you know who *I* am, sweetie? I'm the one who decides whether you get a second pat of butter."

Not all power moves are that blatant. Some leaders dangle others under their authority. I read a classic example of this in Leighton Ford's excellent book, *Transforming Leadership*.

Eli Black, an entrepreneurial businessman, was well-known for two things. The high point of his life was when he engineered the takeover of the United Fruit Company. The end came when he jumped from the forty-second floor of the Pan American Building in New York.

One of his executives, Thomas McCann, wrote about Black in his book *An American Company*. He describes a luncheon meeting with Black and two other managers.

As they sat down, Black smiled and asked if they were hungry. McCann replied that he was starving. Moments later a waiter came with a plate of cheese and crackers. Black reached out and took it, but instead of passing it around he placed it before him and clasped his hands in front of it.

"Now," he asked, "what's on the agenda?"

For several minutes they talked about a building they were going to put up in Costa Rica. McCann, who had not had breakfast, kept his eyes on the cheese and crackers. The only way he could get to them would be to reach across his boss's arm, and Black's body language made it clear that that would be a violation of his territory.

At a brief pause in the discussions, McCann said, "How about some cheese and crackers?" Black never even glanced at McCann, so he rephrased it. "You're not planning on eating those crackers and cheese all by yourself are you, Eli?" Again, no answer. The conversation continued, and McCann leaned back in his chair, giving up all hope of a snack.

Moments later Black made it clear that there was nothing wrong with his hearing. He continued to question and make comments.

Then, says McCann:

He unclasped his hands and picked up the knife. . . . I watched the knife dig down into the bowl of cheese; the other hand reached out and selected a Ritz cracker from the plate and Black poised the cracker on his fingertips as he carefully stroked a rounded, tantalizing mound of cheese across its face.

The cracker remained balanced on the fingertips of Black's left hand for at least the next five minutes. He asked questions about the height of the building from the street and its height above sea level . . . the color and materials . . . the size of the lobby. . . . My eyes never left the cracker. . . .

I leaned back again, this time accepting my defeat.

It was then that Black reached across the table and placed the cracker on my butter plate. He put the knife down where he had found it, and he refolded his hands before him, keeping the food within their embrace for himself alone to dispense or to keep. Black didn't say a word, but his expression made it clear that he felt he had made his point.

Eli Black symbolized perfectly one use of power. Next to truth, the power question is the most important issue for the leader. And it is precisely in relation to power that the leadership of Jesus stands in the greatest contrast to popular understandings of leadership.[4]

Unlike that entrepreneur, Timothy conformed to the Jesus model. He didn't strut his stuff. Like Paul, he served. By sending Timothy to the people of Philippi, Paul felt he was sending *himself.* No fear of offense. No anxiety over how the young man might handle some knotty problem he might encounter. Not even a passing thought that he might throw his weight around, saying, "As Paul's right-hand man. . . ." The aging apostle could rest easy. Timothy was the man for the job. Paul must have smiled when he finally waved good-bye. Friends like Timothy relieve life's pressure and enable us to smile.

A "Brother" Named Epaphroditus

Because the two men were closer, Paul wrote of who Timothy was. But when he mentions this second gentleman, Epaphroditus, he puts his finger on what he did. Another contrast: Timothy would be going to Philippi sometime in the future, but Epaphroditus would be sent immediately, probably carrying this letter Paul was writing.

Epaphroditus had been sent to Rome to minister to Paul, but shortly after arriving the man became terribly ill. Ultimately he recovered, but not before a long struggle where he lingered at death's door. News of his illness might have traveled back to Philippi, and the man was concerned that his friends back home would be worried about him. Furthermore, when he returned earlier than expected, some might think he returned as a quitter, so Paul was careful to write strong words in his defense.

But I thought it necessary to send to you Epaphroditus, my brother and fellow worker and fellow soldier, who is also your messenger and minister to my need; because he was longing for you all and was distressed because you had heard that he was sick. For indeed he was sick to the point of death, but God had mercy on him, and not on him only but also on me, lest I should have sorrow upon sorrow. Therefore I have sent him all the more eagerly in order that when you see him again you may rejoice and I may be less concerned about you. Therefore receive him in the Lord with all joy, and hold men like him in high regard; because he came close to death for the work of Christ, risking his life to complete what was deficient in your service to me.

Philippians 2:25–30

And toward the end of the same letter . . .

But I have received everything in full, and have an abundance; I am amply supplied, having received from Epaphroditus what you have sent, a fragrant aroma, an acceptable sacrifice, well-pleasing to God.

Philippians 4:18

When Epaphroditus first arrived, he brought a gift of money from the Philippians. This tells us the people back home trusted him completely. When he gave the gift to Paul, he brought enormous encouragement to the apostle . . . but shortly thereafter, Epaphroditus fell ill. So the apostle writes with deep affection, referring to him as, "brother . . . fellow worker . . . fellow soldier . . . messenger . . . minister to my need." I'd call those admirable qualities in a friend. Bishop Lightfoot says that Epaphroditus was one in "common sympathy, common work, and common danger and toil and suffering"[5] with the great apostle. When you've got someone near you with credentials like that, life doesn't seem nearly as heavy.

- Why did Paul send Epaphroditus back? To put the people at ease and to cause them to rejoice (there's that word again) upon hearing from Paul by letter.
- What was to be their response back home? Extend a joyful welcome and hold Epaphroditus in high regard.
- Why did he deserve their respect? Because he had risked his life in coming to minister to Paul . . . he had exposed

himself to danger. We would say he had flirted with death to be near his friend.

In those days when people visited prisoners who were held captive under Roman authority, they were often prejudged as criminal types as well. Therefore, a visitor exposed himself to danger just by being near those who were considered dangerous. The Greek term Paul uses here for "risking"—*paraboleuomai*—is one that meant "to hazard with one's life . . . to gamble." Epaproditus did just that.

In the early church there were societies of men and women who called themselves *the parabolani*, that is, *the riskers or gamblers*. They ministered to the sick and imprisoned, and they saw to it that, if at all possible, martyrs and sometimes even enemies would receive an honorable burial. Thus in the city of Carthage during the great pestilence of A.D. 252 Cyprian, the bishop, showed remarkable courage. In self-sacrificing fidelity to his flock, and love even for his enemies, he took upon himself the care of the sick, and bade his congregation nurse them and bury the dead. What a contrast with the practice of the heathen who were throwing the corpses out of the plague-stricken city and were running away in terror![6]

A special joy binds two friends who are not reluctant to risk danger on each other's behalf. If a true friend finds you're in need, he or she will find a way to help. Nor will a friend ever ask, "How great is the risk?" The question is always, "When do you need me?" Not even the threat of death holds back a friend.

This reminds me of the six-year-old girl who became deathly ill with a dread disease. To survive, she needed a blood transfusion from someone who had previously conquered the same illness. The situation was complicated by her rare blood type. Her nine-year-old brother qualified as a donor, but everyone was hesitant to ask him since he was just a lad. Finally they agreed to have the doctor pose the question.

The attending physician tactfully asked the boy if he was willing to be brave and donate blood for his sister. Though he didn't understand much about such things, the boy agreed without hesitation: "Sure, I'll give my blood for my sister."

He lay down beside his sister and smiled at her as they pricked his arm with the needle. Then he closed his eyes and lay silently on the bed as the pint of blood was taken.

Soon thereafter the physician came in to thank the little fellow. The boy, with quivering lips and tears running down his cheeks, asked, "Doctor, when do I die?" At that moment the doctor realized that the naive little boy thought that by giving his blood, he was giving up his life. Quickly he reassured the lad that he was not going to die, but amazed at his courage, the doctor asked, "Why were you willing to risk your life for her?"

"Because she is my sister . . . and I love her," was the boy's simple but significant reply.

So it was between Epaphroditus and his brother in Rome . . . and so it is to this day. Danger and risk don't threaten true friendship; they strengthen it. Such friends are modern-day members of *the parabolani,* that reckless band of friends—riskers and gamblers, all—who love their brothers and sisters to the uttermost. Each one deserves our respect. When we need them, they are there. I have a few in that category. Hopefully, you do too.

THREE PEOPLE WHO DESERVE A RESPONSE

As I think about how all this ties in with our lives today, I am reminded of three categories of special people and how we are to respond to them.

First, there are still a few Timothys left on earth, thank goodness. *When God sends a Timothy into our lives, He expects us to relate to him.* It is often the beginning of an intimate friendship, rarely experienced in our day of superficial companionship. With a Timothy, you won't have to force a friendship; it will flow. Nor will you find yourself dreading the relationship; it will be rewarding. When a Timothy comes along, don't hesitate . . . *relate.*

Second, there may be a modern-day Epaphroditus who comes to your assistance or your rescue. *When God sends an Epaphroditus to minister to us, He expects us to respect him.* This is the type of person who reaches out when he has nothing to gain and perhaps much to lose . . . who gambles on your behalf for no other reason than love. His or her action is an act of grace. Don't question it or try to repay it or make attempts to bargain for it. Just accept it. Grace extended in love is to be accepted with gratitude. The best response to an Epaphroditus? *Respect.*

And there is a third person I haven't said much about in a personal way. But since we are approximately halfway through Paul's letter, as well as this book, it is time I introduced you to this third friend. His name is Jesus Christ. *Since God sent Christ to take away our sins and bring us to heaven, He expects us to receive Him.* If you think a Timothy can mean a lot to you or an Epaphroditus could prove invaluable, let me assure you that neither can compare as a substitute for Jesus. With nail-scarred hands He reaches out to you and waits for you to reach back in faith. I tell you without a moment's hesitation, there is no one you will ever meet, no friend you will ever make, who can do for you what Jesus can do. No one else can change your inner heart. No one else can turn your entire life around. No one else can remove not only your sins but the guilt and shame that are part of that whole ugly package. And now that the two of you have been introduced, only one response is appropriate. Only one. *Receive.*

I began this chapter by stating that people need other people. You need me. I need you. Both of us need a few kindred spirits, people who understand us and encourage us. Both of us need friends who are willing to risk to help us and, yes, at times, to rescue us. Friends like that make life more fun. But all of us—you, me, Timothy-people, Epaphroditus-people, *all of us*—need a Savior. He awaits your response. The everlasting relief He brings is enough to make us not only laugh again, but laugh forever.

8

Happy Hopes for High Achievers

*L*ast night I met a man who told me he needed to work harder at being happier.

He said he had been reared in an ultraserious home. "We didn't talk about our feelings . . . *we worked.* My father, my mother, most of my sisters and brothers bought into that way of life," he sighed. "Somehow we all had the idea that you could achieve whatever you wanted in life if you just worked hard enough and long enough." And then he came to the crux of his concern: "Funny thing . . . in my sixty-plus years I have achieved about everything I dreamed of doing and I have been awarded for it. My problem is that I don't know how to have fun and enjoy all these things hard work has brought me. I cannot remember the last time I laughed—I mean *really* laughed."

As he turned to walk away, I thought this throwaway line was the most revealing thing he said: "I suppose I now need to work harder at being happier."

I reached over, took him by the arm, and pulled him back close enough to put my arms around him for a solid, manly hug. "You've worked hard for everything else in your life," I said quietly. "Why not try a new approach for joy? Trust me on this one—a happy heart is not achieved by hard work and long hours. If it were, the happiest people on earth would be the workaholics . . . and I have never met a work-aholic whose sense of humor balanced out his intensity." We talked a few more minutes, but I'm not sure I made a dent in his thinking. Most likely, at this very moment that high achiever is up and at it (it's early Monday morning) pursuing a game plan to earn happiness. *It ain't gonna happen.*

The problem is that human achievement results in earthly rewards, which fuels the fire for more achievement leading to greater rewards.

109

"Problem . . . what problem?" you and the man I met last night may ask. This: None of that results in deep-down satisfaction, an inner peace, a soul-level contentment, or lasting joy. In the process of achieving more and earning more, few if any learn to laugh more. This is especially true if you're the classic Type A. Hear me out.

Something within all of us warms up to human strokes. We are motivated to do more when our efforts are noticed and rewarded. That is why they make things like impressive trophies and silver platters and bronze plaques and gold medals. Most folks love putting those things on display. Whether it is an athletic letter on a sweater in high school or a Salesperson-of-the-Month plaque on the wall, we like the recognition. What does it do? It drives us on to do more, to gain greater recognition, to achieve more valuable rewards, better pay, or higher promotions.

Virtually every major field of endeavor has its particular award for outstanding achievement. Universities award scholarships; companies give bonuses; the film industry offers the Oscar; the television industry, the Emmy; the music industry, the Grammy; and the writing industry, the Pulitzer Prize. The athletic world has an entire spectrum of honors. Whether garnering individual awards for exceptional achievement or team trophies for championship play, winning players are applauded and record-setting coaches are affirmed (and envied). Furthermore, most folks are awed simply by being around celebrities. Recently I read a funny story that perfectly illustrates this fact:

> A tourist was standing in line to buy an ice cream cone at a Thrifty Drug store in Beverly Hills. To her utter shock and amazement, who should walk in and stand right behind her but Paul Newman! Well the lady, even though she was rattled, determined to maintain her composure. She purchased her ice cream cone and turned confidently and exited the store.
>
> However, to her horror, she realized that she had left the counter without her ice cream cone! She waited a few minutes till she felt all was clear, and then went back into the store to claim her cone. As she approached the counter, the cone was not in the little circular receptacle, and for a moment she stood there pondering what might have happened to it. The she felt a polite tap on her shoulder, and turning was confronted by—you guessed it—Paul Newman. The famous actor then told the lady that if she was looking for her ice cream cone, she had put it into her purse![1]

While I was sitting in the Great Western Forum the other evening watching the Los Angeles Lakers, I looked up toward the ceiling and saw all those NBA championship banners hanging high. I glanced toward one wall bright with spotlights and read the names on jerseys that have been retired: Baylor, Chamberlain, West, Abdul-Jabbar, and, most recently, Johnson. What an honor to have one's name placed on public display for all the world to see! It is society's way of saying, "You are great!"

There is nothing wrong with that as long as we remember it is an earthly system exalting earthly people who are rewarded for earthly accomplishments. But how easy it is to forget that not one of those accomplishments gives a person what he or she may lack deep within—that's why they can't bring lasting satisfaction. And much more importantly, none of them earns God's favor.

THE GREAT TEMPTATION AMONG HIGH ACHIEVERS

All this leads me to a terribly important subject I have been wanting to address. Having had that conversation with Mr. High Achiever last evening, I'm unable to restrain myself any longer . . . and I especially have in mind those of you who can't stand coming in second because you face a great temptation.

What is it? It is the temptation to believe that earthly honors will automatically result in heavenly rewards. This kind of thinking is at the root of a humanistic philosophy of life that says: "By working hard and accomplishing more than most, I will earn God's favor and receive His nod of approval." I don't know of a more subtle, albeit heretical, philosophy than that, yet it is universally accepted as true. And so, the tragedy is, enough is never enough. Life is reduced to work, tasks, effort, an endless list of shoulds and musts . . . minus the necessary fun and laughter that keeps everything in perspective.

Why does it happen? What is it that drives us on so relentlessly? Are you ready? Take a deep breath and allow yourself to tolerate the one-word answer: PRIDE. We work and push and strive so we can prove we are worthy . . . we are the best . . . we deserve top honors. And the hidden message: I can gain righteousness all on my own, by my own effort, ingenuity, and energy. And because I can, I must! And why is this heretical? Because ultimately this philosophy says: (1) I really won't need divine righteousness (after all, God helps those who help themselves, right?), and (2) I will find lasting joy in my own achievement.

111

This will bring me ultimate satisfaction. Both are dead-end roads found on Fantasy Island.

A longtime friend of mine openly confessed:

> Work had always been highly esteemed in our family, and hard work was seen as the primary tool for success. I figured if it were good to work ten hours, it would be even better to work fourteen.
>
> In college, I seemed to have the energy to withstand the pressure. I remember times at Stanford when I wouldn't even go home at night. Instead, I would push a table up near the door of the cafeteria at 3 a.m. and sleep on it, using my books as a pillow. And then in the morning, when I had to be at work, the first person to open the door would knock me off the table, and I'd wake up and start the day. I convinced myself that I was sleeping "faster" than anyone else. . . .
>
> During the years when I was a coach and an area director for Young Life, I would work twelve, fourteen, even fifteen hours a day, six or seven days a week. And I would come home feeling that I hadn't worked enough. So I tried to cram even more into my schedule. I spent more time promoting living than I did living. . . . My life wasn't abundant; it was a frantic sprint from one hour to the next.
>
> I can remember times when fatigue left me feeling isolated and alienated—feelings that previously had been foreigners to me. Unprepared for such parasites on my energy, I became frustrated, and laughter, which had always been my most treasured companion, had silently slipped away. . . .
>
> I was dominated by "shoulds," and "ought to's," and "musts." I would awaken unrefreshed in the morning, with a tired kind of resentment, and hurry through the day trying to uncover and meet the demands of others. Days were not lived but endured. I was exhausted trying to be a hope constantly rekindled for others, straining to live up to their images of me. I had worked hard to develop a reputation as one who was concerned, available, and involved—now I was being tyrannized by it. Often I was more at peace in the eyes of others than in my own.
>
> The Western mind and culture leave little time for leisure, prayer, play, and contemplation. Hurry needs answers; answers need categories; categories need labeling and dissecting. The pace I was trying to maintain had no time for rhythm and awe, for mystery and wonder. I barely had time to care adequately for friends or for myself. In order to keep up my incessant activity, God was simply reduced to fit into my schedule. I suffered, because he didn't fit.[2]

Pride not only expresses itself in high-achieving hard work, but also keeps us from asking for help. We love to leave the impression that no matter what, we can handle it—no help wanted!

I remember when my family and I lived in New England. We weren't accustomed to snow in the winter. It threw us a real nasty curve. We found ourselves somewhat confused when we faced our first wintry blast. For example, I couldn't figure out why people didn't park on the street. I thought, *That's the best place in the world . . . nobody parks there. In fact, there are no "No Parking" signs anywhere.* So I parked on the street. I remember being sort of proud of my original idea when I locked the car for the night. That was about the time the snow began to fall. In fact, it snowed all night. It never even dawned on me that snowplows worked the street all night long, pushing back the fallen snow.

The next morning when I crawled out of our warm bed, I discovered why nobody parked on the street. I looked out front and thought somebody had stolen my car! Stunned to find huge mounds of crusted snow and ice on both sides of the street, I took my pick and shovel and began to do archaeological work in hopes of finding a blue four-door sedan. After digging like mad for at least twenty minutes, I finally got to something hard. When I saw blue I thought, *That's my color . . . must be my car.* About that time a friend drove by. He stopped, smiled, rolled down his window, and asked, "Hey, Chuck, can I help you?" I immediately responded, "No, thanks—I'm doing fine." He shrugged and drove on. About half an hour later I wondered why I hadn't said yes. The simple answer: I was proud. I could dig out my own car, thank you. Stupid pride!

You know what else I did? When I finally got down to my ice-covered car and saw all the ice on the windows, my first thought was, *It's dumb to stand here and scrape off all that ice.* So I went inside and got a bucket of steaming hot water and dumped it over the front window. Trust me, not only did the ice come off, so did my windshield. I was stunned as it shattered with a loud bang and fell into the front seat. I thought, *So that's why everybody scrapes the ice off windshields.* Let me tell you, when I drove the car to the glass shop, I had clear vision! It was ten degrees in the car, but I had clear vision.

Do you know the first thing I did when I broke my front window? I looked around to see if anybody was watching. Why? Pride, plain and simple. I didn't want anyone to know what a foolish thing I had done. Pride encourages us to hide our stupidity rather than admit it. And I remember that throughout the entire episode I did not have much fun. I don't recall laughing either at myself or at my circumstance.

There is always that one telltale sign when pride takes charge: the fun leaves. A driven high achiever may smile on occasion, but it is a surface grin, not a strong, quiet sense of satisfaction. Deep within, he or she is really thinking, *Life is much too busy, much too serious to waste it on silly things like relaxation and laughter.* Staying wound up that tight can cause the mind to snap. G. K. Chesterton was never more correct than when he wrote, "Madmen are always serious; they go mad from lack of humour."[3]

THE HONEST TESTIMONY OF A HIGH-ACHIEVING PHARISEE

All this brings us back to a little letter written to a small band of believers living in ancient Philippi. Because the writer, Paul, felt so close to them, he wasn't afraid to be honest and allow them to see the dark side of his past. But before doing so he underscores the underlying theme of his letter by reminding them to find the joy in living.

Finally, my brethren, rejoice in the Lord. To write the same things again is no trouble to me, and it is a safeguard for you.

Philippians 3:1

The Living Bible says:

Whatever happens, dear friends, be glad in the Lord. I never get tired of telling you this and it is good for you to hear it again and again.

Paul is about to launch into his past—those intense years of his own existence when he worked so hard to impress God. But before he does that, he wants to make sure that they hear yet again the importance of being people of outrageous joy. He calls that "a safeguard." How true. Not only were the pressures of life enough to steal their joy, there were also the ever-present legalists—ancient grace killers—on the loose. And nobody can rob people of joy quicker than a few narrow-minded legalists. Paul's great concern was that his Philippian friends continue to enjoy their freedom in Christ and not allow *anything* or *anyone* to get the best of them. He never got tired of telling them that.

A Warning to His Close Friends

I am not dreaming up the idea that legalists were on the loose. Neither have I been too strong in my comments. Paul himself calls them "dogs . . . evil workers." See for yourself:

> Beware of the dogs, beware of the evil workers, beware of the false circumcision.
>
> *Philippians 3:2*

Strong words! When he refers to them as dogs, Paul doesn't have in mind the little lap dogs we enjoy as pets or those obedient, loyal creatures we pamper and nourish. No, the dogs of his day were dirty, disease-carrying scavengers who ran in packs through the streets and narrow alleys of a city. Unable to be controlled and potentially dangerous, they posed a menacing threat to anyone who got in their way. With that word picture in mind, Paul warns, "Watch out . . . beware! These people will assault you and you will lose your joy."

He goes further: "Beware of evil workers." These legalists taught that people were saved by works—by keeping the Law (an impossibility). Such folks live on to this day, spreading their heresy. Their message is full of exhortations to do more, to work harder, to witness longer, to pray with greater intensity, because enough is never enough. Such folks are "evil workers" who will take away what little bit of joy you may be able to muster. I would also add that when you never know how much is enough to satisfy God, you are left in a continual state of shame and obligation. Your mind never rests. The message of the legalists always finds you lacking. It never brings relief. We need to beware of such messengers. They are, according to Scripture, evil workers.

By calling them "false circumcision" people, Paul meant they believed in mutilation, not merely circumcision, for salvation. They taught, if circumcision was good, castration was even better! One *must* (there's that word again) work exceptionally hard to be acceptable to God—give up, take on, put away, add to, try harder, contribute more—before there could be assurance of divine acceptance. The result of all that? Confidence in the flesh! You worked hard . . . you sacrificed . . . you labored intensely . . . you received it. And in the process you had every reason to be proud of it. I say again . . . heresy!

With quiet and firm reassurance, Paul communicates the simple truth to his friends:

> For we are the true circumcision, who worship in the Spirit of God and glory in Christ Jesus and put no confidence in the flesh.
>
> *Philippians 3:3*

Those last six words—"put no confidence in the flesh"—what a helpful relief! God's grace has again come to our rescue. And in the process He gets the glory. All the credit goes to Him, as certainly it should. When it comes to our vertical and eternal relationship with God, unlike the humanist's message, we put no confidence in the flesh. Salvation through human works? No way. Human pride? No reason. The gift that brings back the laughter—God's gift of eternal life with Him—is based on what He has done for us and not what we have done for Him. Maybe you need to read that sentence again. It explains why we put no confidence in the flesh. Those who do have missed the whole point of grace.

A Revealing of His Proud Record

These words about "confidence in the flesh" triggered a lot of emotion in Paul. While writing them he must have experienced a flashback to the way he was for so many years—in fact, all of his adult life. Before his conversion, he was the personification of a proud Pharisee. Nobody's trophy case was larger. Had they given an award for high achievement in the field of religion, Paul would have won top honors in his nation year after year after year. His wall could have been covered with plaques, diplomas, framed letters from influential individuals, and numerous artifacts—all impressive.

> . . . If anyone else has a mind to put confidence in the flesh, I far more.
>
> *Philippians 3:4*

When he writes those words, Paul is not padding the report or trying to appear important. As we are about to read, he had earned the respect of every law-keeping Judaizer in the known world. When he said, "I far more," he had the record to prove it. For example:

Circumcised the eighth day, of the nation of Israel, of the tribe of Benjamin, a Hebrew of Hebrews; as to the Law, a Pharisee; as to zeal, a persecutor of the church; as to the righteousness which is in the Law, found blameless.

Philippians 3:5–6

That pedigree and brief list of achievements may not seem impressive to you today, especially if you are not Jewish, but do not discount their significance. Paul was the ultimate high achiever of his day. As one New Testament scholar explains:

If ever there was a Jew who was steeped in Judaism, that Jew was Paul. Let us . . . look again at the claims he had to be the Jew *par excellence*. . . . He was circumcised on the eighth day; that is to say, he bore in the body the badge and the mark that he was one of the chosen people, marked out by God as His own. He was of the race of Israel; that is to say, he was a member of the nation who stood in a covenant relationship with God, a relationship in which no other people stood. He was of the tribe of Benjamin. This is a claim which Paul reiterates in *Romans* 11:1. What is the point of this claim? The tribe of Benjamin had a unique place in the history of Israel. It was from Benjamin that the first king of Israel had come, for Saul was a Benjamite . . . . Benjamin was the only one of the patriarchs who had actually been born in the land of promise. When Israel went into battle, it was the tribe of Benjamin which held the post of honour. The battle-cry of Israel was: "After thee, O Benjamin". . . .

In lineage Paul was not only an Israelite; he was of the aristocracy of Israel. He was a Hebrew of the Hebrews; that is to say, Paul was not one of these Jews of the Dispersion who, in a foreign land, had forgotten their own tongue; he was a Jew who still remembered and knew the language of his fathers.

He was a Pharisee; that is to say, he was not only a devout Jew; he was more—he was one of "The Separated Ones" who had foresworn all normal activities in order to dedicate life to the keeping of the Law, and he had kept it with such meticulous care that in the keeping of it he was blameless.

. . . Paul knew Judaism at its best and at its highest; he knew it from the inside; he had gone through all the experiences, both of height and of depth, that it could bring to any man.[4]

Did you observe how Paul categorized his achievements? On an accelerated scale:

- "As to the Law"
- "As to zeal"
- "As to righteousness"

It is the last one that stands out—the ultimate! "When I added up all those things in my mind, I had arrived. When compared to all others, I qualified as *righteous*." Paul outstripped all his contemporaries, eclipsed all other lights. As A. T. Robertson summed up so eloquently, Paul had—

> A marvellous record, scoring a hundred in Judaism.
> . . . He was the star of hope for Gamaliel and the Sanhedrin.[5]

In today's terms, that proud Pharisee known as Saul of Tarsus won all the marbles—the Pulitzer, the Medal of Honor, the Most Valuable Player, the Heisman, the Gold Medal . . . the Nobel of Ancient Jewry. Had they had newspapers or magazines in his day, his picture would have been on the front page, and the headlines would have read, RELIGIOUS ZEALOT OF THE DECADE. His was the name dropped by everybody who was anybody. Any search for a model to follow would have led to the scholar from Tarsus, but you would have to move fast to stay up. He wasn't nearly finished with his plan to rid the world of Christians. The last entry in his Daytimer read, "Next stop: Damascus." On that fateful trip, everything changed.

A Change in His Entire Life

While riding the crest of that wave of international fame, Saul of Tarsus met his match in the person of Jesus Christ. While still on the outskirts of the city of Damascus, he was suddenly struck blind by a blazing light from heaven and silenced by a voice that must have sounded like the roar of a dozen Niagaras: "Saul . . . Saul . . . why are you persecuting Me?" Though blinded by the light, at that moment the Pharisee got his first glimpse of perfect righteousness. And for the first time in his life he was humbled. His robes of self-righteousness were nothing more than filthy rags. All his trophies and plaques and impressive earthly honors were as worthless as wood, hay, and stubble. One glimpse of true, heaven-sent righteousness was enough to convince him forever that he had spent his entire life on the wrong road traveling at breakneck speed toward the wrong destination for all the wrong reasons.

Now we can appreciate the importance of that little word "but" in the midst of Paul's listing of all his achievements:

> But whatever things were gain to me, those things I have counted as loss for the sake of Christ. More than that, I count all things to be loss in view of the surpassing value of knowing Christ Jesus my Lord, for whom I have suffered the loss of all things, and count them but rubbish in order that I may gain Christ, and may be found in Him, not having a righteousness of my own derived from the Law, but that which is through faith in Christ, the righteousness which comes from God on the basis of faith.
>
> *Philippians 3:7–9*

But! God called an abrupt and absolute halt to Saul's maddening pace. His entire frame of reference was altered. His whole perspective changed. His way of thinking and, of course, his way of life were radically transformed from that day forward. He saw, for the first time, how utterly and completely misguided he had been. As this newfound, divine perspective replaced the old hunger for earthly applause and the old drive for human righteousness, he felt himself bankrupt, reduced to ground zero. And all those honors he had worked for and relished for so long? He counted them as "loss" and "rubbish." Having clothed himself in the pride of self-achievement, he now stood stark naked and spiritually bankrupt. Having once set records when evaluated by other men and women, he now realized what a total failure he had been when appraised by his Master and Lord. And at that epochal moment divine righteousness was credited to his empty account, and he saw himself reclothed in the imputed righteousness of Christ. That changed everything within him and about him.

A Statement of His Consuming Passion

Did all of life stop there? Was that all there was to it? Hardly. That was when Paul really started to live. It was at that point the man began to laugh again! With a transformed heart he testified that his desire regarding Christ was that he might—

. . . know Him, and the power of His resurrection and the fellowship of

His sufferings, being conformed to His death; in order that I may attain to the resurrection from the dead.

Philippians 3:10–11

It is difficult to believe that a man as hard-charging and determined as Saul of Tarsus could pen such tender words. Look at them again. Perhaps we could call them Paul's credo. Rather than being driven by confidence in the flesh, his consuming passion was to spend the balance of his years on earth knowing Christ more intimately, drawing upon His resurrection power more increasingly, entering into His sufferings more personally, and being conformed to His image more completely. His dreams of making it all on his own were forever dashed on the solid rock of Jesus Christ.

THE PLAIN TRUTH TO ALL WHO RESPOND

If you are among the high achievers I've been writing to in this chapter, I commend you for reading this far. These are not the kinds of things you normally think about, I realize. Your world doesn't leave much room for personal weakness, does it? You don't rely on help from anything (or anyone) but your own reservoir of resourcefulness, do you? All your life you've been coming on strong, fighting and pushing for top honors and hopefully getting your own sweet way, haven't you? The things you are most proud of are your achievements, naturally, for that's really all you've got to show for all your hard work. In many ways, you've arrived, at least in the opinion of others. Yours is an enviable list of accomplishments. Let me name a few:

- Your respected position with a nice-sounding title
- Your salary with some enviable perks
- Your growing popularity among your peers
- Those awards you've hung on your walls
- That fine automobile sitting in your parking space (and that parking space!)
- A wardrobe full of elegant and stylish clothes
- A nice place to go home to . . . maybe more than a summer home . . . a winter home

120

- The probability of accomplishing and earning more
- A sense of power in knowing you can buy whatever you want any time you want it
- The feeling of accomplishment—you did it!

Granted, those are the kinds of things most folks you know spend their entire lives hoping to achieve. And now you find yourself a member of that elite club: High Achievers Anonymous (except by then they're not usually anonymous). Maybe we could say they are members of the MITTT Club—*Made It to the Top.*

But let's look deeper. Let's look at another list:

- How is your personal life? I'm referring to the real you that's there when nobody's looking . . . like when you're all alone in your car or boat or plane. Are you personally contented and at peace?
- And what about your marriage? And your relationship with your children? Everything okay there?
- While you are allowing me to get this close, may we take a look at your inner person? Are you secure or still rather afraid? Any habits out of control? Any addictions you can't seem to conquer?
- Let me ask a few what ifs: What if you became ill? What if you lost your earning power? What if you lost your title? What if your next physical exam led to the discovery of a lump . . . and that lump proved malignant? What if you had a stroke? Are you ready to die?
- Are there some secrets that haunt you? Are there some terrorizing worries that won't go away . . . that money won't erase?
- Finally, has life become more fun for you? Do you laugh—I mean really laugh—now that you have "arrived"? Or are you still too driven to relax?

If you've answered those questions honestly—or even taken the time to read them—then you're ready to hear the rest.

First, spending your life trusting in your own achievements brings you the glory now but leaves you spiritually bankrupt forever. Read that again, please. And as you do, think of that first-century man we've been reading about, Saul of Tarsus. Think of what his life would have been if he had never responded positively to the claims of Christ.

Second, stopping today and trusting in Christ's accomplishment on the cross will give Him the glory now and provide you with perfect righteousness forever.

You're intelligent, so let me ask you: *Which option makes better sense?* And just in case you think high achievers can't change, remember that man from Tarsus. He didn't merely exchange one religion for another . . . he didn't swap off one system of rites and ceremonies for another system of rules and regulations. The popular opinion these days is that folks need to change their religion or start going to a different church. That is nonsense. Saul didn't get a new religion or merely change churches after his Damascus Road experience. He was thoroughly and radically converted, like the man who wrote these words:

> I had walked life's path with an easy tread,
> Had followed where comfort and pleasure led;
> And then by chance in a quiet place—
> I met my Master face to face.

> With station and rank and wealth for goal,
> Much thought for body but none for soul,
> I had entered to win this life's mad race—
> When I met my Master face to face.

> I had built my castles, reared them high,
> Till their towers had pierced the blue of the sky;
> I had sworn to rule with an iron mace—
> When I met my Master face to face.

> I met Him and knew Him, and blushed to see
> That His eyes full of sorrow were fixed on me;
> And I faltered, and fell at His feet that day
> While my castles vanished and melted away.

> Melted and vanished; and in their place
> I saw naught else but my Master's face;
> And I cried aloud: "Oh, make me meet
> To follow the marks of Thy wounded feet."

My thought is now for the souls of men;
I have lost my life to find it again
Ever since alone in that holy place
My master and I stood face to face.[6]

9

Hanging Tough Together
. . . and Loving It

*O*ne day every year little boys all across America dream big dreams. They may not say so, but inside their heads are mental images of themselves being viewed by millions of people all around the world. In their imaginations they will one day wear the uniform and be a part of some championship team battling for the ultimate prize, a sparkling silver trophy in the shape of a football. We call that day of dreams "Super Bowl Sunday." Amazingly, a few of those little boys who dream big dreams do wind up playing in the big game.

Over twenty-five years ago when the first Super Bowl game was played, a ten-year-old boy sat beside his father in the stands of the Los Angeles Coliseum. As he watched players like Bart Starr, Paul Hornung, Boyd Dowler, Fuzzy Thurston, Carrol Dale, and other outstanding athletes on Vince Lombardi's great Green Bay Packers team dominate their opponents, he daydreamed of one day being down on that gridiron. And that is exactly what happened as James Lofton, a wide receiver for the Buffalo Bills (and the oldest man on the team), finally made it to the top and had his dream come true. Through strong and weak seasons, team changes, and several injuries as a professional football player, Lofton persevered—and his determination paid off. The Bills haven't won a Super Bowl, but James Lofton played in two of them.[1]

I cannot tell you what makes football fans out of other people, but I can tell you why I follow the game with such interest. Far beyond the smashing and the pounding, the aches and pains of the game, I see an analogy between football and life. Those who hang tough, refusing to give up no matter how difficult or demanding or disappointing the challenges may be, are the ones who stand the best chance of winning. They are also the ones who find the greatest satisfaction and delight in their years on earth. Henry David Thoreau said it best:

If one advances confidently in the direction of his dreams, and endeavors to live the life which he has imagined, he will meet with a success unexpected in common hours.[2]

That may sound like the ending to a fairy tale, almost as if some Disney character were telling us to wish upon a star while standing near the castle in Fantasyland, but it is not that at all. I see in Thoreau's statement a long and untiring determination in the same direction. Not a get-rich-quick scheme or some overnight success plan, but a confident advancement in the right direction over the long haul. Dreams are important, no question; yet they must be mixed with the patient discipline of staying at the tough tasks, regardless.

A Brief Stop at Today's Bookshelves

This is not the popular message we hear today. I was struck by this realization recently while browsing through a new bookstore not far from my home. As I wandered through the section on management and motivation, the titles made a bold statement about how society feels regarding patience and long-term diligence:

- *Passport to Prosperity*
- *Winning Moves*
- *True Greed*
- *Leadership Secrets of Attila the Hun*
- *Winning Through Intimidation*
- *Cashing In on the American Dream (How to Retire at 35)*
- *The Art of Selfishness*
- *Techniques That Take You to the Top*
- *How to Get What You Really Want*
- *Secrets to Quick Success*

Who's kidding whom? In spite of all those eye-catching, cleverly worded titles, the so-called secret to quick *anything* beneficial is light-years removed from the truth. In the final analysis, the race is won by right objectives relentlessly pursued. Whether it is an athlete reaching the Super Bowl, parents rearing a houseful of kids, a young woman earning her Ph.D., or a gifted musician perfecting his skill on an instrument, hanging tough over the long haul is still the investment that pays the richest dividends. And, I might add, it brings the greatest joy.

A LINGERING LOOK AT PAUL'S PRESCRIPTION

In the previous chapter we looked at the former life of the apostle Paul. As a young scholar he had won bragging rights over all his peers. His heritage, his schooling, his accomplishments, his zeal, his position, his passion were all part of his being groomed for a seat on the Supreme Court of the Jews, the Sanhedrin. That all-powerful name recognition gave him the edge . . . until he was intercepted by the resurrected, sovereign Christ . . . stunned and crushed by the revelation of the Son of God.

John Pollock, in a work entitled *The Man Who Shook the World*, describes it well.

Paul could not believe what he heard and saw. All his convictions, intellect and training, his reputation, his self-respect, demanded that Jesus should not be alive again. He played for time and replied, "Who are you, Lord?" He used a mode of address which might mean no more than "Your honor."

"I am Jesus, whom you are persecuting. It is hard for you, this kicking against the goad."

Then he knew. In a second that seemed an eternity Paul saw the wounds in Jesus' hands and feet, saw the face and knew that he had seen the Lord, that he was alive, as Stephen and the others had said, and that he loved not only those whom Paul persecuted but Paul: "It is hard for *you* to kick against the goad." Not one word of reproach.

Paul had never admitted to himself that he had felt pricks of a goad as he raged against Stephen and his disciples. But now, instantaneously, he was shatteringly aware that he had been fighting Jesus. And fighting himself, his conscience, his powerlessness, the darkness and chaos in his soul. God hovered over this chaos and brought him to the moment of new creation. It wanted only his "Yes."

Paul broke.

He was trembling and in no state to weigh the pros and cons of changing sides. He only knew that he had heard a voice and had seen the Lord, and that nothing mattered but to find and obey his will.

"What shall I do, Lord?"[3]

I was sitting in chapel back in 1959 at Dallas Theological Seminary, listening to Dr. Alan Redpath, then pastor of the famed Moody Memorial Church. I was taking notes, as I often did while listening to chapel speakers, and suddenly I stopped writing. Dr. Redpath had made a statement that burned its way deeply into the creases of my brain: "When God wants to do an impossible task, He takes an impossible man and crushes him." In the intervening years I have learned how right Dr. Redpath was. That is often the plan God uses when dealing with strong-willed, stubborn people.

Paul was both, so we should not be surprised that he was crushed. "Shattered," says Pollack. That is why verse 7 of Philippians 3 begins with "but." In effect, Paul admits, "I had achieved all those honors, I had won all the awards, I had gotten all the applause, I had impressed all my contemporaries . . . *but* God pulled every one of them off the wall. He put all that into correct perspective as He crushed my pride, won my heart, and came to live within me."

> But whatever things were gain to me, those things I have counted as loss for the sake of Christ. More than that, I count all things to be loss in view of the surpassing value of knowing Christ Jesus my Lord, for whom I have suffered the loss of all things, and count them but rubbish in order that I may gain Christ, and may be found in Him, not having a righteousness of my own derived from the Law, but that which is through faith in Christ, the righteousness which comes from God on the basis of faith.
>
> *Philippians 3:7–9*

I have been justified! God's love has invaded! Christ's presence has taken up residence! He has changed me! The load of sin is lifted . . . the source of righteousness has shifted! My relationship with God now rests on faith, not works. What a relief!

Paul was clearly a changed man. To his own amazement he began to laugh again.

But what now? Had he arrived? Was there nothing more to do but sit around and dream, dream, dream? No. In his own words, "I press on . . . I press on."

> Not that I have already obtained it, or have already become perfect, but I press on in order that I may lay hold of that for which also I was laid

hold of by Christ Jesus. Brethren, I do not regard myself as having laid hold of it yet; but one thing I do: forgetting what lies behind and reaching forward to what lies ahead, I press on toward the goal for the prize of the upward call of God in Christ Jesus. Let us therefore, as many as are perfect, have this attitude; and if in anything you have a different attitude, God will reveal that also to you; however, let us keep living by that same standard to which we have attained.

Philippians 3:12–16

I find his opening lines not a little relieving. With a background like his it would be easy to think he had life by the tail. I've met a few superpious men and women who held a rather inflated opinion of themselves, almost to the point where you wonder if they have started to believe all their own press releases. (I confess, when I come across people like that, I have this strong urge to visit with their married partners and ask them what it is like living with someone who has "arrived." Mates are good at setting the record straight.)

As I read over Paul's comments, which sort of summarize his philosophy of life, five ideas emerge.

1. The plan is progress, not perfection. Twice, right out of the chute, he states that he is far from perfect: "Not that I have obtained it . . . become perfect . . . I do not regard myself as having laid hold of it yet. . . ."

What is "it"? Christlikeness. True and complete godliness in final form, with no room for improvement. Nobody on earth qualifies for this one.

Part of the reason hanging tough is tough is the imperfection that continues to mark our lives. Frequent reminders of our humanity still rear their ugly heads. That is true of ourselves, and it is true of others. We, ourselves, are imperfect, living in an imperfect world, surrounded by imperfect people, who continue to model imperfections on a daily basis. Happy is the person who keeps that in mind. You will find that life is not nearly as galling if you remember that the goal is to press on in spite of the lack of perfection.

Perfectionists have a whale of a battle with this. They want life to be lived flawlessly by everyone. That is why I have said for years that perfectionists are people who take pains—and give them to others.

If a man as capable as Paul freely admitted he had not arrived, we should have little difficulty saying the same. Nevertheless, progress is the main agenda of life. If you can see changes in your own life as compared to, say, a year ago or more, take heart! You are on the right road.

2. *The past is over . . . forget it!* The original word Paul used when he wrote, "forgetting what lies behind," was a Greek term that meant fully forgetting, *completely* forgetting. Actually, it was an ancient athletic term used of a runner who outran another in the same race: Once he got into the lead, he would never turn and look back; he would forget about the other runner. The one in the lead focuses on the tape before him rather than the other runners behind him.

Some of the unhappiest people I have ever known are living their lives looking over their shoulder. What a waste! Nothing back there can be changed.

What's in the past? Only two things: great attainments and accomplishments that could either make us proud by reliving them or indifferent by resting on them . . . or failures and defeats that cannot help but arouse feelings of guilt and shame. Why in the world would anyone want to return to that quagmire? I have never been able to figure that one out. By recalling those inglorious, ineffective events of yesterday, our energy is sapped for facing the demands of today. Rehearsing those wrongs, now forgiven in grace, derails and demoralizes us. There are few joy stealers more insidious than past memories that haunt our minds. Paul says to forget the past! Good advice to all who hope to hang tough.

3. *The future holds out hope . . . reach for it!* I am not the first to point out that Paul may have had in mind the chariot races so popular in the Olympic Games as he wrote of "reaching forward to what lies ahead." He could have been thinking of the chariot racer standing in that small, two-wheeled cart with long, leather reins in his hands, leaning forward to keep his balance. Can you picture it?

The analogy is clear. In this race called life, we are to face forward, anticipating what lies ahead, ever stretching and reaching, making life a passionate, adventurous quest. Life was never meant to be a passive coexistence with enemy forces as we await our heavenly home. But it's easy to do that, especially when we arrive at a certain age (from our mid-fifties on), to sort of shift into neutral and take whatever comes our way.

Let me pause here in midstream and ask you three direct questions:

- Have you left the past—I mean fully moved on beyond it?
- Are you making progress—some kind of deliberate progress with your life?
- Do you passionately pursue some dream—some specific goal?

Robert Ballard suddenly flashes into my mind. Does that name mean anything to you?

Robert Ballard was a man with a quest. He wanted to find the *Titanic.* And on September 1, 1985, he discovered the sunken ship in the North Atlantic, more than 350 miles off the coast of Newfoundland. I get chills when I read his description of the first time he sent down that bright probe light and saw that sight more than two miles below the surface of those cold waters:

> My first direct view of *Titanic* lasted less than two minutes, but the stark sight of her immense black hull towering above the ocean floor will remain forever ingrained in my memory. My lifelong dream was to find this great ship and during the past 13 years the quest for her has dominated my life.[4]

What is your particular quest? For what are you leaning forward? There is something wonderfully exciting about reaching into the future with excited anticipation, and those who pursue new adventures through life stay younger, think better, and laugh louder! I just spoke with a middle-aged man who told me he hopes to teach himself Mandarin, one of the Chinese dialects, so that when he takes an early retirement in a few years he can go to China and teach English as a second language. He was smiling from ear to ear as he shared his plans, and I encouraged him to keep reaching forward for what lies before.

Cynthia and I recently had lunch with a wonderful couple in their thirties who are seriously considering a mid-career change. He will go to seminary and she will go to work to put him through. They have been thinking about it for years. Both are so excited, so motivated. They said we were the first ones to sound enthusiastic; all the others they had mentioned this to were quick to point out all the possible things that could go wrong. All the sacrifices they would have to endure. Why focus on that? I told them to keep reaching forward . . . to pursue their dream. And do I need to mention it? Both were laughing again as they walked away.

- The plan is progress, not perfection.
- The past is over, forget it.
- The future holds out hope, reach for it.

4. The secret is a determined attitude . . . maintain it! Paul specifically mentions having the right attitude. I wrote about this earlier in the book, but perhaps this is a good time to return to it since attitude is such a vital ingredient in the life of anyone who plans to hang tough. Here, the right attitude is important for those who are on the road to maturity . . . who are growing and are ready for the next lesson to be learned.

By the way, I like the gracious way Paul allows others the liberty to grow at their own pace: "If anyone has a different attitude, God will reveal that to him." But as far as the apostle was concerned, hanging tough and maintaining a determined attitude belonged together.

This reminds me of something similar written elsewhere in the New Testament:

> Consider it all joy, my brethren, when you encounter various trials, knowing that the testing of your faith produces endurance. And let endurance have its perfect result, that you may be perfect and complete, lacking in nothing.
>
> *James 1:2–4*

He does not mean that we reach perfection—we have already established that that is not the goal. He has maturity in mind. James says the same thing:

> Dear brothers, is your life full of difficulties and temptations? Then be happy, for when the way is rough, your patience has a chance to grow. So let it grow, and don't try to squirm out of your problems. For when your patience is finally in full bloom, then you will be ready for anything, strong in character, full and complete.
>
> *James 1:2–4 TLB*

I think of the process as a domino effect. Trials and tests come that impact our patience and give it a chance to grow (do they ever!).

As patience begins to develop, strong character is cultivated, moving us ever onward toward maturity. There is no shortcut! But by refusing to squirm out of your problems, you find yourself becoming the man or woman you have always wanted to be. And did you notice that little tidbit of advice? "Then be happy [there's that reminder again!] . . . for when the way is rough . . . you will be ready for anything. . . ." No major change will shock you.

For years all the members of our family lived under the same roof. Even as one after another of our adult children married and moved into their own homes, they still lived nearby. Our lives remained intertwined, and we maintained a close harmony. And then, almost overnight, we were separated. It was as if a bomb exploded and blew us all around the country.

Our older son, Curt, and his wife, Debbie, plus their three children remained nearby. Happily, they were not involved in the wholesale reshuffling of the Swindoll deck. But our older daughter, Charissa, and her husband, Byron, with their two children moved to Atlanta as Byron changed jobs and joined the Ronald Blue Company. Our younger daughter, Colleen, moved to the Chicago area with her husband, Mark, as he began studying for the ministry at Trinity Evangelical Divinity School. And our younger son, Chuck, moved to Orlando to begin his training as a sound engineer at Full Sail Center for the Recording Arts.

All three of those moves happened suddenly within a period of three months . . . boom, boom, boom! As Cynthia and I sat all alone on our sun porch one morning following the sudden scattering of the Swindoll tribe, our heads still swimming in the backwash of it all, we sort of caught our breath and decided that we would neither fight it nor whine about it. We deliberately chose to maintain a good attitude, which meant accepting what had occurred and adjusting to the new challenge of keeping close ties as best we could between Southern California, Chicago, Atlanta, and Orlando.

Since God is sovereign and is in the midst of everything that happens to us, the sudden trial of being so far removed from one another was something we could all endure. And we have. Our long distance phone bill and our travel expenses tell their own tale, I can assure you. But behind it all—on everyone's part—the secret to hanging tough together . . . and loving it has been everyone's attitude. Who knows? We may live to see the day when we're all back in the same geographical region and our home is, once again, filled with wall-to-wall children—

and grandchildren—and we will long for the peace and quiet we had finally gotten used to! No, just kidding.

It occurred to Cynthia and me recently that we had reared our children to keep a close watch over their attitudes. All through their growing-up years we preached and tried hard to model positive attitudes, cooperative attitudes, willing and happy attitudes. Laughter has always been heard in our home, so why not apply all that now? It has worked wonders! Because of that, I have been particularly grateful for the piece Bob Benson wrote several years ago.

Laughter in the Walls

I pass a lot of houses on my way home—
    some pretty,
        some expensive,
            some inviting—
but my heart always skips a beat
    when I turn down the road
and see my house nestled against the hill.
    I guess I'm especially proud
of the house and the way it looks because
    I drew the plans myself.
It started out large enough for us—
    I even had a study—
two teenaged boys now reside in there.
    And it had a guest room—
my girl and nine dolls are permanent guests.
    It had a small room Peg
had hoped would be her sewing room—
    two boys swinging on the dutch door
have claimed this room as their own.
    So it really doesn't look right now
as if I'm much of an architect.
    But it will get larger again—
one by one they will go away
        to work,
            to college,
        to service,
    to their own houses,
and then there will be room—
    a guest room,

a study,
and a sewing room
for just the two of us.
But it won't be empty—
every corner
every room
every nick
in the coffee table
will be crowded with memories.
Memories of picnics,
parties, Christmases,
bedside vigils, summers,
fires, winters, going barefoot,
leaving for vacation, cats,
conversations, black eyes,
graduations, first dates,
ball games, arguments,
washing dishes, bicycles,
dogs, boat rides,
getting home from vacation,
meals, rabbits, and
a thousand other things
that fill the lives
of those who would raise five.
And Peg and I will sit
quietly by the fire
and listen to the
laughter in the walls.[5]

5. *The need is keeping a high standard . . . together.* Those who hang tough do better when doing so with others. That is especially true in times of severe crisis. As Benjamin Franklin said at the signing of the Declaration of Independence: "We must all hang together, or assuredly we shall all hang separately."[6] And while pulling together we need to keep a high standard. As the apostle wrote to his Philippian friends, "Let us keep living by that same standard."

Agreeing on the same basics while encouraging each other to hang in there day after day is one of the many benefits of locking arms in close friendship with a small group of Christians. The group not only holds us accountable, but also reminds us we are not alone. I have found that

I don't get as weary when I pull up close alongside a few like-minded brothers and take the time to cultivate a meaningful relationship. It is practical *and* biblical:

> And let us not lose heart in doing good, for in due time we shall reap if we do not grow weary.
>
> *Galatians 6:9*

> Therefore, my beloved brethren, be steadfast, immovable, always abounding in the work of the Lord, knowing that your toil is not in vain in the Lord.
>
> *1 Corinthians 15:58*

A WORKABLE PLAN FOR EVERYDAY LIVING

Let me see if I can wrap up this chapter in a single statement. Progress is maintained by:

> Forgetting yesterday's glory and grind
> and by
> Focusing on tomorrow's challenging opportunities
> while we
> Keep the right attitude and remember
> we are in it together.

In all honesty, I am convinced that that is a winning game plan for hanging tough . . . and loving it. In fact, I suggest you duplicate that formula on a small sheet of paper or a three-by-five card and tape it to your bathroom mirror or clip it to the sun visor of your car. Repeat it until it gets transferred to your memory and becomes your motto for the month. I have begun doing that, and do you know what? You guessed it—I've started to laugh again . . . even though half the family is still spread across the country.

Let's lock arms and "press on toward the goal for the prize of the upward call of God in Christ Jesus." Is it a deal?

I can still remember sitting as a small boy in a little church in my hometown, El Campo, Texas, listening to those gospel songs sung by some of the simplest and best folks on earth. They were my mom's and dad's Christian friends and family members—people of my simple roots.

One song stands out in my memory above all the rest, a refrain seldom heard in most churches today. It is more than a song. It's a prayer that declares our commitment to enduring the long haul and maintaining a high standard.

> I'm pressing on the upward way,
> New heights I'm gaining every day;
> Still praying as I onward bound,
> Lord, plant my feet on higher ground.
>
> Lord, lift me up and let me stand,
> By faith, on heaven's table-land,
> A higher plane than I have found;
> Lord, plant my feet on higher ground.[7]

10

It's a Mad, Bad, Sad World, But . . .

Right about now a few of you have had it up to here with being told you need to laugh more. All this stuff about being positive and maintaining a good attitude may be starting to wear thin. You might have started to wonder if the two of us—you and I—are living on the same planet. Maybe you are wondering if Swindoll is really in touch with the raw and wicked side of life. If so, let me reassure you—I am.

I live in the Greater Los Angeles area, remember, which is not anyone's idea of a quaint and quiet village filled with caring people living in lovely harmony. Some of the people I am around and some of the sights I see are enough to make me want to get in my car and drive in the other direction. Hopefully, I wouldn't get shot on the freeway trying to get out of town! Acts of violence and the grossest form of criminal behavior are so prevalent that our local television news reporters could easily fill their hour every evening with nothing but that kind of news. Our area is the breeding ground for the full spectrum of human depravity. Sadly, it is here that many cults originate. It is here that one can find every form of pornography, abuse, addiction, and demonic activity, not to mention the ever-present homeless people I see every day. And then there are the tragic emotional breakdowns and marital breakups I hear about on a regular basis. This place is b-a-a-a-a-d!

Do I live on an idyllic island removed from reality where love is abundant and the soft winds of joy blow through the palm trees? Is this the sort of place a person would choose to raise a family who is hoping to escape the harsh realities of a world gone mad? You know better. There are days I would love to pack up and find a nice protected space away from all the noise and nonsense . . . all the fast-lane greed and filthy air . . . all the conflicts and pressures an overcrowded city like ours includes. But then God gets my attention and reminds me that He hasn't called me to Shady Brook Lane where folks sit on the front porch and swing till dark, snapping peas and watching lightning bugs. My world—my mission, my calling—is the city where life gets ugly and people get hostile and kids are exposed to too much too soon. In this area where depravity is relentlessly on display, only the fit survive.

And that is exactly why I've decided to write a book like this. In a world this bad, laughter is the last thing anyone would expect to hear. Trust me, when you laugh in the midst of *this* cesspool environment, people want to know why. "Laughter is hope's last weapon," as I read recently, and I think it is time we put that weapon to use. Out here, only those who are firm in their faith can laugh in the face of tragedy. As Flannery O'Connor wrote:

> Where there is no belief in the soul, there is very little drama. . . . Either one is serious about salvation or one is not. And it is well to realize that the maximum amount of seriousness admits the maximum amount of comedy. Only if we are secure in our beliefs can we see the comical side of the universe.[1]

The Christian is a weird sort, let's face it. We are earthlings, yet the Bible says we are citizens of heaven. This world may not be our home, but it is our residence. Furthermore, we are to live in the world, but we are not to be of the world. And since joy is one of our distinctives, laughter is appropriate even though we are surrounded by all manner of wrong and wickedness. It can get a little confusing, as A. W. Tozer pointed out rather graphically:

> A real Christian is an odd number anyway. He feels supreme love for One whom he has never seen, talks familiarly every day to Someone he cannot see, expects to go to heaven on the virtue of Another, empties himself in order to be full, admits he is wrong so he can be declared right, goes down in order to get up, is strongest when he is weakest, richest when he is poorest, and happiest when he feels worst. He dies so he can live, forsakes in order to have, gives away so he can keep, sees the invisible, hears the inaudible, and knows that which passeth knowledge.[2]

OUR LORD'S STRANGE STRATEGY

In light of all that, doesn't it seem odd of God not to provide an immediate escape route to heaven as soon as we are converted? Why would He leave us in the midst of such an insane, godless setting? I ask you, why? What kind of strange strategy could He have in mind, leaving heaven-bound people riveted to this hell-bound earth?

The answer is worth pursuing, and I don't know of a more qualified source for that answer than Jesus Christ Himself. As I examine His words to His disciples prior to His crucifixion, I find at least three definitive statements that explain what we can expect as we are left on earth.

1. We can have inner peace in the midst of outer pressure and pain. Read Jesus' words slowly and carefully:

> These things I have spoken to you, that you may be kept from stumbling. They will make you outcasts from the synagogue; but an hour is coming for everyone who kills you to think that he is offering service to God.
>
> *John 16:1–2*

> But when He, the Spirit of truth, comes, He will guide you into all the truth; for He will not speak on His own initiative, but whatever He hears, He will speak; and He will disclose to you what is to come.
>
> *John 16:13*

> These things I have spoken to you, that in Me you may have peace. In the world you have tribulation, but take courage; I have overcome the world.
>
> *John 16:33*

If those words mean anything, they provide straight talk about life minus a cushy comfort zone. We won't be sheltered from life's blows. Settle it in your mind once for all: Christians are not supernaturally protected from the blasts, the horrors, the aches, or the pains of living on this globe. Christians can be unfairly treated, assaulted, robbed, raped, and murdered. We can suffer financial reversals, we can be taken advantage of, abused, neglected, and divorced by uncaring mates. Then how can we expect to be joyful, unlike those around us? Because He promises that deep within He will give us peace . . . an unexplainable, illogical inner peace.

2. We are insulated by divine power, yet we are not to live an isolated existence. Again, pay close attention to Jesus' counsel:

These things Jesus spoke; and lifting up His eyes to heaven, He said, "Father, the hour has come; glorify Thy Son, that the Son may glorify Thee, even as Thou gavest Him authority over all mankind, that to all whom Thou hast given Him, He may give eternal life. And this is eternal life, that they may know Thee, the only true God, and Jesus Christ whom Thou hast sent."

John 17:1–3

And I am no more in the world; and yet they themselves are in the world, and I come to Thee. Holy Father, keep them in Thy name, the name which Thou hast given Me, that they may be one, even as We are. While I was with them, I was keeping them in Thy name which Thou hast given Me; and I guarded them, and not one of them perished but the son of perdition, that the Scripture might be fulfilled. But now I come to Thee; and these things I speak in the world, that they may have My joy made full in themselves. I have given them Thy word; and the world has hated them, because they are not of the world, even as I am not of the world. I do not ask Thee to take them out of the world, but to keep them from the evil one.

John 17:11–15

Take another glance at that last statement. Jesus is praying, deliberately asking the Father *not* to remove us from all the earthly garbage, all the daily debris that gathers around this old sin-cursed planet. Then how can any of us ever laugh again? He insulates us! The fires of unrestrained passion may blaze all around us, but He gives us the power of His protective shield to steer us clear of contamination. And don't think the person of the world doesn't notice.

3. We may be unique, but we must be unified. God is pleased with our differences. No two of us are exactly alike, so each person is able to reach out to his or her own sphere of influence. However, our strength comes from our unity.

They are not of the world, even as I am not of the world. Sanctify them in the truth; Thy word is truth. . . . that they may all be one; even as Thou, Father, art in Me, and I in Thee, that they also may be in Us; that the world may believe that Thou didst send Me. . . . I in them, and Thou in Me, that they may be perfected in unity, that the world may know that Thou didst send Me, and didst love them, even as Thou didst love Me.

John 17:16–17, 21, 23

The idea is this: That they (Christians left on earth) may be brought together into a unit—one powerful force for good—in a society weakened by independence and isolation. As people of the world who have no sense of eternal purpose see this unified front, they will realize their own emptiness and seek to find out what makes the difference. What a strategy! All the more reason for Christ's forever family to remain joyfully unified under the authority of His Majesty, King Jesus.

Our world may be a mad, bad, sad place . . . totally out to lunch, spiritually speaking. But impossible to reach and win? Not on your life. Christ's strange strategy is effective because it defies being ignored.

- peace in pressure and pain
- insulated not isolated
- unique but unified

Stop and think. Is it easy to overlook a person who is at peace when you are gripped by panic? And if you are weak within, does someone who seems strangely insulated make you curious? Furthermore, why would anybody laugh in a cesspool society like ours? I repeat, it is an ingenious strategy.

THE CHRISTIAN'S MARCHING ORDERS

All that brings us back to Paul's letter written to his friends in Philippi. He is writing to Christians—peaceful, joyful, strong, insulated people—who live in the real world. He wants them to know how to get a big job done. And so, he tells them, living for Christ means marching in step with His drumbeat.

Brethren, join in following my example, and observe those who walk according to the pattern you have in us. For many walk, of whom I often told you, and now tell you even weeping, that they are enemies of the cross of Christ, whose end is destruction, whose god is their appetite, and whose glory is in their shame, who set their minds on earthly things. For our citizenship is in heaven, from which also we eagerly wait for a Savior, the Lord Jesus Christ; who will transform the body of our humble state into conformity with the body of His glory, by the exertion of the power that He has even to subject all things to Himself. Therefore, my

147

beloved brethren whom I long to see, my joy and crown, so stand firm in the Lord, my beloved.

Philippians 3:17—4:1

Here I find several helpful tips on how to make our lives count . . . how to do more than sit around, waiting for Christ's return. Four specifics come to my mind as I read Paul's wise counsel.

First, *we need examples to follow.*

Brethren, join in following my example, and observe those who walk according to the pattern you have in us.

Philippians 3:17

The bad news is: Ours is an arduous, long, and sometimes tedious journey through Cesspool Cosmos. And, observe, it is a walk, not a sprint. The good news is: We are not alone on this demanding pilgrimage, which means that some folks we are traveling with make awfully good models to follow. So, follow them!

I like it that while Paul invited believers to follow him, he also acknowledged that others were worth being followed as well. This is a good place to be reminded that no one person on earth is to be our single source of instruction or our only object of admiration. When that happens we can easily get tunnel vision and draw dangerously close to idolizing an individual. We are told to follow others' example but not to focus fully on one person, no matter how godly or gifted he or she may be. Happy and balanced are those in God's army who have several mentors and respect many heroes.

What is it we look for when searching for examples to follow? I like the things Paul listed for Timothy:

But you [Timothy] followed my teaching, conduct, purpose, faith, patience, love, perseverance, persecutions, and sufferings, such as happened to me at Antioch, at Iconium and at Lystra; what persecutions I endured, and out of them all the Lord delivered me! And indeed, all who desire to live godly in Christ Jesus will be persecuted.

2 Timothy 3:10–12

And never forget that those we follow are to be diligent followers of Christ Himself. He remains the Master Mentor.

Be imitators of me, just as I also am of Christ.
1 Corinthians 11:1

Before I leave this subject, let me point out a few practical suggestions for determining your role models:

- Choose your mentors slowly.
- Study their private lives carefully.
- Spend time with them regularly.

Some who make a good public impression may lack solid character
qualities behind the scenes. If you ignore that, you can easily be deceived
and disillusioned.

I know from personal experience the downside of following such a
model. Without getting into details, there was a time when I was young
in the faith and terribly vulnerable. A strong leader with a great deal of
charisma sort of swept me off my feet. He became my sole source of
teaching, and for several years his was the only voice of authority I took
seriously. My respect for the man bordered dangerously near idolatry,
though I would have denied it at the time. If he was teaching, I was
there to drink in every word. His interpretations became my convictions.
Even his mannerisms and terminology rubbed off so much that I lost
my own sense of confidence and identity; both were bound up in him.
Looking back, I also realize I became extremely serious—fanatically
serious—about everything. Thankfully, through a chain of events only
the Lord could have orchestrated, all that slowly changed. Several subtle
things came to the surface, causing me to question the man's private life.
And when I challenged some of the things he was teaching, he made it
abundantly clear that no one was *ever* to question him. That did it. My
respect for the man quickly eroded. More importantly, I realized that I
had been looking up to someone who was not the one I should be following, certainly not exclusively. Hard lesson learned, but a good one.

Interestingly, when I broke that fixation, God began to show me
many other things I had been blinded to, and His Word brought fresh
insights. With my spiritual equilibrium restored, a new sense of perspective returned, along with a sense of humor that had lain dormant too long.
In short, it cleared the way for me to become myself rather than a shadow
of someone else. Graciously, in the years that followed, God brought me

several wonderful mentors, who did indeed follow Christ. Each one has contributed immeasurably to my spiritual growth.

So, learn from my mistake. We need examples (plural!) to follow. As we integrate their godly characteristics into our lives, we become better people.

Second, *we live among many who are enemies of the cross.* This fact keeps us from following every strong personality we meet. "Many," says Paul, "are enemies."

> For many walk, of whom I often told you, and now tell you even weeping, that they are enemies of the cross of Christ, whose end is destruction, whose god is their appetite, and whose glory is in their shame, who set their minds on earthly things.
>
> *Philippians 3:18–19*

Paul is firm, but he is not judgmental. He is committed to the truth, which sometimes hurts. But is he proud of the contrast between himself and those he calls enemies? No. He states that what he is saying makes him weep.

If you and I are ever going to get involved in sharing the joys of knowing and walking with Christ, we must come to terms with the fact that people without Christ in their lives are lost—absolutely and undeniably L-O-S-T.

In fact, Paul gives us one of the clearest and most pointed descriptions of the person who is lost. He or she is:

- *Destined for eternal hopelessness.* That is their future. The reality of hell should be enough to prompt *anyone* to turn to Christ.

- *Driven by sensual appetites.* Anyone who is exposed to the world of the unbeliever soon finds out how up-to-date the counsel of Paul really is. The timeworn motto, "Eat, drink, and be merry" is still very much in vogue. Sensuality is the fuel that lights their fire.

- *Dedicated to material things.* Virtually *everything* draws the lost person toward possessions . . . things that have price tags, things that are tangible, things that can be owned and must be maintained. In the words of Paul, they "set their minds on earthly things."

When all this is added up, is it surprising that the sound of laughter has been drowned out? As you read over the list, you realize anew the emptiness, the boredom of such an existence. No laughter here.

Now the point of this analysis of the lost is not to judge or to condemn or to leave the impression that Christians are better than non-Christians. It is to remind us that God has placed us among them. They are, in fact, in the majority! Our mission is not to argue with them or put them down or make them feel ashamed; it is to reach out to them! To *win* them. To help them realize there is much more to life than they have ever known. To model a different lifestyle that is so convincing, so appealing, that their curiosity will be tweaked, so they might discover what they are missing. The non-Christian world may be lost and running on empty, but they are not stupid or unaware of their surroundings. When they come across an individual who is at peace, free of fear and worry, fulfilled, and genuinely happy, no one has to tell them that something is missing from their lives. Ours may be a mad, bad, sad world, but it is not *blind*. And it is certainly not unreachable. Interesting them in something meaningful and different is not an impossibility. Who doesn't want relief? Freedom from addictions? A purpose for living? A reason to laugh again?

I mentioned earlier that I am engaged in a radio ministry, Insight for Living. Frequently listeners will call and/or write to communicate the changes that have happened in their lives as a result of listening to the broadcasts. We have file drawers full of such letters, each one telling how a person was attracted to the program, often because of what was missing in his or her own life.

I shall never forget one such letter from a young woman who had reached the absolute end of her rope. She had checked into a motel, planning to take her life. Throughout the night she sat on the side of the bed and mentally rehearsed her miserable existence. She had endured numerous failed relationships with men and had had several abortions. She was empty, angry, and could see no reason to go on. Finally, just before dawn, she reached in her purse and pulled out a loaded pistol. Trembling, she stuck it in her mouth and closed her eyes. Suddenly the clock radio snapped on. Apparently the previous occupant had set the radio to come on at that precise time on that precise station . . . and the musical theme of "Insight for Living" filled the room. The uplifting sounds startled her. She tried to ignore it, but couldn't. She heard my voice and found herself strangely attracted to the message of new hope and authentic joy that she had never heard in her entire life. Before the thirty-minute broadcast ended, she gave her life to Jesus Christ. When she contacted us to tell us what had happened, she said she could still taste the cold steel from the gun barrel she had pulled from her mouth.

Not all stories are that dramatic. Some call or write, requesting help to get past the horrible scars of years gone by. Some are victims of abuse. Others write of another kind of emptiness—affluent boredom and materialistic greed, where enough was never enough—but they have nothing else to fill the void. Businessmen and women on a maddening pace to get to the top contact us about their lack of happiness and contentment, their dreadful feelings of distance from their mates and children, and their disillusionment with "the system." Many mention extramarital affairs they are not able to stop or addictions they cannot control: alcoholism, drugs, food, sex.

In each case, it seems, they realize that Christ is able to provide what is missing, and they want to or have entrusted their lives to Him. Most mention their feelings of hopelessness and their inability to help themselves. They long to be free . . . free to live rather than merely exist in a revolving door of repeated defeats . . . free enough to laugh again. It is *that* ingredient we notice in virtually all the letters of transformed lives . . . joy—*outrageous* joy.

Third, *we belong to those who are bound for heaven.*

> For our citizenship is in heaven, from which also we eagerly wait for a Savior, the Lord Jesus Christ; who will transform the body of our humble state into conformity with the body of His glory, by the exertion of the power that He has even to subject all things to Himself.
>
> *Philippians 3:20–21*

Isn't that a great thought? "Our citizenship is in heaven." But let's never forget that our involvements are on earth. That may create a little tension now and then, but what a challenging opportunity! Only heaven-bound people are objective enough to make a major difference on earth. While we "eagerly wait for a Savior," we are able to introduce earth-bound people to a whole new way of life. Can you imagine the curiosity that a bunch of us could arouse just by living lives of relaxed laughter, enjoying delightful fun together? Bystanders would stare in wonder and amazement. They couldn't stand it, being left out. They would *have* to know what they were missing and why we are able to have so much fun, and it would be our joy to tell them. *I love it!* Ours may be a mad, bad, sad old world, but impossible to impact? Get serious! No, on second thought, *get happy!*

I have never been able to figure out why heaven-bound citizens of glory have become so grim. In only a matter of time we shall be transformed from our present condition and conformed into Christ's image—what a change! And in light of that, why is a little temporary period of tough times on earth so all-fired important? It's time we looked different and sounded different. It is time we began to laugh again.

Solomon was absolutely right:

> A joyful heart is good medicine,
> But a broken spirit dries up the bones.
>
> *Proverbs 17:22*

Did you know that laughter actually does work like a medicine in our systems? It exercises our lungs and stimulates our circulation. It takes our minds off our troubles and massages our emotions. Laughter decreases tension. When we laugh, a sort of temporary anesthesia is released within us that blocks the pain as our attention is diverted. As I mentioned earlier, laughter is one of the healthiest exercises we can enjoy. It literally brings healing.

Who hasn't heard about Norman Cousins' remarkable experience? In his excellent book, *Anatomy of an Illness as Perceived by the Patient,* he tells about his battle with an "incurable" disease and the pain he endured as his body's collagen was deteriorating. That, by the way, is the fibrous material that holds the body's cells together. In Cousins' own words, he was "becoming unstuck."

He decided to take matters into his own hands and treat himself (with his doctor's approval) by (1) taking vitamins, (2) eating only healthy food, and—are you ready for this?—(3) undergoing "laugh therapy" by watching old, funny Marx Brothers movies, clips from "Candid Camera," and cartoons . . . and anything else that would make him laugh. He found that if he laughed hard for ten minutes straight, he could enjoy about two hours of relief from pain. To his doctor's amazement, Cousins eventually recovered.[3] The man lived many years beyond anyone's expectations . . . anyone's but his! Norman Cousins' remarkable story reminds me of another of Solomon's proverbs, "The cheerful heart has a continual feast" (Prov. 15:15 NIV).

Think of the impact we could have as earth-free citizens of heaven living hilariously enjoyable, responsible, yet wonderfully carefree lives among people who cannot find anything funny in their shattered world of madness, badness, and sadness. If Laurel and Hardy, the Three Stooges, and the Marx Brothers could help Norman Cousins recover, just think of the healing power that could come from the joy of Jesus Christ. No comparison. But we can't forget the key: You and I . . . we must be the ones who model the message if we ever hope to help our world laugh again. It was G. K. Chesterton who wrote:

> I am all in favor of Laughing. Laughter has something in it in common with the ancient winds of faith and inspiration; it unfreezes pride and unwinds secrecy; it makes men forget themselves in the presence of something greater than themselves; something (as the common phrase goes about a joke) that they cannot resist.[4]

Fourth, *we must stand firm, but not stand still.*

> Therefore, my beloved brethren whom I long to see, my joy and crown, so stand firm in the Lord, my beloved.
>
> *Philippians 4:1*

Earlier Paul admonished us to "be confident in the Lord" (1:6). Later, to "have the Lord's attitude" (2:5). Next, to "rejoice in the Lord" (3:1). And now he is saying we are to "stand firm in the Lord" (4:1). All the way through the letter to the Philippians the focus has been not on our circumstances or on others or on ourselves, but on the Lord, our source of life and love, confidence and joy.

Here we are being told to "stand firm." But let's not confuse this with standing still. In a world like ours, it is easy to get caught up in the system and lose our stability, hence the command, "Stand firm." In other words, keep your equilibrium . . . don't let the highs and lows sway you . . . get a firm grip on that eternal relationship you have with the Lord and don't let go. He will give you the strength to go on, and He will continue bringing to your attention the thoughts that will keep you positive, affirming, and winsome.

In the final lines of this chapter, I want to encourage you to be all you can be in this world that long ago lost its way. You may not know it and you may not feel like it, but to someone else you are the only source of light and laughter. They may be mad or they may be bad or they may be sad, but, I repeat, they are not unreachable. The real question is this: Are you willing to do the reaching?

It may be a long reach. And sometimes we get our hands slapped . . . our feelings hurt. That's okay. Hurting people often hurt people. But we have God on our side.

So come on out of your shell and reach. Even though the reachable may sometimes act unreachable, keep on reaching. And remember, a good mixture of compassion and realism is essential.

I like the wry comment Barbara Johnson makes in her book, *Splashes of Joy in the Cesspools of Life:*

> The rain falls on the just and also on the unjust, but
> chiefly on the just,
> Because the unjust steals the just's umbrella.[5]

No problem . . . like I've been saying, it's a mad, bad, sad world. Even if you get wet doing it, keep reaching, and, for sure, keep laughing.

11

Defusing Disharmony

*I*n a parable she entitles "A Brawling Bride," Karen Mains paints a vivid scene, describing a suspenseful moment in a wedding ceremony. Down front stands the groom in a spotless tuxedo—handsome, smiling, full of anticipation, shoes shined, every hair in place, anxiously awaiting the presence of his bride. All attendants are in place, looking joyful and attractive. The magical moment finally arrives as the pipe organ reaches full crescendo and the stately wedding march begins.

Everyone rises and looks toward the door for their first glimpse of the bride. Suddenly there is a horrified gasp. The wedding party is shocked. The groom stares in embarrassed disbelief. Instead of a lovely woman dressed in elegant white, smiling behind a lace veil, the bride is limping down the aisle. Her dress is soiled and torn. Her leg seems twisted. Ugly cuts and bruises cover her bare arms. Her nose is bleeding, one eye is purple and swollen, and her hair is disheveled.

"Does not this handsome groom deserve better than this?" asks the author. And then the clincher: "Alas, His bride, THE CHURCH, has been fighting again!"[1]

Calling them (and us) "the church," the apostle Paul writes to the Ephesians:

> Christ . . . loved the church and gave Himself up for her . . . to make her holy and clean . . . so that He could give her to Himself as a glorious church without a single spot or wrinkle or any other blemish, being holy and without a single fault.
>
> *Ephesians 5:25–27 NASB/TLB*

Wonderful plan . . . but hardly a realistic portrayal. I mean, can you imagine what the wedding pictures would look like if Christ claimed

159

His bride, the church, *today?* Try to picture Him standing next to His brawling bride. It is one thing for us to survive the blows of a world that is hostile to the things of Christ, but to be in disharmony with one another, fighting and arguing among ourselves—unthinkable.

Puritan Thomas Brookes once penned these words: "For wolves to worry lambs is no wonder, but for lambs to worry one another, this is unnatural and monstrous."[2]

Unthinkable and unnatural though it may seem, the bride has been brawling for centuries. We get along for a little while and then we are back at each others' throats. After a bit we make up, walk in wonderful harmony for a few days, then we turn on one another. We can switch from friend to fiend in a matter of moments.

In a "Peanuts" cartoon, Lucy says to Snoopy: "There are times when you really bug me, but I must admit there are also times when I feel like giving you a big hug."

Snoopy replies: "That's the way I am . . . huggable and buggable."

And so it is with us and our relationships within the ranks of God's family. I'm not referring to the variety of our personalities, gifts, tastes, and preferences—that's healthy. The Master made us like that. It's our mistreatment of each other, the infighting, the angry assaults, the verbal misrepresentations, the choosing of sides, the stubborn wills, the childish squabbles. An objective onlooker who watches us from a distance could wonder how and why some of us call ourselves Christians. "Well," you ask, "must we always agree?" No, absolutely not. But my question is this: Why can't we be *agreeable?* What is it that makes us so ornery and nitpicking in our attitudes? Why so many petty fights and ugly quarrels? Why so little acceptance and tolerance? Aren't we given the direct command to "keep the unity of the Spirit in the bond of peace"? What makes Christ's bride forget those words and have so many verbal brawls?

ANALYZING CONFLICT'S CAUSE AND EXTENT

James asked similar questions back in the first century—which tells us that disharmony is not solely a twentieth-century malady. Even back in the days when life was simple and everyone's pace was slower, there were squabbles.

What is the source of quarrels and conflicts among you? Is not the source your pleasures that wage war in your members? You lust and do not have; so you commit murder. And you are envious and cannot obtain; so you fight and quarrel. You do not have because you do not ask. You ask and do not receive, because you ask with wrong motives, so that you may spend it on your pleasures.

James 4:1–3

James never was the type to beat around the bush. With penetrating honesty he asks and answers the critical question. The terms he uses are extremely descriptive: "quarrels and conflicts." The first term is from the Greek word for "war." It conveys a scene of broad and bloody hostility between opposing parties. The second represents smaller skirmishes, local and limited battles, even a chronic state of disharmony. During World War II there were two massive "theaters" of warfare, vast territories on opposite sides of our country: the European theater of war and the Pacific theater of war. Within both numerous skirmishes and individual battles took place. That is the idea here.

The same can be seen to this day within the ranks of religion. England and Ireland have sustained their territorial and denominational "quarrel" for centuries. People on both sides are still being killed and crippled by real bombs and real bullets. Less bloody perhaps, but no less real are the denominational quarrels in our own land—fights and splits within the ranks. Seminaries quarrel as one theological position takes up arms against another. The disputes appear civil and sophisticated as each side publishes its position in journals and books, but behind the veil of intellectualism is a great deal of hostility.

And then there are those "conflicts" between local churches as well as among members of the same church. Small, petty battles . . . arguments, power struggles, envyings, catty comments, silent standoffs, and even lawsuits between members of the body of Christ. These may not be on the national news, but they can get ugly.

A pastor from another state recently told me that some of the members of his board of elders had not spoken to one another for over a year. A concerned board member from a different church in another state said he had recently resigned because he had gotten exhausted from doing nothing but "putting out fires" and "trying to keep church members happy." His particular church had been through two major splits in the past seven years over reasons that would make you smile and shake your head in disbelief. Such are the "conflicts among us."

Why We Have Them

James points to "the source" as he addresses the issue. His answer may seem strange: "Is not the source your pleasures that wage war in your members?"

"Pleasures" doesn't sound very hostile, does it? Maybe not in our English language, but the Greek word is the one from which we get "hedonism." It means the strong desire to get what one does not have, which includes the idea of satisfying oneself . . . the passion to get what one wants, regardless. Such an intense craving drives us to shameful and selfish actions. As James puts it, such pleasures lead us to "wage war"—*strateuo*—from which we get "strategy." Our desire to get what we want prompts us to strategize: to put a plan in motion that will result in *my* getting *my* way.

Is this a determined effort? Look again at what James writes:

> You lust and do not have; so you commit murder. And you are envious and cannot obtain; so you fight and quarrel. You do not have because you do not ask.
>
> *James 4:2*

I'd call that determined! If it calls for a fight, *fight!* If it means an argument, *argue!* If it will require getting other people to back me up, *enlist!* If stronger words will help me reach my objective and get what I want, *murder!*

I realize we don't carry weapons to church—not literally. That is not necessary, since the muscle behind our teeth is always ready to launch its killing missiles. We may not bring blood from another's body, but we certainly know how to make them squirm and hopefully surrender. And we never admit it is because we are selfish or because we crave our own way—there's always a principle at stake or a cause worth fighting for that's bigger than personalities. Sure, sure.

I realize that on a few occasions conflicts will arise. There *are* those times when it is essential to stand one's ground and refuse to compromise biblical principles. But more often than not the nasty infighting among us is embarrassingly petty. And, unfortunately, the world has a field day watching us fight and quarrel for the silliest of reasons.

Ways We Express Our Disharmony

Rationalizing our wrong attitudes and actions, we Christians will go to amazing lengths to get our way. The history of the church is strewn with the litter of battle. I repeat, some of those fights were unselfish and necessary. To have backed away would have meant compromising convictions clearly set forth in the Scriptures. But more often than not the "quarrels and conflicts" have expressed themselves in personal power plays, political maneuvering, strong-minded and selfish parishioners determined to get their own way, stubborn pastors who intimidate and bully others, unbending and tightfisted board members who refuse to listen to reason, and, yes, those who seem to delight in stirring up others through rumor and gossip. It's just a mess! Sometimes I wonder how the Shepherd puts up with us. We can be such wayward, stubborn sheep! And to think He sees it all—each and every cutting word or ugly act—yet loves us still. Only because of His grace are we able to continue on.

Marshall Shelley, in his book *Well-Intentioned Dragons,* talks about disharmony in the church from another perspective. Sometimes it is from folks who don't necessarily mean to be difficult, but they are.

Dragons, of course, are fictional beasts—monstrous reptiles with lion's claws, a serpent's tail, bat wings, and scaly skin. They exist only in the imagination.

But there are dragons of a different sort, decidedly real. In most cases, though not always, they do not intend to be sinister; in fact, they're usually quite friendly. But their charm belies their power to destroy.

Within the church, they are often sincere, well-meaning saints, but they leave ulcers, strained relationships, and hard feelings in their wake. They don't consider themselves difficult people. They don't sit up nights thinking of ways to be nasty. Often they are pillars of the community— talented, strong personalities, deservingly respected—but for some reason, they undermine the ministry of the church. They are not naturally rebellious or pathological; they are loyal church members, convinced they're serving God, but they wind up doing more harm than good.

They can drive pastors crazy . . . or out of the church.

Some dragons are openly critical. They are the ones who accuse you of being (pick one) too spiritual, not spiritual enough, too dominant, too laid back, too narrow, too loose, too structured, too disorganized, or ulterior in your motives.

These criticisms are painful because they are largely unanswerable. How can you defend yourself and maintain a spirit of peace? How can you possibly prove the purity of your motives? Dragons make it hard to disagree without being disagreeable.

Relationships are both the professional and personal priority for pastors—getting along with people is an essential element of any ministry—and when relationships are vandalized by critical dragons, many pastors feel like failures. Politicians are satisfied with 51 percent of the constituency behind them; pastors, however, feel the pain when one vocal member becomes an opponent.

Sightings of these dragons are all too common. As one veteran pastor says, "Anyone who's been in ministry more than an hour and a half knows the wrath of a dragon." Or, as Harry Ironside described it, "Wherever there's light, there's bugs."[3]

LOOKING THROUGH THE KEYHOLE
OF A FIRST-CENTURY CHURCH

I would be a lot more discouraged about the problem of disharmony among believers if I didn't remember that it has been around since the church began. Those early churches were anything but pockets of perfection. Christians in places like Corinth and Galatia, Rome and Thessalonica had their troubles just like those living in towns and cities all around our world today. Even Philippi—as fine a group of Jesus People as they were—had their own skirmishes, one of which Paul pinpointed in his letter to them.

Therefore, my beloved brethren whom I long to see, my joy and crown, so stand firm in the Lord, my beloved.

I urge Euodia and I urge Syntyche to live in harmony in the Lord. Indeed, true comrade, I ask you also to help these women who have shared my struggle in the cause of the gospel, together with Clement also, and the rest of my fellow workers, whose names are in the book of life.

Philippians 4:1–3

In his typical fashion, Paul starts with a general principle before he addresses a specific concern; then he wraps things up as he makes a request. Behind it all is his unspoken desire that the Philippians defuse the disharmony and begin to laugh again. When disharmony persists, the first thing to go is the sweetest sound that can be heard in a church—laughter.

Perhaps it had been too long since the Philippians had enjoyed the presence of one another. Paul's hope is that once this difficulty is cleared up, their joy might return.

A Primary Principle

Solving problems that grow out of disharmony among believers calls for a return to standing firm in the things of the Lord, not satisfying self.

> Therefore, my beloved brethren whom I long to see, my joy and crown, so stand firm in the Lord, my beloved.
>
> *Philippians 4:1*

Earlier in the letter Paul had written:

> Only conduct yourselves in a manner worthy of the gospel of Christ; so that whether I come and see you or remain absent, I may hear of you that you are standing firm in one spirit, with one mind striving together for the faith of the gospel.
>
> *Philippians 1:27*

Actually, the idea of standing firm is one of the apostle's favorite topics. For example:

"Stand firm in the faith" (1 Cor. 16:13).
"Keep standing firm" (Gal. 5:1).
"Now we really live, if you stand firm in the Lord" (1 Thess. 3:8).
"So then, brethren, stand firm" (2 Thess. 2:15).

Why place such an emphasis on standing firm in the Lord? What's the big deal? Let me suggest to you that it is one of the most foundational principles of maintaining harmony:

STANDING FIRM IN THE LORD

PRECEDES

RELATING WELL IN THE FAMILY

What would standing firm include? Following Christ's teachings. Respecting His Word. Modeling His priorities. Loving His people.

Seeking and carrying out His will. It has been my observation that those who are committed to these things have little difficulty relating well to other members of God's family. Not surprisingly the very next issue Paul brings up has to do with two in the church at Philippi who needed to "live in harmony" with one another. But before I go into that, this might be a good time for you to ask yourself, "Am I one who stands firm *in the Lord?*" Other options create havoc: Standing firm *for what I want* . . . or, standing firm *in honor of tradition* . . . or, standing firm *with a couple of my friends.*" Unquestionably, those three positions represent the antithesis of "standing firm in the Lord."

A Relational Need

Having stated the principle, Paul puts his finger on the specific conflict at Philippi. He even names names.

> I urge Euodia and I urge Syntyche to live in harmony in the Lord.
>
> *Philippians 4:2*

Let me mention several observations:

1.   These are two women in the church at Philippi (feminine names).

2.   They are mentioned nowhere else in the Scriptures.

3.   The specific details of their dispute are not explained.

4.   Paul's counsel is to urge them toward harmony: "I urge . . . I urge" (he neither rebukes them nor pontificates).

5.   He appeals to their conscience . . . their hearts (intrinsic motivation).

I am just as impressed with what Paul does not do.

He does not spell out a step-by-step process; that was for the two women to work out on their own. Equally impressive, he does not pull rank by adding a warning or a threat, like, "I'll give you two weeks to clear this up," or "If you don't straighten up, I will. . . ."

Paul handled the matter with dignity and grace. While he was deeply concerned ("I urge . . . I urge"), he did not attempt to take charge of the situation from a distance. If anyone is tempted to think Paul was too passive or should have said more, a quick reading of other renderings may help:

- "I plead with . . . I plead with . . ." (NIV).
- "Please, please, with the Lord's help, quarrel no more—be friends again." (TLB).
- "Euodias and Syntyche, I beg you by name to make up your differences as Christians should!" (PHILLIPS).

By repeating the verb ("I urge . . . I urge"), Paul leaves the impression that there was fault on both sides. In fact, the Vulgate, the Latin version of Scripture, uses different verbs in the appeal, which seems to emphasize mutual wrong.

I have seldom seen an exception to this: When disharmony arises between two people or two groups, there is some measure of fault on both sides. The road leading to a breakdown in harmony is never a one-way street. Both parties must be encouraged to see each other's fault, each other's failure . . . and meet on common ground with a mutual willingness to listen and to change.

And what is that common ground? The statement Paul makes includes the answer: "live in harmony in the Lord." Just as we are to "stand firm" in Him, so are we to find agreement in Him. Both sides need to make Him their focus if a solution is ever going to be found. It is as if the Apostle of Grace is saying, "It is important that both release their grudge and state their forgiveness and adopt the same attitude as their Lord when He unselfishly came from heaven to earth to be our Savior. Only then will there be renewed harmony."

One more thought before moving on. Everything we know of these two women is: They quarreled. Down through the centuries the only answer that could be given to the question: "Who were Euodia and Syntyche?" has been "They were two women from Philippi who lived in disharmony." That prompts me to ask you: If *your* life were to be summed up in a single statement, what would that statement be?

An Affirming Request

Occasionally a dispute is so deep and longstanding that it calls for a third party—an objective, unprejudiced arbitrator—to come between those in conflict to help bring restoration. That is Paul's request here:

> Indeed, true comrade, I ask you also to help these women who have shared my struggle in the cause of the gospel, together with Clement also, and the rest of my fellow workers, whose names are in the book of life.
>
> *Philippians 4:3*

All sorts of suggestions have been made as to the identity of the one called "true comrade." One scholar suggested Barnabas. If so, why didn't Paul call him by name? Another said it could have been Epaphroditus. But, again, one wonders why he would have been called by name earlier yet referred to as "true comrade" here. A curious suggestion has been a person named Sunzugos, which is the Greek transliteration of "comrade." One fanciful idea is that the person was one of their husbands (I doubt that either husband would have relished that role) . . . another, that it was Paul's wife!

The name of the mediator is not nearly as important as the help that he or she could bring ("help these women"). Why did this mean so much to Paul that he included it in his letter? Because these women were important. They had "shared in the struggle" with Paul, and they belonged to the same spiritual family. Their clash was hurting the fellowship among the Christians at Philippi, so it needed resolution . . . soon. The bride needed to stop brawling!

Someone has said that Christians trying to live in close harmony is the next thing to impossible. The scene is not unlike the old forest folktale where two porcupines were huddled close together on a cold, cold night up in northern Canada. The closer they got to stay warm, the more their quills pricked each other, making it virtually impossible for them to remain side by side. Silently, they scooted apart. Before long, they were shivering in the wintry gale, so they came back together. Soon both were poking and jabbing each other . . . so they separated again. Same story . . . same result. Their action was like a slow-moving, monotonous dance—back and forth, back and forth.

Those two women in Philippi were like the Canadian porcupines; they needed each other, but they kept needling each other. Unfortunately, the disruptive dance of disharmony did not stop in that first-century church.

May I speak to you heart-to-heart, as friend-to-friend, before ending this chapter? In all honesty, have my words opened an old wound that has never healed? Did the imaginary scene of a brawling bride bring back a few ugly memories of an unresolved conflict in your past . . . or maybe several of them? Is there someone you continue to blame for the hurt you had to endure, bringing pain that never got reconciled? If so, do you have any idea how much emotional energy you are burning up nursing that wound? And while I'm asking questions: Are you aware of the joy-stealing effect an unforgiving spirit is having on your life? If your bitterness is deep enough, you've virtually stopped living. It is no wonder you have also stopped laughing!

Please listen to me. *It is not worth it.* You need to come to terms with this lingering, nagging issue *now.* The peace and contentment and joy that could be yours are draining away, like water down the drain of an unplugged bathtub. It is time for you to call a halt to the dispute; the disharmony must be defused. But it won't happen automatically. You are an essential part of the healing equation. You must do something about it.

Start by telling God how much it hurts and that you need Him to help you to forgive the offense. If you have a friend who is close enough to you to help you work your way through the process, reach out and say so. Get rid of all the poison of built-up anger and pour out all the acid of long-term resentment. Your objective is clear: Fully forgive the offender. Once that is done, you will discover that you no longer rehearse the ugly scenes in your mind. The revengeful desire to get back and get even will wane, and in its now-empty space will come such an outpouring of relief and a new spirit of joy that you won't feel like the same person. That deep frown on your brow and those long lines on your face will slowly disappear. And before too long you will get reacquainted with a sound you haven't made for months, maybe years. It is called laughter.

A resentful, unforgiving spirit and a carefree, happy heart never existed in the same body. Until you take care of the former you won't be able to enjoy the latter.

Considering the Lessons This Teaches Us . . .

I can think of at least four practical lessons we have learned from the things we have been considering.

1. Clashes will continue to occur. I wish I could promise you otherwise, but as long as depravity pollutes humanity, we can forget about a

conflict-free environment. So, don't be surprised when another skirmish breaks out.

2. Not all conflicts are wrong. Not all disagreements require reconciliation. As I recall, it was Jesus who said that He brings "a sword" into certain relationships. Occasionally it is right to be defiant and to fight. When critical biblical lines are drawn and the issues at stake have nothing to do with personal preferences or individual personalities, surrendering to a cause that would lead to wrong is wrong.

3. If the disagreement *should* be resolved and *could* be resolved but is not, then stubbornness and selfishness are at the core. We may be adults in age and height, but we can be awfully childish in attitude. Come on, give in. To persist in this lack of harmony brings hurts far greater than the small radius of your relationship.

4. Should you be the "comrade" needed to assist in the reconciliation, remember the threefold objective:

- The ultimate goal: Restoration (not discipline)
- The overall attitude: Grace (not force)
- The common ground: Christ (not logic or the church or tradition or your will)

There is something magnanimous about the name of Jesus that softens our attitude and defuses disharmony. Somehow the insertion of His name makes it inappropriate to maintain a fighting spirit.

The truth of that was underscored when I read of something that happened over one hundred years ago.

Charles H. Spurgeon, Baptist minister of London, England, had a pastor-friend, Dr. Newman Hall, who wrote a book entitled, *Come to Jesus*. Another preacher published an article in which he ridiculed Hall, who bore it patiently for a little while. But when the article gained popularity, Hall sat down and wrote a letter of protest. His answer was full of retaliatory invectives that outdid anything in the article which attacked him. Before mailing the letter, Hall took it to Spurgeon for his opinion.

Spurgeon read it carefully then, handing it back, asserted it was excellent and that the writer of the article deserved it all. "But," he added, "it just lacks one thing." After a pause Spurgeon continued,

"Underneath your signature you ought to write the words, 'Author of *Come to Jesus.'*"

The two godly men looked at each other for a few minutes. Then Hall tore the letter to shreds.[4]

12

Freeing Yourself Up to Laugh Again

Cynthia and I are into Harley-Davidson motor-cycles.

I know, I know . . . it doesn't fit our image. Who really cares? We stopped worrying about our image years ago. We should be ashamed of ourselves? We aren't. We're having a mutual mid-life crisis? We hope so. We should be better examples to the youth? They love it! Actually, it's only a few crotchety adults who don't. What are we going to say to our grand-kids? "Hey, kids, wanna ride?" And how are we supposed to explain it to "the board?" They don't care either. This is *California*, remember?

We are having more fun than anybody can imagine (except fellow Harley riders). One of the best things about the whole deal is that those guys and gals down at the bike shop don't have a clue as to who we are. We have *finally* found a place in our area where we can be out in public and remain absolutely anonymous. If anybody down there happens to ask our names, we'll just tell 'em we're Jim and Shirley Dobson. Those Harley hogs don't know them either.

You should have been in the showroom when I first sat on one of those big bikes. Cynthia stood a few feet away and just stared. She didn't know whether to laugh out loud or witness to me. She compromised and hopped on behind after I winked at her. She couldn't resist. As soon as she leaned forward and whispered in my ear, "Honey, I could get used to this," I knew it wouldn't be long before we'd be truckin' down the asphalt without a worry in the world.

We sat there and giggled like a couple of high school sweethearts sipping a soda through two straws. She liked the feel of sitting close to me (she couldn't resist, naturally), and I liked the feel of her behind me and that giant engine underneath us. And that inimitable Harley *roar.* Man, it was great!

Suddenly, sitting on that shiny black Heritage Softail Classic with thick leather saddlebags, we were on the back streets of Houston in 1953 all over again, roaring our way to a Milby High School football game. She was wearing my letterman's sweater and red-and-white saddle oxfords, and I had a flattop with a ducktail and a black leather jacket with fringe and chrome studs!

When we came back to our senses, we realized that somehow we were sorta misfits. I mean, a responsible senior pastor and radio preacher in a suit and tie with a classy, well-dressed woman who is executive vice president of Insight for Living perched on a Harley-Davidson in a motorcycle showroom. Everybody else was wearing t-shirts, torn jeans, boots, black leather stuff, and sported tattoos. I saw one guy who had a tattoo on each arm . . . one was of a snarling bulldog with a spiked collar and the other was the Marine insignia—the eagle, globe, and anchor of the Corps! A few folks were glancing in our direction as if to say, "Get serious!" And Cynthia leaned up again and whispered, "Do you think we ought to be in here?"

"Of course, honey, who cares? After all, *I'm a Marine!* What I need is a pair of black jeans and leather chaps and all you need is a tattoo, and we'll blend right in." The jeans and chaps for me, probably someday. But Cynthia with a tattoo? I rather doubt it. Somehow I don't think it would go over very big at formal church dinners and the National Religious Broadcasters banquets.

We have had one hilarious time with this in our family. Especially since I raised all four of our kids with only one unchangeable Swindoll rule: "You will not *ever* ride on or own a motorcycle!" Now the old man and his babe are roaring all around town. And it's our now-grown kids who are trying to figure out what's happened to their parents and what to say to *their* kids when they see their grandparents tooling down the freeway like a couple of gray-haired teenagers. Actually, we're getting concerned lately that our children may be a little too strict with *their* kids. "Ya gotta lighten up, guys," as they say down at the Harley hangout. The only one of the bunch who fully understands is our youngest, Chuck—but that makes sense. He rides a Harley too.

What's happening? What would ever possess me to start messing around with a motorcycle, cruising some of the picturesque roads down by the ocean, or taking off with my son for a relaxed, easygoing two or three hours together? What's this all about?

It's about forgetting all the nonsense that every single moment in life is serious. It's about breaking the thick and rigid mold of predictability. It's about enjoying a completely different slice of life where I don't have to concern myself with living up to anyone else's expectations or worry about who thinks what. It's about being with one of our kids in a world that is totally on his turf (for a change), not mine, in a setting that is just plain fun, not work. It's about being me, nobody else.

It's about breaking the bondage of tunnel vision. It's about refusing to live my life playing one note on one instrument in one room and finding pleasure in a symphony of sounds and sights and smells. It's about widening the radius of a restrictive and demanding schedule where breathing fresh air is sometimes difficult and thinking creative thoughts is occasionally the next thing to impossible.

Bottom line, it's about freedom. That's it, plain and simple. It's about being free.

It's about entering into a tension-free, worry-free world where I don't have to say something profound or fix anyone or do anything other than feel the wind and smell the flowers and hug my wife and laugh till we're hoarse. That's it in a nutshell . . . it's about freeing ourselves up to laugh again.

In Jesus' day He took His twelve disciples across a lake to enjoy some R&R alone on a mountainside. Who knows what they did for fun? Maybe they climbed rocks or swam in a cool lake or sat around a campfire and told a few jokes. Whatever, you can count on this—they laughed. Today, Cynthia and I prefer to hop on the old Harley. If Jesus lived on earth today, He might ride with us. But something in me says He probably wouldn't get a tattoo. Then again, who knows? He did a lot of other stuff that made the legalists squirm. He knew the truth . . . and the truth had really set Him free.

Getting Serious About Being Set Free

Americans did not invent the idea of freedom. Even though we have fought wars for it and built monuments to it, it is not original with us. It began with God, way back in the Garden of Eden when He made Adam and Eve. God made them—and He has made you and me—to enjoy the pleasures and the responsibilities of freedom. How?

- God made us with a mind . . . that we might think freely.
- God made us with a heart . . . that we might love freely.
- God made us with a will . . . that we might obey freely.

Let me analyze those three factors from a strictly human viewpoint. By making us in His image, God gave us capacities not given to other forms of life. Ideally, He made us to know Him, to love Him, and to obey Him. He did not put rings in our noses that He might pull us around like oxen, nor did He create us with strings permanently attached to our hands and feet like human marionettes to control and manipulate our every move. What pleasure would He have in the love of a puppet or the obedience of a dumb animal?

No, He gave us freedom to make choices. By His grace we are equipped to understand His plan because we have a mind with which we can know Him. We are also free to love and adore Him because we have emotions. He takes pleasure in our affection and devotion. We can obey His instructions, but we are not pawns on a global chessboard. It is in the voluntary spontaneity of our response that He finds divine pleasure. When His people *freely* respond in worship and praise, obedience and adoration, God is glorified to the maximum.

There is a downside to all this, however. Because we are free to do these things, we are also free *not* to do them. We are free to make wrong choices—how well we know! In fact, we can continue to make them for so long we can wind up in our own self-made prison of consequences. That prison of our own choosing can hold us in such bondage that we are unable to escape. When that occurs, we experience the ultimate in earthly misery. It is called *addiction.* If you have ever been in such bondage or worked with someone who is, you know firsthand how horrible an existence it can be. Strange as it may seem, an addiction is the tragic consequence of freedom . . . freedom out of control . . . freedom gone to seed.

What God Has Promised

It is at this point that God is ultragracious. He takes no cruel delight in seeing us squirm, trapped in a dungeon of our own making. In fact, that is a large part of the reason He sent His Son to this earth. He sent Him on a mission of mercy to set the captives free. One of the earliest declarations of Christ's Great Commission (His mission statement) is found in Isaiah's ancient prophecy. Though written seven centuries before His birth, this was the coming Messiah's "job description":

> The Spirit of the Lord GOD is upon me,
> Because the LORD has anointed me
> To bring good news to the afflicted;
> He has sent me to bind up the brokenhearted,
> To proclaim liberty to captives,
> And freedom to prisoners;
> To proclaim the favorable year of the LORD,
> And the day of vengeance of our God;
> To comfort all who mourn,
> To grant those who mourn in Zion,
> Giving them a garland instead of ashes,
> The oil of gladness instead of mourning,
> The mantle of praise instead of a spirit of fainting.
> So they will be called oaks of righteousness,
> The planting of the LORD, that He may be glorified.
>
> *Isaiah 61:1–3*

Don't miss those words, "To proclaim liberty to captives and freedom to prisoners."

Lest you think the prophet was writing of himself, notice what Jesus did and said more than seven hundred years later when He was beginning His ministry in Nazareth. Read these words carefully as you imagine the scene:

> And He came to Nazareth, where He had been brought up; and as was His custom, He entered the synagogue on the Sabbath, and stood up to read. And the book of the prophet Isaiah was handed to Him. And He opened the book, and found the place where it was written,
>
> "THE SPIRIT OF THE LORD IS UPON ME,
> BECAUSE HE ANOINTED ME TO PREACH THE
>   GOSPEL TO THE POOR.
> HE HAS SENT ME TO PROCLAIM RELEASE TO THE
>   CAPTIVES,
> AND RECOVERY OF SIGHT TO THE BLIND,
> TO SET FREE THOSE WHO ARE DOWNTRODDEN,
> TO PROCLAIM THE FAVORABLE YEAR OF THE LORD."

And He closed the book, and gave it back to the attendant, and sat down; and the eyes of all in the synagogue were fixed upon Him. And He began to say to them, "Today this Scripture has been fulfilled in your hearing."

Luke 4:16–21

Isn't that interesting? Of all the Scriptures He could have read, Jesus selected that section from Isaiah. He not only stated that "release to the captives" and "setting free those who are downtrodden" were on His earthly agenda, but that He was beginning to fulfill Isaiah's prophecy that very day.

Hundreds of years before the Messiah came, God promised that He would set the captives free. Obviously He wasn't referring to opening all prison doors and breaking the bars on every jail. The captives He had in mind were those in bondage to sin. And He also stated that He would provide sight for the blind, physically and spiritually. What grand promises!

Let's glance briefly at one more New Testament scene.

Jesus therefore was saying to those Jews who had believed Him, "If you abide in My word, then you are truly disciples of Mine; and you shall know the truth, and the truth shall make you free." They answered Him, "We are Abraham's offspring, and have never yet been enslaved to anyone; how is it that You say, 'You shall become free'?" Jesus answered them, "Truly, truly, I say to you, everyone who commits sin is the slave of sin. And the slave does not remain in the house forever; the son does remain forever. If therefore the Son shall make you free, you shall be free indeed."

John 8:31–36

What I find significant is the promise from Jesus' lips; namely, that a knowledge of the truth is freeing . . . and once freed, we "shall be free indeed." This refers to a deeply personal freedom, an inner emancipation from what has bound you long enough. What a marvelous thought!

How We Have Responded

If the truth could be known, we have only halfheartedly believed God's promise to us. Even though He has made us to be free and to be released from whatever binds us, many have chosen to live enslaved. By opting for bad choices, they have given all sorts of addictions opportunity to take control. And instead of enjoying the benefits of freedom, many live in its backwash as helpless, hopeless captives.

Jean Jacques Rousseau, the eighteenth-century French philosopher, was never more correct than when he said, "Man was born free, and everywhere he is in chains."[1]

THE MOST UNIVERSAL OF ALL ADDICTIONS

It is time to get specific. So far I have dealt in generalities and not once zeroed in on any one addiction, so you probably feel safe. No longer. Lest you and I start to feel a little smug, thinking we are safe because we don't have a habit so captivating that we are held in bondage, I might as well go to the one addiction that tops all others—worry. Anxiety addicts abound!

The trouble with worry is that it doesn't seem all that harmful. It is a little like the first few snorts of cocaine. A person may know down inside it is not good, but surely it can't be as bad as some have made it out to be. Foolish thinking.

When it comes to worry, we blithely excuse it. For example, one evening we say to a friend, "Hey, don't worry," Our friend responds, "Well, maybe I shouldn't, but you know me. I'm just the worrying type." We answer back, "Yeah, well, I sure understand. I myself am a worrier. Can't blame somebody for feeling a little concerned tonight."

What if we changed that conversation to refer to drinking too much alcohol. Imagine this: "Hey, things will work out." Our friend responds, "Well, maybe I shouldn't, but you know me. I'm just the liquor-drinking type." Answering back, we say, "Yeah, well, I sure understand. I myself drink too much. Can't blame somebody for drinking a couple extras tonight." Suddenly, worry takes on a new significance.

Analyzing the Problem

Of all the joy stealers that can plague our lives, none is more nagging, more agitating, or more prevalent than worry.

We get our English word *worry* from the German word *wurgen*, which means "to strangle, to choke." Our Lord mentioned that very word picture when He addressed the subject on one occasion.

The sower sows the word. And these are the ones who are beside the road where the word is sown; and when they hear, immediately Satan comes and takes away the word which has been sown in them. And in a similar way these are the ones on whom seed was sown on the rocky places, who, when they hear the word, immediately receive it with joy; and they have no firm root in themselves, but are only temporary; then, when affliction or persecution arises because of the word, immediately they fall away. And others are the ones on whom seed was sown among the thorns; these are the ones who have heard the word, and the worries of the world, and the deceitfulness of riches, and the desires for other things enter in and choke the word, and it becomes unfruitful.

Mark 4:14–19

In other words, when worry throttles our thinking, choking out the truth, we are unable to bear fruit. Along with becoming mentally harassed and emotionally strung out, we find ourselves spiritually strangled. Worry cuts off our motivation and lifeline of joy.

In spite of all these consequences, more people are addicted to worry than all other addictions combined. Are you one of them? If you are, you might as well put on hold all the things I have been saying in this book about being more joyful and carefree with an optimistic attitude. You will need to come to terms with your anxiety addiction before you find yourself freed up enough to laugh again.

I know what I'm writing about, believe me. There was a time in my own life when worry controlled me and the tentacles of tension choked much of the fun out of my life. I cared too much about what people thought and said, so I ran a little scared on a daily basis. And then I wasn't sure about my future either. So I worried about that. The churning intensified after I joined the Marines. Cynthia and I had not been married very long. Where would we be stationed? What if I got sent overseas? How would Cynthia do without me . . . and vice versa? The worry list grew once I got my orders—*Okinawa!* Why would God allow this to happen? I mean, the recruiting office promised me that would *never* happen (you're smiling, right?). One by one, day after day, my worries intensified as my joy faded. Prayer was only a formality.

It was while Cynthia and I were separated by the Pacific Ocean for well over a year that I was forced to come to terms with my anxiety addiction. I finally determined to stop that nonsense. I began taking God and His Word much *more* seriously and myself a lot *less* seriously (we usually get those two reversed). I found that prayer was never meant to be a ritual but an actual calling out to God for help . . . and each time I did, He came through. I also discovered that He was in control of life's circumstances as well as the details of my life and my wife. In fact, she was in better care under His sheltering wings than she ever could have been under my roof. She and I both did just fine; matter of fact, *incredibly well*. I kept a journal and I also wrote her letters, sometimes four or five a week. Looking back, I realize it was in the midst of that lonely, involuntary separation that I began to cultivate an interest in writing. (Who would have ever guessed what that letter writing in a little Quonset hut at Camp Courtney, not far from Naha, Okinawa, would lead to?) As I gave my anxieties to God, He took them and solved every one of the things I placed in His care. As I relaxed the tension, He moved in with sovereign grace. It was *wonderful*.

The major turning point occurred when I did an in-depth study of Philippians 4:4–9, which I can still vividly remember. It was then I began . . .

Understanding God's Therapy

Do you realize that God has a sure-cure solution to worry? Has anyone ever told you that if you perfect the process you will be able to live a worry-free existence? Yes, you read that correctly. And if you know me fairly well, you know that I seldom make statements anywhere near that dogmatic. But in this one I am confident. If you will follow God's stated procedure, you will free yourself to laugh again.

First, let's let the Scriptures speak for themselves:

> Rejoice in the Lord always; again I will say, rejoice! Let your forbearing spirit be known to all men. The Lord is near. Be anxious for nothing, but in everything by prayer and supplication with thanksgiving let your requests be made known to God. And the peace of God, which surpasses all comprehension, shall guard your hearts and your minds in Christ Jesus.
>
> *Philippians 4:4–7*

Next, let's get six words clearly fixed in our minds. These six words form the foundation of God's therapeutic process for all worrywarts.

WORRY ABOUT NOTHING,
PRAY ABOUT EVERYTHING

Say that over and over until you can say it without looking. Say the six words aloud. Close the book. Close your eyes. Picture the words in your mind. Spend a minute or more turning them over in your head. What qualifies as a worry? Anything that drains your tank of joy—something you cannot change, something you are not responsible for, something you are unable to control, something (or someone) that frightens and torments you, agitates you, keeps you awake when you should be asleep. All of that now needs to be switched from your worry list to your prayer list. Give each worry—one by one—to God. Do that at this very moment. Tell the Lord you will no longer keep your anxiety to yourself.

Now then, once you buy into this all-important plan God has provided for those who wish to be free, you will begin to have time left in your day . . . lots of extra time and energy. Why? Because you used to spend that time worrying. Your addiction, like all addictions, held you captive. It took your time, it required your attention, it forced you to focus on stuff you had no business trying to deal with or solve.

So what now? How do you spend the time you used to waste worrying? Go back to the words from Paul to the Philippians. As I read them over, I find three key words emerging:

> . . . **rejoice** (v. 4)
>> . . . **relax** (v. 5)
>>> . . . **rest** (v. 7)

They look pretty easy, but for someone who has worried as long as *you* have, they are not. You haven't done much of any of these three lately, have you?

To begin with, REJOICE! Worry about nothing . . . pray about everything, and *REJOICE!*

> Rejoice in the Lord always; again I will say, rejoice!
>
> *Philippians 4:4*

Because we have repeated the term and several synonyms throughout the book so often, the whole idea could begin to lose its edge. Don't let it. Rejoicing is clearly a scriptural command. To ignore it, I need to remind you, is disobedience. In place of worry, start spending time enjoying the release of your humor. Find the bright side, the sunny side of life. Deliberately look for things that are funny during your day. Loosen up and laugh freely. Laugh more often. Consciously stay aware of the importance of a cheerful countenance. Live lightheartedly! Stop reading only the grim sections of the newspaper. Watch less television and start reading more books that bring a smile instead of a frown. That's exactly why you picked up this one! We put a cover on it that would attract your attention (I think my publisher did a bang-up job, don't you?), and as you thumbed through it you probably thought something like, *I need to quit being so serious—maybe this book will help.* Don't stop with this book. Choose others like it. Feed your mind more uplifting "thought food."

Locate a few acquaintances who will help you laugh more at life. Ideally, find Christian friends who see life through Christ's eyes, which is in itself more encouraging. Have fun together. Share funny stories with each other. Affirm one another.

> Shared laughter creates a bond of friendship. When people laugh together, they cease to be young and old, master and pupils, worker and driver. They have become a single group of human beings, enjoying their existence.[2]

Fred Allen, one of my favorite humorists of yesteryear, used to say that it was bad to suppress your laughter because when you do, he said, it goes down and spreads your hips.[3] Maybe that explains those extra pounds.

Solomon writes that "a cheerful heart has a continual feast" (Prov. 15:15), and he is right. I find that a spirit of cheer spreads rapidly. Before you know it, others have joined you at the table. Choose joy! There are very few days in my life during which I find nothing to laugh at. Laughter is the most familiar sound in the hallway where my staff and I work alongside each other. And what a contagious thing is outrageous joy . . . everybody wants to be around it. So, rejoice!

Next, RELAX! Worry about nothing . . . pray about everything, and *RELAX!*

> Let your forbearing spirit be known to all men. The Lord is near.
>
> *Philippians 4:5*

Where do I find "relax" in Paul's statement? See that unusual expression, "forbearing spirit"? It means "gentleness," or "easy." We would say "easygoing." It is "sweet reasonableness" . . . the idea of a relaxed, easygoing lifestyle. A worry-filled world can increase your tension to a dangerous level. Physically, it can take a serious toll on your health.

Lighten up! So much of what we get nervous about and jumpy over never happens anyway. Let me get downright specific. Relax more with your children. Take it easy, especially if they are junior highers (whom my friend, Kenny Poure, calls "pre-people"). If your son or daughter is struggling through a stage in the stormy adolescent years, have a heart. Back off. Loosen the strings. You will realize later that God was there all along—in control—taking care of business, His business. Oh, if only I had applied more of this when our children were younger. Every once in a while, during one of my unrelaxed, high-tension, tightwire acts, one of our kids would say, "Just take a deep breath, Dad." Ouch! When I took their advice, my "forbearing spirit" resurfaced.

My dear friend, Ruth Harms Calkin, describes our dilemma with this insightful reminder:

Spiritual Retreat

This was my calculated plan:
I would set aside my usual schedule—
The menial tasks that wedge in routinely.
In the peace and quiet of my living room
I would relax in Your glorious presence.
How joyfully I envisioned the hours—
My personal spiritual retreat!
With Bible and notebook beside me
I would study and meditate—
I would intercede for the needy world.

But how differently it happened, Lord:
Never has the phone rung so persistently.
Sudden emergencies kept pouring in
Like summer cloudbursts.
My husband came home ill.
There were appointments to cancel
Plans to rearrange.
The mailman brought two disturbing letters
A cousin whose name I couldn't remember
Stopped by on her way through town.
My morning elation became drooping deflation.

And yet, dear Lord
You were with me in it all!
I sense Your vital presence—
Your sure and steady guidance.
Not once did You leave me stranded.
Perhaps, in Your great wisdom
You longed to teach me a practical truth:
When *You* are my Spiritual Retreat
I need not be a spiritual recluse.[4]

And then, REST! Worry about nothing . . . pray about everything, and *REST!*

> Be anxious for nothing, but in everything by prayer and supplication with thanksgiving let your requests be made known to God. And the peace of God, which surpasses all comprehension, shall guard your hearts and your minds in Christ Jesus.
>
> *Philippians 4:6–7*

I know of few Scriptures that have helped me more than the words you just read. Go back and read them once again, this time slower. Maybe seeing them in The Living Bible will help. That's where I picked up the idea of resting.

> Don't worry about anything; instead, pray about everything; tell God your needs and don't forget to thank him for his answers. If you do this you will experience God's peace, which is far more wonderful than the human mind can understand. His peace will keep your thoughts and your hearts quiet and at rest as you trust in Christ Jesus.
>
> *Philippians 4:6–7* TLB

Paul writes of God's peace which "shall guard your hearts and your minds." When he mentions peace as a "guard," he uses a military term for "marching sentry duty" around something valuable and/or strategic. As we rest our case, as we transfer our troubles to God, "Corporal Peace" is appointed the duty of marching as a silent sentry around our minds and our emotions, calming us within. How obvious will it be to others? Go back and check—it will "surpass all comprehension." People simply will not be able to comprehend the restful peace we will model. In place of anxiety—that thief of joy—we pray. We push the worrisome, clawing, monster of pressure off our shoulders and hand it over to God in prayer. I am not exaggerating; I must do that hundreds of times every year. And I cannot recall a time when it didn't provide relief. In its place, always, comes a quietness of spirit, a calming of the mind. With a relieved mind, rest returns.

Rejoice. Relax. Rest. The three substitutes for worry. And impatience. And turmoil.

Correcting Our Perspective

Three simple exercises will help you stay worry free.

1. Feed your mind positive thoughts.

Finally, brethren, whatever is true, whatever is honorable, whatever is right, whatever is pure, whatever is lovely, whatever is of good repute, if there is any excellence and if anything worthy of praise, let your mind dwell on these things.

Philippians 4:8

No matter what you're dealing with or how bad things seem to be or why God may be permitting them, deliberately letting your mind dwell on positive, uplifting thoughts will enable you to survive. Literally. I frequently quote those words from Philippians 4:8 to myself. I say things like, "Okay, Chuck, it's time to let your mind dwell on better things." And then I go over the list and deliberately replace a worry with something far more honorable or pure or lovely, something worthy of praise. It never fails; the pressure I was feeling begins to fade and the peace I was missing begins to emerge.

2. Focus your attention on encouraging models.

The things you have learned and received and heard and seen in me, practice these things.

Philippians 4:9a

In the Philippians' case, Paul was their model. From his example, there were things to be learned and received and heard and seen. What a demonstration of encouragement he provided!

In your case and mine, it will help to focus our attention on someone we know and/or admire. That life, that encouraging model will give us a boost, a quick charge when our battery starts getting low.

3. *Find "the God of Peace" in every circumstance.*

> . . . and the God of peace shall be with you.
>
> *Philippians 4:9b*

This is the crowning achievement of recovering from anxiety addiction. Instead of living in the grip of fear, held captive by the chains of tension and dread, when we release our preoccupation with worry, we find God's hand at work on our behalf. He, our "God of peace," comes to our aid, changing people, relieving tension, altering difficult circumstances. The more you practice giving your mental burdens to the Lord, the more exciting it gets to see how God will handle the things that are impossible for you to do anything about. And as a result—you guessed it—you will begin to laugh again.

A Principle . . . A Parrot

What is it, in the final analysis, that makes worry such an enemy of joy? Why does anxiety addiction take such a devastating toll on us? I have been thinking about that for months, and I believe I have the answer, which we might call a principle. At first it may seem simplistic, but this *is* the crux of the problem. This is exactly why anxiety holds us in such bondage.

WORRY FORCES US TO FOCUS ON THE WRONG THINGS

Instead of essentials, we worry about nonessentials. Rather than looking at the known blessings that God provides today—so abundantly, so consistently—we worry about the unknown and uncertain events of tomorrow. Invariably, when we focus on the wrong things, we miss the main thing that life is all about.

That fact is vividly illustrated by one of my favorite stories. After more than forty years of marriage, this woman's husband suddenly died. For several months she sat alone in her house with the shades pulled and the door locked. Finally she decided she needed to do something about her situation. The loneliness was killing her.

She remembered that her husband had a friend who owned a nice pet store—a pet might be good company. So she dropped in one afternoon to look over the selection. She looked at dogs, cats, goldfish—even snakes! Nothing seemed quite right. She told the store owner she wanted a pet that could be a real companion—"almost like another human being in the house."

Suddenly he thought of one of his prized parrots. He showed her the colorful bird.

"Does it talk?"

"Absolutely . . . a real chatterbox. Everybody who comes in the store is astounded by this parrot's friendly disposition and wide vocabulary. That's why it's so expensive."

"Sold!" She bought the expensive parrot and hauled it home in a large, elegant cage. At last she had a companion she could talk to, who could answer back. Perfect!

But there was a problem. A full week passed without the bird's saying one word. Beginning to worry, she dropped by the pet shop.

"How's the parrot doing? Quite a talker, huh?"

"Not one word. I haven't been able to get a sound out of that bird. I'm worried!"

"Well, did you buy a *mirror* when you got the parrot and the cage last week?"

"Mirror? No. There's no mirror in the cage."

"That's your problem. A parrot needs a mirror. It's funny, but while looking at itself, a parrot starts to feel comfortable. In no time it will begin to talk." So she bought the mirror and put it into the cage.

Time passed, still nothing. Each day the woman talked to the bird, but not a peep came out of its beak. For hours on end she would talk as the parrot stared in silence. Another week passed without a word. By now she was really getting worried.

"The parrot isn't talking," she told the pet store owner. "I'm worried. All that money, the mirror—and still nothing."

"Say, did you buy a *ladder* when you got the cage?"

"A ladder? No. I didn't know it needed a ladder. Will that make it talk?"

"Works like a charm. The parrot will look in the mirror and get a little exercise, climbing up and down this ladder several times. Before long you won't believe what you hear. Trust me, you need the ladder."

She bought the ladder and put it into the cage next to the mirror . . . and waited. And waited. Another seven, eight days, still nothing. By now her worry was approaching the panic stage. "Why doesn't it talk?" That was all she could think about. She returned to the store in tears . . . with the same complaint.

"Did you buy a *swing?*"

"A swing! No. I have the cage, a mirror, and a ladder—I thought I had everything. I had no idea I needed a swing."

"Ya gotta have a swing. A parrot needs to feel completely at home. It glances in the mirror, takes a stroll up and down the ladder, and before long it's on the swing enjoying itself—and bingo! I've found that parrots usually talk when they are perched on a swing."

The woman bought the swing. She attached it to the top of the cage near the ladder and coaxed the parrot up the ladder and onto the swing. Still, absolute silence. For another ten days not one sound came from the cage.

Suddenly she came bursting into the pet store, really steaming. The owner met her at the counter.

"Hey, how's the parrot? I'll bet—"

"It died! My expensive bird is dead in the bottom of the cage."

"Well, I can't believe that. I'm just shocked. Did it ever say anything at all?"

"Yes, as a matter of fact, it did. As it lay there taking its last few breaths, it said very faintly, 'Don't they have any *food* down at that store?'"

There is no greater waste of our time and no greater deterrent to our joy than worry. By turning our attention to the wrong things, worry leads us to live our lives for the wrong reasons . . . and God is grieved. As I mentioned earlier in the book, God gives to His beloved even in our sleep. As we rejoice, relax, and rest, He relieves, renews, and restores.

A weary Christian lay awake one night trying to hold the world together by his worrying. Then he heard the Lord gently say to him, "Now you go to sleep, Jim; I'll sit up."[5]

13

Don't Forget to Have Fun As You Grow Up

I like the question once asked by Satchel Paige, that venerable alumnus of baseball: "How old would you be if you didn't know how old you were?" An honest answer to that question depends on an honest admission of one's attitude. It has nothing to do with one's age. As someone young at heart has written:

> Remember, old folks are worth a fortune—silver in their hair, gold in their teeth, stones in their kidneys, lead in their feet, and gas in their stomachs.
>
> I have become a little older since I saw you last, and a few changes have come into my life since then. Frankly, I have become quite a frivolous old gal. I am seeing five gentlemen every day.
>
> As soon as I wake up, Will Power helps me get out of bed. Then I go to see John. Then Charlie Horse comes along, and when he is here he takes a lot of my time and attention. When he leaves Arthur Ritis shows up and stays the rest of the day. He doesn't like to stay in one place very long, so he takes me from joint to joint. After such a busy day I'm really tired and glad to go to bed with Ben Gay. What a life!
>
> P.S. The preacher came to call the other day. He said at my age I should be thinking about the hereafter. I told him, "Oh, I do all the time. No matter where I am—in the parlor, upstairs, in the kitchen, or down in the basement—I ask myself what am I here after?"[1]

The longer I live the more I become convinced that our major battle in life is not with age but with maturity. All of us are involuntary victims of the former. There is no choice involved in growing older. Our challenge is the choice of whether or not to grow up. It was Jesus who asked, "Who of you by worrying can add one inch to your height. . . or subtract one day from your age?" (Matt. 6:25–31). In other words, don't waste your time worrying about how old you are getting. Age is a matter of fact. Maturity, on the other hand, is a matter of choice.

You may be thinking, *Well, Chuck, that is all well and good, but you can't teach an old dog new tricks.* To which I respond with two reminders:

1. I am not writing to "old dogs." You are a person who has the capacity to think and to decide. Furthermore, if you are a Christian, you have the power of Christ within you, which means sufficient inner dynamic to effect incredible changes. If you are not a Christian, there is no time like the present to take care of that.

2. I am not teaching "tricks." The things you are reading are attainable and meaningful techniques that, when applied, can help you break old habits and form new ones. Admittedly the process of change may not come easy, but many have done it and you can too. The real question is not, "Am I able?" but, "Am I willing?"

Our becoming more mature is toward the top of the list on God's agenda for us. Repeatedly He mentions it in His Book:

> As a result, we are no longer to be children, tossed here and there by waves, and carried about by every wind of doctrine, by the trickery of men, by craftiness in deceitful scheming; but speaking the truth in love, we are to grow up in all aspects into Him, who is the head, even Christ.
>
> *Ephesians 4:14–15*

> Therefore, putting aside all malice and all guile and hypocrisy and envy and all slander, like newborn babes, long for the pure milk of the word, that by it you may grow in respect to salvation.
>
> *1 Peter 2:1–2*

> But solid food is for the mature, who because of practice have their senses trained to discern good and evil. Therefore leaving the elementary teaching about the Christ, let us press on to maturity, not laying again a foundation of repentance from dead works and of faith toward God.
>
> *Hebrews 5:14—6:1*

You and I are growing older. That's automatic. But that does not necessarily mean we are growing up. How important it is that we do so! And it will not happen unless we get control of our attitude, which turns us in the right direction. Let me urge you not to feed your mind with thoughts like: *I'm too far gone to change;* or, *Having been through all the things I've been through, there is no way I can alter my attitude.* Wrong!

It is childish to play in the traffic of fear or let the hobgoblins of habit impede our progress. No one can win a race by continually looking back at where he or she has been. That will only demoralize, immobilize, and ultimately paralyze. God is for us. God's goal is that we move toward maturity, all our past failures and faults and hangups notwithstanding. I have seen many adults who thought they couldn't change begin to change. So I'm no longer willing to sit back and let anyone stay riveted to yesterday, thinking, *Woe is me.* Some of the most sweeping changes in my own life have occurred in my adult years. If it can happen in me, there is an enormous amount of hope for you. Attitudes can soar even if our circumstances lag and our past record sags.

God's specialty is bringing renewal to our strength, not reminders of our weakness. Take it by faith, He is well aware of your weaknesses; He just sovereignly chooses not to stop there. They become the platform upon which He does His best work. Cheer up! There is great hope. You won't be the first He helped from puberty to maturity.

THAT ELUSIVE QUALITY CALLED MATURITY

If maturity is all that important, we need to understand it better. The clearer it is in our minds, the easier it will be to get a focus on the target.

Exactly What Is It?

To be mature is to be fully developed, complete, and "grown up." Becoming mature is a process of consistently moving toward emotional and spiritual adulthood. In that process we leave childish and adolescent habits and adopt a lifestyle where we are fully responsible for our own decisions, motives, actions, and consequences. I heard someone say recently that maturity is developed and discerning competence as to how to live appropriately and to change rightly. In a word, it is *stability*. We never "arrive." We are always in the process of moving toward that objective. I have also observed that when maturity is taking place, balance replaces extremes and a seasoned confidence replaces uneasy feelings of insecurity. Good choices replace wrong ones.

How Is It Expressed?

Several things come to mind when I think of how all this works its way out. Marks of maturity are emerging—

- When our concern for others outweighs our concern for ourselves
- When we detect the presence of evil or danger before it is obvious
- When we have wisdom and understanding as well as knowledge
- When we have more than high ideals but also the discipline to carry them out
- When our emotions are tempered by responsibility and thoroughness
- When our awareness of needs is matched by our compassion and involvement
- When we not only understand a task but also have the fortitude to stay at it until it is done
- When we have a willingness to change, once we are convinced that correction is in order
- When we have the ability to grow spiritually by an independent intake of God's Word

One person summarized it in these words:

> Maturity is the ability to do a job whether you are supervised or not; finish a job once it's started; carry money without spending it. And last, but not least, the ability to bear an injustice without wanting to get even.[2]

TWO SIDES OF THE SAME QUALITY

Most folks I know would agree that those things describe where we would like to be personally. When we think of growing up, that is what we have in mind. Once we are there, who wouldn't have reason to rejoice? But the fact is, if we maintain the right attitude we are able to rejoice while in the process of getting there. That is what is so exciting about Paul's words to his friends in Philippi. Throughout the letter he has continued to emphasize and encourage outrageous joy in spite of difficult circumstances, because of Christ. In fact, that is exactly where this next section begins.

> But I rejoiced in the Lord greatly, that now at last you have revived your concern for me; indeed, you were concerned before, but you lacked opportunity.
>
> *Philippians 4:10*

Who is saying this? Some young turk who has just turned the deal on his first million? A superstar who recently signed an unbelievable contract? Some guy in his twenties about to set sail on a magnificent adventure? Not on your life. Would you believe, a sixty-plus-year-old Jew chained to a Roman guard under house arrest, not knowing if tomorrow he will be killed, brought to court, or set free? Though getting up in years, he is rejoicing. Though without the comforts of home and the privileges of privacy, he is happy. Though he doesn't have a clue regarding his future, he is smiling at life. Though he is set aside, forced to stay in one place, completely removed from the excitement of a broader minisry, he is still rejoicing, still laughing. No matter what happened to him, Paul refused to be caught in the grip of pessimism.

Maturity of Paul

We are able to get a pretty good glimpse here of the man who truly practiced what he preached. I find in this section of his letter at least four characteristics of maturity in Paul's life.

1. He is affirming.

> But I rejoiced in the Lord greatly, that now at last you have revived your concern for me; indeed, you were concerned before, but you lacked opportunity.
>
> *Philippians 4:10*

The words could sound mysterious if you didn't understand that behind them is the financial support of the Philippians. When he writes that they had revived their concern for him, Paul means that they had sent another contribution to help him press on. Don't miss a little detail here. When he says, "You were concerned before, but you lacked opportunity," he means they had wanted to send an offering to him earlier, but they either didn't know where he was or they had no way to get it to him. Normally it is the other way around! We have an opportunity to send our support, but we lack concern.

I am impressed with Paul's affirmation of his friends. This is a thank-you letter . . . a "receipt letter," if you will. The implication is so thoughtful: Even when I didn't hear from you, you were concerned for me. Paul thought better of others, not less. He upheld their intentions. Even when he didn't hear from his friends, he did not doubt that they cared.

We appreciate what people do. We affirm who they are. When we say thank you to someone who completes a task, we are expressing our appreciation. But when we acknowledge and express our gratitude for what others are—in character, in motive, in heart—we are affirming them personally. A mark of maturity is the ability to affirm, not just appreciate. How easy to see people (especially family members and fellow workers at our place of employment) as doers of tasks, but a task-oriented mentality is incomplete. And as important as appreciation for a job well done may be, it too is incomplete. People are not human tools appointed to accomplish a set of tasks, but human beings with souls, with feelings. How essential it is to recognize and affirm the unseen, hidden qualities that make an individual a person of worth and dignity. The best leaders (like Paul) appreciate and affirm.

Max DePree is chairman and chief executive officer of Herman Miller, Inc., the furniture maker that was named one of *Fortune* magazine's ten best managed and most innovative companies. It was also chosen as one of the hundred best companies to work for in America. In his book, *Leadership Is an Art,* DePree touches on the importance of understanding and acknowledging the diversity of people's inner gifts and unseen talents. What he describes has to do with affirmation.

> My father is ninety-six years old. He is the founder of Herman Miller, and much of the value system and impounded energy of the company, a legacy still drawn on today, is a part of his contribution. In the furniture industry of the 1920s the machines of most factories were not run by electric motors, but by pulleys from a central drive shaft. The central drive shaft was run by the steam engine. The steam engine got its steam from the boiler. The boiler, in our case, got its fuel from the sawdust and other waste coming out of the machine room—a beautiful cycle.
>
> The millwright was the person who oversaw that cycle and on whom the entire activity of the operation depended. He was a key person.
>
> One day the millwright died.
>
> My father, being a young manager at the time, did not particularly

know what he should do when a key person died, but thought he ought to go visit the family. He went to the house and was invited to join the family in the living room. There was some awkward conversation—the kind with which many of us are familiar.

The widow asked my father if it would be all right if she read aloud some poetry. Naturally, he agreed. She went into another room, came back with a bound book, and for many minutes read selected pieces of beautiful poetry. When she finished, my father commented on how beautiful the poetry was and asked who wrote it. She replied that her husband, the millwright, was the poet.

It is now nearly sixty years since the millwright died, and my father and many of us at Herman Miller continue to wonder: Was he a poet who did millwright's work, or was he a millwright who wrote poetry?

In our effort to understand corporate life, what is it we should learn from this story? In addition to all of the ratios and goals and parameters and bottom lines, it is fundamental that leaders endorse a concept of persons. This begins with an understanding of the diversity of people's gifts and talents and skills.[3]

2. He is contented.

> Not that I speak from want; for I have learned to be content in whatever circumstances I am.
>
> *Philippians 4:11*

As valuable as affirmation may be, maturity is never more obvious than when an individual evidences contentment. And no one was a better model than Paul, who "learned to be content," regardless of his situation. To him it made no difference whether he was freed or bound to a soldier . . . whether the day was hot and humid or bleak and frigid . . . whether the Philippians sent a gift or failed to make contact. How wonderfully refreshing. How incredibly mature!

Some people are thermometers. They merely *register* what is around them. If the situation is tight and pressurized, they register tension and irritability. If it's stormy, they register worry and fear. If it's calm, quiet, and comfortable, they register relaxation and peacefulness.

Others, however, are thermostats. They *regulate* the atmosphere. They are the mature change-agents who never let the situation dictate to them.

You are probably thinking, *I wish I had that "contentment gift."* Wait.

It isn't a gift. It is a learned trait. Paul admits that he has developed the ability to accept and to adapt. Remember? He wrote, "I have *learned* to be content."

That reminds me of the comment we heard from several men who had been prisoners of war during the Vietnam War and survived the horrors of Hanoi. A number of those brave men said the same thing: "We learned after a few hours what it took to survive, and we just adapted to that." They didn't whine and complain because they had been captured. They didn't eat their hearts out because the conditions were miserable and the food was terrible. They chose to adapt.

Interestingly, the Greek term translated "content" does not mean, "I don't care what happens—I'll remain indifferent, numb." No, this unusual term suggests "self-sufficient," and in the context of this letter it means being at peace in Christ's sufficiency. How could Paul adapt and endure? What was it that relieved the tension and allowed him to be so relaxed within? He was convinced that Christ was in the midst of his every day, pouring His power into him. When we believe that, *anything* is bearable. *Nothing* is out of control. When we genuinely have that attitude, laughter comes easily, naturally.

3. He is flexible.

> I know how to get along with humble means, and I also know how to live in prosperity; in any and every circumstance I have learned the secret of being filled and going hungry, both of having abundance and suffering need.
>
> *Philippians 4:12*

What an enviable list. Three strong contrasts illustrate the man's ability to adapt.

In the yo-yo of life, it is essential to flex. Paul wasn't ticked off because he was on the street, sleeping under a bridge with a growling stomach. Neither was he uneasy in the penthouse, enjoying delicious meals in abundance. When without, he didn't grumble. And when blessed he didn't act unworthy and ashamed. Mature men and women can handle both without disturbing their spiritual or emotional equilibrium.

For some strange reason, most Christians I know struggle more with having an abundance than with suffering great need. Maybe that explains the tendency among Christians to judge and criticize other believers who have wealth and lovely possessions, even though they earned it honestly and hold it all loosely. What graceless immaturity! For some weird reason we would rather brag about how little we have than thankfully relax in a context of God-given prosperity. Am I promoting some kind of "prosperity" gospel? In no way; I think such teaching is heresy. But my concern here is that we be just as willing "to rejoice with those who rejoice" as we are "to weep with those who weep" (Rom. 12:15). When I meet those who cannot do both with equal passion and support, I realize that the problem is immaturity. What concerns me the most is the lack of interest in learning to change in that area.

4. He is confident.

I can do all things through Him who strengthens me.

Philippians 4:13

I mentioned earlier that Paul demonstrated self-sufficiency in his contentment. Here is the statement I referred to when I said that he was sufficient in Christ's sufficiency. The Living Bible puts it this way:

For I can do everything God asks me to with the help of Christ who gives me the strength and power.

No statement in Scripture speaks more clearly of the indwelling Christ. Our Savior not only *lives* within each of His people, He also *pours His power* into us. And that alone is enough to make us confident.

Consider again Paul's statement. Whatever we may substitute for "Christ" fails to fit the statement. Let's try several.

"I can do all things through *drugs.*" No.

"I can do all things through *education.*" No.

"I can do all things through *money.*" No.

"I can do all things through *success.*" No.

"I can do all things through *friends.*" No.

"I can do all things through *positive thinking.*" No.

"I can do all things through *political office.*" No.

Nothing else fits . . . only Christ. Why? Because nothing and no one else is able to empower us and provide the strength we need. Because the Christian has the Lord Himself dwelling within, the potential for inner strength (i.e., confidence) is unlimited. This explains why those who gave their lives for whatever righteous cause down through the ages did so with such courage. Often they were physically weak individuals, small in stature, but they refused to back down. Only the indwelling, empowering Christ can give someone that much confidence. It is almost as if He gives us a feeling of victorious invincibility. That kind of mature confidence enables us to laugh in the face of resistance.

Maturity of the Philippians

We found four qualities of maturity in Paul.

- Affirming others
- Contented, regardless
- Flexible, whatever the situation
- Confident through Christ

I find it interesting that his Christian friends in Philippi, according to what he wrote of them, also demonstrated maturity. I find at least three characteristics in their lives.

1. Personal compassion.

> Nevertheless, you have done well to share with me in my affliction. And you yourselves also know, Philippians, that at the first preaching of the gospel, after I departed from Macedonia, no church shared with me in the matter of giving and receiving but you alone.
>
> *Philippians 4:14–15*

Paul had numerous needs as he traveled on his missionary journeys. He endured hardship and disappointments, heartaches and afflictions. Through it all, the Philippians lent their support. In fact, no other church demonstrated such personal compassion—a mark of maturity. They never second-guessed the apostle in his decision to move on; they supported him. They neither judged him when things went well nor complained when times were hard and he had no fruit to show for his labor; they supported him. They felt pain when he hurt, they prayed for him when he was unable to stay in touch, and they sent friends to comfort him when he was in prison. What a church! No wonder he felt such affection for them.

2. Financial generosity.

> For even in Thessalonica you sent a gift more than once for my needs. Not that I seek the gift itself, but I seek for the profit which increases to your account.
>
> *Philippians 4:16–17*

There is perhaps no finer evidence of maturity than financial generosity. When people graciously and liberally release their treasure to the cause of Christ, it is a sign that they are growing up. The people of Philippi were models of this—"even in Thessalonica." That was a wealthier city than Philippi. Yet even when Paul was there, the Philippians kept right on giving.

By the way, don't rush over that second sentence ("Not that I seek . . .") too quickly. Paul wasn't interested in getting their money; rather, he was seeking their best interest. Am I saying he didn't need their financial contributions? On the contrary. He probably could not have survived without them.

We need a whole new mentality when it comes to thinking clearly about money. The greed of this era has caused the subject of money to be tainted and misunderstood. Money, however, is not evil. It is immature to think it is. While it can be abused and can become the cause for all sorts of evil (1 Tim. 6:10), how one handles this medium of exchange is often a good barometer of one's spiritual and emotional growth. Very few things get accomplished in the realm of ministry without the presence of generous financial support from God's choice servants. Let's face it, money and ministry often flow together. There is nothing unspiritual about admitting the need for money in our lives. To quote the great Sophie Tucker:

> From birth to eighteen, a girl needs good parents.
> From eighteen to thirty-five, she needs good looks.
> From thirty-five to fifty-five, she needs a good
> personality.
> From fifty-five on, she needs cash.[4]

Paul's need was for cash, no question about it. Because his friends were mature, they responded generously.

3. Sacrificial Commitment.

> But I have received everything in full, and have an abundance; I am amply supplied, having received from Epaphroditus what you have sent, a fragrant aroma, an acceptable sacrifice, well-pleasing to God.
>
> *Philippians 4:18*

As Paul took stock of his situation, he realized he couldn't have been better taken care of. As he put it, he was "amply supplied." He had more than enough. Thanks to the sacrificial commitment of the Philippians, his needs were wonderfully met. And isn't that the way it is supposed to be? As the gift is given, prompted by the Spirit of God, it comes as "a fragrant aroma," giving God great delight.

It is as if Paul's heart suddenly bursts forth with gratitude as he writes this splendid promise to his friends:

> And my God shall supply all your needs according to His riches in glory in Christ Jesus.
>
> *Philippians 4:19*

When God is in our hearts of compassion, prompting us to get involved in helping others . . . when He is in our acts of generosity, honoring our support of those engaged in ministry . . . and when He is in our strong commitment, using our sacrifices to bless other lives, He does not forget us in our need. It is all so beautiful, so simple, so right. It is enough to make every one of us *laugh out loud!*

But there is a flip side to all this where something meant to be simple and beautiful can become slick and ugly. The whole subject of finances and fund raising and remaining pure, humble, and grateful in the handling of money is a heavy weight hanging on the thin wires of integrity and accountability. Because a few ministries, rare negative examples, have made the news over the misuse of funds, some would discredit all ministries who need the support of God's people. That is both unfortunate and unfair. All physicians are not viewed with suspicion because a few have been guilty of malpractice. God honors the sacrificial commitment of His people and promises His blessing on those who give that His work might go on.

It is as if Paul is summing up his thoughts with the final verse:

My God . . .

your needs . . .

His riches. . . .

When those three ingredients blend together under the control of the Holy Spirit, it is *something* to behold!

Before we bring this chapter to a close, I want to address the importance of earning the respect of those who continue to support a ministry. As Paul maintained a life of trust and faith and quiet confidence in God, the people in Philippi did not hesitate to stand with him financially. Though he occasionally enjoyed times of abundance and prosperity, Paul never became enamored by his success. He assumed nothing and continued to walk humbly with his God. He refused to believe his own press clippings or lose sight of God's hand in it all.

When the PTL scandal grabbed the attention of the national media, so many in the church, including myself, watched in embarrassed disbelief. As one disgraceful act after another became public knowledge, our disbelief turned to shock and shame. All of us wondered how such things could have happened in a ministry. Some of the answers were provided in an interview *Christianity Today* did with Richard Dortch, who was on staff as PTL grew in popularity. Of special interest to me was his description of how the managers of that organization came to define success:

> It is all tied to how many stations we have on our network or how big our building is. It is so easy to lose control, to compromise without recognizing it. At PTL, there was not time taken for prayer or family because the show had to go on. We were so caught up in God's work that we forgot about God.[5]

With unusual candor, Mr. Dortch also mentioned the incredible impact of television on the one up-front under the bright lights, always before an applauding audience:

> A television camera can change a preacher quicker than anything else. Those who sit on the sidelines can notice the changes in people once they get in front of a camera. It turns a good man into a potentate. It is so easy to get swept away by popularity: Everybody loves you, cars are waiting for you, and you go to the head of the line. That is the devastation of the camera. It has made us less than what God has wanted us to become.[6]

Mr. Dortch's words sound forth another grim reminder that maturity, integrity, and accountability must remain present if we hope to know the blessing of God. People's support is a sacred trust, never to be taken lightly.

MAKING MATURITY A PERSONAL MATTER

How can these truths get lifted from the printed page and transferred to our lives? What's necessary if we hope to break the selfish syndrome and accelerate our growth toward maturity? Let me leave you three bones to chew on:

1. Look within . . . and release. What is it down inside you that is stunting your growth? When you probe around and find something you are hanging onto too tightly, deliberately let go. Yes, you can. You just read it from Paul's pen. You "can do all things through Christ." Let Him help you pry your fingers loose. Inner joy begins when you have "no other gods before you."

2. Look around . . . and respond. Don't wait for someone else. Act on your own, spontaneously. The Philippians saw Paul in his need and they responded . . . again and again. Even though other churches did not follow their example, those folks from Philippi saw the need and responded. Is there some need you can help meet? Risk responding.

3. Look up . . . and rejoice. You are the recipient of His riches—enjoy them! Realize anew all He has done for you; then rejoice in the pleasure of getting involved with others. Among the happiest people are those who voluntarily serve others to the glory of God. Some of the saddest are people who have ceased all contact with those in need.

A comment from Jeanne Hendricks' fine volume, *Afternoon,* has helped me remember this:

> Living is not a spectator sport. No one, at any price, is privileged to sit in the stands and watch the action from a distance. Being born means being a participant in the arena of life, where opposition is fierce and winning comes only to those who exert every ounce of energy.[7]

Laughter is definitely connected to staying involved with people. Stay involved! You will never regret it. Furthermore, it will help you grow up as you find yourself growing old. And the more involved you remain, the less concern you will have for how old you are.

By the way, how old *would* you be if you didn't know how old you were?

14

A Joyful, Grace-Filled Good-bye

*T*his has been the most enjoyable book I have written. The chapters have flowed together (an author's dream!), and the theme of outrageous joy and laughter has lifted my own spirits immensely. I am convinced the Lord knew I needed a dose of my own medicine. With all the heaviness and "bad-news blues" I have had to wade through lately, I was ready for a lighthearted shot in the arm. It worked. I hope it has for you too.

All that prompts a confession: I get weary of believers who live their entire lives with such long faces and nothing but woe-is-me words pouring from their mouths. I realize that life isn't one continually blooming rose garden (mine certainly isn't), but surely it is more than Lamentations Lane. I look at some who claim to be "happy within," and I wonder if maybe they were baptized in freshly squeezed lemon juice. When did we buy into that nonsense? Each time I look up and see Dr. Dryasdust and his wife Grimly making their way toward me, I find myself wanting to run and hide or, better, be raptured out!

Reminds me of a cartoon every mother of small children will appreciate. A little freckled-faced boy, five or six years old, is standing in his pajamas outside his parents' bedroom door—which is shut *and locked.* He looks like the type who would keep six or seven healthy adults jumping. The bottom of his pajamas is unsnapped, his diaper is bagging and soaked, his teddy bear has had its nose torn off and one button-eye is dangling, the other missing. He is staring at a sign, hanging from the doorknob, on which his mom has scribbled

CLOSED FOR BUSINESS!
MOTHERHOOD OUT OF ORDER

There are days I'm tempted to do the same on my study door. Only my sign would read something like:

I'VE HEARD ENOUGH!

MINISTER OUT OT ORDER

GONE RIDIN' ON MY HARLEY

BE BACK IN TWO DAYS—MAYBE

There are days a guy like me (and perhaps you can identify) starts running out of ideas on how to help folks fix their messed-up lives. Sometimes the more I try, the worse the mess. Ever had that happen? Then you understand. But maybe not as well as a fellow named R. D. Jones. "Dear Abby" mentioned him in one of her newspaper columns several months ago. It had to do with a typographical error in the classified section of a small-town newspaper and the subsequent disastrous attempts to correct it. Things went from bad to worse to *horrible*.

Monday: FOR SALE—R. D. Jones has one sewing machine for sale. Phone 948–0707 after 7 p.m. and ask for Mrs. Kelly who lives with him cheap.

Tuesday: NOTICE—We regret having erred in R. D. Jones' ad yesterday. It should have read: One sewing machine for sale. Cheap. Phone 948–0707 and ask for Mrs. Kelly who lives with him after 7 p.m.

Wednesday: NOTICE—R. D. Jones has informed us that he has received several annoying telephone calls because of the error we made in his classified ad yesterday. His ad stands corrected as follows: FOR SALE—R. D. Jones has one sewing machine for sale. Cheap. Phone 948–0707 p.m. and ask for Mrs. Kelly who loves with him.

Thursday: NOTICE—I, R. D. Jones, have NO sewing machine for sale. I SMASHED IT. Don't call 948–0707, as the telephone has been disconnected. I have not been carrying on with Mrs. Kelly. Until yesterday she was my housekeeper, but she quit.[1]

I suggest that R. D. Jones pick up a copy of my book on Friday and start reading right away. And Mrs. Kelly should spend the whole weekend in it, nonstop.

At times like that we need to find relief from life's blistering winds of disappointment and discouragement. For me, nothing works better than a break in the schedule where hearty laughter and a whole change of pace takes my mind off the demands and deadlines. And of all the books in the Bible that help bring a fresh perspective, Philippians tops the list. Again and again it reminds us that we can choose joy regardless of our circumstances, our financial status, our occupation, our past failures, or our current distresses. Thank goodness, things don't have to be perfect or nearly perfect in order for us to focus on the bright side of life.

WHERE HAVE WE BEEN?

Since we have come to the last few words Paul wrote his friends at Philippi, this is a good time to do a little review of where we have been. Threaded through the fabric of this delightful letter has been an overriding theme of joy and rejoicing.

- In chapter 1 of the letter we found *joy in living.* Can you remember? It was there the Apostle of Grace communicated, "For me to live is Christ" (1:21). As long as Christ is central in my life, nothing can steal that joy He brings.

- In chapter 2 of Philippians we discovered there is *joy in serving.* And from whom do we learn this? Again, Christ is the model. With an attitude of submission and acceptance, He left the splendor of heaven in order to come and serve others on earth.

- In chapter 3 *joy in submitting* was the prominent message. Christ, according to that chapter, is our goal. Paul lists all his accomplishments and human effort then admits that, compared to Christ, those things he "counted as loss." Zero. Compared to Christ's righteousness, human effort is nothing more than cotton candy.

- In chapter 4 we learned there is *joy in resting.* Why? Because Jesus Christ is our cause for contentment. We can rest in Him, and as we do, He pours His power into us. When He does that our confidence is re-ignited and restored.

This little letter, the most upbeat of all those Paul wrote, never fails to silence the naysayers and lift our spirits. Surrounded by so many who are down in the mouth, convinced we are headed for doom (with statistics to prove it), we need the reminder that Christ is still triumphant. Our circumstances may be challenging, but God is not wringing His hands, wondering how He is going to work things out. That kind of negative reasoning deserves one of my favorite Greek words in response: *Hogwash.*

I love the way G. Campbell Morgan addresses all this:

> I have no sympathy with people who tell us today that these are the darkest days the world has ever seen. The days in which we live are appalling, but they do not compare with conditions in the world when Jesus came into it. Historians talk of the *Pax Romana* and make much of the fact that there was peace everywhere, the Roman peace. Do not forget that the Roman peace was the result of the fact that the world had been bludgeoned brutally into submission to one central power. . . .
>
> Notwithstanding the prevailing conditions, the dominant note of these Letters, revealing the experience of the Church, is a note of triumph. The dire and dread facts and conditions are never lost sight of—indeed, they are there all the way through. The people are seen going out and facing these facts—and suffering because of these facts—but we never see them depressed and cast down, we never see them suffering from pessimistic fever. They are always triumphant. That is the glory of Christianity. If ever I am tempted to think that religion is almost dead today, it is when I listen to the wailing of some Christian people: "Everything is wrong," or "Everything is going wrong." Oh, be quiet! Think again, look again, judge not by the circumstances of the passing hour but by the infinite things of our Gospel and our God. And that is exactly what these people did.[2]

I love his spunk when encountering the grumblers and doomsayers: "Oh, be quiet!"

HOW DO WE PROCEED?

Let's take a look at Paul's closing comments. Read his words slowly, deliberately pausing at the important terms he uses:

> And my God shall supply all your needs according to His riches in glory in Christ Jesus. Now to our God and Father be the glory forever and ever. Amen.

Greet every saint in Christ Jesus. The brethren who are with me greet
you. All the saints greet you, especially those of Caesar's household.
The grace of the Lord Jesus Christ be with your spirit.

Philippians 4:19–23

Unlike the fanfares of a grand symphonic cadence, Paul says
farewell in an understated manner. I find about four staccatolike statements.

First, *he writes of the glory of the Lord's plan.* Hidden in the throne
room of God's celestial existence are "riches in glory." He blesses us and
He provides for us according to those riches. He draws upon that infinite
supply base as He meets our every need. And when He does, He gets the
corresponding glory . . . forever. Look how Paul puts it:

> And it is he who will supply all your needs from his riches in glory,
> because of what Christ Jesus has done for us. Now unto God our Father
> be glory forever and ever. Amen.
>
> *Philippians 4:19–20 TLB*

God gives from His "riches in glory," and, in turn, He receives the
glory. We would say He gets the credit. Need a few examples?

- When your boss walks in and congratulates you—you are
  being promoted—God gets the glory. Of course you feel
  good about it and you worked hard for it, but the credit is
  God's.

- An illness has plagued you for weeks, perhaps months.
  While you prayed and sought qualified medical attention
  during that time, little changed. To your own amazement,
  God steps in and solves the dilemma. Who can ever explain
  the healing that He miraculously performed? We cannot
  explain it, but we *can* give Him the glory. And because we
  can, we *must*.

- One of your children has been a special challenge. Virtually
  since birth, he (or she) has been difficult. About the time you
  are ready to throw up your hands and say, "I've had it!" the
  Lord steps in and "supplies all your need according to His
  riches in glory," and your almost-grown challenge suddenly
  changes and begins to model manners, responsibility, and

courtesy. As a result, God gets the glory . . . as you begin
to laugh again.

How happy are those to whom God demonstrates His glory.
Second, *he mentions the greeting of the saints.*

> Greet every saint in Christ Jesus. The brethren who are with me greet
> you. All the saints greet you, especially those of Caesar's household.
>
> *Philippians 4:21–22*

As you can imagine, those words have spurred imaginations for
centuries. The intriguing part is Paul's reference to "Caesar's household."
Could he have in mind the emperor's wife and children? Would it be
broader than that and encompass the in-laws and distant relatives? Does
Paul mean the *literal* household?

The most reliable scholarship suggests that it is a reference to an
incredibly large body of people in Italy and the surrounding provinces,
slaves and free citizens alike . . . members of the elite Imperial Guard
that waited on Caesar, doing his special work. And we should not forget
the network of executives and administrators, secretaries and courtiers in
and about Caesar's royal palace.

If you find this fascinating, as I certainly do, the following quotations
will tweak your interest further.

J. B. Lightfoot writes:

> It has been assumed that this phrase must designate persons of high
> rank and position, powerful minions of the court, great officers of state, or
> even blood relations to the Emperor himself. . . . The 'domus' or 'familia
> Caesaris' . . . includes the whole of the imperial household, the mean-
> est [lowest] slaves as well as the most powerful courtiers. . . . In Rome
> itself . . . the 'domus Augusta' must have formed no inconsiderable
> fraction of the whole population; but it comprised likewise all persons in
> the emperor's service, whether slaves or freemen, in Italy and even in the
> provinces.[3]

William Ramsey, in his fascinating classic, *St. Paul, the Traveller and
the Roman Citizen,* adds this:

> The new movement made marked progress in the vast Imperial
> household. . . . The Imperial household was at the centre of affairs and

in most intimate relations with all parts of the Empire. . . . There can be no doubt that . . . Christianity effected an entrance into Caesar's household before Paul entered Rome; in all probability he is right also in thinking that all the slaves of Aristobulus (son of Herod the Great) and of Narcissus (Claudius's favourite freedman) had passed into the Imperial household, and that members of these two *familiae* are saluted as Christians by Paul (Rom. 16:10–16).[4]

One other, from Alfred Plummer of Trinity College at Oxford:

There were many Jews among the lower officials in Nero's household, and it was perhaps among them that the Gospel made its first converts.[5]

Legend has it that while Nero was out of town, his wife listened to the Christian message and turned her life over to Christ. When Nero returned and discovered she had been converted to Christ, his anger knew no bounds! Perhaps it was that which led to his rash decision to behead Paul.

The point I am making is that the remarkable spread of the gospel is enough to make all of us laugh out loud! Christ had invaded and infiltrated the very citadel of unbelief. Isn't that a great thought? In the very rooms where His name had been an unmentionable, Christ as Lord was now being openly discussed. And all of that was happening right under Nero's nose—yet he couldn't stop it!

Our minister of music at the church I serve, Howie Stevenson, and his wife, Marilyn, along with several friends from our church and many others from the United States, had the privilege of taking their talents to Moscow during the Russian Orthodox Easter in 1991. It was a vast gathering of Christians and non-Christians alike. The actual place of ministry was the Palace of Congress where the Supreme Soviet had met for years. You've seen the massive room on television, with the enormous oversize picture of Lenin hung before all in attendance. Except, in this case, Lenin's portrait was covered. And instead of communism's propaganda being proclaimed, Bill Bright, of Campus Crusade for Christ, preached the gospel. Howie, accompanied by his wife and two of my favorite musical artists, Stephen Nielson and Ovid Young, on dual pianos, led a large choir who presented the praises of Jesus Christ in the very stronghold of atheism.

The halls were filled with the majestic music of the Messiah, Jesus Christ, whose message of forgiveness and grace was announced by television to millions of viewers in the land of Russia . . . the very place where a few years ago you would be immediately arrested for merely mentioning the name of Jesus Christ.

On Sunday afternoon the group went into Red Square and distributed more than a hundred thousand pamphlets that conveyed the message of Christ, including Testaments and Bibles in the language of the people. (Actually they were warned against doing that too aggressively because they might be mobbed by people starving for more information about Christ.)

Isn't that great! They announced in music and spoken word that Jesus Christ is the Savior, the Lord, the risen Supreme One. We could say that Christ was proclaimed "even in Lenin's household." I must confess, when Howie reported on the marvelous success of their trip and everyone in our church applauded vigorously, I thought, *In your face, Lenin! Our God reigns.*

As I write this I am smiling. The thought of that triumphant message being publicly proclaimed in a once-forbidden region of our world is enough to make me laugh out loud. I cannot help but wonder if Paul, chained to that uniformed and armed guard in his little house in Rome, didn't smile with delight as he pictured the irresistible, life-changing movement of Christianity pushing its way into the least likely areas of Nero's domain. Yes, *our God reigns!*

Third, *Paul reaffirms the grace of the Savior.* We would expect this from him, wouldn't we? Grace had become the very theme of his life by now. Law had come by Moses, but grace came through Jesus Christ. It was grace that reached Paul en route to Damascus. It was grace that saved him as he realized all those accomplishments of his past were deeds done in the flesh. It became obvious to him that grace would be his message as he was used by God to minister to Gentiles and offer them the hope of sins forgiven and a home in heaven. And it was grace that assured him of his own eternal destiny. Any man whose life had been transformed so radically, so completely, because of God's matchless grace would naturally shout it from the housetop for the rest of his life.

As John Newton wrote with equal passion centuries later:

> Through many dangers, toils, and snares,
> I have already come;
> 'Tis grace hath brought me safe thus far,
> And grace will lead me home.[6]

I never sing that grand old hymn without thanking God anew that in spite of all those things He could have held against me, He accepted me, forgave me, included me in His family, and will some day receive me into glory. If that isn't enough to make us laugh again, I don't know what is.

What a magnificent letter Paul wrote from Rome to his friends far away in Philippi. I can imagine the gray-haired apostle reaching his manacled arm over to Epaphroditus, taking the stylus from his hand . . . and forming these closing words with his own fingers:

> To our God and Father be the glory forever and ever. Greet every saint in Christ Jesus. . . . All the saints greet you, especially those of Caesar's household. . . . Grace . . . be with your spirit. Amen.
> Paulos

And with that Paul rolled up the scroll, embraced his friend with a smile, and sent him on his way with letter in hand, having prayed for journey mercies. I can see Paul smiling as he waved a joyful, grace-filled good-bye to a man he would never see again on earth.

A TREASURED LEGACY

When I completed my own study of the letter to the Philippians, I experienced a nostalgic serendipity. As I was putting away my research materials along with pen and paper, an old book by F. B. Meyer, one of my favorite authors, caught my attention. It happened to be his work on Philippians, but I had not consulted it throughout my months of study.

Thinking there might be something in it to augment my study, I decided to pull it from the shelf and leaf through it before I went home for the day. I turned off the overhead light in my study, and, with only the light from my desk lamp, I leaned back in my old leather desk chair and opened Meyer's book.

To my unexpected delight, it was not the words of F. B. Meyer that spoke to me that evening, but the words of my mother. For as I began looking through it, I realized this book was one of the many volumes which had found their way from her library into mine after her death back in 1971. Little did she know when she wrote in it years before that her words would become a part of her legacy to me, her youngest. I sat very still as I took in the wonder.

In her own inimitable handwriting, my mother had made notes in the text and along the margins throughout the book. When I got to the end, I noticed she had penned these words on the inside of the back cover, "Finished reading this May 8, 1958."

I looked up in my dimly lit study and pondered, *1958*. My mind took me back to a tiny island in the South Pacific where I had spent many lonely months as a Marine. I recalled that it was *in May of 1958* that I had reached a crossroad in my own pilgrimage. In fact, I had entered the following words in my journal: "The Lord has convinced me that I am to be in His service. I will begin to make plans to prepare for a lifetime of ministry." Amazingly, it was in the same month of that very year that my mother had finished reading Meyer's book. As I looked back over the pages, I found one reference after another to her prayers for me as I was away . . . her concern for my spiritual welfare . . . her desire for God's best in my life. And occasionally she had inserted a clever quip or humorous comment.

Turning back to the front of the book, I found another interesting entry, also with a date. It read, "Chart of Philippians mailed to me by Charles when he was ministering in Massachusetts, 1966." As I glanced over the chart, another memory swept over me. I recalled putting that chart together and sending it to her during my years in New England. Once again I looked up and momentarily relived those years between 1958 and 1966. What a significant passage! All through that time, I now realize my mother had prayed for me and loved me and sought God's best for me.

Across the room in my study hangs an original oil painting with a light above it, shedding a golden glow down over the colorful canvas. The painting was my mother's gift to me some years after I entered the ministry. She had painted it. It is of a shepherd surrounded by a handful of sheep on a green hillside.

I had looked at this painting countless times before, but this time was unique. In the bottom right corner I looked at her name and the date . . . only days before she passed into the Lord's presence. Caught in that nostalgic time warp, I turned off my desk lamp and stared at the lighted painting. There I sat, twenty years after she had laid the brush aside, thanking God anew for my mother's prayers, my pilgrimage, and especially His presence. Faithfully, graciously, quietly He had led me and helped me and blessed me. I bowed my head and thanked Him for His sustaining grace . . . and I wept with gratitude.

Suddenly the shrill sound of the telephone broke the silence. My younger son, Chuck, was on the line wanting to tell me something funny that had happened. I quickly switched gears and enjoyed one of those delightful, lighthearted father-son moments. As we laughed loudly together, he urged me to hurry home.

Following his call I placed the F. B. Meyer book back on the shelf. As I was leaving my study, I paused beside the painting and thought of the significant role my parents had played in those formative years of my life . . . and how the torch had been passed on from them to Cynthia and me to do the same with our sons and daughters . . . and they, in turn, with theirs.

As I switched off the light above the painting, I smiled and said, "Good-bye, Mother." In the darkness of that room I could almost hear her voice answering me, "Good-bye, Charles. I love you, Son. I'm still praying for you. Keep walking with God . . . and don't forget to have some fun with your family tonight."

What a treasured legacy: devoted prayers, lasting love, hearty laughter. That's the way it ought to be.

Conclusion

God's sense of humor has intrigued me for years. What amazes me, however, is the number of people who don't think He has one. For the life of me, I can't figure out why they can't see it. He made you and me, didn't He? And what about all those funny-looking creatures that keep drawing us back to the zoo? If they aren't proof of our Creator's sense of humor, I don't know what is. Have you taken a close look at a wombat or a two-toed sloth, a giant anteater or a warthog lately? They're hilarious! Every time I look at a camel I chuckle, recalling the words of some wag who said it reminded him of a horse put together by a committee. I honestly wonder if God didn't laugh Himself as He dropped some of those creatures on our planet eons ago.

God's humor, unfortunately, does not occupy any significant place in serious works of theology. I know; I've been checking them for years and been disappointed. In my four intensive years of study in an excellent graduate school of theology, I don't recall one time that any prof addressed the subject of God's sense of humor. And in all my reading since then— thirty years of searching—seldom have I found anything more than a lighthearted throwaway line on the subject.

That's too bad. Because the impression we are left with is that our Lord is an all-too-serious Sovereign who has no room in His character for at least a few moments of fun. At best this frowning, uptight caricature suggests He is a heavenly representation of some venerable, earthly theologian—only older and wiser. Please!

Surely it is not blasphemous to think that laughter breaks out in heaven on special occasions. Why shouldn't it? There is every reason to believe that would happen in His infinite, holy presence, where all is well and no evil abides. After all, God sees everything that transpires in this human comedy of errors . . . He understands it all.

He must have smiled, for example, when Elijah mocked the false prophets on Mount Carmel, asking whether their gods had gone on a journey or fallen asleep or were *indisposed* (1 Kings 18:27)! And what about that fellow named Eutychus who listened to Paul preach and fell out of a third-story window (Acts 20:9)? Don't worry, he recovered . . . but are you going to sit there and tell me God didn't find humor in that scenario?

Think of how many times preachers have gotten their tongues twisted and blurted out stupid stuff. Once while I was explaining that many of the people in Christ's day expected Him to come and break the yoke of Rome, out came "roke of Yome." But that wasn't nearly as bad as the time I was describing the unusual strategy Joshua and his warriors employed to bring down the walls of Jericho. Instead of saying they were to march around the wall, I chose to say that they circumscribed the wall, but inadvertently it came out, "circumcised the wall" . . . which brought the house down. You're telling me God didn't laugh?

One of my mentors tells me that he was once introduced by a country preacher as "the professor of the Suppository Preaching Department." I asked him what he did after he got up to preach. He smiled and said, "Well, Chuck, I just stood up and supposited the Word, like I always do." Surely the God we serve finds those moments as funny as we do.

And what about those embarrassing typos and misworded announcements that appear in church bulletins, like:

- This afternoon there will be a meeting in the north and south ends of the church. Children will be baptized at both ends.
- The choir will be participating in the local community sing, which is open to everyone. They will be sinning at 6:00 p.m. this Sunday.
- There will be a sin-in at the Johnsons' home this evening, immediately following the pastor's message, "Intimate Fellowship."
- Affirmation of Faith No. 738: "The Apostles' Greed"
- Solo: "There Is a Bomb in Gilead"
- Order of Service: Silent Prayer and Medication

- This was printed after a church potluck: "Ladies, if you have missing bowels, you will find them in the church kitchen."
- Pastor Brown will marry his son next Sunday morning.

Such stories abound! And you will never convince me that God doesn't get a kick out of such things and laugh with some of us in our well-meant seriousness.

I believe He fully understands us in our imperfect humanity. He understands little children who pick their noses in church because they are bored stiff. It's no big deal to Him. He must smile at some of the notes children send their pastor, too, like this one I read recently:

Dear Pastor,
    I know God loves everybody, but He never met my sister.

Yours sincerely,
Arnold

A friend of mine told me about another one that read:

Dear Paster,
    My father couldn't give more $$money$$ to the chrch. HE is a good chrischen but has a *cheap* boss.

Ronald

Surely God smiles with understanding when he hears prayers like the one Erma Bombeck says she has prayed for years: "Lord, if you can't make me thin, then make my friends look fat."

Isn't God the One who urges us to "Make a joyful noise unto the Lord"? Why do we always think that means singing? Seems to me the most obvious joyful noise on earth is laughter. We say we believe in laughing and having a happy countenance. I'm not sure. I've seen folks quote verses like "Rejoice in the Lord always" while their faces look like they just buried a rich uncle who willed everything to his pregnant guinea pig. Something is missing.

We all *look* so much better and *feel* so much better when we laugh. I don't know of a more contagious sound. And yet there are so many who never weary of telling us, "Life is no laughing matter." It may not be for them, but I must tell you, it often is for me. Knowing that God is causing "all things to work together for good," and remembering that we, His people, are on our way to an eternal home in the heavens without fears or tears, takes the sting out of this temporary parenthesis of time called earthly life.

The returning prodigal was absolutely amazed by his father's immediate acceptance, reckless forgiveness, and unconditional love. Having been so distant, so desperate, so utterly alone, he knew no way to turn but homeward. Then, at the end of his rope, he found himself suddenly safe in his dad's embrace, smothered with kisses, and surrounded by extravagant grace. The fatted calf . . . a soft, warm robe, comfortable new sandals, and the costliest ring were all his . . . no strings attached . . . no probation required. Not surprisingly, that home was soon filled with "music and dancing." As Jesus told the story, He was careful to add, "And they began to be merry."

Then why shouldn't we?

Throughout these pages I have been urging you to lighten up. I could not have done so without knowing that Someone, like the prodigal's father, is diligently searching for you. Every day He scans the horizon and waits patiently for you to appear. He has spared no expense. A blood-smeared cross on which His Son died is now a painful memory, but it was essential to solve the sin problem.

Every day He says to our world, "All is forgiven . . . come on home." His arms are open, and there is a wide, wide smile on His face. The band is tuning up. The banquet is ready to be served. All that is needed is you.

Come on home. You will be so glad you did. In fact, before you know it, you'll begin to laugh again.

Notes

Introduction

1. James S. Huett, ed., *Illustrations Unlimited* (Wheaton, Ill.: Tyndale, 1988), 101.

Chapter 1 / Your Smile Increases Your Face Value

1. G. K. Chesterton, *Orthodoxy* (New York: Dodd, Mead and Co., 1954), 298.
2. Adapted from "The Chair Recognizes Mr. Buckley," quoted in *Tabletalk* 17, no. 1 (March 1992): 9.
3. Jane Canfield, in *Quote/Unquote*, comp. Lloyd Cory (Wheaton, Ill.: Victor Books, 1977), 144.
4. Helen Mallicoat, "I Am," in Tim Hansel, *Holy Sweat* (Waco, Tex.: Word Books, 1987), 136. Used by permission.
5. Hansel, *Holy Sweat*, 58–59.

Chapter 2 / Set Your Sails for Joy

1. Ella Wheeler Wilcox, "The Wind of Fate," in *The Best Loved Poems of the American People*, comp. Hazel Felleman (Garden City, N.Y.: Garden City Books, 1936), 364.
2. Kenneth S. Wuest, *Philippians in the Greek New Testament* (Grand Rapids, Mich.: William B. Eerdmans Publishing Co., 1942), 26–27.
3. William Griffin, "On Making Saints," *Publishers Weekly*, 5 October 1990, 34.
4. Anonymous.
5. John Powell, *Why Am I Afraid to Tell You Who I Am?* (Chicago, Ill.: Argus Communications Co., 1969), 54–55.
6. Ibid., 56.
7. Ibid., 56–57.
8. Ibid., 57–58.

9. Ibid., 61–62.

10. Howard Taylor and Mary G. Taylor, *Hudson Taylor's Spiritual Secret* (Chicago: Moody Press, 1932), 152.

11. Wilcox, "The Wind of Fate," 364.

Chapter 3 / What a Way to Live!

1. G. W. Target, "The Window," from *The Window and Other Essays* (Boise, Idaho: Pacific Press Publishing Association, 1973), 5–7.

2. Stuart Briscoe, *Bound for Joy: Philippians—Paul's Letter from Prison* (Glendale, Calif.: Regal Books, 1975), 25.

3. Samuel Johnson to Lord Chesterfield, 19 September 1777, cited in John Bartlett, *Familiar Quotations*, ed. Emily Morison Beck (Boston, Mass.: Little, Brown and Co., 1980), 355.

4. Anonymous.

Chapter 4 / Laughing Through Life's Dilemmas

1. From "Jesus Is All the World to Me," Will L. Thompson [1847–1909].

2. Horatius Bonar, "Thy Way, Not Mine," *Baker's Pocket Treasury of Religious Verse,* ed. Donald T. Kauffmann (Grand Rapids, Mich.: Baker Book House, 1962), 219. Used by permission.

3. Anonymous.

4. Quoted by J. Foster, *Then and Now* (London, 1945), 83, cited in Ralph P. Martin, *The Epistle of Paul to the Philippians* (Grand Rapids, Mich.: William B. Eerdmans Publishing Co., 1959), 88.

5. "God's Gargoyle: An Interview with Malcolm Muggeridge," *Radix/Right On* (May 1975): 3.

Chapter 5 / The Hidden Secret of a Happy Life

1. Canfield, *Quote/Unquote,* 23.

2. From "When I Survey the Wondrous Cross," Isaac Watts [1674–1748].

3. Harry A. Ironside, *Notes on the Epistle to the Philippians* (Neptune, N.J.: Loizeaux Brothers, 1922), 38–39.

4. D. Martyn Lloyd-Jones, *The Life of Joy: An Exposition of Philippians 1 and 2* (Grand Rapids, Mich.: Baker Book House, 1989), 142–43.

5. Ironside, *Notes on the Epistle to the Philippians,* 47.

6. From "Holy, Holy, Is What the Angels Sing," Rev. Johnson Oatman, Jr.

Notes

Chapter 6 / While Laughing, Keep Your Balance!

1. "Advice to a (Bored) Young Man," cited in Ted W. Engstrom, *Motivation to Last a Lifetime* (Grand Rapids, Mich.: Zondervan, 1984), 23–24.

2. Mark Twain, *Pudd'nhead Wilson* [1894], "Pudd'nhead Wilson's Calendar," cited in Bartlett, *Familiar Quotations,* 624.

3. Jimmy Bowen, cited in Sharon Bernstein, "When Entertainment LipSyncs Modern Life," *Los Angeles Times,* 29 November 1990, F1.

4. Ibid.

5. Eugene H. Peterson, *Five Smooth Stones for Pastoral Work* (Atlanta, Ga.: John Knox Press, 1980), 47.

6. J. B. Priestly in *Macmillan Dictionary of Quotations* (Norwalk, Conn.: Easton Press, 1989), 120.

7. "World May End with a Splash," *Los Angeles Times,* 9 October 1982.

8. Julia Seton, *Quote/Unquote,* 67.

9. Laurence Peter and Bill Dana, *The Laughter Prescription* (New York: Ballantine Books, 1987), 8.

10. Jim McGuiggan, *The Irish Papers* (Fort Worth, Tex.: Star Bible Publications, 1992), 42.

11. John Wooden, *They Call Me Coach* (Waco, Tex.: Word Books, 1972), 184.

12. Source unknown.

Chapter 7 / Friends Make Life More Fun

1. Michael LeBoeuf, *How to Win Customers and Keep Them for Life* (New York: Berkley Books, 1987), 84–85.

2. "How Important Are You," © United Technologies Corporation, 1983. Used by permission.

3. Briscoe, *Bound for Joy,* 92–93.

4. Leighton Ford, *Transforming Leadership* (Downers Grove, Ill.: InterVarsity Press, 1991), 139–41.

5. J. B. Lightfoot, *St Paul's Epistle to the Philippians* (London: Macmillan and Co., 1908), 123.

6. William Hendriksen, *New Testament Commentary* (Grand Rapids, Mich.: Baker Book House, 1962), 144–45.

Chapter 8 / Happy Hopes for High Achievers

1. Joe Lomusio, *If I Should Die Before I Live* (Fullerton, Calif.: R. C. Law & Co., 1989), 144–45.

2. Tim Hansel, *When I Relax I Feel Guilty* (Elgin, Ill.: David C. Cook Publishing Co., 1979), 20–22.

3. G. K. Chesterton, *The Napoleon of Notting Hill* (New York: Paulist Press, 1978), 37.

4. William Barclay, *The Mind of St Paul* (New York: Harper and Brothers Publishers, 1958), 17–19.

5. Archibald T. Robertson, *Word Pictures in the New Testament*, vol. 4 (Nashville, Tenn.: Broadman Press, 1931), 453.

6. "I Met My Master," *Poems That Preach*, ed. John R. Rice (Wheaton, Ill.: Sword of the Lord Publishers, 1952), 18. Used by permission.

Chapter 9 / Hanging Tough Together . . . and Loving It

1. *Los Angeles Times,* 27 January 1991.

2. Henry David Thoreau, cited in Bartlett, *Familiar Quotations,* 590.

3. John Pollock, *The Man Who Shook the World* (Wheaton, Ill.: Victor Books, 1972), 18.

4. Robert Ballard, "A Long Last Look at Titanic," *National Geographic* 170, no. 6 (December 1986): 698–705.

5. Bob Benson, *Laughter in the Walls* (Nashville, Tenn.: Impact Books, 1969), 16–17. Used by permission.

6. Benjamin Franklin, at the signing of the Declaration of Independence [4 July 1776], cited in Bartlett, *Familiar Quotations,* 348.

7. From "Higher Ground," Johnson Oatman, Jr. [1856–1926].

Chapter 10 / It's a Mad, Bad, Sad World, But . . .

1. Flannery O'Connor, *Mystery and Manners* (New York: Farrar, Straus and Giroux, 1969), 167.

2. A. W. Tozer, *The Root of Righteousness* (Harrisburg, Pa.: Christian Publications, 1955), 156.

3. Norman Cousins, *Anatomy of an Illness as Perceived by the Patient* (New York: Norton, 1979), 25–43.

4. G. K. Chesterton, *The Common Man* (New York: Sheed and Ward, 1950), 157–58.

5. Barbara Johnson, *Splashes of Joy in the Cesspools of Life* (Dallas, Tex.: Word Publishing, 1992), 65.

Chapter 11 / Defusing Disharmony

1. Karen Mains, *The Key to a Loving Heart* (Elgin, Ill: David C. Cook, 1979), 143–44.

2. Thomas Brookes, *The Golden Treasure of Puritan Quotations,* ed. I. D. E. Thomas (Chicago, Ill.: Moody Press, 1975), 304.

3. Marshall Shelley, *Well-Intentioned Dragons* (Waco, Tex.: Word Books/CTi, 1985), 11–12.

Notes

4. Leslie B. Flynn, *You Don't Have to Go It Alone* (Denver, Colo.: Accent Books, 1981), 117.

Chapter 12 / Freeing Yourself Up to Laugh Again

1. Jean Jacques Rousseau, *Du Contrat Social* [1762], bk. 1, chap. 1, cited in Bartlett, *Familiar Quotations*, 358.
2. W. Grant Lee, in Bartlett, *Familiar Quotations*, 174.
3. Fred Allen, in *Quote/Unquote*, 174.
4. Ruth Harms Calkin, "Spiritual Retreat," *Lord, You Love to Say Yes* (Elgin, Ill.: David C. Cook, 1976), 16–17. Used by permission.
5. Quoted by Ruth Bell Graham, *Prodigals and Those Who Love Them* (Colorado Springs, Colo.: Focus on the Family Publishing, 1991), 44.

Chapter 13 / Don't Forget to Have Fun As You Grow Up

1. Anonymous.
2. Fred Cook, in *Quote/Unquote*, 200.
3. Max DePree, *Leadership Is an Art* (New York: Dell Publishing, 1987), 7–10. Used by permission of Doubleday, a division of Bantam Doubleday Dell Publishing Group, Inc.
4. Sophie Tucker, quoted in Rosalind Russell and Chris Chase, *Life Is a Banquet* (New York: Random House, 1977), 2.
5. Quoted in "I Made Mistakes," interview with Richard Dortch, *Christianity Today*, 18 March 1988, 46–47.
6. Ibid.
7. Jeanne Hendricks, *Afternoon* (Nashville, Tenn.: Thomas Nelson Publishers, 1979), 103.

Chapter 14 / A Joyful, Grace-Filled Good-bye

1. From the California Newspaper Association.
2. G. Campbell Morgan, *The Unfolding Message of the Bible* (Westwood, N.J.: Fleming H. Revell Co., 1961), 367.
3. J. B. Lightfoot, *Notes on the Epistle to the Philippians*, 171.
4. W. M. Ramsay, *St Paul, the Traveller and the Roman Citizen* (London: Hodder and Stoughton, 1895), 352–53.
5. Alfred Plummer, *A Commentary on St Paul's Epistle to the Philippians* (London: Robert Scott Roxburghe House, 1919), 107.
6. From "Amazing Grace," John Newton [1725–1807].

HOPE AGAIN

I dedicate this book to two of my closest colleagues and
faithful friends on the leadership team at
Dallas Theological Seminary:

Dr. Wendell Johnston
and
Dr. Charlie Dyer

Without their invaluable assistance, there is no way these
recent years could have been so satisfying and
rewarding. These men have given me
fresh encouragement to press on . . . to finish strong
. . . to hope again.

Contents

✦

Acknowledgments

I WANT TO ACKNOWLEDGE, with great gratitude, my longstanding friendship with several important people.

First, my friends on the leadership team at Word Publishing: Byron Williamson, Kip Jordon, Joey Paul, and David Moberg. There are others I could name, but these four have been especially encouraging and helpful on this particular project. Thank you, men, for continuing to believe in me and for knowing how to turn dreams into books.

I also want to express my gratitude to writer Ken Gire for his excellent work many years ago on our Insight for Living study guide on 1 Peter. I found several of his insights and illustrations helpful as I worked my way through this volume.

Judith Markham has again proven herself invaluable to me as my editor. Her ability to transform my primitive lines and disjointed phrases into understandable sentences and meaningful paragraphs is something to behold! I am especially grateful for her wise and seasoned counsel throughout this process. Without her help this book would have been twice as long and half as interesting.

Although I've already mentioned them in my dedication, I want to repeat my thanks to Wendell Johnston and Charlie Dyer for giving me hope again and again on numerous occasions since I began my work as president of Dallas Theological Seminary back in the summer of 1994. The Dallas heat during that July was enough to wilt the most stouthearted, but there they were right from the start, smiling, serving, and sweating alongside me, giving constant affirmation and providing plenty of wind beneath my wings. Without their whole-hearted commitment and assistance, rather than soaring like an eagle, I would have wandered around those halls like a turkey wondering where to roost. So thank you, men, for your faithful and supportive presence.

Finally, I want to acknowledge the encouragement of my wife, Cynthia, and express my thanks for her unswerving loyalty and compassionate understanding. We have been through a whale of a transition (we're still in it!), but because I haven't had to travel alone, the journey hasn't been nearly as difficult as it could have been. Having her by my side and knowing she is always in my corner and excited about my work has freed me up to finish what I started, regardless of the time and effort required. Thanks to her, I never felt the challenging task of finishing another project this extensive was hopeless.

CHUCK SWINDOLL

DALLAS, TEXAS

The Old Fisherman's Letter

HOPE IS A wonderful gift from God, a source of strength and courage in the face of life's harshest trials.

- When we are trapped in a tunnel of misery, hope points to the light at the end.
- When we are overworked and exhausted, hope gives us fresh energy.
- When we are discouraged, hope lifts our spirits.
- When we are tempted to quit, hope keeps us going.
- When we lose our way and confusion blurs the destination, hope dulls the edge of panic.
- When we struggle with a crippling disease or a lingering illness, hope helps us persevere beyond the pain.
- When we fear the worst, hope brings reminders that God is still in control.
- When we must endure the consequences of bad decisions, hope fuels our recovery.
- When we find ourselves unemployed, hope tells us we still have a future.
- When we are forced to sit back and wait, hope gives us the patience to trust.
- When we feel rejected and abandoned, hope reminds us we're not alone... we'll make it.

- When we say our final farewell to someone we love, hope in the life beyond gets us through our grief.

Put simply, when life hurts and dreams fade, nothing helps like hope.

Webster defines hope: "Desire accompanied by expectation of or belief in fulfillment . . . to desire with expectation of obtainment . . . to expect with confidence." How vital is that expectation! Without it, prisoners of war languish and die. Without it, students get discouraged and drop out of school. Without it, athletic teams fall into a slump and continue to lose . . . fledgling writers, longing to be published, run out of determination . . . addicts return to their habits . . . marriage partners decide to divorce . . . inventors, artists, entertainers, entrepreneurs, even preachers, lose their creativity.

Hope isn't merely a nice option that helps us temporarily clear a hurdle. It's essential to our survival.

Realizing the vital role hope plays in life, I decided several years ago to do a serious, in-depth study on the subject. To my surprise, one of the best sources of information was a letter located toward the end of the New Testament that was written by the old fisherman himself, Peter. He should know the subject well, having found himself in great need of hope at a critical moment in his own life—when he failed miserably.

And so . . . here it is, a book for all who sincerely search for ways to hope again . . . when your life hurts and when your dreams fade.

1

Hope Beyond Failure

The Broken
Man Behind
the Book

THIS IS A BOOK ON HOPE. *Hope.* It is something as important to us as water is to a fish, as vital as electricity is to a light bulb, as essential as air is to a jumbo jet. Hope is that basic to life.

We cannot stay on the road to anticipated dreams without it, at least not very far. Many have tried—none successfully. Without that needed spark of hope, we are doomed to a dark, grim existence.

How often the word "hopeless" appears in suicide notes. And even if it isn't actually written, we can read it between the lines. Take away our hope, and our world is reduced to something between depression and despair.

There once lived a man who loved the sea. Rugged, strong-willed, passionate, and expressive, he did nothing halfheartedly. When it came to fishing, he was determined—and sometimes obnoxious. But he was loyal when it came to friendships . . . loyal to the core, blindly courageous, and overconfident, which occasionally caused him to overstate his commitment. But there he stood, alone if necessary, making promises with his mouth that his body would later be unable to keep.

As you probably realize by now, the man's name was Peter, not just one of the Twelve, but the spokesman for the Twelve (whether they liked it or not). Once he decided to follow Christ, there was no turning back. As time passed, he became all the more committed to the Master, a devoted and stubborn-minded disciple whose loyalty knew no bounds.

Ultimately, however, his commitment was put to the test. Jesus had warned him that Satan was hot on his heels, working overtime to trip him up. But Peter was unmoved. His response? "Lord, with You I am ready to go both to prison and to death!" (Luke 22:33). Jesus didn't buy it. He answered, "Peter, the cock will not crow today until you have denied three times that you know Me" (Luke 22:34). Though that prediction must have stung, Peter pushed it aside . . . self-assured and overly confident that it would never happen.

Wrong. That very night, Jesus' words turned to reality. The loyal, strong-hearted, courageous Peter failed his Lord. Deliberately and openly he denied that he was one of the Twelve. Not once or twice but three times, back to back, he turned on the One who had loved him enough to warn him.

The result? Read these words slowly as you imagine the scene.

And the Lord turned and looked at Peter. And Peter remembered the word of the Lord, how He had told him, "Before a cock crows today, you will deny Me three times." And he went out and wept bitterly. (Luke 22:61–62)

No longer loyal and strong, far from courageous and committed, the man was suddenly reduced to heaving sobs. What guilt he bore! How ashamed he felt! Words cannot adequately portray his brokenness. Emotionally, he plunged to rock bottom, caught in the grip of hopelessness; the effect on Peter was shattering. Every time he closed his eyes he could see the face of Jesus staring at him, as if asking, "How could you, Peter? Why would you?" That look. Those words. The man was haunted for days. The Savior's subsequent death by crucifixion must have been like a nail driven into Peter's heart.

The one thing he needed to carry him on was gone...gone forever, he thought. *Hope.* Until that glorious resurrection day, the first Easter morn, when we read not only of Jesus' miraculous, bodily resurrection from the dead but also those great words of grace, "Go, tell His disciples and Peter..." (Mark 16:7). *And Peter!* The significance of those two words cannot be overstated.

They introduced hope into the old fisherman's life...the one essential ingredient without which he could otherwise not recover. Upon hearing of his Savior's resurrection and also his Savior's concern that *he* especially be given the message, Peter had hope beyond his failure. Because of that, he could go on.

And, not surprisingly, he would later be the one who would write the classic letter of hope to those who needed to hear it the most...those who were residing "as aliens, scattered" across the vast landscape of the Roman Empire (1 Pet. 1:1).

Between his earlier failure and his writing this letter, Peter had been used of God as the catalyst in the formation of the early church. But having been broken and humiliated, his leadership was altogether different than it would have been without his failure. Now that he had been rescued by grace and restored by hope, he had no interest in playing "king of the mountain" by pushing people around. Rather, he became a servant-hearted shepherd of God's flock.

I like the way Eugene Peterson describes Peter in his introduction to 1 and 2 Peter:

> The way Peter handled himself in that position of power is even more impressive than the power itself. He kept out of the center of attention, he didn't parade his power, because he kept himself under the power of Jesus. He could have easily thrown around his popularity, power, and position to try to take over, using his close association with Jesus to promote himself. But he didn't. Most people with Peter's gifts couldn't have handled it then *or* now, but he did. Peter is a breath of fresh air.[1]

I cannot speak for you, but I certainly can for myself—this is a time when I could use some of Peter's "fresh air" in the form of a big dose of hope! These past two and a half years of my life and ministry have been anything but relaxed and settled. Having left a thriving, flourishing church where I had ministered for almost twenty-three years with a staff many would consider among the best in the country, and having stepped into a whole new arena of challenges—including endless commuting, facing the unknown, and accepting responsibilities outside the realm of my training, background, and expertise—I have found myself more than ever in need of hope. Solid, stable, sure hope. Hope to press on. Hope to endure. Hope to stay focused. Hope to see new dreams fulfilled.

And so it follows naturally that a book with this title has begun to flow from my pen. I trust that you who once smiled with me as we learned to laugh again by working our way through Paul's words to the Philippians are ready to travel with me through Peter's words as we now learn to hope again.

The journey will be worth the effort, I can assure you. We'll find hope around the corner of many of life's contingencies: hope beyond suffering and temptation . . . hope beyond immaturity and bitterness and the realities of our culture . . . hope beyond our trials and beyond times of dissatisfaction, guilt, and shame, to name only a few.

Best of all, we'll be guided on this journey by one who knew hopelessness firsthand, thanks to his own failures . . . and who experienced, firsthand, what it was like to hope again and again and again.

If that sounds like the kind of journey you need to take, read on. It will be a pleasure to travel with you, to be your companion on a road that leads to the healing of hurts and dreams fulfilled.

A Prayer for Hope Beyond Failure

Dear Father, every person reading these words, including the one writing them, has experienced failure. It has left us broken and disappointed in ourselves. And there are times when a flashback of those failures returns to haunt us. How sad it makes us when we recall those moments! Thank You for the remarkable transformation made possible by forgiveness. Thank You for understanding that "we are but dust," often incapable of fulfilling our own promises or living up to our own expectations.

Renew our hope—hope beyond failure—as we read and reflect on the words of Peter, with whom we can so easily identify. Remind us that, just as You used him after he had failed repeatedly, You will also use us, by Your grace.

May we find fresh encouragement from his words and new strength from his counsel as we journey together with Peter as our guide. We look to You for the ability to hope again, for You, alone, have the power to make something beautiful and good out of lives littered with the debris of words we should never have said and deeds we should never have done.

Our only source of relief comes through Your grace. Bring it to our attention again and again as we discover the truths You led the old fisherman to write so many years ago. In the gracious name of Jesus, I ask this.

AMEN

2

❖

Hope Beyond Suffering

How We Can
Smile Through
Suffering

WE DON'T LOOK ALIKE. We don't act alike. We don't dress alike. We have different tastes in the food we eat, the books we read, the cars we drive, and the music we enjoy. You like opera; I like country. We have dissimilar backgrounds, goals, and motivations. We work at different jobs, and we enjoy different hobbies. You like rock climbing; I like Harleys. We ascribe to a variety of philosophies and differ over politics. We have our own unique convictions on child-rearing and education. Our weights vary. Our heights vary. So does the color of our skin.

But there is one thing we all have in common: We all know what it means to hurt.

Suffering is a universal language. Tears are the same for Jews or Muslims or Christians, for white or black or brown, for children or adults or the elderly. When life hurts and our dreams fade, we may express our anguish in different ways, but each one of us knows the sting of pain and heartache, disease and disaster, trials and sufferings.

Joseph Parker, a great preacher of yesteryear, once said to a group of aspiring young ministers, "Preach to the suffering and you will never lack a congregation. There is a broken heart in every pew."

Truly, suffering is the common thread in all our garments.

This has been true since the beginning, when sin entered the world and Adam and Eve were driven from the Garden. It shouldn't surprise us, therefore, that when the apostle Peter wrote his first letter to fellow believers scattered throughout much of Asia Minor he focused on the one subject that drew all of them together. Suffering. These people were being singed by the same flames of persecution that would take the apostle's life in just a few years. Their circumstances were the bleakest imaginable. Yet Peter didn't try to pump them up with positive thinking. Instead, he gently reached his hand to their chins and lifted their faces skyward—so they could see beyond their circumstances to their celestial calling.

> Peter, an apostle of Jesus Christ, to those who reside as aliens, scattered throughout Pontius, Galatia, Cappadocia, Asia, and Bithynia, who are chosen according to the foreknowledge of God the Father, by the sanctifying work of the Spirit, that you may obey Jesus Christ and be sprinkled with His blood: May grace and peace be yours in fullest measure. (1 Pet. 1:1–2)

The men and women Peter wrote to knew what it was like to be away from home, not by choice but by force. Persecuted for their faith, they had been pushed out into a world that was not only unfamiliar but hostile.

Warren Wiersbe, in a fine little book entitled *Be Hopeful*, says this about the recipients of the letter:

> The important thing for us to know about these "scattered strangers" is that they were going through a time of suffering and persecution. At least fifteen times in this letter, Peter referred to suffering; and he used eight different Greek words to do so. Some of these Christians were suffering because they were living godly lives and doing what was good and right.... Others were suffering reproach for the name of Christ... and being railed at by unsaved people.... Peter wrote to encourage them

to be good witnesses to their persecutors, and to remember that their suffering would lead to glory.[1]

Take another look at the beginning of that last sentence: "Peter wrote to encourage them to be good witnesses to their persecutors." It is so easy to read that. It is even easier to preach it. But it is extremely difficult to do it. If you have ever been mistreated, you know what a great temptation it is to retaliate, to defend yourself, to fight back, to treat the other person as he or she has treated you. Peter wants to encourage his fellow believers to put pain in perspective and find hope beyond their suffering.

While most of us are not afflicted by horrible persecution for our faith, we do know what it means to face various forms of suffering, pain, disappointment, and grief. Fortunately, in the letter of 1 Peter we can find comfort and consolation for our own brand of suffering. Just as this treasured document spoke to the believers scattered in Pontius or Galatia or Cappadocia or Asia, so it speaks to us in Texas and California, Arizona and Oklahoma, Minnesota and Maine.

The first good news Peter gives us is the knowledge that we are "chosen by God." What a helpful reminder! We aren't just thrown on this earth like dice tossed across a table. We are sovereignly and lovingly placed here for a purpose, having been chosen by God. His choosing us was *according to His foreknowledge, by the sanctifying work of the Spirit, that we may obey Jesus Christ, having been sprinkled with His blood.* Powerful words!

God has given us a purpose for our existence, a reason to go on, even though that existence includes tough times. Living through suffering, we become sanctified—in other words, set apart for the glory of God. We gain perspective. We grow deeper. We grow up!

Can you imagine going through such times without Jesus Christ? I can't. But frankly, that's what most people do. They face those frightening fears and sleepless nights in the hospital without Christ. They struggle with a wayward teenager without Christ. Alone, they endure the awful words from a mate, "I don't want to live with you any longer. I want my freedom. I don't love you any more. I'm gone." And they go through it all without Christ.

For souls like these, life is one painful sting after another. Just imagining what life must be like without Christ, I am surprised that more people who live without hope don't take their own lives. As appalled as I am by Jack Kevorkian and his death-on-demand philosophy, I am not surprised. What surprises me is that more people don't simply put an end to it all.

Yet if we will only believe and ask, a full measure of God's grace and peace is available to any of us. By the wonderful, prevailing mercy of God, we can find purpose in the scattering and sadness of our lives. We can not only deal with suffering but rejoice through it. Though our pain and our disappointment and the details of our suffering may differ, there is an abundance of God's grace and peace available to each one of us.

These truths form the skeleton of strong doctrine. But unless the truths are fleshed out they remain hard and bony and difficult to embrace. Knowing this, Peter reminds his readers of all they have to cling to so that they can actually rejoice in times of suffering, drawing on God's grace and peace in fullest measure.

Rejoicing Through Hard Times

As I read and ponder Peter's first letter, I find six reasons why we as believers can rejoice through hard times and experience hope beyond suffering.

We Have a Living Hope

> Blessed be the God and Father of our Lord Jesus Christ, who according to His great mercy has caused us to be born again to a living hope through the resurrection of Jesus Christ from the dead. (1 Pet. 1:3)

As difficult as some pages of our life may be, nothing that occurs to us on this earth falls into the category of "the final chapter." That chapter will not be completed until we arrive in heaven and step into the presence of the living God. Our final meeting is not with the antagonist in our life's story but with the author Himself.

"Who can mind the journey," asks the late, great Bible teacher James M. Gray, "when the road leads home?"

How can we concern ourselves that much over what happens on this temporary planet when we know that it is all leading us to our eternal destination? Peter calls that our "living hope," and he reminds us that it is based on the resurrection of Jesus Christ. If God brought His Son through the most painful trials and back from the pit of death itself, certainly He can bring us through whatever we face in this world, no matter how deep that pit might seem at the time.

Do you realize how scarce hope is to those without Christ? One cynical writer, H. L. Mencken, an American newspaperman during the early half of this century, referred to hope as "a pathological belief in the occurrence of the impossible."

To the unsaved, hope is nothing more than mental fantasy, like wishing upon a star. It's the kind of Disneyland hope that says, "I sure hope I win the lottery." . . . "I hope my boy comes home someday." . . . "I hope everything works out OK." That's not a living hope. That's wishful thinking.

But those who are "born again" in the Lord Jesus Christ have been promised a living hope through His resurrection from the dead.

So if you want to smile through your tears, if you want to rejoice through times of suffering, just keep reminding yourself that, as a Christian, what you're going through isn't the end of the story . . . it's simply the rough journey that leads to the right destination.

"Hope is like an anchor," someone has said. "Our hope in Christ stabilizes us in the storms of life, but unlike an anchor, it does not hold us back."

We Have a Permanent Inheritance

Blessed be the God and Father of our Lord Jesus Christ, who according to His great mercy has caused us . . . to obtain an inheritance which is

257

imperishable and undefiled and will not fade away, reserved in heaven for you. (1 Pet. 1:3–4)

We also can rejoice through suffering because we have a permanent inheritance—a secure home in heaven. And our place there is reserved under the safekeeping, under the constant, omnipotent surveillance of Almighty God. Nothing can destroy it, defile it, diminish it, or displace it. Isn't that a great relief?

Have you ever had the disconcerting experience of finding someone else in the theater or airplane seat you had reserved? You hold the proper ticket, but someone else is in your seat. At best it's awkward; at worst it can lead to an embarrassing confrontation.

Have you ever made guaranteed reservations at your favorite hotel for a "nonsmoking" room and arrived late at night to find they have given it to someone else? What a disappointment! You give them your guaranteed reservation number and they punch endless information into the computer, then they look at you as though you've just landed from Mars. Your heart sinks. You force a smile and ask to speak to the manager. He comes out, stares at the same computer screen, then gives you the same look with a slightly deeper frown. "Sorry," he says. "There must be some kind of mistake."

Well, that's not going to happen in glory! God will not look at you like, "Now, what did you say your name was again?" The living God will ultimately welcome you home to your permanent, reserved inheritance. Your name is on the door.

I don't know what that does to you, but it sure gives me a reason to rejoice. The more difficult life gets on this earth, the better heaven seems.

We Have a Divine Protection

[We]... are protected by the power of God, through faith for a salvation ready to be revealed in the last time. (1 Pet. 1:5)

Under heaven's lock and key, we are protected by the most efficient security system available—the power of God. There is no way we will be lost in the process of suffering. No disorder, no disease, not even death itself can weaken or threaten God's ultimate protection over our lives. No matter what the calamity, no matter what the disappointment or depth of pain, no matter what kind of destruction occurs in our bodies at the time of death, our souls are divinely protected.

Our world is filled with warfare, with atrocities, with terrorism. Think of those men and women, especially those precious, innocent children, whose lives were shattered in an instant on that April 1995 morning in Oklahoma City when the world blew up around them. What happens in such times of tragic calamities? Is our eternal inheritance blown away with our bodies? Absolutely not. Even through the most horrible of deaths, He who made us from the dust of the earth protects us by His power and promises to deliver us to our eternal destination.

"God stands between you and all that menaces your hope or threatens your eternal welfare," James Moffatt wrote. "The protection here is entirely and directly the work of God."

Two words will help you cope when you run low on hope: *accept* and *trust.*

Accept the mystery of hardship, suffering, misfortune, or mistreatment. Don't try to understand it or explain it. Accept it. Then, deliberately *trust* God to protect you by His power from this very moment to the dawning of eternity.

We Have a Developing Faith

In this you greatly rejoice, even though now for a little while, if necessary, you have been distressed by various trials, that the proof of your faith, being more precious than gold which is perishable, even though tested by fire, may be found to result in praise and glory and honor at the revelation of Jesus Christ. (1 Pet. 1:6–7)

Here is the first of several references in Peter's letter to rejoicing. The words "even though" indicate that the joy is unconditional. It does not depend on the circumstances surrounding us. And don't

259

overlook the fact that this joy comes *in spite of* our suffering, not because of it, as some who glorify suffering would have us believe. We don't rejoice because times are hard; we rejoice in spite of the fact that they are hard.

These verses also reveal three significant things about trials.

First, trials are often necessary, proving the genuineness of our faith and at the same time teaching us humility. Trials reveal our own helplessness. They put us on our face before God. They make us realistic. Or, as someone has said, "Pain plants the flag of reality in the fortress of a rebel heart." When rebels are smacked by reality, it's amazing how quickly humility replaces rigidity.

Second, trials are distressing, teaching us compassion so that we never make light of another's test or cruelly force others to smile while enduring it.

How unfair to trivialize another person's trial by comparing what he or she is going through with what someone else has endured. Even if you have gone through something you think is twice as difficult, comparison doesn't comfort. It doesn't help the person who has lost a child to hear that you endured the loss of two.

Express your sympathy and weep with them. Put your arm around them. Don't reel off a lot of verses. Don't try to make the hurting person pray with you or sing with you if he or she is not ready to do that. Feel what that person is feeling. Walk quietly and compassionately in his or her shoes.

Third, trials come in various forms. The word *various* comes from an interesting Greek term, *poikolos,* which means "variegated" or "many colored." We also get the term "polka dot" from it. Trials come in a variety of forms and colors. They are different, just as we are different. Something that would hardly affect you might knock the slats out from under me—and vice versa. But God offers special grace to match every shade of sorrow.

Paul had a thorn in the flesh, and he prayed three times for God to remove it. "No," said God, "I'm not taking it away." Finally Paul said, "I've learned to trust in You, Lord. I've learned to live with it."

It was then God said, "My grace is sufficient for that thorn." He matched the color of the test with the color of grace.

This variety of trials is like different temperature settings on God's furnace. The settings are adjusted to burn off our dross, to temper us or soften us according to what meets our highest need. It is in God's refining fire that the authenticity of our faith is revealed. And the purpose of these fiery ordeals is that we may come forth as purified gold, a shining likeness of the Lord Jesus Christ Himself. That glinting likeness is what ultimately gives glory and praise and honor to our Savior.

We Have an Unseen Savior

> And though you have not seen Him, you love Him, and though you do not see Him now, but believe in Him, you greatly rejoice with joy inexpressible and full of glory. (1 Pet. 1:8)

Keep in mind that the context of this verse is suffering. So we know that Peter is not serving up an inconsequential, theological hors d'oeuvre. He's giving us solid meat we can sink our teeth into. He's telling us that our Savior is standing alongside us in that furnace. He is there even though we can't see Him.

You don't have to see someone to love that person. The blind mother has never seen her children, but she loves them. You don't have to see someone to believe in him or her. Believers today have never seen a physical manifestation of the Savior—we have not visibly seen Him walking among us—but we love Him nevertheless. In times of trial we sense He is there, and that causes us to "greatly rejoice" with inexpressible joy.

Some, like the struggling, reflective disciple Thomas, need to see and touch Jesus in order to believe. But Jesus said, "Blessed are they who did not see, and yet believed" (John 20:29). Even though we can't see Jesus beside us in our trials, He is there—just as He was when Shadrach, Meshach, and Abednego were thrown into the fiery furnace.

We Have a Guaranteed Deliverance

> ...obtaining as the outcome of your faith the salvation of your souls. (1 Pet. 1:9)

How can we rejoice through our pain? How can we have hope beyond our suffering? Because we have a living hope, we have a permanent inheritance, we have divine protection, we have a developing faith, we have an unseen Savior, and we have a guaranteed deliverance.

This isn't the kind of delivery the airlines promise you when you check your bags. ("Guaranteed arrival. No problem.") I'll never forget a trip I took a few years ago. I went to Canada for a conference with plans to be there for eight days. Thanks to the airline, I only had my clothes for the last two! When I finally got my luggage, I noticed the tags on them were all marked "Berlin." ("Guaranteed arrival. No problem." They just don't guarantee when or where the bags will arrive!) That's why we now see so many people boarding airplanes with huge bags hanging from their shoulders and draped over both arms. Don't check your bags, these folks are saying, because they probably won't get there when you do.

But when it comes to spiritual delivery, we never have to worry. God guarantees deliverance of our souls, which includes not only a deliverance from our present sin but the glorification of our physical bodies as well. Rejoice! You're going to get there—guaranteed.

Rejoicing, Not Resentment

When we are suffering, only Christ's perspective can replace our resentment with rejoicing. I've seen it happen in hospital rooms. I've seen it happen in families. I've seen it happen in my own life.

Our whole perspective changes when we catch a glimpse of the purpose of Christ in it all. Take that away, and it's nothing more than a bitter, terrible experience.

Nancy and Ed Huizinga in Grand Rapids, Michigan, know all about this. In December 1995, while they were at church rehearsing for the annual Christmas Festival of Lights program, their home burned to the ground. But that wasn't their only tragedy that year. Just three months earlier, Nancy's long-time friend, Barb Post, a widow with two children, had died of cancer. Nancy and Ed had taken her two children, Jeff and Katie, into their home as part of their family, something they had promised Barb they would do. So when Ed and Nancy's house burned to the ground just before Christmas, it wasn't just their home that was lost; it was the home of two teenagers who had already lost their mother and father.

As circumstances unfolded, irony went to work. The tragedy that forced the Huizingas from their home allowed Jeff and Katie to move back to theirs. Since their home had not yet been sold following their mother's death, they and the Huizinga family moved in there the night after the fire.

On the following Saturday, neighbors organized a party to sift through the ashes and search for anything of value that might have survived. One of the first indications they received of God's involvement in their struggle came as a result of that search. Somehow a piece of paper survived. On it were these words: "Contentment: Realizing that God has already provided everything we need for our present happiness."

To Nancy and Ed, this was like hearing God speak from a burning bush. It was the assurance they needed that He was there ... and He was not silent.

Nancy's biggest frustration now is dealing with insurance companies and trying to assess their material losses. Many possessions, of course, were irreplaceable personal items such as photographs and things handed down from parents and grandparents. But her highest priority is Jeff and Katie, along with her own two children, Joel and Holly. The loss has been hardest on them, she says.

"They don't have the history of God's faithfulness that Ed and I have. We've had years to make deposits in our 'faith account,' but they haven't. We've learned that if you fail to stock up on faith when you don't need it, you won't have any when you do need it. This has been our opportunity to use what we've been learning."

While the world might view this as a senseless tragedy, deserving of resentment, Nancy and Ed have seen God reveal Himself to them and refine them through this fire as He pours out a full measure of grace and peace.[2]

Suffering comes in many forms and degrees, but His grace is always there to carry us beyond it. I've lived long enough and endured a sufficient number of trials to say without hesitation that only Christ's perspective can replace our resentment with rejoicing. Jesus is the central piece of suffering's puzzle. If we fit Him into place, the rest of the puzzle—no matter how complex and enigmatic—begins to make sense.

Only Christ's salvation can change us from spectators to participants in the unfolding drama of redemption. The scenes will be demanding. Some may be tragic. But only then will we understand the role that suffering plays in our lives. Only then will we be able to tap into hope beyond our suffering.

A Prayer for Hope Beyond Suffering

Lord, mere words about hope and encouragement and purpose can really fall flat if things aren't right in our lives. If we're consumed by rage and resentment, somehow these words seem meaningless. But when our hearts are right, we hear with new ears. Then, rather than resisting these words, we appreciate them, and we love You for them.

Give us grace to match our trials. Give us a sense of hope and purpose beyond our pain. And give us fresh assurance that we're not alone, that Your plan has not been aborted though our suffering intensifies.

Help those of us who are on our feet right now to maintain a compassion for those who aren't. Give us a word of encouragement for others living in a world of hurt.

Let us never forget that every jolt in this rugged journey from earth to heaven is a reminder that we're on the right road.

I ask this in the compassionate name of the Man of Sorrows who was acquainted with grief.

AMEN

3

Hope Beyond Temptation

Staying Clean
in a
Corrupt Society

WOULDN'T IT BE wonderful if God would save us and then, within a matter of seconds, take us on to glory? Wouldn't that be a great relief? We would never have any temptations. We would never have to battle with the flesh. We would never even have the possibility of messing up our lives. We could just be whisked off to glory—saved, sanctified, galvanized, glorified! Trouble is, I have a sneaking suspicion that many, if not most, would wait until fifteen minutes before takeoff time to give their lives to Christ and then catch the jet for glory.

Since that's not an option and since it's clearly God's preference that we prove ourselves blameless and innocent and above reproach, we obviously have to come up with an alternative route. Some have suggested sanctification by isolation, believing the only way to keep evil and corruption from rubbing off on you is to withdraw from the world. After all, how can you walk through a coal mine without getting dirty? The logic seems irrefutable.

But God, in His infinite wisdom, has deliberately left us on this earth. He has sovereignly chosen to give many of us more years *in* Christ than *out* of Christ—many more years to live for Him "in the midst of a crooked and perverse generation, among whom you appear as lights in the world" (Phil. 2:15). Or, as one of my mentors, the late Ray Stedman, so succinctly put it, "Crooked and perverse simply means we are left in a world of crooks and perverts." That's the kind of world God left us in on purpose.

Don't think for a minute, however, that the Lord has made a mistake leaving us here. We are His lights in a dark world. In fact, just minutes before Jesus' arrest and ultimate death on the cross, He prayed this for His disciples and for us:

> I have given them Thy word; and the world has hated them, because they are not of the world, even as I am not of the world. I do not ask Thee to take them out of the world, but to keep them from the evil one. (John 17:14–15)

Think about that. "I'm not asking You to take them out from among the midst of a crooked and perverse generation," Jesus said. "But I do ask You to guard them, to protect them." Jesus doesn't ask the Father to isolate His disciples from the world but to insulate them, "to keep them from the evil one."

He has left us in the world on purpose and for His purpose. In a world where the majority are going the wrong way, we are left as lights—stoplights, directional lights, illuminating lights—as living examples, as strong testimonies of the right way. We are spiritual salmon swimming upstream.

The Seductive Cosmos Mentality

Few things are more awesome than pictures of earth the astronauts have taken from space. Our big, blue-and-white marble planet stands out so beautifully against the deep darkness of space. However, that's not the "world" Jesus has in mind here. He's not talking about the visible planet named Earth; He's talking about a philosophy that envelopes earthlings. It's not a place but a system—a system that finds its origin in the Enemy himself. It's a figure of speech that encapsulates the mind-set and morality of the unregenerate. It's what John calls the *cosmos*.

> Do not love the world, nor the things in the world. If anyone loves the world, the love of the Father is not in him. For all that is in the world [the *cosmos*], the lust of the flesh and the lust of the eyes and the boastful pride of life, is not from the Father, but is from the world. And the world is passing away, also its lusts; but the one who does the will of God abides forever. (1 John 2:15–17)

The physical world upon which we have our feet planted is visible. It can be measured. It can be felt. It has color and odor and texture. It's tangible...obvious. What is not so obvious is the system that permeates and operates within lives on this earth. It is a world-system manipulated by the pervasive hand of Satan and his demons, who pull the strings to achieve the adversary's wicked ends. If we are ever to extricate ourselves from those strings, we must be able to detect them and understand where they lead.

So what is this system? What is its philosophy? What is the frame of reference of the *cosmos*—its thinking, its drives, its goals?

The first thing we need to know is that it is a system that operates apart from and at odds with God. It's designed to appeal to us, to attract us, to seduce us with its sequined garb of fame, fortune, power, and pleasure. God's ways are often uncomfortable, but the world-system is designed to make us comfortable, to give us pleasure, to gain our favor, and ultimately to win our support. The philosophy of the world-system is totally at odds with the philosophy of God.

Greek grammarian Kenneth Wuest wrote:

> *Kosmos* refers to an ordered system...of which Satan is the head, his fallen angels and demons are his emissaries, and the unsaved of the human race are his subjects....Much in this world-system is religious, cultured, refined, and intellectual. But it is anti-God and anti-Christ.

...This world of unsaved humanity is inspired by "the spirit of the age," ...which Trench defines as follows: "All that floating mass of thoughts, opinions, maxims, speculations, hopes, impulses, aims, aspirations, at any time current in the world, which it may be impossible to seize and accurately define, but which constitutes a most real and effective power, being the moral, or immoral atmosphere which at every moment of our lives we inhale, again inevitably to exhale."[1]

You want to know what we are inhaling? Pay close attention to the commercials on television and observe what they're advertising and how virtually every word, picture, and sound is designed to pull you in, to make you dissatisfied with what you have and what you look like and who you are. The great goal is to make you want whatever it is that is being sold.

But it's not just on television. The world-system, the cosmos philosophy, is everywhere. It's going on all the time, even when you can't see it, and especially when you're not thinking about it. It's whistling its appeal, "Come on. Come on. You'll love it. This is so much fun. It'll make you look so good. It'll make you feel so good." It motivates us by appealing to our pride and to that which pleases us, all the while cleverly seducing us away from God.

And over all this realm, don't forget, Satan is prince.

A Challenge to Be Different

The pull of the world is every bit as strong and subtle as gravity. So invisible, yet so irresistible. So relentlessly there. Never absent or passive.

Unless we realize how strong and how subtle the world's influence really is, we won't understand the passion behind Peter's words.

Living in Holiness

Therefore, gird your minds for action, keep sober in spirit, fix your hope completely on the grace to be brought to you at the revelation of Jesus Christ. As obedient children, do not be conformed to the former lusts

272

which were yours in your ignorance, but like the Holy One who called you, be holy yourselves also in all your behavior; because it is written, "You shall be holy, for I am holy." (1 Pet. 1:13–16)

Reading these statements, we can't help but catch something of Peter's assertive spirit. He seems to be saying that this is no time to kick back; this isn't a day to be passive. In fact, I think Peter really bears down with his pen at this point. Look at the forcefulness of his phrases: "gird your minds for action" ... "keep sober" ... "fix your hope." He spits them out in staccato form. Today we might say, "Straighten up!" ... "Get serious!" And then the clincher command from God, saying, in essence: "Be holy like I am."

It's easy to let the world intoxicate us and fuzz our minds. But if we're to shake ourselves out of that dizzying spell, we must resist the power it exerts on us.

I think Peter is saying, "You have to realize that even though you're living in the cosmos, your mind, your eyes, *your focus* must be beyond the present." Kenneth Wuest suggests this: "Set your hope perfectly, unchangeably, without doubt and despondency."

That goes back to what we were thinking about in the previous chapter. No matter how bad things get, fix your mind beyond what's happening around you and what's happening to you. Otherwise you'll erode into the cosmos mentality.

I love the way verse 14 begins, "As obedient children...." Isn't that affirming? Rather than coming down on his fellow believers, assuming they're disobedient, Peter assumes just the opposite here. "You're obedient children."

Through the years, my wife, Cynthia, and I found that if we referred to our children as good kids, obedient kids, kids we were proud of, that attitude instilled in them a sense that Mom and Dad had confidence and trust in them. And that's the attitude Peter employs when he tells the believers scattered throughout the ancient world: "As obedient children, do not be conformed." This also reminds me of Paul's words to believers in Romans 12:2: "And do not be conformed to this world, but be transformed...."

How easy it is to allow the world, the cosmos, to suck you into its system. If you do, if you conform, then you are adopting the kind of lifestyle that was yours when you were in ignorance, when you didn't know there was another way to live. That was back when the cosmos was your comfort zone.

Have you been in Christ so long that you have forgotten what it was like to be without Him? Remember, He has called us to follow in His footsteps—to be *holy* "like the Holy One who called you, be holy yourselves also in all your behavior; because it is written, 'YOU SHALL BE HOLY, FOR I AM HOLY.'" We have a Father who is holy, and as His children, we're to be like Him.

But what does it mean to be *holy*? That's always a tough question to answer. Stripped down to its basics, the term *holy* means "set apart" in some special and exclusive way. Perhaps it will help if we think of it in another context. In holy matrimony, for example, a man and a woman are set apart, leaving all others as they bond exclusively to each other.

When I was a young man and a young husband serving in the marines, I was eight thousand miles away from my wife. I knew Cynthia existed. I could read her letters and occasionally hear her voice on the phone, but I couldn't see her or touch her. I had only the memory of our standing together three years earlier before God and a minister who had pronounced us husband and wife, setting us apart exclusively to each other for the rest of our lives. We were wed back in June 1955, but regardless of how long ago it was, we stood together and committed ourselves to a *holy* intermingling of our lives. To be intimate with another woman would break that holy relationship, that exclusive oneness. Remembering that helped keep me faithful to my wife while we were apart those many months...and it still helps over forty-one years later!

Church ordinances or sacraments, such as baptism and communion, are often called *holy*. In Holy Communion, for example, the bread and wine are set apart from common use and set aside to God alone. The same meaning lies behind the word *sanctify* in 1 Peter 3:15: "But sanctify Christ as Lord in your hearts." I love that. We are to "set Him apart" as Lord in our hearts.

What a successful way to deal with the cosmos! To begin the morning by saying, "Lord, I set apart my mind for You today. I set apart my passion. I set apart my eyes. I set apart my ears. I set apart my motives. I set apart my discipline. Today I set apart every limb of my body and each area of my life unto You as Lord over my life." When we start our day like that, chances are good that temptation's winks will not be nearly as alluring.

Walking in Fear

And if you address as Father the One who impartially judges according to each man's work, conduct yourselves in fear during the time of your stay upon earth. (1 Pet. 1:17)

Another secret of living a godly life in the midst of a godless world involves the way we conduct ourselves hour by hour through the day. Peter says we are to do it "in *fear*." We don't hear much about the *fear* of God today, and when we do, some may think only of images of a fire-and-brimstone preacher pounding a pulpit. We need a better perspective. Perhaps the word *reverence* gives us a clearer picture of what Peter means here. In fact, the New International Version translates this phrase "live your lives as strangers here in reverent fear." The point is, if we're going to address God as Father, then we should conduct ourselves on earth in a way that reflects our reverence for Him as our Father.

Also, if you're going to address Him as your Father, if you're going to have a one-on-one relationship with Him in fellowship and in prayer, then conduct yourself as one who knows that you will someday have to account to Him for your life. Why? Well, in case you didn't know, "each one of us shall give account of himself to God" (Rom. 14:12).

When we die, we will be brought before the judgment seat of Christ where we will independently account for our lives before God. He will see us as our lives pass in review, and He will reward us accordingly. It's not a judgment to see if we get into heaven. That's taken care of. As we saw in the previous chapter, we can't lose our salvation. We can, however, lose our reward. At the judgment seat, Christ will judge our works and determine whether they were done in the power of the Spirit or in the energy of the flesh. We will all give an account of the deeds we have done in this life, and God will "test the quality of each man's work" (1 Cor. 3:13). That thought, alone, will instill a big, healthy dose of the fear of God in us!

We don't know how God is going to do this, but it helps me to put it into an everyday image we can understand. So I picture myself in the future standing there all alone before my heavenly Father. Along comes an enormous celestial dump truck, piled high with stuff. The truck backs up, the bed lifts up, and the whole load is dumped out in front me. The Lord and I talk about all the wood, hay, and stubble that's piled there, and then He begins digging through it. "Oh, there's a piece of gold," He says. "Hmm, here's some silver." With that He begins setting aside all the precious and permanent stuff. Then, *whoosh!* The wood, hay, and stubble are gone, instantly consumed by fire. Only the gold, silver, and precious stones that remain are rewarded.

In the 1988 Summer Olympics in Seoul, South Korea, Ben Johnson of Canada won the one-hundred-meter dash, setting a new Olympic record and a new world record. Our American contender, Carl Lewis, came in second, and most were shocked that he hadn't won the gold. After the race, the judges learned that Johnson had had an illegal substance in his body. He ran the race illegally, so the judges took away his medal. Though he ran faster and made an unforgettable impression, he did not deserve the reward.

Though the world and even our fellow Christians may be impressed with and applaud our deeds, let's not forget that God is the final judge! He searches our hearts; He alone knows our motivation. And He will be the One to say, "This deserves a reward. Ah, but that does not."

That's why we conduct ourselves in fear. That's why we walk in reverence. Because we know that He is checking for illegal substances. He knows whether down deep inside we have gotten sucked into the cosmos, whether we have bought into the system. He knows whether our noble acts and deeds are done out of pride and self-aggrandizement or whether they have been carried out in the power of the Spirit. He knows whether our inner, unseen thoughts and motives match our external words and works. He is pleased when our lives honor Him—inside and out. He is grieved when they do not. And it is *His* smile we want. It is *His* reward, not the reward of this world, not the applause of those around us, not the superficial spotlight of fame or fortune or power.

This Christian life is a tough fight. Earlier in this century, Donald Grey Barnhouse, a well-known minister and radio preacher, wrote an entire book on this subject, *The Invisible War*. This conflict is not a war fought with Uzis or tanks or smart bombs or ground-to-air missiles. The land mines, ambushes, and traps set by our enemy are much more subtle than that—and even more deadly, for they aim at the soul. And they are everywhere.

But with the pride and pleasures of the cosmos so alluring, how can weaklings like us run the race without being disqualified and forfeiting our reward? How can we win the battle over an enemy we can't see? The solution to that problem rests within our minds.

Focusing Your Mind

> …knowing that you were not redeemed with perishable things like silver or gold from your futile way of life inherited from your forefathers, but with precious blood, as of a lamb unblemished and spotless, the blood of Christ. For He was foreknown before the foundation of the world, but has appeared in these last times for the sake of you who through Him are believers in God, who raised Him from the dead and gave Him glory, so that your faith and hope are in God. (1 Pet. 1:18–20)

I'm convinced that the battle with this world is a battle within the mind. Our minds are major targets of the Enemy's appeal. When the world pulls back its bowstring, our minds are the bull's-eyes. Any arrows we allow to become impaled in our minds will ultimately poison our thoughts. And if we tolerate this long enough, we'll end up acting out what we think. So the third technique for counteracting that poison, for dealing with the seduction of the cosmos, the world around us, is to focus our minds on Christ. We can do this by remembering what our Savior has done for us. Or, to paraphrase 1 Peter, "remember what your inheritance cost your Savior."

The first thing Christ did for us was to deliver us from slavery—slavery to a "futile way of life." Whether we knew it or not, we were trapped in a lifestyle that had only empty pleasures and dead-end desires to offer. We were in bondage to our impulses spawned from our sinful nature. In such a condition, we were hopelessly unable to help ourselves. The only way for us to be emancipated from that slavery was to have someone redeem us. That ransom price was paid by Christ, not with gold or silver, but with His precious blood. In doing so, He broke the chains that bound us to this world. He opened the door and said, "Now you're free to live for Me and serve Me." That single emancipation proclamation made possible a life of hope beyond temptation.

The second thing Christ did for us was to come near and make Himself known; He "appeared in these last times for the sake of you who through Him are believers in God...so that your faith and hope are in God" (vv. 20–21). That makes the whole thing personal, doesn't it? He realized the enormity of our earth-born emptiness. He knew our inability to free ourselves. And He willingly stepped out of His privileged position in heaven to pay the ransom...for us! He gave Himself, not only so we could become free, but so we could be secure, with our faith and hope resting not precariously on our own shoulders but securely on His.

What is life like without Christ? Look at 1 Peter 4:3–4.

> For the time already past is sufficient for you to have carried out the desire of the Gentiles, having pursued a course of sensuality, lusts, drunkenness, carousels, drinking parties and abominable idolatries. And in all this, they are surprised that you do not run with them into the same excess of dissipation, and they malign you.

That's a pretty vivid description of the futile lifestyle of the lost. That's what we see around us every day—a lifestyle promising to satisfy, to bring happiness and pleasure and contentment. Yet it brings just the opposite. This lifestyle leads only to another hangover or another bout with guilt—if there is even enough conscience left for guilt. It's one "happy hour" (strange name!) after another. One high after another. One snort after another. One drug after another. One affair after another. One abortion after another. One partner after another. It's life lived for the highs, which are nothing more than temporary breaks in the lows. It's empty. It's hollow. It's miserable. It's exactly as Peter describes it: a "futile way of life."

And we've been redeemed from that, not with silver or gold, "but with precious blood, as of a lamb unblemished and spotless, the blood of Christ."

Techniques to Remember

When we're in the comfortable conclave of Christian fellowship, it's relatively easy to be holy, to conduct our lives in the fear of God, and to focus our minds on the Savior (at least externally). But when we're out in the world, when we're in the minority, it's different, isn't it?

If you want to stay clean, even when you're walking alone in the dark, low-ceilinged coal mine of the corrupt and secular culture, you need to remember a few practical things—four come to mind.

First, pay close attention to what you look at. This takes us back to verse 13, where we are told to gird our minds for action, keep sober in spirit, and fix our hope completely on the grace that's revealed in Jesus Christ.

Our eyes seem to be the closest connection to our minds. Through our eyes we bring in information and visual images. Through our eyes we feed our imaginations. Through our eyes we focus on things that are alluring and attractive and, don't kid yourself, extremely pleasurable for a while... *for a while.* Remember, the Bible says that Moses, by faith, gave up the "passing pleasures of sin" to walk with the people of God (Heb. 11:24–26). The cosmos offers pleasures, no doubt about it, but they are passing....

If then you have been raised up with Christ, keep seeking the things above, where Christ is, seated at the right hand of God. Set your mind on things above, not on the things that are on earth. (Col. 3:1–2)

Second, give greater thought to the consequences of sin rather than to its pleasures. One of the characteristics of the cosmos is that nobody ever mentions the ugly underside of pleasurable sins. If you're thinking about having an affair, if you are getting caught in that lustful trap, I strongly suggest that you walk through the consequences in your mind. Stroll slowly . . . ponder details. Think through the effects of that act in your life and in the lives of others whom your life touches.

In a *Leadership* magazine article titled "Consequences of a Moral Tumble," Randy Alcorn says that whenever he is feeling "particularly vulnerable to sexual temptation," he finds it helpful to review the effects such action could have. Some of things he mentions are:

- Grieving the Lord who redeemed me. . . .
- One day having to look Jesus . . . in the face and give an account of my actions. . . .
- Inflicting untold hurt on . . . your best friend and loyal wife. . . . losing [her] respect and trust.
- Hurting my beloved daughters. . . .
- Destroying my example and credibility with my children, and nullifying both present and future efforts to teach them to obey God. . . .
- Causing shame to my family. . . .
- Creating a form of guilt awfully hard to shake. Even though God would forgive me, would I forgive myself?
- Forming memories and flashbacks that could plague future intimacy with my wife.
- Wasting years of ministry training and experience for a long time, maybe permanently. . . .

- Undermining the faithful example and hard work of other Christians in our community.

- Bringing great pleasure to Satan, the enemy of God and all that is good. . . .

- Possibly bearing the physical consequences of such diseases as gonorrhea, syphilis, chlamydia, herpes, and AIDS; perhaps infecting [my wife] or, in the case of AIDS, even causing her death.

- Possibly causing pregnancy, with the personal and financial implications, including a lifelong reminder of my sin. . . .

- Causing shame and hurt to my friends, especially those I've led to Christ and discipled.[2]

And that's just a partial list of the consequences! It doesn't even begin to factor in the consequences for the other person in the affair and the number of people affected by his or her sin.

Take a realistic look at the other side of a moral tumble. For a change, force yourself to give greater thought to the painful consequences than to the passing pleasures of sin.

Third, begin each day by renewing your sense of reverence for God. Start each new day by talking to the Lord, even if that early-morning talk has to be brief.

"Lord, I'm here. I'm Yours. I want You to know that I'm Yours. Also I want to affirm that I reverence You. I give You my day. I will encounter strong seductive forces that will allure me. Since I am frail and fragile, I really need Your help."

If you know of some challenges you'll be facing that day, rehearse the areas of need. If you know a real test is coming, talk to the Lord about it. Then trade off with Him. Hand over your fragility and receive His strength in return. Reverence Him as the source of your power.

Fourth, periodically during each day focus fully on Christ. In his book *Spiritual Stamina*, Stuart Briscoe cites a good example of this:

It's fun watching young men in love. It can be even more fun when the romance is long distance.

You can predict what will happen. There'll be hours of late-night, heart-pounding telephone conversations. The postal service will be overrun with love notes crossing each other in the mail. Pillows will be soaked with tears.

But the most telling symptom is the glazed, faraway look in Romeo's eyes. I'm sure you've seen it. You ask the man a question and you get a blank stare. He's not at home. He's elsewhere. He's in another land. He's with his sweetheart.

You might say his heart is set on things afar, where Juliet is seated right by the telephone.[3]

That's being focused fully on another person. I challenge you to do this with your Lord. Deliberately set aside a few minutes every day when your eyes glaze over, when you don't realize where you are, when a telephone ring means nothing because you are focusing fully on Christ. Imagine Him as he walks with His disciples, touching those who were sick, praying for them in John 17, going to the cross, sitting with His disciples at the seashore and having broiled fish for breakfast. Then imagine Him as He is thinking about you, praying for you, standing with you, living in you.

These four techniques will help you stay clean in a corrupt society—to be in the world but not of it.

A Prayer for Hope Beyond Temptation

Thank You, Father, for Your truth preserved through the centuries. Thank You for the careful concern of a man like Peter who knew both sides of life on planet Earth: what it was to live in this old world and what it was to walk with the Savior, Your Son.

Lord, since You don't save us then suddenly take us home to glory, hear our prayer this day as we ask You to bring to our attention those things that will assist us in staying clean in a corrupt world. Give us an intense distaste for things that displease You and a renewed pleasure in things that bring You honor and magnify Your truth. As You do this, we will have what we need so much, hope beyond temptation.

I ask this for the honor of Him who consistently and victoriously withstood the blast of the Devil's temptations without relief, Jesus our Lord.

AMEN

4

◈

Hope Beyond Division

Reasons for
Pulling Together

BEFORE ANDREW JACKSON became the seventh president of the United States, he served as a major general in the Tennessee militia. During the War of 1812 his troops reached an all-time low in morale. As a result they began arguing, bickering, and fighting among themselves. It is reported that Old Hickory called them all together on one occasion when tensions were at their worst and said, "Gentlemen! Let's remember, the enemy is over *there!*"

His sobering reminder would be an appropriate word for the church today. In fact, I wonder if Christ sometimes looks down at us and says with a sigh, "Christians, your Enemy is over there! Stop your infighting! Pull for one another. Support one another. Believe in one another. Care for one another. Pray for one another. Love one another."

One of the most profound comments made regarding the early church came from the lips of a man named Aristides, sent by the Emperor Hadrian to spy out those strange creatures known as "Christians." Having seen them in action, Aristides returned with a mixed report. But his immortal words to the emperor have echoed down through history: "Behold! How they love one another."

How often do we hear such words today from those who don't know Christ but who have watched those of us who do? I'm inclined to think that it's much more likely that they say, "Behold! How they hurt one another!" . . . "Behold! How they judge one another!" . . . "Behold! How they criticize one another!" . . . "Behold! How they fight with one another!"

This is the generation that has given new meaning to the shameful practice of brother-bashing and sister-smashing. You would think we were enemies rather than members of the same family. Something is wrong with this picture.

The mark of the Christian should be a spirit of unity and genuine love for others, but the church today rarely demonstrates those qualities. We are looked on by the world as self-seeking and factious rather than loving and unified. You question that? Just step into a Christian bookstore and scan the shelves. What impression do you get? Do the books reflect love and unity within the body of Christ? Or do they reflect polarization, criticism, and judgment of one another? Better yet, sit back and observe what's going on in your own church. Are you overwhelmed with the love and unity that exudes from your local body of believers? Or are you saddened and disappointed by the political power plays and petty disagreements that block our ability to get along with one another?

Unity: An Almost Forgotten Virtue

To underscore this important quality, let's consider Jesus' words in John 13, where we find Him with His twelve disciples for the last time. They have met together for a meal in a second-floor room in the city of Jerusalem. Jesus notices that the men have come into the room with dirty feet—not surprising in that rocky, dusty land. What must have been disappointing was that none of the Twelve had voluntarily washed the others' feet. So during supper Jesus arose from the table and poured water into a basin and proceeded to go around the table and wash the disciples' feet.

What a scene it must have been! To this day, I shake my head when I imagine the Savior washing the dirty feet of His disciples.

> And so when He had washed their feet, and taken His garments, and reclined at the table again, He said to them, "Do you know what I have done to you?" (John 13:12)

Understand, He wasn't fishing for the obvious answer, "You've washed our feet, Master." He was looking for the answer He has to explain to them a few moments later:

> You call Me Teacher and Lord; and you are right, for so I am. If I then, the Lord and the Teacher, washed your feet, you also ought to wash one another's feet. For I gave you an example that you also should do as I did to you. (John 13:13–15)

I think most of Jesus' disciples would have gladly returned the favor and washed *His* feet. Peter out of embarrassment. John out of devotion. That would be easy to do. After all, they loved Him. Why wouldn't they take an opportunity to wash His feet—if only to make a good impression? But that is not what Jesus told them to do. Instead He said, *"Wash one another's feet."*

Then, a bit later, in their final hours together, He changed the subject from washing feet to showing love.

> A new commandment I give to you, that you love one another, even as I have loved you, that you also love one another. By this all men will know that you are My disciples, if you have love for one another. (John 13:34–35)

It's easy to love Christ for all He is, for all He's done. It's not so easy, however, to love other Christians. Yet that is the command we have been given. That compelling mark of the Christian will be a powerful witness to non-Christians. It has nothing to do with talking to the lost about their spiritual condition. It has everything to do with how we treat one another. If you want to make an impact on the world around you, this rugged society that is moving in the wrong direction more rapidly every year, He said, "love one another." That's how they'll know that you're different. Your love will speak with stunning eloquence to a lost world.

Then, as the oil lamps flickered away the last hour before His arrest and trial, Jesus prayed to the Father on behalf of His disciples.

> I do not ask in behalf of these alone [the disciples], but for those also who believe in Me through their word [that's you and me]; *that they may all be one*; even as Thou, Father, art in Me, and I in Thee, that they also may be in Us; that the world may believe that Thou didst send Me. And the glory which Thou hast given Me I have given to them; that they may be one, just as We are one; I in them, and Thou in Me, that they may be perfected in unity, that the world may know that Thou didst send Me, and didst love them, even as Thou didst love Me. (John 17:20–23, italics mine)

Look at that! Believe it or not, He was praying for us during those final hours. He was praying that you and I might make an impact on the world because of our unity with Him and with each other.

The margin notes of the New American Standard Bible gives this literal translation: "That they may be perfected *into a unit*." A unit is a team, folks. No more brother-bashing. No more sister-smashing. No more ugly gossip groups. No more sarcastic, judgmental put-downs. Jesus prayed that we would support and encourage and love and forgive each other until we are perfected into a unit.

Unity. That's what He desires for us. Not uniformity, but unity; oneness, not sameness. We don't have to look alike. We don't even have to think alike. The body is made up of many different parts. He doesn't even pray for unanimity. We can disagree. Every vote doesn't have to be 100 percent. But we must be a unit: our eyes on the same goal, our hearts in the same place, our commitment at the same level. And we must love each other.

If there is anything that would keep me away from Christ these days, if I were lost, it would be the attitude Christians have toward one another. That would do it. While there is much wonderful fellowship in the church where the fire of friendship warms and affirms us, there are still too many places where for the life of me I don't know how people stay in ministry. The conditions in which some men and women labor are occasionally beyond belief.

Paul wrote to the Philippians:

> Do nothing from selfishness or empty conceit, but with humility of mind let each of you regard one another as more important than himself; do not merely look out for your own personal interests, but also for the interests of others. (Phil. 2:3–4)

Selfishness and conceit and pride are the things that break down our fellowship and erode our unity. Everything you need to know about getting along well in a family, to say nothing of getting along well in a church, is right here in these verses.

If you're on a church board and you're wondering what's going wrong, what's missing, what's happened to the unity you once had, I'll guarantee somebody isn't abiding by these verses.

You want to pull together as the family of God? It's merely a matter of obeying Philippians 2:3–4. Stop looking for credit. Stop looking for what you can get out of it. Think about the other person instead of yourself. Don't be selfish. Sounds like something a teacher would say to a roomful of kindergartners, doesn't it? Yet how many adult problems could be solved if the elementary truths woven into these two verses were the driving force in our relationships with one another? How many committees could resolve their disputes? How many couples could reconcile their marital differences?

Love: A Never-to-Be-Forgotten Command

With the teachings of Christ and Paul as a backdrop, we are better able to understand and appreciate Peter's comments about love and unity. Remember, he was writing to hurting people. They were scattered, many of them far from home (see 1 Pet. 1:1). They were "distressed," living in extreme situations (1:6). They were being "tested" by "various trials" (1:6–7). Some of them were running for their lives. With the madman Nero on the throne in Rome, it was a dangerous time to be a Christian. Some, no doubt, were tempted to conform, compromise, or give up altogether.

When I was a kid and an argument broke out in our home, my dad always used to say, "We may have a few differences inside these walls, but just remember, we're family. If your brother or your sister needs you, you take care of 'em. You love 'em. You pull for 'em." Good advice for the church as well!

When people hurt—and we've all been there—it's easy to get a little thin on love. But that's what these people needed. They needed to pull together and support each other. They needed a community where they could find acceptance and unity. They needed to conduct themselves as members of the family of God.

Following his strong words encouraging fellow believers to live holy lives, Peter gives them a pep talk, explaining exactly how they have been freed to support each other. He says, in effect, "You have everything you need that makes it possible; you don't have to live in lonely isolation." Read his counsel carefully:

> Since you have in obedience to the truth purified your souls for a sincere love of the brethren, fervently love one another from the heart, for you have been born again not of seed which is perishable but imperishable, that is, through the living and abiding word of God. (1 Pet. 1:22–23)

As we read Peter's uplifting words, we see that he specifies three things that encourage mutual support. First, obedience to the truth. Second, purity of soul. Third, a lack of hypocrisy.

Being obedient to the truth means that we don't have to look at others through the distorted lenses of our own biases. We can see them as God sees them and love them as He loves them. This has a purifying effect on us. It purges us, not only from a limited perspective, but from prejudice, resentment, hurt feelings, and grudges. Such purity of soul helps us love each other without hypocrisy and with a sincere love. It doesn't blind us to each other's faults; it gives us the grace to overlook them.

The glue—the bonding element—that holds all this together is love: "Fervently love one another from the heart." Peter writes with a strong, emotional, passionate commitment that is difficult to pick up on in the English.

Two Greek words are used predominantly in the New Testament to describe love, and Peter uses both of them here. One is *philos*, which generally refers to a brotherly love or the love of a friend. That is the word he uses for "love of the brethren." The other is *agape*, a higher form of love, a more divine type of love, which is the word he uses for "love one another." Peter then intensifies both with passionate modifiers: "sincere," "fervently," and "from the heart."

> These Christians to whom Peter was writing already had a fondness and an affection for one another.... But if these Christians would blend the two kinds of love, saturate the human fondness and affection with the divine love with which they are exhorted to love one another, then that human affection would be transformed and elevated to a heavenly thing. Then the fellowship of saint with saint would be a heavenly fellowship, glorifying to the Lord Jesus, and most blessed in its results to themselves. There is plenty of the *phile* fondness and affection among the saints, and too little of the *agape* divine love.[1]

Maybe it's time to pause and take a look inside your own heart. Are you "fervently loving one another from the heart"? When I am snippy or negative, judgmental or ugly toward a brother or a sister, I look at myself with honesty, shining God's light of truth on my own attitude, and I invariably find that it's my heart that's not right. The old spiritual hymn says it well:

> It's not my brother nor my sister
> but it's me, O Lord,

Standin' in the need of prayer.
It's not the preacher nor the deacon
but it's me, O Lord,
Standin' in the need of prayer.

Support: Four Much-Needed Reminders

What kind of love and support do we need? What kind of love and support do we give? What about a "love one another" support group, in which we offer—and receive from—our brothers and sisters in the family of God this same kind of love and lack of judgmental spirit, this true affection, this arm around your shoulder, saying, "I'm in your corner"?

Many churches have support groups of various kinds in which individuals are actively involved in each other's lives. Through the years I've talked with lots of individuals who say they couldn't survive without such support groups.

Some are struggling through the backwash of a divorce, trying to gain self-respect and a sense of dignity again. Aided by the support of others who are going through, or have gone through, the same turmoil, they work through their feelings of rejection, sadness, and loneliness...then emerge stronger and more stable.

Some attend support groups because they are in the grip of an awful addiction. Right now they're clean or dry, but they realize they're just a day away, just an hour away, from the same old habit. The support of others keeps them strong and helps them hope again.

Most of these groups are not highly visible, but they're there for those who need them, week in and week out. With consistent regularity people keep coming because they find refuge in this safe and supportive harbor. They find love, acceptance, and a lack of judgmental spirit. They find tolerance and accountability. They find care and encouragement—and a word of affirmation from a sincere heart and an arm of support around the shoulder mean more than a thousand words from some frowning preacher.

What is it about the family of God that gives us this sense of one-ness and support? Since we don't have to look alike and we don't all have the same temperament and we don't all vote the same way at election time, what is it that draws believers together?

We Are Children of the Same Father

For you have been born again not of seed which is perishable but imperishable, that is, through the living and abiding word of God. (1 Pet. 1:23)

In the human family, there are various kinds of birth experiences. But in God's family, everybody begins the same way. We are all ad-opted. We all have the same Father. We all come to Him the same way—through His Son, Jesus Christ. We are all members of the same family. Our background, our education, our social connections, our job, or how much money we have in the bank—all these things are irrelevant. We've all been born anew. We're all brothers and sisters in the Lord.

We Take Our Instruction from the Same Source

Not of seed which is perishable but imperishable, that is, through the living and abiding word of God. For,
"All flesh is like grass,
And all its glory like the flower of grass.
The grass withers,
And the flower falls off,
But the word of the Lord abides forever."
And this is the word which was preached to you. (1 Pet. 1:23b–25)

The seed is the Word of God, our reliable source of truth, and we all get our instruction from this source. But for that seed to grow and produce fruit in our lives, it must be embraced and applied.

There's nothing automatic about being exposed to the same source of truth. We may all hear the same Sunday morning message, but unless our ears are attentive and our hearts prepared, that seed will be picked up in Satan's beak and winged right out of our lives.

You can sit and listen to truth being delivered, and it can change your life in a moment's time. Yet someone sitting right next to you, hearing the same insightful information, can go right on living against the will of God.

We have a responsibility, not only to hear the truth, but to apply it. Just being exposed to the truth will not change us. You can put me in a room with a dozen beautiful Steinway pianos and leave me there for hours, but I still won't be able to sit down and play. You could put an accomplished pianist at every one and expose me to hours of exquisite music, but even in that stimulating environment I wouldn't be able to sit down and play. Bringing beautiful music from those black-and-white keys takes work—commitment, dedication, private lessons, and untold hours of practice.

We Have the Same Struggles

> Therefore, putting aside all malice and all guile and hypocrisy and envy and all slander.... (1 Pet. 2:1)

In case you've ever wondered what breaks down the fellowship, what keeps us from pulling together, there's your list. Read each one slowly and form pictures in your mind: malice, guile, hypocrisy, envy, and slander. In weaker moments we fall back on them, but God says, "put them aside"—get rid of them. If you want to move beyond your divisions, beyond your differences, if you want to become one in the Lord, lose them. And, by His grace, let them go!

Let's return to this list and probe a little deeper.

Malice. The Greek word here is a general word for the wickedness that characterizes unbelievers entrenched in the world system. These are the sins that hurt and injure others.

Guile. The Greek word means two-facedness, deception, or trickery. In its earliest form, this word meant "to catch with bait." It refers to a deception that is aimed at attaining one's own end—a hidden agenda.

Hypocrisy. The Greek word here means to act a part, to hide behind a mask, to appear to be someone else. This is what happens when we try to be someone or something we are not.

Some family members have a tendency to be envious of those who are going through "good times." Others have a tendency to slander those who are going through a bad patch. The next two sins are kind of the flip side of each other, and we are told to put both aside.

Envy is not only hidden resentment over another's advantage, but wanting that same advantage for yourself. According to Webster, it is "painful or resentful awareness of an advantage enjoyed by another joined with a desire to possess the same advantage." In other words, someone has something you don't have and you long to have it yourself. Edward Gordon Selwyn comments on the Greek term, saying that this sin is "a constant plague of all voluntary organizations, not least religious organizations, and to which even the Twelve themselves were subject at the very crisis of our Lord's ministry."[2]

Slander is even more vicious. Literally the word means "evil speaking." It occurs most often when the victim is not there to offer a defense or set the record straight. Often disguised as rumor or bad news or just passing on information, slander is disparaging gossip that destroys one's confidence in another, discoloring or harming that person's reputation. It can be as mild as bad-mouthing or as vile as backstabbing. When the tongue is used for slander, it becomes a lethal weapon.

Peter commands us to "strip off" these five outdated garments that once belonged to our old natures! If all of us in God's family were mutually committed to such behavior, can you imagine the pleasure we could enjoy together? But it'll never happen until we "strip off" the old garments that keep us carnal.

We Focus on the Same Objectives

Like newborn babes, long for the pure milk of the word, that by it you may grow in respect to salvation, if you have tasted the kindness of the Lord. (1 Pet. 2:2–3)

What is the objective of all this? Maturity. "Grow up," Peter says. And our model? The Lord Himself.

For three and a half years Peter followed Jesus everywhere He went. Why? Because he had "tasted the kindness of the Lord."

Nourished by that kindness, Peter grew toward greater maturity, and so can we!

What do people think of after they have had a conversation or a meal with you? What do they think after they have worked alongside you? Do they think, "How kind he is. What a kind person she is"? Selflessly giving ourselves to one another is the key to unity. Our relationships with others are to be built upon the example of the selflessness Christ first demonstrated.

It's so basic, isn't it? It reminds me of Robert Fulghum's *All I Really Need to Know I Learned in Kindergarten*, which I read when it originated as an article in the *Kansas City Times*. In it he said, "Share everything. Play fair. Don't hit people. Put things back where you found them. Clean up your own mess. Don't take things that aren't yours. Say you're sorry when you hurt somebody.... And it is still true, no matter how old you are: When you go out into the world, it is best to hold hands and stick together."

Come on, let's pull together. Let's support each other. In doing so, remember Paul's closing words in Ephesians 4. I like the way Eugene Peterson paraphrases that final verse:

> Make a clean break with all cutting, backbiting, profane talk. Be gentle with one another, sensitive. Forgive one another as quickly and thoroughly as God in Christ forgave you. (Eph. 4:31 MSG)

Think of somebody in the family of God—just one person you know—who could really use a word of support. Then give it! Don't wait . . . give it this week. Don't just think about it or write it in your journal. Do it. *Do it today.*

Pray for that individual you were thinking about a moment ago. Ask God to give you just the right word, just the right method of approaching that person. Maybe you need to write a note. Maybe you need to make a phone call. Maybe you need to take the person out for a cup of coffee or invite him or her over for a meal. Who knows? Your action could be the catalyst that causes that individual to gain hope beyond division.

Remember, "The enemy is over *there!*" Behold! How we need to love one another!

A Prayer for Hope Beyond Division

Forgive us, oh, forgive us, our Father, for the hours we have spent in the wasteland of malice and guile, hypocrisy and envy and slander. What grimy garments we've worn! Show us the joy of kindness, the long-lasting benefits of unity, grace, and support. Remind us that it all begins with genuine love prompted by forgiveness. Start a work within us so that our love flows from a pure heart, not from a desire to win friends or impress people.

Most of all, Lord, make us like Your Son. Kind. Meek. Humble. Gracious. May we grow up into His kindness, may we model His meekness, may we walk with His humility. May we reflect His grace so that others gain new hope. What we're really asking is that You help us grow up!

We're so glad to be in Your family, so grateful for Your forgiveness. Use us this week, perhaps even today, to help someone else feel grateful that he or she, too, is a part of this family. Through Christ, who prayed for our unity.

AMEN

5

Hope Beyond Guilt

Becoming
Living
Stones

FOR SOME STRANGE REASON, those of us who have known the Lord since we were young have a tendency to outgrow a close friendship with Him. When we were children, we felt free and open with our heavenly Father. But when we became adults, we seemed to take a few giant steps backward in that relationship.

When we were young, we talked to Him freely. With a child's faith, knowing He loved us, we trusted Him with the details of our life. Nothing was too small and, for sure, nothing was too big to ask of Him. In unguarded innocence, we prayed for *anything*!

The ease with which we once approached God can be seen in the letters written to Him by children. See if the ones below don't take you back to a time of innocence and openness in your own relationship with Him.

Dear Lord,
Thank you for the nice day today. You even fooled the TV weatherman.
Hank (age 7)

Dear Lord,
   Do you ever get mad?
   My mother gets mad all the time but she is only human.
                                             Yours truly,
                                             David (age 8)

Dear Lord,
   I need a raise in my allowance. Could you have one of your angels
tell my father?
                                             Thank you.
                                             David (age 7)[1]

Dear God,
   Charles my cat got run over. And if you made it happen you have to
tell me why.
                                             Harvey

Dear God,
   Can you guess what is the biggest river of all of them? The Amazon.
You ought to be able to because you made it. Ha, ha.
                                             Guess who[2]

Wouldn't it be interesting to compile an assortment of adult letters to God? Undoubtedly the childhood innocence would be lost as
well as the candor and ease of approach. The words would be more
guarded. We would be sophisticated. Fear and feelings of worthless-
ness would underscore the halting sentences. Shame, guilt, and regret would punctuate the paragraphs. We have lost much, haven't
we, on the road to adulthood?

We can learn a great deal from children about simple faith and
simple hope. Yet we have had years to experience those truths. We
can look back at the many times He has taken our brokenness and
made something beautiful of our lives. Our greatest failures, our
deepest sorrows, have offered opportunities for the operation of His
mercy and grace. How can we forget that?

God's Appraisal of Us

The Bible is filled with reminders of how much God cares for us, His plans for our welfare, and what our relationship with Him should be. Take, for example, the familiar words of the psalmist. Though an adult, he writes of God with free-flowing delight.

> Bless the LORD, O my soul;
> And all that is within me, bless His holy name.
> Bless the LORD, O my soul,
> And forget none of His benefits;
> Who pardons all your iniquities;
> Who heals all your diseases;
> Who redeems your life from the pit;
> Who crowns you with lovingkindness and compassion;
> Who satisfies your years with good things,
> So that your youth is renewed like the eagle....
>
> For as high as the heavens are above the earth,
> So great is His lovingkindness toward those who fear Him.
> As far as the east is from the west,
> So far has He removed our transgressions from us.
> Just as a father has compassion on his children,
> So the LORD has compassion on those who fear Him.
>
> For He Himself knows our frame;
> He is mindful that we are but dust. (Ps. 103:1–5, 11–14)

What a list! What a relief! Our Lord understands our limits. He realizes our struggles. He knows how much pressure we can take. He knows what measures of grace and mercy and strength we'll require. He knows how we're put together.

Frankly, His expectations are not nearly as unrealistic as ours. When we don't live up to the agenda we have set, we feel like He is going to dump a truckload of judgment on us. But that will not happen. So why do we fear it could? Because we forget that He "knows our frame; He is mindful that we are but dust."

What, then, is God's agenda for us? What does He want for us this afternoon, tomorrow morning, or next week? Well, His plans for us are clearly set forth. He wrote them originally to Israel, but they apply to us too.

> "For I know the plans that I have for you," declares the LORD, "plans for welfare and not for calamity to give you a future and a hope. Then you will call upon Me and come and pray to Me, and I will listen to you." (Jer. 29:11–12)

Isn't that wonderful? "I have plans for you, My son, My daughter," God says. "And they are great plans. Plans for your welfare and not for your calamity. Plans to give you a future and a hope." It is God's agenda that His people never lose hope. Each new dawn it's as if He smiles from heaven, saying, "Hope again... hope again!"

After the fall of Jerusalem, the prophet Jeremiah reminded himself of God's hope-filled plans.

> This I recall to my mind,
> Therefore I have hope.
> The LORD's lovingkindnesses indeed never cease,
> For His compassions never fail.
> They are new every morning;
> Great is Thy faithfulness.
> "The LORD is my portion," says my soul,
> "Therefore I have hope in Him."
> The LORD is good to those who wait for Him,
> To the person who seeks Him.
> It is good that he waits silently
> For the salvation of the LORD. (Lam. 3:21–26)

Right now you may be waiting for something from the Lord. Matter of fact, most people I meet are in some sort of holding pattern. (I certainly am!) They have something on the horizon that they're trusting God for. (I certainly do!) And their hope is not misplaced. He is good to those who wait for Him. He is good to those who seek Him. We have nothing to fear. And we certainly have no reason for living each day crushed by guilt or shame.

He has redeemed us, given us an inheritance, and shown us forgiveness. The most succinct summary of God's appraisal of our relationship as His children can be found in Romans 8:31–32. Many years ago I memorized the concluding paragraph in Romans 8, which begins with these two verses. I cannot number the times I have had my hope renewed by quoting these words to myself.

What then shall we say to these things? If God is for us, who is against us? He who did not spare His own Son, but delivered Him up for us all, how will He not also with Him freely give us all things?

Contrary to popular opinion, God doesn't sit in heaven with His jaws clenched, His arms folded in disapproval, and a deep frown on His brow. He is not ticked off at His children for all the times we trip over our tiny feet and fall flat on our diapers. He is a loving Father, and we are precious in His sight, the delight of His heart. After all, He "has qualified us to share in the inheritance of the saints in light" (Col. 1:12). Think of it! He's put us in His inheritance!

Remember that the next time you think God is coming down on you. You have reason to give thanks. You don't have to qualify yourself for His kingdom. His grace has rescued you. He has already qualified you by accomplishing a great deliverance in your life. That brings to mind another verse I love to quote:

For He delivered us from the domain of darkness, and transferred us to the kingdom of His beloved Son, in whom we have redemption, the forgiveness of sins. (Col. 1:13–14)

He has literally transferred us from the dark domain of the Enemy of our souls into the light of the kingdom of His Son. He considers us there with Him, surrounded by love, receiving the same treatment He gives His Son.

Sometimes it's encouraging just to thumb through the Scriptures and find all the promises that tell us what God thinks of us, especially in a world where folks are continually telling us all the things they have against us and all the things they see wrong with us.

God is not only "for us," according to Romans 8, He is constantly giving great gifts to us.

Every good thing bestowed and every perfect gift is from above, coming down from the Father of lights, with whom there is no variation, or shifting shadow. (James 1:17)

Literally, that last phrase means "shadow of turning." In other words, there is no alteration or modification in His giving, regardless of how often we may turn away. No shifting shadow on our part causes Him to become moody and hold back His gifts to us. Talk about grace!

God is for us. I want you to remember that.

God is for us. Say those four words to yourself.

God is for us.

Remember that tomorrow morning when you don't feel like He is. Remember that when you have failed. Remember that when you have sinned and guilt slams you to the mat.

God is for you. Make it personal: *God is for me!*

Never ever, ever tell your children that if they do wrong, God won't love them. That is heresy. There's no grace in that. Grace says, "My child, even though you do wrong, God will continue and I will continue to love you. God is for you, and so am I!"

I thought of this the other day as I was humming the children's tune, "Jesus loves the little children, all the children of the world." I thought, well, what about all the grownups? So I changed the words of that little song.

Jesus loves His adult children,
All the grownups of the world.
Red and yellow, black and white,
We are precious in His sight.

Jesus loves all the teens and adults of the world.
[Just thought I should include the teenagers too!]

Why do we think His love is just for the little children, innocent and disarming as they are? He loves all of His people. Let me repeat it once more: God is for us.

In Peter's letter, we catch a glimpse of the delight God takes in us as the apostle paints six beautiful word pictures of us, vivid pen portraits of God's children.

And coming to Him as to a living stone, rejected by men, but choice and precious in the sight of God, you also, as living stones, are being built up as a spiritual house for a holy priesthood, to offer up spiritual sacrifices acceptable to God through Jesus Christ. For this is contained in Scripture:
"Behold I lay in Zion a choice stone, a precious
      corner stone,
And he who believes in Him shall not be disappointed."
This precious value, then, is for you who believe. But for those who disbelieve,
"The stone which the builders rejected,
this became the very corner stone,"
and,
"A stone of stumbling and a rock of offense";
for they stumble because they are disobedient to the word, and to this doom they were also appointed. (1 Pet. 2:4–8)

We Are Living Stones in a Spiritual House

The metaphor woven through the fabric of this passage is that of a building, Christ being the cornerstone and we, His children, being the living stones that make up the building. (The apostle Paul uses this same image in Ephesians 2:19–22.)

Each time someone trusts Christ as Savior, another stone is quarried out of the pit of sin and fitted into the spiritual house He's building through the work of the Holy Spirit. And carefully overseeing the construction is Christ, who is the hands-on contractor of this eternal edifice.

We are His living stones, being built up as a spiritual house.

Think of it this way. There's a major construction project going on through time as Jesus Christ builds His family. It's called the *ekklesia*, the "church," those who are called out from the mass of humanity to become a special part of God's forever family. And you, as a Christian—a follower of Christ—have been picked, chosen, and called out to be one of them.

He has quarried you from the pit of your sin. And now He is chiseling away, shaping you and ultimately sliding you into place. You are a part of His building project.

All kinds of prophets of doom wonder about the condition of God's building. They see it as condemned property, worn out, dilapidated, and derelict rather than as a magnificent edifice that is being constructed on schedule. The truth is, God is the master architect, and every stone is being placed exactly where He designed it to fit. The project is right on schedule. Never forget, even on those blue days, we are living stones in a spiritual house. But there's more....

We Are Priests in the Same Temple

Peter refers to us both as a "holy priesthood" and as a "royal priesthood." It's true that we're not all preachers or evangelists or gifted teachers. But we *are* all priests, belonging to a kingly order that has been set apart by God.

The role of priest implies more than meets the eye, for priests have specific responsibilities delineated in Scripture. Priests offer up prayers, bring spiritual sacrifices, intercede to God on behalf of others, and stay in tune with the spiritual side of life. All this applies to every believer, regardless of age, regardless of sex, regardless of social standing. Perhaps you never thought of this before, but it's really true; we are priests in the same temple. But there's more....

We Are a Chosen Race

Our heads might have a tendency to swell at being chosen to be on God's team, so it might behoove us to take a quick glance at exactly why God chose the Hebrews to be His people. This will help us put the whole idea of being chosen by God into perspective. Here Moses is addressing the nation Israel, preparing them to enter the Promised Land.

> For you are a holy people to the LORD your God; the LORD your God has chosen you to be a people for His own possession out of all the peoples who are on the face of the earth. The LORD did not set His love on you nor choose you because you were more in number than any of the peoples, for you were the fewest of all peoples, but because the LORD loved you and kept the oath which He swore to your forefathers, the LORD brought you out by a mighty hand, and redeemed you from the house of slavery, from the hand of Pharaoh king of Egypt. (Deut. 7:6–8)

Why did God choose Israel? Because of their strength? No. Because of their numbers? Because of their mental or moral superiority? No. He chose them not because they deserved it, but simply because of His grace—a kindness shown to them entirely without merit on their part. Simply "because the Lord loved you."

Why did God choose us? For the same reason. Not because we did anything that impressed Him. It wasn't the size of our faith... or the sincerity. It wasn't the goodness of our heart... or the greatness of our intellect. It certainly wasn't because we first chose Him. It was entirely by grace. Grace prompted by love.

The Lord chooses us because He chooses to choose us. Period. He sets His love upon us because out of the goodness and grace of His own heart He declares, "I want you to be Mine."

311

I love that! Not only because it exalts the grace of God, but because God gets all the glory in it. We won't walk around heaven with our thumbs under our suspenders outbragging one another. Instead, we'll be absolutely amazed that we are privileged to be there.

John 15:16 says, "You did not choose Me, but I chose you." We didn't hunt Him down. He hunted us down. He is the eternal Hound of Heaven. We didn't work half our lives to find Him; He gave His life to find us. Being chosen by God says a lot more about Him than it does about us! He is the Good Shepherd who gives His life for the sheep. When you find yourself slumping in shame or giving way to guilt, remind yourself of this: You have been chosen by the Good Shepherd. He wants you in His flock. But there is more. . . .

We Are a Holy Nation

Holy can be an intimidating word. Though meant to be sacred, it can seem scary. Remember, earlier we explained that the word means "to be set apart." But let's look at it another way.

I'm sitting in my study right now, and I'm wearing a suit and a tie because I'm going to an important meeting in a couple hours. This morning when I was getting dressed, I looked on my tie rack and I selected a tie. I had a number to choose from, but I chose this particular one. I pulled it off the rack, put it around my neck, and tied the knot, and at that moment the tie became holy. Doesn't look holy. I can assure you, it doesn't feel holy. (As a matter of fact, I can see a small spot on it. Must have gotten some gravy on it when I wore it last.) But it's still the tie I set apart for this particular purpose. In the broadest sense of the word, the tie I'm wearing is "holy." It's set apart for a special purpose.

You and I are a holy nation. We make up a body of people set apart for a special purpose: to be ambassadors for Jesus Christ, the King of the church. We are a people set apart for His special purpose and glory.

If we seem out of step with the rest of the world, it is because we march to the beat of a different drummer. We sing a different national anthem and pledge our allegiance to a different flag—because our citizenship, our true citizenship, is in heaven. You and I are parts of His holy nation. But there's more....

We Are God's Own Possession

Possessions of the powerful, wealthy, or famous, no matter how common, can become extremely valuable, even priceless. Napoleon's toothbrush sold for $21,000. Can you imagine—paying thousands of dollars for someone's cruddy old toothbrush? Hitler's car sold for over $150,000. Winston Churchill's desk, a pipe owned by C. S. Lewis, sheet music handwritten by Beethoven, a house once owned by Ernest Hemingway. At the Sotheby's auction of Jackie Kennedy Onassis's personal belongings, her fake pearls sold for $211,500 and JFK's wood golf clubs went for $772,500. Not because the items themselves are worthy but because they once belonged to someone significant.

Are you ready for a surprise? We fit that bill too. Think of the value of something owned by God. What incredible worth that bestows on us, what inexplicable dignity! We belong to Him. We are "a people for God's own possession" (1 Pet. 2:9).

I love that expression—"a people for God's own possession." And I'm glad this verse is correctly translated in the version of the Bible I'm using. For the longest time I used a version that said, "We are a peculiar people." (Actually, I saw all kinds of evidence of that around me, as if Christians were supposed to be odd or weird or strange.) But the correct rendering is far more encouraging. Weird or not, we're His possession...owned by the living God.

The price paid for us was unimaginably high—the blood of Jesus Christ—and now we belong to Him. We have been bought with a price. That's enough to bring a smile to anyone's face. But there is more...one more.

We Are a People Who Have Received Mercy

Have you lived so long in the family of God that your memory has become blurred? Have you forgotten what it was like when you weren't?

> ... for you once were not a people, but now you are the people of God; you had not received mercy, but now you have received mercy. (1 Pet. 2:10)

As a result of God's mercy, we have become a people who are uniquely and exclusively cared for by God. The fact that we are the recipients of His mercy makes all the difference in the world as to how we respond to difficult times. He watches over us with enormous interest. Why? Because of His immense mercy, freely demonstrated in spite of our not deserving it. What guilt-relieving, encouraging news!

Of all the twelve disciples, none could have been more grateful than Peter... or, if he had allowed it, none more guilt-ridden. Called to serve his Savior, strong-hearted, determined, zealous, even a little cocky on occasion, the man had known the heights of ecstasy but also knew the aching agony of defeat.

Though warned by the Master, Peter announced before His peers, "Even though all may fall away... I will never fall away" (Matt. 26:33). And later... "Lord, with You I am ready to go both to prison and to death!" (Luke 22:33). Yet only a few hours later he denied even knowing Jesus... three times!

What bitter tears he wept when the weight of his denials crushed his spirit. But our Lord refused to leave him there, wallowing in hopeless discouragement and depression. He found the broken man and forgave him... and used him mightily as a leader in the early church. What grace... what mercy!

Charles Wesley beautifully captures the theology of such mercy in the second stanza of his magnificent hymn, "And Can It Be?"

> He left His Father's throne above,
> So free, so infinite His grace!

Emptied Himself of all but love,
And bled for Adam's helpless race!
'Tis mercy all, immense and free,
For, O my God, it found out me.

Our Lives Are Being Watched

Beloved, I urge you as aliens and strangers to abstain from fleshly lusts, which war against the soul. Keep your behavior excellent among the Gentiles, so that in the thing in which they slander you as evildoers, they may on account of your good deeds, as they observe them, glorify God in the day of visitation. (1 Pet. 2:11–12)

Peter begins his practical summary of this section with the words, "Beloved, I urge you." He feels passionate about this—and there's a warning here. Peter is telling us that in light of all that we are as God's children, in light of our roles as living stones in a building that will never be destroyed, and in light of our being these things he's described—a royal priesthood, a chosen race, a holy nation, a people for His own possession, those who have received mercy, we are to live in a certain way. Our earthly behavior is to square with our divinely provided benefits.

For unbelievers, earth is a playground where the flesh is free to romp and run wild. But for believers, earth is a battleground. It's the place where we combat the lusts that wage war against our souls. For the brief tour of duty we Christians have on this earth, we cannot get stalled in sin or, for that matter, incapacitated by guilt. To live the kind of life God requires, Peter offers four suggestions.

First, live a clean life. Don't think for a moment that it makes no difference to unbelievers how Christians live. We live out our faith before a watching world. That's why Peter urges us to abstain from fleshly lusts, "in order to get their attention" and to prove that what we believe really works.

You and I don't know how many non-Christians are watching us this very day, determining the truth of the message of Christianity strictly on the basis of how we live, how we work, how we respond to life's tests, or how we conduct ourselves with our families.

Every time I hear of a pastor or Christian leader or well-known Christian artist who has failed morally, it breaks my heart. Not just because it scandalizes the church and possibly destroys his or her family, although those are certainly tragedies enough. But I think of what it says to unbelievers who read it in the headlines or hear it joked about on television talk shows. Living a clean life isn't merely a nice option to consider; it's the least we can do to demonstrate our gratitude for God's deliverance.

Second, leave no room for slander. When the ancient Greek philosopher Plato was told that a certain man had begun making slanderous charges against him, Plato's response was, "I will live in such a way that no one will believe what he says."[3]

The most convincing defense is the silent integrity of our character, not how vociferously we deny the charges.

Third, do good deeds among unbelievers. It's easy for Christians to have such tunnel vision that we limit all of our good deeds to the family of God. But if you're driving along and see someone with a flat tire, you don't roll down your window and say, "Hey there ... you with the flat tire! Are you a Christian?" ... then determine if you should help. We would do well to extend our good deeds to those outside the family.

What makes the story of the Good Samaritan so compelling? The merciful deeds were done on behalf of a total stranger. That is how we win the right to be heard—not by a slick mass-advertising campaign but by our compassionate and unselfish actions.

Notice that Peter says, "on account of your good *deeds*," not your good *words*. The unsaved are watching our lives. When our good deeds are indisputable the unbeliever says, "There must be something to it." Chances are good that at that point the person will hear what we have to say.

Fourth, never forget—we are being watched. The world is watching us to see if what we say we believe is true in our lives. Warren

Wiersbe tells a brief but powerful story that illustrates this beautifully.

> In the summer of 1805, a number of Indian chiefs and warriors met in council at Buffalo Creek, New York, to hear a presentation of the Christian message by a Mr. Cram from the Boston Missionary Society. After the sermon, a response was given by Red Jacket, one of the leading chiefs. Among other things, the chief said...
>
> "Brother, we are told that you have been preaching to the white people in this place. These people are our neighbors. We are acquainted with them. We will wait a little while and see what effect your preaching has upon them. If we find it does them good, makes them honest and less disposed to cheat Indians, we will then consider again what you have said."[4]

Whew! That's laying it on the line. I wonder how many people are looking at us and saying to themselves, "I hear what he's saying. Now I'm going to watch how he lives. I'll see if what he says is what he does."

Let's Not Forget—God Is for Us

This has been a searching chapter to write. I've not attempted to soften Peter's words, lest we miss the punch in his points. For whatever it's worth, I've felt a few stinging reproofs as well. Sometimes an author has to swallow some of his own medicine... except in this case, God is giving the medicine through Peter's pen, not mine! And so, you and I both have taken it on the chin. Hopefully, it will make a difference.

But let's not forget the good news: There is hope beyond guilt! May I remind you of that oft-repeated line from Romans 8? "God is for us." In devoted love He chose us. In great grace He stooped to accept us into His family. In immense mercy He still finds us wandering, forgives our foolish ways, and (as He did with Peter) frees us to serve Him even though we don't deserve such treatment.

So... away with guilt! If you need a little extra boost to make that happen, read Eugene Peterson's paraphrase of Romans 8:31–19. Read it slowly, preferably *aloud*. As a good friend of mine once put it, "If this don't light your fire, you got wet wood!"

So, what do you think? With God on our side like this, how can we lose? If God didn't hesitate to put everything on the line for us, embracing our condition and exposing himself to the worst by sending his own Son, is there anything else he wouldn't gladly and freely do for us? And who would dare tangle with God by messing with one of God's chosen? Who would dare even to point a finger? The One who died for us—who was raised to life for us!—is in the presence of God at this very moment sticking up for us. Do you think anyone is going to be able to drive a wedge between us and Christ's love for us? There is no way! Not trouble, not hard times, not hatred, not hunger, not homelessness, not bullying threats, not backstabbing, not even the worst sins listed in Scripture:
"They kill us in cold blood because they hate you.
We're sitting ducks; they pick us off one by one."

None of this fazes us because Jesus loves us. I'm absolutely convinced that nothing—nothing living or dead, angelic or demonic, today or tomorrow, high or low, thinkable or unthinkable—absolutely *nothing* can get between us and God's love because of the way that Jesus our Master has embraced us. (Rom. 8:31–39 MSG)

A Prayer for Hope Beyond Guilt

Father... dear gracious Father, we're our own worst enemy.
We focus on our failures rather than on Your rescues... on our
wrongs rather than on Your commitment to making us
right... on our puny efforts rather than on Your powerful

plans for our good. Even our attempts at being devoted to You can become so self-centered. Turn our attention back to You.

- *Remind us of our exalted position in Christ.*
- *Refresh us with frequent flashbacks—"God is for us."*
- *Renew our spirits with the realization that we're your possession.*

Then, with those joyful thoughts to spur us on, slay the dragon of guilt within us so we might enjoy, as never before, your ultimate embrace. Through Christ I pray.

AMEN

6

Hope Beyond Unfairness

Pressing on
Even Though
Ripped Off

EVER BOUGHT A LEMON of a used car? Ever sent away for some marvelous $16.95 gadget displayed on an infomercial and ended up with about 85 cents worth of plastic?

Who hasn't been hoodwinked by a smooth-talking salesman with styled hair and patent-leather shoes? Who hasn't been burned by a glitzy ad campaign that promises more than it delivers? Who hasn't, at some point, been taken advantage of or "ripped off"?

Yet we recover relatively easily and quickly from ripoffs like those. What's really difficult to endure is the kind of abuse or victimization that gets personal—when someone slanders our reputations, pulls the economic rug out from under us, or even threatens our lives. It's hard enough to deal with the consequences of our own missteps, miscalculations, and stupid mistakes. But it seems unbearable to suffer the consequences of something that wasn't our fault or that we didn't deserve.

If you've ever been treated like that, you're in good biblical company. David was ripped off by Saul, Esau was duped by Jacob,

323

Joseph was mistreated by his brothers, and Job was victimized by the Sabeans and Chaldeans.

David, as a young shepherd boy, killed Goliath and helped rout the Philistine enemy. After that, David became overwhelmingly popular among the people. He also became the object of King Saul's rage. David had done only good for Saul and his people. Therefore, the people appropriately sang their praises to David: "Saul has slain his thousands, and David his ten thousands" (1 Sam. 18:7). That popular song sent Saul into such a revengeful rage against the young hero that for more than a decade David ran for his life while Saul hunted and haunted him. David didn't deserve this, but it happened.

Joseph didn't ask to be his father's favorite, but when Jacob showed favoritism to his youngest son, Joseph's brothers, in a moment of absolute hatred, sold him into slavery. Although Joseph triumphed over his circumstances, he was initially ripped off by his brothers.

Earlier, Joseph's father, Jacob, had cheated his own brother, Esau, out of his birthright. Admittedly Esau was rash and irresponsible, but Jacob took advantage of his brother in a vulnerable moment.

And what about that good man Job? According to the Scriptures, he was "blameless" and "upright" and had taken unfair advantage of no one ... but because Satan used him as a guinea pig, Job lost all his land, servants, possessions, and above all, his ten children.

While God ultimately used all these circumstances for the believers' good and His honor, initially all of these men could have said, "What is happening here? This is unfair! I don't deserve this!"

So while we may be in good company—and misery does love company—company doesn't alleviate the pain of unfair treatment.

Natural Reactions to Unfair Treatment

It's been my observation that when we're treated unfairly, we respond with three common, knee-jerk reactions.

First, there is the aggressive pattern: we blame others. This reaction not only focuses on the person who ripped us off and keeps a running tally of wrongs done against us, it also engineers ways to get back. This reaction says, "I don't just get mad, I get even." In the process, aggression grows from simple anger all the way to rage. It starts with the seed of resentment, germinates into revenge, and in the process nurtures a deep root of bitterness that tenaciously wraps around our hearts. When allowed to grow to full size, it leaves us determined to get back at *every* person who has done anything against us.

It's like the fellow who was bitten by a dog and was later told by his physician, "Yes, indeed, you do have rabies." Upon hearing this, the patient immediately pulled out a pad and pencil and began to write.

Thinking the man was making out his will, the doctor said, "Listen, this doesn't mean you're going to die. There's a cure for rabies."

"I know that," said the man. "I'm making a list of people I'm gonna bite."

It is probable that a few who read these words are making lists right now of people you're gonna bite the very next chance you get. Some of you are already engaged in doing just that. The blame game may temporarily satisfy an aggressive inner itch, but it doesn't lead to a lasting solution. Small wonder God warns us: "Never take your own revenge . . . 'Vengeance is Mine, I will repay,' says the Lord" (Rom. 12:19).

Second, there is the passive pattern: we feel sorry for ourselves. We throw a pity party, complaining to anyone who will lend a sympathetic ear. "Life just isn't fair," we whine. But if we wallow in this slough of despondency too long, we become depressed and immobile, living the balance of life with the shades drawn and the doors locked. Like quicksand, feeling sorry for ourselves will suck us under.

Though you may be holding back, there's a lot of anger in this passive pattern as well. Give in to this temptation, and I can assure you, you'll not be vulnerable to anybody ever again.

Reminds me of some fellows in the military who were stationed in Korea during the Korean War. While there, they hired a local boy to cook and clean for them. Being a bunch of jokesters, these guys soon took advantage of the boy's seeming naiveté. They'd smear Vaseline on the stove handles so that when he'd turn the stove on in the morning he'd get grease all over his fingers. They'd put little water buckets over the door so that he'd get deluged when he opened the door. They'd even nail his shoes to the floor during the night. Day after day the little fella took the brunt of their practical jokes without saying anything. No blame... no self-pity... no temper tantrums.

Finally the men felt guilty about what they were doing, so they sat down with the young Korean and said, "Look, we know these pranks aren't funny anymore, and we're sorry. We're never gonna take advantage of you again."

It seemed too good to be true to the houseboy. "No more sticky on stove?" he asked.

"Nope."

"No more water on door?"

"No."

"No more nail shoes to floor?"

"Nope, never again."

"Okay," the boy said with a smile... "no more spit in soup."

Even in a passive mode, you can spit in somebody's soup.

Third, there is the holding pattern: we postpone or deny our feelings. We might call this the Scarlett O'Hara syndrome: "I'll think about it tomorrow." Every boiling issue is left to simmer on the back burner over a low flame. On the surface all seems calm—"Doesn't bother me"—but underneath, our feelings seethe, eating away at us like acid. This failure to deal with the problem forthrightly leads only to doubt and disillusionment and weakens the fiber of our lives. Furthermore, it's physically unhealthy to sustain feelings of resentment.

An Alternative That Honors God

Though they are all very common, don't expect to find any of these reactions in Peter's wonderful letter where he informs us how to have hope beyond unfairness. Expect instead an alternative reaction to unfair treatment.

The Command

> Submit yourselves for the Lord's sake to every human institution, whether to a king as the one in authority, or to governors as sent by him for the punishment of evildoers and the praise of those who do right. (1 Pet. 2:13–14)

It's important to understand the historical context of this command. The Roman Empire, throughout which the readers of Peter's letter were scattered, was not a benevolent monarchy. It was a dictatorship ruled by the insane demagogue Nero, who was especially notorious for his wickedness and his cruelty to Christians. Many of the believers who received Peter's letter had suffered persecution. The bodies of their friends and loved ones had bloodied the sand of the Roman coliseum. Their corpses, soaked in oil, had lit that vast stadium. So it was altogether natural and fitting that Peter would address the subject of unfair treatment. These believers had been the target of the grossest kind of mistreatment by government, by their fellow citizens, and by their neighbors.

Should these Christians pick up arms and resist a government with such a leader at its helm? No, said Peter. Incredibly, in the midst of all this, he had the audacity to say, "Submit."

God does not promote anarchy. Jesus said, "Render to Caesar the things that are Caesar's and to God the things that are God's" (Matt. 22:21). And Paul exhorts us to pray for those who are in authority over us (see 1 Tim. 2:1–2). Nowhere in Scripture is overt insurrection against the government recommended. The believer was not put on earth to overthrow governments but to establish in the human heart a kingdom not of this world.

There may be instances, of course, when we must stand our ground, when we must stand firm and disobey a law that is disobedient to the law of God. We are not to buckle under by compromising our convictions or renouncing our faith. But those are the exceptions, not the normal rule. Whenever possible we are to render unto Caesar the coin of civil obedience, pray for those in authority, pay our taxes, obey the laws of the land, and live honorably under the domain of earthly elected leaders.

The way to live honorably, Peter says, is to "submit." The Greek word is *hupotasso*, a military term that means "to fall in rank under an authority." It's composed of two words: *tasso*, meaning "to appoint, order, or arrange," and *hupo*, meaning "to place under or to subordinate." In this particular construction it conveys the idea of subjecting oneself or placing oneself under another's authority.

This recognition of existing authority, coupled with a willingness to set aside one's own personal desires, shows a deep dependency upon God. This submission to authority is not only in respect to God, the foremost human authority, but to lesser officials as well, such as kings and governors as well as law officers and teachers.

I'm convinced in my heart that if we were good students of submission we would get along a lot better in life. But I am also convinced that it is the one thing, more than any other, that works against our very natures, which argue, "I don't want to submit. I don't want to give in. I won't let him have his way in this." And so we live abrasively.

Let's get something very clear here. Our problem is not understanding what submission means. Our problem is doing what it says.

Because submission is so difficult, we need to look at the reason behind Peter's command.

The Reason

For such is the will of God that by doing right you may silence the ignorance of foolish men. (1 Pet. 2:15)

The Greek word translated "silence" here means "to close the mouth with a muzzle." You see, Christians in the first century were the targets of all kinds of slanderous rumors. "They're a secret sect," people said. "They are people of another kingdom." . . . "They follow another god." . . . "They have plans to overthrow us." Throughout the Roman Empire people gossiped about their secret meetings, their subversive ideologies, their loyalty to another kingdom, their plans to infiltrate, indoctrinate, and lead an insurrection. This kind of paranoia was common, all the way to Nero. To muzzle these rumors, Peter encouraged submission to the powers that be. By submitting, Peter said, by doing right before God, they would muzzle the mouths of those passing around such rumors.

Let's translate it into today's terms. We live in a city where the government is run by civil authorities. Our church building is located in that city. Now, those civil authorities have no right to tell us what to preach, what to teach, or which philosophy to adopt as a church. If they attempt to do that, we have a right—in fact, it's a duty—to rebel, because there is a higher law than their law, the higher law relating to the declaration of truth. However, they do have the right to say, "In this room you may put 150 people and no more. If you go beyond that you are violating the fire code and will be subject to a fine and possibly other penalties." It is neither right nor wise for us to break this civil law. It does not violate God's law and is, in fact, there for our protection. So we must submit to that law.

In the church I pastored in Fullerton, California, we had to abide by local laws, one of which stated that we could not use folding seats in the worship auditorium; the seats had to be fixed to the floor. Also, the local law mandated a certain predetermined ratio between how many cars were parked in a parking lot measured against how many people could sit in an auditorium. Any church that constructed a worship center had to provide parking for "X" number of people in the worship gathering. We agreed to cooperate with that.

By submitting to this civil authority, we muzzled any rumors that we were just a maverick group, that we did as we pleased, thank you. We would have gained nothing by rebelling against the civic authorities. In fact, we would have lost in many ways by doing so.

The Principle

Act as free men, and do not use your freedom as a covering for evil, but use it as bondslaves of God. Honor all men; love the brotherhood, fear God, honor the king. (1 Pet. 2:16–17)

It's important that we keep the right perspective on the principle here. We do not submit because we necessarily agree. We do not submit because deep within we support all the rules, codes, and regulations. At times they may seem petty and galling, terribly restrictive, and even prejudicial. We submit because it is the "will of God" and because we are "bondslaves of God."

Now, you see, the principle comes to the surface: "Do not use your freedom as a covering for evil." Do not use or abuse grace so that your freedom becomes a cloak for evil.

In little staccato bursts, Peter gives us several commands in verses 16 and 17: act as free men; honor all men; love the brotherhood; fear God; honor the king. And wrapped around the commands is that main principle: "Do not use your freedom as a covering for evil."

We must forever be aware of the temptation to abuse liberty. It's so easy to stretch it; so easy to make it work for ourselves rather than for the glory of God.

An Example and *the* Example

Servants, be submissive to your masters with all respect, not only to those who are good and gentle, but also to those who are unreasonable. For this finds favor, if for the sake of conscience toward God a man bears up under sorrows when suffering unjustly. For what credit is there if, when you sin and are harshly treated, you endure it with patience? But if when you do what is right and suffer for it you patiently endure it, this finds favor with God. For you have been called for this purpose. (1 Pet. 2:18–21a)

To understand the full import of what Peter is saying we must understand something of the nature of slavery in the time of the early church. William Barclay sheds some historical light on this.

In the time of the early church . . . there were as many as 60,000,000 slaves in the Roman Empire.

It was by no means only menial tasks which were performed by slaves. Doctors, teachers, musicians, actors, secretaries, stewards were slaves. In fact, all the work of Rome was done by slaves. Roman attitude was that there was no point in being master of the world and doing one's own work. Let the slaves do that and let the citizens live in pampered idleness. The supply of slaves would never run out.

Slaves were not allowed to marry; but they cohabited; and the children born of such a partnership were the property of the master, not of the parents, just as the lambs born to the sheep belonged to the owner of the flock, and not to the sheep.

It would be wrong to think that the lot of slaves was always wretched and unhappy, and that they were always treated with cruelty. Many slaves were loved and trusted members of the family; but one great inescapable fact dominated the whole situation. In Roman law a slave was not a person but a thing; and he had absolutely no legal rights whatsoever. For that reason there could be no such thing as justice where a slave was concerned.... Peter Chrysologus sums the matter up: "Whatever a master does to a slave, undeservedly, in anger, willingly, unwillingly, in forgetfulness, after careful thought, knowingly, unknowingly, is judgment, justice and law." In regard to a slave, his master's will, and even his master's caprice, was the only law.[1]

That was the reality of the first-century world when Peter addressed slaves and told them to "be submissive" to their masters. It would have been easy for slaves who became Christians to think that their Christianity gave them the freedom to break with their masters. Peter, under the Holy Spirit's inspiration, stated that this was not so.

Centuries later, Christianity pervaded the culture and overcame slavery, but it didn't happen in the first century. This is a good lesson for us regarding God's timing versus our timing, even when it comes to adversity. While He certainly commands us to be salt and light and thus bring about justice and change in our culture, His ultimate priority is changing the individual human heart.

It's difficult for us in America to read some of these verses. Our frame of reference is so different—so Western, so twentieth century—that we sometimes try to rewrite God's Word to make it fit us. We can't do that. We must let it speak for itself.

"Well, that's great if you have a good master," you say. It's wonderful if you're a slave of Saint Francis of America . . . or Mother Teresa of your community. If you're working for some marvelous, saintlike boss, everything is cool. You're happy to submit. But what if your taskmaster fits the description in the last part of the verse—what if you work for "those who are unreasonable"?

Do you have an uncaring boss? Do you have a supervisor or a manager who isn't fair? Do you have to deal with unreasonable people? You may not want to hear this today, but there is a lot of truth for you in verses 18 and 19, none of which will ever appear in your local newspaper or on a television talk show.

The natural tendency of the human heart is to fight back against unfair and unreasonable treatment. But Peter's point is that seeking revenge for unjust suffering can be a sign of self-appointed lordship over one's own affairs. Revenge, then, is totally inappropriate for one who has submitted to the lordship of Jesus Christ. Christians must stand in contrast to those around them. This includes a difference in attitude and a difference in focus. Our attitude should be "submissive," and our focus should be "toward God." And how is this change viewed by God? It "finds favor" with Him.

Our focus, then, should not be consumed with getting the raise at the office but with getting the praise from God, not with getting the glory for ourselves but with giving the glory to Him.

> For what credit is there if, when you sin and are harshly treated, you endure it with patience? But if when you do what is right and suffer for it you patiently endure it, this finds favor with God. (1 Pet. 2:20)

The contrast is eloquent. There's no credit due a person who suffers for what he has coming to him. If you break into a house and steal, you will be arrested, and you could be incarcerated. And if you patiently endure your jail sentence, no one is going think you are wonderful for being such a good and patient prisoner. You won't get elected "Citizen of the Year."

But if you are a hard-working, faithful employee, diligent, honest, productive, prompt, caring, working for a boss who is belligerent, stubborn, short-sighted, and ungrateful, and if you patiently endure that situation—aha! That "finds favor" with God! (I told you this wasn't information generally embraced by the public!) Actually another meaning for the word translated "favor" is *grace*. So when you endure, you put grace on display. And when you put grace on display for the glory of God, you could revolutionize your workplace or any other situation.

Can you see why the Christian philosophy is absolutely radical and revolutionary? We don't work for the credit or the prestige or the salary or the perks! We work for the glory of God in whatever we do. The purpose of the believer in society is to bring glory and honor to the name of Christ, not to be treated well or to have life be easy or even to be happy, as wonderful as all those things are. Again, this is not promoted in today's workplace.

> For you have been called for this purpose, since Christ also suffered for you, leaving you an example for you to follow in His steps. (1 Pet. 2:21)

You are "called for this purpose." That's the reason you're in that company. That's the reason you're filling that role. That's the reason these things are happening to you. Why? So that you might follow in the steps of our Lord Jesus, who suffered for us.

I deliberately left Christ off the list of biblical examples at the beginning of the chapter because I wanted to mention Him here. No one was ever more "ripped off" than our Savior. Absolutely no one. Jesus of Nazareth was the only perfect Man who ever lived, yet He suffered continually during His brief life on this planet. He was misunderstood, maligned, hated, arrested, and tortured. Finally, they crucified Him.

And Peter says we are to walk in the steps of Jesus.

> Since Christ also suffered for you, leaving you an example for you to follow in His steps, who committed no sin, nor was any deceit found in His mouth; and while being reviled, He did not revile in return; while

suffering, He uttered no threats, but kept entrusting Himself to Him who judges righteously; and He Himself bore our sins in His body on the cross, that we might die to sin and live to righteousness; for by His wounds you were healed. (1 Pet. 2:21b–24)

In these verses Peter shifts from *an* example of unfair treatment to *the* example we should follow—from that of a servant to that of the Savior.

John Henry Jowett writes of Jesus' perfection.

> The fine, sensitive membrane of the soul had in nowise been scorched by the fire of iniquity. "No sin!" He was perfectly pure and healthy. No power had been blasted by the lightning of passion. No nerve had been atrophied by the wasting blight of criminal neglect. The entire surface of His life was as finely sensitive as the fair, healthy skin of a little child.... There was no duplicity. There were no secret folds or convolutions in His life concealing ulterior motives. There was nothing underhand. His life lay exposed in perfect truthfulness and candour. The real, inner meaning of His life was presented upon a plain surface of undisturbed simplicity. "No sin!" Nothing blunted or benumbed. "No guile!" Therefore nothing hardened by the effrontery of deceit.[2]

That's the sinless Christ. But still they mocked Him and bruised Him and beat Him and *crucified* Him. When Peter tells us He is our example, that's saying something!

Consider His focus. He "kept entrusting Himself to Him who judges righteously."

That's a good thing to do throughout your day. "Lord, this is a hard moment for me. I'm having a tough time today. Here I am again, dealing with this unreasonable person, this person who is treating me unfairly. Lord, help me. I entrust myself to You. I give You my struggle. Protect me. Provide the wisdom and self-control I need. Help me do the right thing."

We must understand that the purpose of Jesus' suffering was different from ours. I know there comes a point where subjection to certain situations can become absolutely unwise and unhealthy. No argument there. But most of us don't get anywhere near that. We are so quick to defend ourselves. We are a fight-back generation. We know our lawyers' phone numbers better than we know verses of Scripture on self-restraint. Quick to get mad! Quick to fight back! Quick to answer back! Quick to threaten a lawsuit! "Don't you DARE step across that line...I've got my rights!"

When was the last time you deliberately, for the glory of Christ, took it on the chin, turned the other cheek, kept your mouth shut, and gave Him all the glory?

A Benefit That Accompanies Such Obedience

For you were continually straying like sheep, but now you have returned to the Shepherd and Guardian of your souls. (1 Pet. 2:25)

Staring in horror at the cross, one can't help but become dizzy from a swarm of questions. Why? Why should this innocent man endure such unjust suffering? Why should we? Why shouldn't we resist the thorns and the lash we are forced to bear? Why should we submit to the hammer blows, to the piercing nails, to the cross of unjust suffering?

Because it causes us to return to our Savior for protection rather than defending ourselves or fighting for "our rights." That kind of reaction has become so much a part of our lifestyle and culture that we don't even realize it when we react that way. We don't even recognize that we should be different from those around us.

By the way, see the words, "by His wounds you were healed"? Talk about vivid! Peter had seen firsthand the yoke of unjust suffering placed upon Jesus' shoulders. No doubt he was remembering. He could see it as clearly as though it were yesterday—that moment when he saw his Master's bruised and bleeding body staggering along the narrow streets of Jerusalem on the way to Golgotha. And as he remembered that scene, he said, "by that He heals us."

Are you feeling the splinters of some cross of unjust suffering? Has a friend betrayed you? Has an employer impaled you? Has a disaster dropped on your life that's almost too great to bear? If so, don't fight back. Unjust suffering can be a dizzying experience. To keep your balance in those times when things are swirling around you, it's important to find a fixed reference point and focus on it. Return to the protection and guardianship of the Good Shepherd who endured the cross and laid down His life . . . for you.

It was because David refused to take vengeance on King Saul that we remember his story to this day. It was because Joseph was so willing to forgive his brothers that we admire him to this day. And it was because Job did not waver in his faith, in spite of all those unfair calamities, that we are impressed to this day.

If you'd just as soon be forgotten because you lived consumed with blame and self-pity, keep fighting back. Get even. Stay angry.

But if you hope to be remembered, admired, and rewarded, press on even though you've been ripped off.

A Prayer for Hope Beyond Unfairness

Dear Lord, find within us a yielded and quiet spirit of submission. To make that happen, we need You to come in like a flood. Occupy us as water finding empty spaces. Occupy reserved portions of our lives where anger is festering and the secret places where grudges are being stored. Sweep through our houses . . . don't miss one room or a single area—cleanse every dark closet, look under every rug. Let nothing go unnoticed as You take full control of our motives as well as our actions. Deep within our hearts we pray that You would sweep us clean of blame and revenge, of self-pity and keeping score. Enable each one of us to be big enough to press on regardless of what unfair treatment we've had to endure. Take away the scars of ugly treatment and harsh words. Forgiveness comes hard . . . but it's essential. Help us forgive even those who never acknowledge their wronging and hurting us! Give us peace in place of turmoil and erase the memories that keep us offended. We need fresh hope to go on! I ask this in the name of Him who had no sin and did no wrong, but died, the just for the unjust: Jesus Christ our Lord.

AMEN

7

⬧

Hope Beyond "I Do"

The Give-and-Take
of
Domestic Harmony

A WEDDING IS ONE thing. A marriage is another. What a difference between the way things start in a home . . . and the way they continue.

In his book *Secrets to Inner Beauty*, Joe Aldrich humorously describes the realities of married life.

> It doesn't take long for the newlyweds to discover that "everything in one person nobody's got." They soon learn that a marriage license is just a learner's permit, and ask with agony, "Is there life after marriage?"
>
> An old Arab proverb states that marriage begins with a prince kissing an angel and ends with a bald-headed man looking across the table at a fat lady. Socrates told his students, "By all means marry. If you get a good wife, twice blessed you will be. If you get a bad wife, you'll become a philosopher." Count Herman Keyserling said it well when he stated that "The essential difficulties of life do not end, but rather begin with marriage."[1]

Marriage begins like a romantic, moonlight sleigh ride, smoothly gliding over the glistening snow. It's living together after the honeymoon that turns out to be rough backpacking across rocks and hot sand. For two people to live in domestic harmony, it takes a lot of give-and-take. If you need any confirmation of this outside your own life, just look at the statistics. No, forget statistics. Just look about you. On the job. In the office. Around your neighborhood. At church. Broken marriages. Separations. Divorces. Fractured homes. Some children have so many stepparents they can't keep track of them.

A wedding is one thing. A marriage is something else entirely.

I am a realist, not an idealist. I've been married for forty-one years, and they have been years of learning and growth, years of difficulty and ecstasy, years of delight and discovery, years of heartache and hardship, years of having children and losing children (two miscarriages), years of growing together and, I must confess, some days in which it seemed we were growing apart.

At first, of course, deceived by the rose-colored glasses of romantic love, we didn't see any of this. And looking back through the fog of disappointment, we see very few things clearly.

In an essay on the theme of "arranged marriages," writer Philip Yancey offers these insights.

> In the U.S. and other Western-style cultures, people tend to marry because they are attracted to another's appealing qualities: a fresh smile, wittiness, a pleasing figure, athletic ability, a cheerful disposition, charm. Over time, these qualities can change; the physical attributes, especially, will deteriorate with age. Meanwhile, surprises may surface: slatternly housekeeping, a tendency toward depression, disagreements over sex. In contrast, the partners in an arranged marriage [over half of all marriages in our international global village fit this description] do not center their relationship on mutual attractions. Having heard your parents' decision, you accept that you will live for many years with someone you now barely know. Thus the overriding question changes from "Whom should I marry?" to "Given this partner, what kind of marriage can we construct together?"[2]

Truthfully, that is the kind of attitude we need if we are going to move beyond romance into reality to build a strong and lasting life together. The apostle Peter gives us some helpful advice. He offers hope beyond "I do."

Tucked away in the heart of his letter is a little gem of truth, like a diamond in a ring. Without the right setting to enhance its beauty, this little gem would get lost; but viewed in its proper setting it becomes a sparkling delight. In the Bible, this setting is called the scriptural context.

The overall setting begins at 1 Peter 2:13 and continues through the end of chapter 3. These many verses challenge us to respond correctly, even in unfair circumstances. Some of those circumstances are briefly illustrated: citizens in various situations (2:13–17), slaves with unjust masters (2:18–20), wives with unfair husbands (3:1–6), and Christians in an unchristian society (3:13–17).

The key term in this context is the word *submit*, which we defined and analyzed in the previous chapter. You'll recall it is translated from a Greek military term meaning "to fall in rank under the authority of another... to subject oneself for the purpose of obeying or pleasing another." Some men have taken this word to the extreme in marriage, promoting cowering and servile behavior by women in the face of the worst kinds of abuse. Others have gone to the opposite extreme and labeled these passages dated and therefore culturally obsolete, saying that they apply only to the era in which they were originally written. The balance of the biblical position lies somewhere between these two poles.

Wise Counsel to Wives

The first six verses of our "gem of truth" passage refer to wives, and the seventh verse refers to husbands. One New Testament scholar gives a good explanation of this seeming inequity.

> It may seem strange that Peter's advice to wives is six times as long as that to husbands. This is because the wife's position was far more

difficult than that of the husband. If a husband became a Christian, he would automatically bring his wife with him into the Church.... But if a wife became a Christian while her husband did not, she was taking a step which was unprecedented and which produced the acutest problems.[3]

Despite that explanation, I know this passage is probably one of the hottest potatoes in Scripture, especially for women. Let me put some of you at ease. I do not believe this or any other part of Scripture admonishes a wife to stay in a situation where her health is being threatened or where her life—or the lives of her children—is in danger. That is not what submission is all about. So please don't run to that extreme and hide there, thinking you can avoid or deny the importance of submission in every other area or at any other level.

I find no fewer than three implied imperatives woven into the fabric of these important verses. They are reasonable and doable commands. They aren't culturally irrelevant. Best of all, they work!

Analyze Your Actions

In the same way, you wives, be submissive to your own husbands so that even if any of them are disobedient to the word, they may be won without a word by the behavior of their wives, as they observe your chaste and respectful behavior. (1 Pet. 3:1–2)

Many wives tend to view their roles as conditional; their behavior depends on the behavior of their husbands. "Sure, I'll be the kind of wife I should be if he's the kind of husband he should be." On the surface, that sounds great. Turnabout is fair play. There's only one problem: This passage isn't written just to wives who have husbands who play fair. Peter doesn't let us off the hook that easily. The passage is written to all wives, even those whose husbands are "disobedient to the word." In fact, by implication this paragraph is directed to women who live with disobedient husbands—husbands who are going their own way, husbands who care little about the things of God, husbands who would even mock the things of Christ. In short, these are husbands who aren't measuring up to God's standard.

Having to exhibit godly behavior under such circumstances can, however, cause wives to substitute secret manipulation for a quiet spirit. This may take many forms: pouting, sulking, scheming, bargaining, nagging, preaching, coercing, or humiliating. Wives who use this strategy are not trusting God to change their husbands' lives. They're trusting themselves.

You see, a wife is not responsible for her husband's life. She is responsible for her life. You cannot make your husband something he is not. Only God can do that.

I think it was the evangelist's wife, Ruth Graham, who once said, "It is my job to love Billy. It is God's job to make him good." I'd call that a wonderful philosophy for any wife to embrace.

Wife, it is your job to love your husband. It is God's job to change his life.

And wives who are truly obedient to Christ will find that He will honor their secure spirit. Yes, submission is a mark of security. It is not a spineless cringing, based on insecurity and fear. It is a voluntary unselfishness, a willing and cooperative spirit that seeks the highest good for one's husband.

"Well, that sounds like a dead-end street, Chuck," some of you might be saying. "If you only knew what I am living with, what a rascal, what a reprobate, what an ungodly man he really is."

But notice what Peter says: "they may be won without a word by the behavior of their wives, *as they observe your chaste and respectful behavior.*" The Greek term for *observe* suggests that this is a keen and careful observation, not a casual glance. As a "disobedient" husband observes his wife's godly behavior, his heart will eventually soften toward spiritual things. Such a lifestyle has been called "the silent preaching of a lovely life."

Watch Your Adornment and Your Attitude

And let not your adornment be merely external—braiding the hair, and wearing gold jewelry, or putting on dresses, but let it be the hidden person of the heart, with the imperishable quality of a gentle and quiet spirit, which is precious in the sight of God. (1 Pet. 3:3–4)

Obviously Peter is drawing a sharp contrast between inner beauty and outer beauty, or as Peter puts it, between outer adornment (verse 3) and inner adornment (verse 4).

It's easy in our shop-'til-you-drop culture to get carried away with the externals, ladies. Catalogs for every conceivable item of clothing pour into our homes, with their 800 numbers eager to take your order at any hour of the day or night. If that isn't convenient enough, we have entire television channels devoted to shopping and stores available on the Internet. Ready...set...*charge*!

The point of the contrast here is to restore the balance. Peter isn't prohibiting the braiding of hair or the wearing of jewelry any more than he's prohibiting the wearing of dresses. He merely wants to put those things in the background and bring the woman's character into the foreground. Perspective is the key.

Taken to an unrealistic extreme, you can really miss the mark in your external adornment. I have seen some women who think that it is a mark of spirituality to look like an unmade bed. That is not what God has in mind. On the other hand, if externals get overemphasized, appearance, cosmetics, and clothing take on too much significance. You can become preoccupied with your external adornment, and you can begin judging yourself and others solely by appearance, which is often what our culture does.

External beauty is ephemeral. Internal beauty is eternal. The former is attractive to the world; the latter is pleasing to God. Peter describes this inner beauty as "a gentle and quiet spirit." This might be paraphrased "a gentle tranquility." Without question, this is any woman's most powerful quality—true character. And such character comes from within—from the hidden person of the heart—because you know who you are and you know who you adore and serve, the Lord Christ. God values this kind of inner beauty as "imperishable" and "precious."

Outward adornment doesn't take a great deal of time. I've seen women do it in a few minutes on their way to work in the morning. (Ever been driving behind a woman putting on her makeup in the car as she's driving to work? It's an amazing process! And dangerous. I always cringe and wonder—what happens if she hits a pothole?) It may take only a few hours to prepare yourself for the most elegant of evenings, but it takes a lifetime to prepare and develop the hidden person of the heart.

Adornment is important but not nearly as important as attitude. If the internal attitude is right, it's amazing how much less significant one's external appearance becomes. Wise is the wife who watches both.

Evaluate Your Attention

For in this way in former times the holy women also, who hoped in God, used to adorn themselves, being submissive to their own husbands. Thus Sarah obeyed Abraham, calling him lord, and you have become her children if you do what is right without being frightened by any fear. (1 Pet. 3:5–6)

The fact that Sarah called her husband her lord (Gen. 18:12) reveals much about their relationship. It shows that she respected him, was attentive to his needs, cooperated with his wishes, and adapted herself to his desires.

Wives, are you patterning yourself after Sarah's role model? Take a look at where you place most of your attention, where you spend your time, what the focus of your prayer life is. Is your husband at the top of your earthly list?

I would encourage you wives to evaluate where you place most of your attention, and this is especially true for women who are busy raising a family. It is so easy in the press of caring for the constant needs of your children to put the needs of your husband on hold. Experience has taught me that is often where a breakdown in a marital relationship begins.

Peter says, "Sarah obeyed Abraham." A good paraphrase might be, "She paid attention to him."

*

Strong Commands to Husbands

You husbands likewise, live with your wives in an understanding way, as with a weaker vessel, since she is a woman; and grant her honor as a fellow heir of the grace of life, so that your prayers may not be hindered. (1 Pet. 3:7)

The final verse in this section turns the spotlight on husbands. It's short, but penetrating. I find that it is packed with three strong imperatives.

First, live with your wife. The Greek term here is a compound word composed of *sun* (with) and *oikeo* (to dwell/abide); put together they obviously mean "to dwell together." Now, you're probably thinking, "Well, certainly, I live with my wife. I'm *married* to her." But that is not what Peter is talking about. He's talking about a "close togetherness." *Sunoikeo* suggests much more than merely living under the same roof. There is a depth, a sense of intimacy, in the word. He is saying that husbands are responsible for that in the relationship. Providing a good living should never become a substitute for sharing deeply in life. The husband needs to be "at home with" his wife, understanding every room in his wife's heart and being sensitive to her needs. "Dwelling together" definitely means more than eating at the same table, sharing the same bed, and paying for the same mortgage.

Second, know your wife. Peter exhorts husbands to live with their wives "in an understanding way." That phrase literally means, "according to knowledge"—not an academic knowledge, but a thorough understanding of how your wife is put together.

"Oh, I know my wife," you may say. "Brown hair. Blue eyes. Weight. Height. I know what she likes for supper. Her favorite color is blue. I know where she likes to go for dinner." It's not that kind of knowledge either. Any man can know those things about her!

Your wife is a unique vessel, carefully crafted and beautifully interwoven by her Creator. To "know your wife" means you know the answers to those complex questions about her. What is her innermost makeup? What are her deepest concerns and fears? How do you help her work through them in the safety and security of your love? What does she need from you? Why does she respond as she does?

There's no handbook for those insights into her life. Even your father-in-law can't give you this inside information. You have to find it out in the intimacy of marriage and in the process of cultivating your life together. It takes time. It takes listening. It takes paying attention, concentrating, praying for insight, seeking understanding. Most wives long for that. Some of them die longing for it. Few things give a woman more security than knowing that her husband really knows her. That's what results in intimacy. That's what turns romance into a deep, lifelong love. That's what keeps her focused on and committed to you, longing to have you there, delighting in your presence, your words, your listening ear.

By the way, we need to address another phrase that occurs here: "living with your wife in an understanding way, *as with a weaker vessel.*" Now a word of caution: This has nothing to do with weakness of character or intelligence.

> The woman is called the "weaker vessel" (*skeuos*, lit., "vessel"); but this is not to be taken morally, spiritually, or intellectually. It simply means that the woman has less physical strength. The husband must recognize this difference and take it into account.[4]

Sometimes this is a bit difficult to comprehend when we consider what a woman goes through in bearing children. There's no doubt about the kind of strength women have within them when it comes to enduring pain. When my daughter gave birth to her second child, our fourth grandchild, she had natural childbirth. (Seemed strange to me—"natural" childbirth—and I was thankful I never had to go through that. I've never heard of anybody having a natural appendectomy or requesting a natural root canal!) What strength she demonstrated!

But when it comes to actual physical strength, Dr. Robert Kerlan, orthopedic surgeon and sports medicine specialist, says: "If the battle of the sexes was reduced to a tug-of-war with a line of 100 men on one side of the trench and 100 women on the other, the men would win." What makes the difference, he says, is muscle makeup.[5]

God's goal for us as husbands is to be sensitive rather than to prove how strong and macho we are. We need to love our wives, listen to them, adapt to their needs. We need to say no to more and more in our work so we can say yes to more and more in our homes . . . so we can say yes to the needs of our children and our families. (How else will your children learn what it means to be a good husband and father?)

Mind you, this is not to be a smothering kind of attention—the kind that says a husband is so insecure he cannot let his wife out of his sight. Instead, this is the kind of love that means your wife can't come back fast enough to your arms. Which brings us to the third imperative.

Third, honor your wife. To "grant her honor" is to assign her a place of honor. The same word translated "honor" here in 3:7 refers to the blood of Christ as "precious" in 1:19. I'd call that a rather significant analogy, wouldn't you?

Authors Gary Smalley and John Trent define this word well in their book *The Gift of Honor*.

> In ancient writings, something of honor was something of substance (literally, heavy), valuable, costly, even priceless. For Homer, the Greek scholar, "The greater the cost of the gift, the more the honor." . . .
> Not only does it signify something or someone who is a priceless treasure, but it is also used for someone who occupies a highly respected position in our lives, someone high on our priority list.[6]

That's how husbands are to treat their wives—to honor them by assigning them the top priority on their list of human relationships . . . in their schedules . . . and most importantly, in their hearts.

May I ask a few very personal questions? How do you treat your wife on an average day? Do you honor her? Do you give her a place of significance? Does she know she's your "top priority"? And do you communicate that in both actions and words? Honoring another is never something we keep to ourselves.

This is a magnificent truth, and you'll only get it from the Scriptures. It revolutionized my home. That's why I know it works. I didn't come from a model home and my wife didn't come from a home where her mother was honored. Cynthia and I knew that if we were going to make our marriage work, we had to go God's way, which meant we both had to be willing to change. We determined to do just that. And I'll freely admit, of the two of us, I have had to change more. About the time I think I've got things in good shape, another area emerges, and I have to deal with that! The journey toward marital maturity is a long one! And each year there are always some changes that must occur.

Let me summarize what Peter has written. Wives, your actions, your adornment, your attitudes, your attention are crucial in your marriage. Husbands, living with your wife, getting to know your wife, and honoring your wife are imperative if your marriage is going to be what it should be in God's eyes. Marriage is a two-way street. Both sides must be maintained.

A Promise to Both Partners

To seal this "heavenly bargain," Peter closes with a promise to both partners: "So that your prayers may not be hindered." This is an added incentive for husband and wife to live together in domestic harmony.

If you and your mate hope to cultivate an effective prayer life, the secret lies in your relationship with each other. Your prayers will not be hindered if you cultivate a close and caring relationship. Could that explain why your prayers are not being answered now?

A Project to Add Hope to Your Home

During the next week I'd like you to work on a very practical project. It will involve your doing two things. *First*, write down four qualities you appreciate most about your mate. After thinking them through, tell your spouse what they are and why they come to mind. Give examples. Take your time. Spell them out. Genuinely affirm your partner. *Second*, using this section of 1 Peter as your guide, admit the one thing you would most like to change about yourself. Don't be afraid to be vulnerable. Your mate will appreciate your willingness to be transparent.

Now don't get those two reversed. Don't mention four things you want your partner to change and the one thing you like most about yourself!

Talk truth. Refuse to blame. Guard against this becoming an evening of confrontation. Make it an evening of getting back together. Go ahead . . . be willing to risk.

You may be amazed to discover how quickly new hope for your marriage can return. The secret isn't that profound. A good marriage isn't so much finding the right partner as it is being the right partner.

And that starts with you.

A Prayer for Hope Beyond "I Do"

Lord, marriage was Your original idea. You hold the patent on this one. You brought the first couple together and gave Adam and Eve wise instruction on how to make their marriage flourish.

I believe You are still bringing men and women together . . . all around this big world. But today I pray specifically for those who read this chapter. For some, their hopes are dim. They don't know where to start or how to rekindle the flame that once burned brightly. For others, starting over seems too great a hurdle . . . too huge a mountain to climb . . . too much to face.

Somehow, Lord, break down the barriers. Bring back the "want to." Restore a glimmer of hope, especially in the lives of that one couple who think they will never make it. May Your Spirit miraculously renew their hope at this moment. I ask this in the name of Christ, in whom nothing is impossible.

AMEN

8

Hope Beyond Immaturity

Maturity Checkpoints

DURING MY MOST obnoxious years as a teenager I frequently received two admonitions. The first one was an abrupt, "Shut up!" The second was, "Grow up!"

Though I found it difficult on occasion, I usually managed to accomplish the first rather quickly. But I must confess, there are still days when I struggle with the second piece of advice.

En route to maturity, we all spill our milk, say things we shouldn't, and fail to act our age. At times we act like a two-year-old throwing a temper tantrum. At other times we pout like a pubescent child or go through sweeping mood swings like an awkwardly adjusting teenager.

This process is called "growing up." Let's not minimize the truth—it's painful. We struggle through it more by trial and error than by unfaltering charm-school grace. Consequently, every now and then we skin an elbow, bruise a knee, or bloody a nose from falling on our faces.

Growing up. Sooner or later we all have to do it. The sooner we do, the easier it will be to walk the uneven and sometimes uncertain sidewalks of faith.

Problem is, how do we determine whether we are grown up? Does it mean our hair starts to turn gray? No, that means we're growing older but not necessarily wiser. I've met people with snow-white hair who are still immature. Signs of aging do not necessarily mean we are showing signs of maturity.

If you think it's easier to tell from the inside out, forget it. How do you know that you are more mature this year than you were last year? Has living twelve months longer made any difference? We know we're growing older, but how do we know we're growing up? And is growing up something God even requires of us? Maybe He just wants us to live in His family, sort of exist between now and eternity, then He's planning to take us home. No, that's not the way it works. Growing up is a stated objective for every member of God's family. God says so in His Word.

The writer of Hebrews addresses this very matter when he takes his readers to task for their lack of maturity. They had grown older in the faith, but they had not yet grown up. Instead of building on the foundation laid by the apostles, they were still playing with blocks.

> For though by this time you ought to be teachers, you have need again for someone to teach you the elementary principles of the oracles of God, and you have come to need milk and not solid food. For everyone who partakes only of milk is not accustomed to the word of righteousness, for he is a babe. But solid food is for the mature, who because of practice have their senses trained to discern good and evil.
>
> Therefore leaving the elementary teaching about the Christ, *let us press on to maturity,* not laying again a foundation of repentance from dead works and of faith toward God, of instruction about washings, and laying on of hands, and the resurrection of the dead, and eternal judgment, and this we shall do, if God permits. (Heb. 5:12–6:3, italics added)

Do you notice the Lord's concern that some seem perpetually immature? "You have need *again* for someone to teach you the elementary principles of the oracles of God," says the writer (italics added). "You have come to need milk and not solid food." How interesting that he puts it like that. We would say, "You're back on baby food."

I've had grocers tell me that they sell more baby food to the aging than to the parents of infants in their community. As we get older, in many ways we revert back to childhood. Physically that can't be helped—as we age and grow infirm, our bodies deteriorate. But spiritually, immaturity is something we must not allow. God wants us to get beyond the elementary matters of the faith and set out on a life-long pursuit of maturity. He longs for us to grow up in the faith.

Leave behind elementary teachings, says the letter to the Hebrews. Press on to maturity.

By "elementary teachings," the writer is very likely referring to the Old Testament signs and sacrifices. "We've gone beyond that now," he says. In today's terms we could say, "Move beyond the gospel. You have heard the gospel, you have responded to the gospel, you have believed the gospel, now go on. Grow up. Get into areas of teaching and learning that probe much deeper into your life." That kind of solid food results in spiritual strength. In fact, I've heard it rendered, "We are to leave the ABCs of the faith." In other words, we need to quit playing blocks and sucking milk from a bottle and wanting to be entertained. Leave the things that characterize infancy and get on with a grown-up lifestyle.

Few things are more pathetic to behold than those who have known the Lord for years but still can't get in out of the rain doctrinally and biblically. To put it succinctly, they have grown old, but they haven't grown up.

Do you feed yourself regularly on the Word of God or must you have the teaching of someone else to keep growing? Now, don't get me wrong; I don't decry teaching and preaching. How could I? That's my job security! All of us have a need for someone to instruct and exhort us in the things of God. But it isn't because we have no way of taking it in on our own. Teaching and preaching are more like nutritional food supplements.

Let me ask you several penetrating questions. Are you digging into the Word of God? Are you truly searching the Scriptures on your own? Are you engaged in a ministry of concerted and prevailing prayer? Can you handle pressure better than you could, say, three years ago? Are you further along on your own growth chart than you were a year ago, two years ago, five years ago?

Checkpoints for Maturity

How can we know we're growing up? Outwardly we have various signs of physical growth and aging. But when it comes to spiritual maturity, we need another kind of growth chart, and Peter, in his letter of hope, offers us a series of checkpoints to help us know we're growing up and getting on in spiritual life.

In the past three years I have flown on more airplanes than ever before in my life, commuting from California to Texas and back again, plus dozens of other destinations. When people ask Cynthia and me where we live, I sometimes reply, "Seats 16C and D, American Airlines." We're now on a first-name basis with many of the airline personnel.

As a result of this unusual transitional lifestyle, I have had ample occasions to watch the procedure pilots go through as they prepare for an upcoming flight. You may have observed it as well. The next time you're taking a trip, stand in the terminal and look out the windows into the cockpit of the airplane parked at the gate. You'll see the pilot sitting there with a clipboard, checking off all the instruments and systems. He'll also get out and check the outside of the aircraft, walking all around it. This is a seasoned pilot, with perhaps tens of thousands of hours in the air. Still, every time, before he takes that airplane up, he runs through his preflight checklist. We're thankful he does!

Look at 1 Peter 3:8–12, and you'll find another kind of checklist—a checklist for spiritual maturity. It helps us evaluate how we're doing on this pilgrimage from earth to heaven.

To sum up, let all be harmonious, sympathetic, brotherly, kind-hearted, and humble in spirit; not returning evil for evil, or insult for insult, but giving a blessing instead; for you were called for the very purpose that you might inherit a blessing. For,

"Let him who means to love life and see good days
refrain his tongue from evil and his lips from speaking guile.
"And let him turn away from evil and do good;
let him seek peace and pursue it.
"For the eyes of the Lord are upon the righteous,
and his ears attend to their prayer,
but the face of the Lord is against those who do evil."
(1 Pet. 3:8–12)

If I count correctly, there are no fewer than eight checkpoints in this section of Scripture. They help us determine how we're doing in our growth toward maturity.

Unity

The first checkpoint is unity: "Let all be harmonious." This refers to a oneness of heart, a similarity of purpose, and an agreement on major points of doctrine.

Please remember, this quality is not the same as *uniformity*, where everyone must look alike and think alike, form identical convictions and prefer the same tastes. That's what I call a cracker-box mentality. Peter isn't promoting uniformity. Nor is he referring to *unanimity*, where there is 100 percent agreement on everything. And it is not the same as *union*, where there is an affiliation with others but no common bond that makes them one at heart.

The secret to this kind of harmony is not to focus on petty peripheral differences but to concentrate on the common ground of Jesus Christ—His model, His message, and His mission.

How mature are you in the area of unity? Are you at harmony with other believers in the family of God? Are you one who works well *with* others?

Mutual Interest

The second checkpoint is mutual interest: "Let all be . . . sympathetic." The Greek root gives us our word *sympathy*, meaning "to feel with."

This means that when others weep, you weep; when they rejoice, you rejoice. It connotes the *absence* of competition, envy, or jealousy toward a fellow Christian.

Romans 12:15–16 states it well: "Rejoice with those who rejoice, and weep with those who weep. Be of the same mind toward one another. . . ." Believers who are growing toward maturity share in mutual feelings—mutual woes and mutual joys.

This is one of the best benefits of being part of the body of Christ and a major reason why we need to be involved in a local church. In that local community we have a context in which we can rejoice with each other and weep with one another. Think what happens when you move to a new community, a new home. Sadly you leave the church that has been your home, your spiritual family, where God has used you and encouraged you. But then He leads you to another. When you move to a new town or city, as a Christian one of the first things you do is search for a new church home, one where your new brothers and sisters welcome you and receive you into their fellowship and life. Right away you're surrounded by a family.

How's your maturity level on this second checkpoint? Can you truly say you enter the feelings of the other person? When others hurt, do you hurt? When they enjoy life, do you really enjoy it with them? When God blesses them with material prosperity or some significant award or promotion, do you rejoice with them or do you envy them? When they lose, do you feel the loss with them, or do you feel just a tiny pinprick of satisfaction?

I've heard it said, "Maturity begins to grow when you can sense your concern for others outweighing your concern for yourself."

Maturing believers care very much about the things others are experiencing.

Affectionate Friendship

The third checkpoint is friendship and affection: "Let all be...brotherly."

The word translated here as "brotherly" is from the Greek word *philos*, which has in mind the love of an affectionate friend. The poet Samuel Coleridge once described friendship as "a sheltering tree." When you have this quality, the branches of your friendship reach out over the lives of others, giving them shelter, shade, rest, relief, and encouragement.

Much has been written about the importance of friendship. James Boswell said, "We cannot tell the precise moment when friendship is formed. As in filling a vessel drop by drop, there is at last a drop which makes it run over; so in a series of kindnesses there is at last one which makes the heart run over." Longfellow wrote, "Ah! How good it feels, the hand of an old friend." Isn't that true!

Friends give comfort. We find strength near them. They bear fruit that provides nourishment and encouragement. When something troublesome occurs in our life, we pick up the phone and call a friend, needing the comfort he or she provides. I think there are few things more lonely than having no friend to call. Friends also care enough about us to hold us accountable...but we never doubt their love or respect.

Are you cultivating such friends? Are you being a friend? Are there a few folks who will stand near you, sheltering you with their branches?

Jay Kesler, my long-time friend and currently the president of Taylor University, has said that one of his great hopes in life is to wind up with at least eight people who will attend his funeral without once checking their watches. I love it! Do you have eight people who'll do that?

As we mature, it is healthy for us to have a circle of friends who lovingly hold us close, regardless...who care about our pain, who are there for us when we can't make it on our own. The flip side of that is equally healthy—our being friends like that to others. Works both ways. As we mature our friendships deepen.

Kindheartedness

The fourth checkpoint is kindheartedness: "Let all be . . . kindhearted." The Greek term here can also be translated "compassionate," and it is used in the Gospels to describe Jesus.

And seeing the multitudes, He *felt compassion* for them, because they were distressed and downcast like sheep without a shepherd. (Matt. 9:36, italics added)

As a good shepherd, Jesus looked at humanity's lost sheep who were scattered, frightened, and hungry. What He saw pulled at His heartstrings. He was full of tenderness for them. He had compassion for them. Just as these hurting people touched the heart of the Savior, so should hurting people today touch our hearts. If they do, it's a definite sign of spiritual growth. No one who is mature is ever so important that the needs of others no longer matter.

I've just finished reading a fascinating volume, *Character Above All*. It is a compilation of ten essays on the ten United States presidents from Franklin Roosevelt in the 1930s to George Bush in the 1990s, each written by people who knew those presidents well—friends, speechwriters, fellow politicians, and other colleagues who worked alongside them.

My favorite was the chapter on Ronald Reagan, who served our country from 1981–1989. His speechwriter, Peggy Noonan, wrote the piece and captured the essence of his character in twenty-two pages. Wonderful reading!

She concludes with a story about, in her words, "the almost Lincolnian kindness that was another part of Reagan's character . . . everyone who worked with Reagan has a story about his kindness." Before I retell that story, go back and read those eleven words. Wouldn't it be great if that could be said about each of us? Wouldn't it be wonderful to be remembered for our kindness?

In highlighting this quality in Reagan's character, Noonan tells the story of Frances Green, an eighty-three-year-old woman who lived by herself on social security in a town just outside San Francisco.

She had little money, but for eight years she'd been sending one dollar a year to the Republican National Convention.

Then one day Frances got an RNC fund-raising letter in the mail, a beautiful piece on thick, cream-colored paper with black-and-gold lettering. It invited the recipient to come to the White House to meet President Reagan. She never noticed the little RSVP card that suggested a positive reply needed to be accompanied by a generous donation. She thought she'd been invited because they appreciated her dollar-a-year support.

Frances scraped up every cent she had and took a four-day train ride across America. Unable to afford a sleeper, she slept sitting up in coach. Finally she arrived at the White House gate: a little elderly woman with white hair, white powder all over her face, white stockings, an old hat with white netting, and an all-white dress, now yellow with age. When she got up to the guard at the gate and gave her name, however, the man frowned, glanced over his official list, and told her that her name wasn't there. She couldn't go in. Frances Green was heartbroken.

A Ford Motor Company executive who was standing in line behind her watched and listened to the little scenario. Realizing something was wrong, he pulled Frances aside and got her story. Then he asked her to return at nine o'clock the next morning and meet him there. She agreed. In the meantime, he made contact with Anne Higgins, a presidential aide, and got clearance to give her a tour of the White House and introduce her to the president. Reagan agreed to see her, "of course."

The next day was anything but calm and easy at the White House. Ed Meese had just resigned. There had been a military uprising abroad. Reagan was in and out of high-level secret sessions. But Frances Green showed up at nine o'clock, full of expectation and enthusiasm.

The executive met her, gave her a wonderful tour of the White House, then quietly walked her by the Oval Office, thinking maybe, at best, she might get a quick glimpse of the president on her way out. Members of the National Security Council came out.

High-ranking generals were coming and going. In the midst of all the hubbub, President Reagan glanced out and saw Frances Green. With a smile, he gestured her into his office.

As she entered, he rose from his desk and called out, "Frances! Those darn computers, they fouled up again! If I'd known you were coming I would have come out there to get you myself." He then invited her to sit down, and they talked leisurely about California, her town, her life and family.

The president of the United States gave Frances Green a lot of time that day—more time than he had. Some would say it was time wasted. But those who say that didn't know Ronald Reagan, according to Peggy Noonan. He knew this woman had nothing to give him, but she needed something he could give her. And so he (as well as the Ford executive) took time to be kind and compassionate.[1]

In our high-tech, cyberspace era it is so easy to become distant. We can live our lives untouched and untouchable. In a fast-lane world it isn't difficult to become uncaring and preoccupied with our own agendas. The freeway of life requires that we keep moving, no matter what we see happening around us. The pace at which we travel does not allow us to stop easily. And even if we could, we've seen the stories in the news about people who stopped to help and were rebuffed, mugged, or carjacked—even murdered. So we learn to keep our eyes straight ahead and keep going...fast! The homeless person on the sidewalk? The mentally disturbed stranger at the mall? Hurry past. Just keep looking straight ahead, moving past them, down the road of life.

Of course, we need to be wise; we must use discernment. Still, is there no place for kindheartedness and compassion in our world? Is there no time for tender mercies?

Read again the words that appear at the end of Ephesians 4:

> And be kind to one another, tender-hearted, forgiving each other, just as God in Christ also has forgiven you. (Eph. 4:32)

Maturing people are tender people. How valuable they are in a busy society like ours!

Humility

The fifth checkpoint is humility: "Let all be... humble in spirit." The phrase "humble in spirit" literally means "lowly" or "bowed down" in mind. It speaks of an internal attitude rather than an external appearance. Humility isn't a show we put on; in fact, if we think we're humble, we're probably not. And in our day of self-promotion, self-assertion, spotlighting "celebrities of the faith," and magnifying the flesh, this quality—so greatly valued by the Lord Jesus—is a rare commodity indeed. Oswald Chambers writes of this so insightfully:

> We have a tendency to look for wonder in our experience, and we mistake heroic actions for real heroes. It's one thing to go through a crisis grandly, yet quite another to go through every day glorifying God when there is no witness, no limelight, and no one paying even the remotest attention to us. If we are not looking for halos, we at least want something that will make people say, "What a wonderful man of prayer he is!" or "What a great woman of devotion she is!" If you are properly devoted to the Lord Jesus, you have reached the lofty height where no one would ever notice you personally. All that is noticed is the power of God coming through you all the time.
>
> We want to be able to say, "Oh, I have had a wonderful call from God!" But to do even the most humbling tasks to the glory of God takes the Almighty God Incarnate working in us.[2]

If you are blessed with abilities, if you are gifted, if you are used by God, it is easy to start believing your own stuff. Yet one of the marks of a truly mature life is humility of spirit.

> It can be said without qualification that no human being can consider himself mature if he narrows the use of his efforts, talents, or means to his own personal advantage. The very concept of maturity rests on the degree of inner growth that is characterized by a yearning within the individual to transcend his self-concentration by extending himself into the lives of others. In other words, maturity is a stage in his development when to live with himself in a satisfying manner it becomes imperative for him to give as well as to receive.[3]

A truly humble person looks for opportunities to give himself freely to others rather than holding back, to release rather than hoarding, to build up rather than tearing down, to serve rather than being served, to learn from others rather than clamoring for the teaching stand. How blessed are those who learn this early in life.

Carl Sandberg once related the story about a mother who brought her newborn son to General Robert E. Lee for a blessing. The southern gentleman tenderly cradled the lad in his arms then looked at the mother and said, "Ma'am, please teach him that he must deny himself."[4]

Forgiveness

Thus far, Peter has written about how maturity affects how we think and how we feel. In his last three checkpoints, found in verses 9 through 11, he tells us how maturity affects *what we do and what we say*. In verse 9 he tells us not to return evil for evil. In other words, be willing to forgive.

> ...not returning evil for evil, or insult for insult, but giving a blessing instead; for you were called for the very purpose that you might inherit a blessing. (1 Pet. 3:9)

Isn't that a great statement? It touches all the important bases regarding forgiveness. Just look at the four steps in it; observe the process.

First, when we have true forgiveness in our hearts, we refuse to get back or get even.

Second, we restrain from saying anything ugly in return.

Third, we return good for evil, "giving a blessing instead [of evil or insult]."

And fourth, we keep in mind that we were called to endure such harsh treatment.

It's easy to miss that last one, isn't it? I thought at first I was misreading it, and then I went back to chapter 2 and found that's what Peter says over there too. So he must mean it. Do you remember his earlier comment?

What credit is there if, when you sin and are harshly treated, you endure it with patience? But if when you do what is right and suffer for it you patiently endure it, this finds favor with God. For you have been called for this purpose. (1 Pet. 2:20–21a)

What is a sure sign that I'm growing up? When I stop fighting back. When I take the chip off my shoulder. When I stop working on my clever answer so I can punch back with a sarcastic jab.

Whenever the urge to get even comes over us, it's important for us to realize that retaliation is a sign of adolescence while restraint is a mark of maturity.

A Controlled Tongue

"Let him who means to love life and see good days
refrain his tongue from evil and his lips from speaking guile."
(1 Pet. 3:10)

You knew we'd get around to this one, didn't you? The tongue . . . what a battle! Warnings about the tongue are threaded throughout the Bible. In fact, in this verse and the one that follows Peter is quoting from Psalm 34:12–16.

Here he says to "refrain" your tongue from evil. Actually the psalmist used a little more forceful language: "Keep your tongue from evil." The idea is to get control of your tongue, or, as James puts it, put a bridle on it. It's the idea of holding it back from galloping headlong into greater evil (see James 3:1–10). Control your tongue!

Show me a person who has learned to refrain from gossip, to refrain from passing on confidential information, to refrain from making an unverified comment, and I'll show you somebody who is well on his or her way to maturity.

You really want to love life? You want to see good days? Gain better control of your tongue. Life will be happier for you. It'll even be easier for you. You'll see better days.

Some never learn this lesson. Remember the classic grave marker from jolly old England?

Beneath this sod,
this lump of clay,
lies Arabella Young,
who, on the 24th of May
began to hold her tongue.

Will it take death to control your tongue? It need not! Pray that God will control your tongue, starting today! Pray that He will muzzle your mouth when someone says, "Please don't share this with anyone else." When someone speaks to you in confidence, seal the information in the secret vault of your mind.

Believe me, I'm a preacher, and I know how tempting it is to use real-life examples in my sermon illustrations, especially family-related examples. I heard recently about a preacher up in the Northwest who pays his kids a royalty of a dollar every time he uses them in an illustration! He asks permission, they approve, he tells the story, they get a buck. That'll curb a loose tongue real quick!

A mark of maturity is a controlled tongue.

A verse in Psalm 141 puts all of this so clearly. It's from the ancient writings of David, and I've often thought of it as a great prayer with which to begin each day.

Set a guard, O LORD, over my mouth;
Keep watch over the door of my lips. (Ps. 141:3)

How are you doing on the checklist so far? Unity. Mutual interest. Friendship and affection. Kindheartedness and compassion. Humility. Forgiveness. A controlled tongue. Pretty convicting list, isn't it? But if we wish to have hope beyond our immaturity, these qualities are worth our time and attention. And there's one more twofold checkpoint.

Purity and Peace
"And let him turn away from evil and do good;
let him seek peace and pursue it.
"For the eyes of the Lord are upon the righteous,

And his ears attend to their prayer,
But the face of the Lord is against those who do evil."
(1 Pet. 3:11–12)

Look again at Peter's counsel. "Turn away from evil and do good."
That's purity. "Seek peace and pursue it." That's peace. And then he
tells us that the Lord is watching us and listening to us. Why? Because He cares about our modeling these qualities.

The eyes and ears of the Lord are emblematic of God's providential care for His people. What a wonderful reason for pursuing purity and peace—the promise of God's providential care!

A Final Glance at the Checklist

That's quite a checklist, isn't it? Eight distinct notches to mark our
Christian maturity. How do you measure up?

We're told to grow up. We're told to press on to maturity. But
growing up is never easy. We all have areas of trouble, setbacks, stumbling points along the way. (I don't know of one item on this list that
isn't a struggle for me at various times in my own life.) So those are
the things that we pray about, for "His ears attend to our prayers."

Here's a practical suggestion. Go over that list at the end of every
month. Write it out and stick it where you will see it. Put it under a
refrigerator magnet. Tape it to your mirror. Ask God for strength in
these eight areas.

As children of God moving toward maturity, let's be committed
to harmony, to a spirit of unity. Let's engage in a mutual interest in
each other's lives. Let's develop friendships marked by affection, by
"touchable love"—love that is genuine and demonstrative. Let's be
kindhearted and compassionate. Let's exhibit humility of spirit and
a mind that is concerned about others instead of ourselves. Finally,
let's forgive, control our tongues, and pursue purity and peace.

I am grateful airline pilots take the time to check their lists before
we take off. I'm especially glad they don't shrug their shoulders when

they see a bulge on one of the tires and say, "Well, we'll just hope for the best." I'm glad they don't ignore the smallest detail, even though they've gone down the same list hundreds of times in their careers. I'm glad they don't take my life and safety for granted. That's why they are willing to return to that list again and again and again.

We dare not take our Christian maturity for granted either. That's why we must return to God's checklist again and again and again.

We dare not do any less if we hope to get beyond a life of immaturity.

A Prayer for Hope Beyond Immaturity

Father, thank You for the reminder today of things that are such an important part of our lives. Though none of these qualities is new, we continue to need the reminder. How often we have come asking for help in one or more of these areas. You've heard our pleas on many occasions. We so want to be growing toward maturity . . . but the journey takes forever! And so, this very moment, we thank You for the Lord Jesus Christ, our model and our master, who fulfilled each of these marks of maturity and dozens of other character qualities to perfection, though fully man. Thank You for the hope we have that Your Holy Spirit will be with us each step of our way on our road to maturity. We certainly need His empowerment to keep us going and growing.

I would ask, finally, that You give us hope beyond our immaturity. Guard us from discouragement as we look back over the checklist and realize how far we have to go. Remind us that we've come a long way toward the goal, by Your grace. Through Jesus Christ I pray.

AMEN

9

Hope Beyond Bitterness

When Life
"Just Ain't Fair"

AN OLD FRENCH fairy tale tells the story of two daughters—one bad and the other good. The bad daughter was the favorite of her mother, but the good daughter was unjustly neglected, despised, and mistreated.

One day, while drawing water from the village well, the good daughter met a poor woman who asked for a drink. The girl responded with kind words and gave the woman a cup of water. The woman, actually a fairy in disguise, was so pleased with the little girl's kindness and good manners that she gave her a gift.

"Each time you speak," said the woman, "a flower or jewel will come out of your mouth."

When the little girl got home, her mother began to scold her for taking so long to bring the water. The girl started to apologize, and two roses, two pearls, and two diamonds came out of her mouth.

Her mother was astonished. But after hearing her daughter's story and seeing the number of beautiful jewels that came out in the telling, the mother called her other daughter and sent her forth to get the same gift. The bad daughter, however, was reluctant to be seen performing the lowly task of drawing water, so she grumbled sourly all the way to the well.

When the bad daughter got to the well, a beautiful queenly woman—that same fairy in another disguise—came by and asked for a drink. Disagreeable and proud, the girl responded rudely. As a result, she received her reward too. Each time she opened her mouth, she emitted snakes and toads.[1]

How's that for poetic justice!

There's something in each one of us that longs for circumstances to be fair, isn't there? Maybe that's why fairy tales are so appealing. Good people receive their rewards and "live happily ever after" while bad people are soundly punished. Life works out, justice is done, and fairness reigns supreme.

Unfortunately, real life doesn't usually turn out that way. Every child needs to be taught, "Fairness is rare." Every epitaph could read, "Life is difficult."

Our lives are haunted by unfairness when we want fairness. Instead of justice we are surrounded by injustice. We want deceit exposed, dishonesty revealed, and truth rewarded. But things don't work out that way. At least not as we perceive them.

Some families have been racked by unfairness. A mate leaves a loving, faithful partner. Disease steals a loved one prematurely. An unfair situation at work or at school keeps escalating.

Life just doesn't turn out fair for some . . . for most!

Truly, life *is* difficult. But therein lies some of life's best lessons.

I was reminded of those words when I read this astonishing statement by a well-known British writer and radio personality:

> Contrary to what might be expected, I look back on experiences that at the time seemed especially desolating and painful with particular satisfaction. Indeed, I can say with complete truthfulness that everything I have learned in my seventy-five years in this world, everything that has truly enhanced and enlightened my existence, has been through affliction and not through happiness. In other words, if

it ever were to be possible to eliminate affliction from our earthly existence by means of some drug or other medical mumbo jumbo...the result would not be to make life delectable, but to make it too banal and trivial to be endurable. This, of course, is what the Cross signifies. And it is the Cross, more than anything else, that has called me inexorably to Christ.[2]

Now it is one thing to read those words from a man like Malcolm Muggeridge and almost be moved to tears. It's another thing to embrace them in our own lives. I know there isn't a person reading this who hasn't, at some point, had reason to become bitter because of the way you were treated by someone or because of some "unfair" affliction or experience. Everyone can blame someone for something!

As Christians we know that, ultimately, good will triumph over evil and that our God is just and kind and fair. But what can we do with the injustices and unfairnesses in the meantime? How can we keep pressing on in spite of such mistreatment?

Two Different and Distinct Perspectives

Our response to unfairness, as with all other issues, is based on our perspective—the particular vantage point from which we look at life. Basically, in this case, we have two perspectives to choose from: the human perspective or the divine.

The Human Perspective

Our natural, human perspective contends, "Since life isn't fair, I'm going to get my share. I'm going to look out for number one. I'm going to spend my energy getting my own back or setting things straight or making it right. I'm not going to take it any longer."

Our world is full of literature and counselors who will help you carry out this agenda. The problem is, you may get even but you won't get peace. You may feel better for the short term, but you won't get lasting satisfaction. You may find a way to channel your anger, but if retaliation is your major goal, you will not glorify God. Those who live their lives from this perspective are more likely to end their lives as bitter, cynical, hostile people. Tragically, I have just described how the majority of Americans choose to live.

The Divine Perspective

Fortunately, we do have another option, and we find it clearly spelled out for us in 1 Peter.

> "For the eyes of the Lord are upon the righteous,
> And His ears attend to their prayer,
> But the face of the Lord is against those who do evil."
> (1 Pet. 3:12)

The principle that Peter gives us is this: God misses nothing. He's looking out for us. He's listening to our prayers. And He is completely aware of the evil that is happening to us.

Don't ever think He has missed the evil. He sees, and He remembers. He may be long-suffering, but He doesn't compromise His justice. Not only is His eye on the righteous, His face is against evil. Ultimately, good will overcome evil. In the end, God wins!

But if this is true, we wonder, why doesn't He do something about evil? Why does He let it go on so long? Because God's time line is infinite—He doesn't close His books at the end of the month. It may take a lifetime—or longer—before justice is served. But in the end, count on it, *God will be just*. In the end, He will "work everything together for good" and for His glory.

That thought gives us hope beyond bitterness. If we don't believe that and if we don't focus on that, we become the loser. We spend our years like a rat in a sewer pipe, existing in the tight radius of cynicism and bitterness. Ultimately, we become, in our aging years, angry old men and jaded old women.

*

Psalm 34:15-16

. STRONG STATEMENT - SOMETHING the WORD OF GOD
HAS EMPHASIZED A GREAT DEAL.

#1 GOD HAS GUARANTEED to HEAR the PRAYERS
OF THOSE WHO ARE HIS OWN. HE HAS NOT GUARANTEED to HEAR
the PRAYER of Those who ARE NOT HIS.

THE only PRAYER A SINNER CAN PRAY IS to ADMIT
to the LORD HE/SHE IS A SINNER, AND ACCEPT JESUS CHRIST
AS SAVIOR. THIS PRAYER GOD will HEAR AND ANSWER.

MANY BELIEVE YOU CAN LIVE ANYWAY YOU CHOOSE AND WHEN IN
NEED EXPECT GOD to HEAR AND ANSWER. It is A FALSE idea
to think YOU CAN CALL ON GOD UNDER ANY CIRCUMSTANCE WHEATHER
OR NOT YOU ARE HIS CHILD — GOD DOES NOT PROMISE to hear
the PRAYERS OF Those who DO NOT BELONG to HIM.

It is NOT UNTIL YOU ARE RIGHT WITH GOD YOU CAN
live life to its FULLEST.

Some Helpful Insights and Techniques to Keep Hope Alive

Building on this divine perspective, Peter gives us five ways we can live in an unfair and inequitable world. But first there's a general principle we need to underscore.

A General Principle

And who is there to harm you if you prove zealous for what is good? (1 Pet. 3:13)

If we were to paraphrase this verse, we could say that those who live honest lives will not usually suffer harm. *Usually.* There are exceptions, of course, to almost every rule, as we will see below. But as a general rule, if you live a life of purity and integrity, in the long run you usually won't suffer as much as those who habitually traffic in evil.

For example, if you pay your debts, chances are good that you won't get into financial trouble. If you pay all your taxes on time, you probably won't have the IRS on your case. If you take care of your body—get sufficient exercise and sleep, watch your diet and your stress level—chances are good that you will live a healthier life than those who don't. If you help others, chances are good that when you are in need someone will be there to help you. To paraphrase Peter's principle, those who do what is right are usually not in harm's way. *Usually* that's the rule.

Occasional Inequities

However, to return to reality, because life is difficult, there are times when life "just ain't fair." So there will be times when, despite that general principle, despite your righteous life, despite your faithful walk with God, situations turn on you. And it's these exceptions to the rule that Peter is addressing in chapter 3, verses 11 through 17. He begins with a general summation of the condition.

But even if you should suffer for the sake of righteousness, you are blessed. (1 Pet. 3:14a)

Before going on, notice the words, "But even if you should." In New Testament Greek, there are four conditions introduced by the word *if*. Three were quite common. The first-class condition, meaning "assumed as true," was a common usage (see Matt. 4:3, 6); the second-class condition, meaning "assumed as not true," was also commonly used (see Gal. 1:10); the third-class condition, meaning "maybe, maybe not," was frequently employed by writers (as seen earlier in 1 Pet. 3:13). The fourth-class condition, meaning "unlikely but possible," is rarely used in Scripture. Interestingly, this is the condition Peter uses here in verse 14. It could be paraphrased, "It is unlikely that you should suffer for the sake of righteousness, but if you should...." That, alone, ought to give us a boost of fresh hope!

Then Peter goes on to suggest five ways you and I should respond if this happens. Remember, this is not my advice; this is God's advice. Human advice says, "Kick 'em in the teeth. Get even." That's not good advice, but it's often heard. So we need to know what God has to say about how to respond when we have done what is right but wrong is done to us in return.

It might help if you wrote these responses down on a three-by-five card and keep them handy. I'd suggest that you look at the card at least once a day. You might want to stick it on your bathroom mirror or slide it under the glass of your desktop.

How are we to respond when the exception to the rule occurs?

First, consider yourself uniquely blessed by God.

As far as the injustice itself is concerned, Peter's surprising advice is, "Be happy! Consider yourself blessed!" James tells us something similar in the first chapter of his letter.

> When all kinds of trials and temptations crowd into your lives, my brothers, don't resent them as intruders, but welcome them as friends! (James 1:2 PHILLIPS)

Sure sounds nice, you may say, but honestly now, how can we be happy and consider ourselves blessed when we've just been punched in the eye with the fist of injustice?

Well, we can do this by remembering two things: first, as we saw in chapter 6, we are called to patiently endure unfair treatment (see 1 Pet. 2:21; 3:9) so that when it comes we can know we're still experiencing God's plan and fulfilling our calling. Such treatment reminds us that God's hand is still on our lives. And second, someday we will be rewarded for our endurance of these undeserved trials (see Matt. 5:10–12; James 1:12).

Anybody can accept a reward graciously, and many people can even take their punishment patiently when they have done something wrong. But how many people are equipped to handle mistreatment after they've done right? Only Christians are equipped to do that. That is what makes believers stand out. That's our uniqueness. And, yes, there are occasions in life when we will be called for that very purpose. In the mystery of God's sovereign plan, we will be singled out. Then later, like Job, we will be rewarded for enduring those trials we did not deserve.

Remember Jesus' instruction?

"Blessed are those who have been persecuted for the sake of righteousness, for theirs is the kingdom of heaven. Blessed are you when men cast insults at you, and persecute you, and say all kinds of evil against you falsely, on account of Me. Rejoice, and be glad, for your reward in heaven is great, for so they persecuted the prophets who were before you." (Matt. 5:10–12)

Because of these promises (there are many similar ones throughout the Scriptures) Christians can do something different from all the rest of humanity. We can respond to injustice with a positive attitude. When we do, mouths drop open . . . and we're frequently given an opportunity to explain why we're not eaten up with revenge.

Second, don't panic and don't worry.

And do not fear their intimidation, and do not be troubled. (1 Pet. 3:14b)

It doesn't take a linguistic scholar to interpret that counsel. Peter puts his finger on two common responses. Panic and worry. I do both of those things when I operate in the flesh, don't you? But observe what Peter says.

First, look at the word *fear*. It comes from the original term *phobos*, from which we also get our word *phobia*. This kind of fear is the fear that seizes us with terror and causes us to take flight, running away from the pressure. Peter says, "Don't do that. There's no reason to run. Don't attempt to escape the trial. Don't panic."

In the second phrase he tells us that we don't need to "be troubled." The word *troubled* in Greek means "to be agitated, uneasy," the idea of feeling inner turmoil or agitation. Remember John 14:1, "Let not your heart be troubled"? Same root word here.

The energy and effort we expend worrying never solves a thing. In fact, it usually makes the situation worse for us, creating a terrible inner turmoil which, if allowed to intensify, can paralyze us.

Peter's counsel to us is that, even when trials are pressing in and people are trying to intimidate us, we can have a calmness of spirit. As far as the persecutor or instigator is concerned, we can be free from panic and worry. How? Why? Because we know that God is on our side.

Third, acknowledge Christ as Lord even over this event.

> But sanctify Christ as Lord in your hearts... (1 Pet. 3:15a)

We often overlook the first phrase of this verse in our concentration on the second part:

> ...always being ready to make a defense to everyone who asks you to give an account for the hope that is in you. (1 Pet. 3:15b)

We usually apply those words to some public defense of the faith. While they may be used in that way, the verse actually appears in a context of wrong having come to us as a result of our doing what is right. And it says, "Do not fear... but in your hearts set apart [sanctify] Christ as Lord" (NIV).

You and I can do that in prayer. When we think a wrong has been done to us that we don't deserve, we can respond, "Lord, You're with me right now. You are here, and You have Your reasons for what is happening. You will not take advantage of me. You're much too kind to be cruel. You're much too good to be unjust. You care for me too much to let this get out of hand. Take charge. Use my integrity to defend me. Give me the grace to stay calm. Control my emotions. Be Lord over my present situation." In such a prayer, we "set apart Christ as Lord" in our hearts.

If I have prayed that sort of prayer once, I must have prayed it dozens of times. "Lord, there is no way I can set the record straight, it seems. It's getting more complicated and I find myself completely at Your disposal... at Your mercy. Take over, Lord. You be the sovereign Master over this moment. I can't change this person... I can't alter these circumstances. You be the Lord over this scene."

When our older daughter, Charissa, was in high school, she was on the cheerleading squad. One day at the church office I got an emergency call from her school. She had accidentally fallen from the top of a pyramid of the other cheerleaders during practice and landed on the back of her head. To her and everyone else's amazement, she couldn't move. It took me about fifteen minutes to drive from my study at the church to the school campus. I was praying that kind of prayer all the way. "Lord, You are in charge of this situation. I have no idea what I'm going to face. You be the Lord and Master. I am trusting You in all this."

When I got to the school, they already had Charissa immobilized on a wrap-around stretcher. I slipped to my knees beside her.

"Daddy, I can't move my fingers. My feet and legs are numb," she said. "I can't feel anything in my body very well. It's kind of tingling."

At that moment, I confess I had feelings of fear. But I leaned closer to Charissa and whispered in her ear, "Sweetheart, I will be with you through all of this. But more importantly, Jesus is here with you. He is Lord over this whole event."

Her mother and I were totally helpless. We had absolutely no control over the situation or over the healing of our daughter's body. She was at the mercy of God. I can still remember the deliberateness with which I acknowledged Christ as Lord in my heart and encouraged her to do the same. Cynthia and I waited for hours in the hospital hallway as extensive X-rays were taken and a team of physicians examined our daughter. We prayed fervently and confidently.

Today, Charissa is fine. She recovered with no lasting damage. She did have a fracture, but thankfully it wasn't an injury that resulted in paralysis. Had she been permanently paralyzed, we would still believe that God was in sovereign control. He would still be Lord!

A good example of someone who sanctified Christ as Lord in his heart is Stephen. When he gave an eloquent and penetrating defense of Jesus before the Jewish Sanhedrin, this infuriated many who heard him. Their hatred raged out of control. Do you remember his response?

> But being full of the Holy Spirit, he gazed intently into heaven and saw the glory of God, and Jesus standing at the right hand of God; and he said, "Behold, I see the heavens opened up and the Son of Man standing at the right hand of God." (Acts 7:55–56)

They wouldn't listen to him. They covered their ears and rushed upon him. They drove him out of the city and violently stoned him to death.

As Stephen died, "he called upon the Lord and said, 'Lord Jesus, receive my spirit!' And falling on his knees, he cried out with a loud voice, 'Lord, do not hold this sin against them!'" (Acts 7:59–60). And then he died.

Stephen didn't deserve their savage attack. He certainly didn't deserve death. Because of that, he could have died in bitterness and cynicism. He could have died with curses on his lips. Instead, he sanctified the moment to God and died with a prayer on his lips, asking forgiveness for those who so mercilessly killed him. When those men looked into Stephen's face, they didn't find their own hatred reflected back at them; they saw the reflection of the Savior's grace and love.

Like Stephen, we need to acknowledge Christ's control over our unfair circumstances and do our best to see that He is glorified in them. That is the only thing that will bring us lasting, peaceful satisfaction.

Fourth, be ready to give a witness.

. . . . always being ready to make a defense to everyone who asks you to give an account for the hope that is in you, yet with gentleness and reverence. (1 Pet. 3:15b)

I'm intrigued by this. Some of us are so anxious to give a witness that we press it on others even when it isn't appropriate or when the timing isn't right. But this says we are to be ready *when they ask us* to give an account. And believe me, if you are handling mistreatment or unfairness or suffering for the glory of God, people will ask.

"How do you do it?" . . . "How do you handle this?" . . . "How do you live with it?" . . . "Why is it you haven't lost your joy?" . . . "What keeps you on your feet?" . . . "Why haven't you just turned tail and run?" . . . "Why haven't you fought back?" Common questions from curious onlookers.

"Be ready to make a defense . . . to give an account." The word *defense* comes from the term *apologia*. We get our word *apology* from this Greek word. It refers to making a verbal statement of defense. And *account* comes from the word *logos*, translated elsewhere in Scripture, "the word." At such times we are to be ready to give a verbal witness . . . a gentle and yet pointed declaration of the truth.

Stop and consider. Mistreatment is a perfect platform for a witness. Your neighbors will want to know how you stay calm in the midst of it, how you go through it without strongly reacting. Your friend at work will want to know, "How do you pull it off?"

Be ready to make a defense, to give an answer, to witness to anyone who asks. Seldom will there be a more opportune time to share your faith than when you are suffering and glorifying Him through it. Others who know what you are enduring will listen. You have earned the right to be heard. But don't miss the way you should testify: "with gentleness and reverence." Wise counsel from Peter, a man who had been broken.

William Barclay gives an excellent explanation of what our "defense" and "account" should be like.

> It must be *reasonable*. It is a *logos* [account] that the Christian must give, and a *logos* is a reasonable and intelligent statement of his position.... To do so we must know what we believe; we must have thought it out; we must be able to state it intelligently and intelligibly....
>
> His defence must be given with *gentleness*.... The case for Christianity must be presented with winsomeness and with love.... Men may be wooed into the Christian faith when they cannot be bullied into it.
>
> His defence must be given *with reverence*. That is to say, any argument in which the Christian is involved must be carried on in a tone which God can hear with joy.... In any presentation of the Christian case and in any argument for the Christian faith, the accent should be the accent of love.[3]

And fifth, keep a good conscience.

Here Peter digs below the surface, turning up the rich soil of inner character. And what is the precious gem he is trying to unearth? *Integrity*.

> And keep a good conscience so that in the thing in which you are slandered, those who revile your good behavior in Christ may be put to shame. (1 Pet. 3:16)

Nothing speaks louder or more powerfully than a life of integrity. Absolutely nothing! Nothing stands the test like solid character. You can handle the blast like a steer in a blizzard. The ice may form on your horns, but you keep standing against the wind and the howling, raging storm because Christ is at work in your spirit. Character will always win the day. As Horace Greeley wrote: "Fame is a vapor, popularity an accident, riches take wing, and only character endures."

There is no more eloquent and effective defense than a life lived continually and consistently in integrity. It possesses invincible power to silence your slanderers.

The Underlying and Unwavering Principle

For it is better, if God should will it so, that you suffer for doing what is right than for doing what is wrong. (1 Pet. 3:17)

Simply stated, the principle is this: Unjust suffering is always better than deserved punishment. And sometimes—though we cannot fully explain why—it is God's will that His people should suffer for doing what is right.

An old Hebrew story tells of a righteous man who suffered undeservedly. He was a man who had turned away from evil, took care of his family, walked with God, and was renown for his integrity. But suddenly, without warning, and seemingly without reason, he lost everything he had: his flocks, his cattle, his servants, his children, and finally his health. This old Hebrew story is no fairy tale. It is the real account of a real person—Job.

Though he suffered terribly, and though he could never have foreseen it himself or understood it when it happened, Job has been remembered down through the ages and to this very day as a model of patient endurance. "The patience of Job" remains one of our axiomatic phrases.

I would not wish the life of Job on anyone. But, then, I'm not God. I've never been too good at directing anyone else's life. I have a hard enough time keeping my own on track. But I have observed a few "Jobs" in my years in ministry. They come under that fourth-class condition: "If He should will it so . . . it's unlikely but possible."

If you are one of those modern-day "Jobs," don't waste your time trying to figure out *why*. Someday all will be made clear. For now, follow the five responses outlined by Peter.

Dr. Bruce Waltke was my Hebrew professor during three of my years at Dallas Seminary. He has since become something of a mentor and friend. He is a brilliant man with a tender heart for God. When I was going through a very difficult time in my senior year in seminary and wanted some answers to the *whys,* Bruce said something like this: "Chuck, I've come to the place where I believe only on very rare occasions does God tell us why, so I've decided to stop asking." I found that to be very helpful counsel. From that point on, I began to acknowledge that I am not the "answer man" for events in life that don't make logical, human sense. I'm now convinced that even if He did explain His reasons, I would seldom understand. His ways are higher and far more profound than our finite minds can comprehend. So I now accept God's directions, and I live with them as best I can. And frankly, I leave it at that. I've found that such a response not only relieves me, it gives me hope beyond bitterness.

If God has called you to be a Job—a rare calling—remember that the Lord is not only full of compassion, He is also in full control. He will not leave you without hope. He offers us His promises:

> "For My thoughts are not your thoughts,
> Neither are your ways My ways," declares the Lord.
> "For as the heavens are higher than the earth,
> So are My ways higher than your ways,
> And My thoughts than Your thoughts." (Isa. 55:8–9)

> When a man's ways are pleasing to the Lord,
> He makes even his enemies to be at peace with him. (Prov. 16:7)

Listen to the counsel of Peter. Calmly and quietly let these five bits of counsel sink in.

- Consider yourself uniquely blessed by God.
- Do not run in panic or sit and worry.

- Acknowledge Christ as Lord even over this event.
- Be ready to give a witness.
- Keep a good conscience.

A Prayer for Hope Beyond Bitterness

Our Father, as we acknowledge Your Son as Lord, it is with a sigh, because we cannot deny the pain or ignore the difficulty of earthly trials. For some who read these words, the reality of this is almost unbearable. But being sovereign and being the One with full capacity to handle our needs, it is not beyond Your strength to take the burden and, in return, to give us the perspective we need.

Quiet our spirits. Give us a sense of relief as we face the inevitable fact that life is difficult and that there will be those rare moments when it will not be at all fair. Erase any hint of bitterness. Enable us to see beyond the present, to focus on the invisible, and to recognize that You are always there. Remind us, too, that Your ways are higher and far more profound than ours.

Thank You for the joy of this day. Thank You for the pleasure of a relationship with You and a few good, caring, loving friends. And especially, Father, thank You for the truth of Your Word that lives and abides forever. In the strong name of Him who is higher, Jesus the Lord.

AMEN

10

Hope Beyond the Creeds

Focusing Fully
on
Jesus Christ

WHEN I WAS a little boy, my family moved to Houston, where my father had been hired to work at what was called, in those days during World War II, a "defense plant." Houston is a city of industry, and during those war years many of the industries retooled in order to manufacture implements, ammunition, and equipment for the war. The particular place where my father worked built transmissions for the rugged Sherman tank and landing gears for the powerful B-17 "Flying Fortresses."

We didn't see much of my dad during those five years because he was working ten to fifteen, sometimes even eighteen, hours a day, from six to seven days a week. Since our family had only one car, which Dad used each day to drive himself and several coworkers to the shop, the rest of our family had to walk to the grocery store, to school, and to church.

The closest church was a Methodist church at the end of our street. I still remember sitting in those wooden pews almost every Sunday. And every Sunday, as part of the worship-service liturgy of that particular Methodist church, we recited the Apostles' Creed.

I don't remember one sermon that was preached during those five years. I cannot recall any church-sponsored event that made an impact on me. But I clearly remember repeating the Apostles' Creed. In fact, I memorized that statement of faith in a matter of months simply because we repeated it Sunday after Sunday. You, too, may know these words well:

> I believe in God the Father Almighty, maker of heaven and earth;
> And in Jesus Christ, His only begotten Son, our Lord, who was conceived by the Holy Spirit, born of the Virgin Mary, suffered under Pontius Pilate, was crucified, dead and buried; He descended into hell; the third day He rose again from the dead; He ascended into heaven, and sits at the right hand of God the Father Almighty; from thence He shall come to judge the living and the dead.
> I believe in the Holy Spirit, the holy catholic church, the communion of saints, the forgiveness of sins, the resurrection of the body, and the life everlasting. Amen.

Even though I was only a small boy when I recited the creed, there were two statements in it that troubled me. My first concern was, "I believe in the holy catholic church." I knew our family wasn't Catholic, so how could I keep saying I believed in the Holy Catholic Church? Then, at some point, a youth worker explained to me that catholic (small "c") really meant "universal," so what we were really saying was, "I believe in the universal church." No problem.

More difficult to resolve, however, was the part where we said that Jesus Christ "descended into hell." That troubled me. There was nobody around who could answer that for me, not even my mother. Interestingly, it was almost twenty years later in a Greek class in seminary that I experienced a flashback to those days as a little boy in the Methodist church. We were digging into the text at the end of 1 Peter 3, and I came across the verse that described in Scripture what I had stated as a little boy but had never understood.

Let me remind you of the last five verses in 1 Peter 3:

For Christ also died for sins once for all, the just for the unjust, in order that He might bring us to God, having been put to death in the flesh, but made alive in the spirit; in which also He went and made proclamation to the spirits now in prison, who once were disobedient, when the patience of God kept waiting in the days of Noah, during the construction of the ark, in which a few, that is, eight persons, were brought safely through the water. And corresponding to that, baptism now saves you—not the removal of dirt from the flesh, but an appeal to God for a good conscience—through the resurrection of Jesus Christ, who is at the right hand of God, having gone into heaven, after angels and authorities and powers had been subjected to Him. (1 Pet. 3:18–22)

Isn't that a grand statement of faith? It's almost like another creed that we might recite in church from Sunday to Sunday.

Our Example

I have found in my study of the Bible that one of the best rules to follow if I'm going to understand any particular section of Scripture is to look at the whole scene (the context) before I try to work my way through each verse. Sort of like looking at the forest before examining the trees.

Following that rule, we first need to answer a primary question: What's the main subject of this paragraph? As you may recall from the subject we dealt with in chapter 9, it is unjust suffering. Remember the words of Peter?

For it is better, if God should will it so, that you suffer for doing what is right rather than for doing what is wrong. (1 Pet. 3:17)

If unjust suffering is the main subject, what's the point of the whole paragraph? Clearly, it is this: blessings follow suffering for well-doing.

Now at this point, immediately after Peter has written verse 17, the Spirit of God prompts him to mention the One who best exemplifies that truth. Who in every believer's mind would best exemplify blessing following unjust suffering? Obviously, Christ. And that's why Peter at verse 18 says, "For Christ." He doesn't say so, but we could insert in parentheses, "As an example."

> For Christ (as an example) also died for sins... the just for the unjust, in order that He might bring us to God....

What is the blessing that came to us following Christ's unjust suffering? Our salvation. And what was the blessing for Him, personally, following His unjust suffering? His resurrection. That is stated at the end of verse 20.

The focus of attention here is Jesus Christ, not the recipients of the letter or those who would read it centuries later. It is Jesus Himself. He alone is the focal point. Look at this great statement of faith regarding the Lord Jesus.

Verse 18: He "died for sins." That's His *crucifixion*.

Verse 19: "He... made *proclamation*."

Verse 21: "through the *resurrection* of Jesus Christ."

Verse 22: "who is at the right hand of God... after angels and authorities and powers had been subjected to Him." That's *exaltation*.

What we have here, in brief, is a survey of the crucifixion, proclamation, resurrection, and exaltation of the Lord Jesus Christ. Peter is clearly and openly highlighting some major doctrines related to Jesus Christ. So far, so good. But the paragraph also includes a digression (see verses 19–21).

Sometimes while writing a letter you'll mention a subject that is important to you, which reminds you of something not as pertinent as the subject but since it completes the picture, you add it. It might take another paragraph to do so, or it might just take a sentence or two. In this instance, Peter completes the overall thought regarding Christ by adding some details... things seldom mentioned elsewhere in the Bible. In fact, there are two knotty issues here that every serious student of the New Testament struggles with. One of them has to do with Christ's "descent into hell" (see verses 19–20), and the other has to do with what appears to be an affirmation of baptismal regeneration, "baptism now saves you" (verse 21)—more about these later.

Our Entree

Having considered the overall context, then, let me come to the central theme of the passage. Look back again at verse 18. This is one of those all-encompassing verses that states the gospel in its briefest and most concentrated form. That concentrated statement concerning the Lord Jesus is beautiful: "Christ also died for sins once for all." We don't have to relive or redo the death of Christ. We don't have to anticipate His dying another time or several other times. He has died "once for all." It was the death of all deaths, permanently solving the sin problem.

When Christ came, He was the perfect substitute for sin. And as a lamb without spot and without blemish, He hung on the cross and died. His blood became the one-and-only, all-sufficient payment to God for sins. The anger of God was satisfied, because Christ's payment for sin settled the account, once for all. Furthermore, all the debt against us was wiped away as Christ's righteousness was credited to our account. It wasn't fair for Him to die. He was just. He died, "the just for the unjust."

You may not know it, but you're mentioned (by implication) in Scripture on a number of occasions. And here is one of those times. Your name could appear in the place of the words "the unjust."

Let me state it in my case: "For Christ also died for sins once for all, the just for Chuck Swindoll. . . ."

Or you could put *your* name there: "The just for [your name]."

Why did He do it? "In order that He might bring us to God." One very careful student of the New Testament calls this "an entree." Our Lord Jesus Christ, in dying on the cross, provided us with "an entree" into heaven. He gave us access. As a result of His death, the access to heaven is now permanently paved. It is available to all who believe in the Lord Jesus Christ.

He "was put to death in the flesh, but made alive in the Spirit." So what is He doing now? "He is at the right hand of God." Maybe you didn't know that—a lot of people don't know what Christ is currently doing. He has ascended from this earth, and He has gone back to the place of glory in bodily form. (He is the only member of the Godhead who is visible. God the Father is in spirit form. God the Spirit is in spirit form. The only visible member of the Trinity is the Lord Jesus Christ.) He sits at the right hand of God making intercession for us. He's praying for us. He is moved by our needs; He is touched with the feelings of our infirmities. He is there for us, His people, and He is interceding for us. Since He is at the right hand of God, there is no question of His place of authority.

The Apostles' Creed is correct when it says, "He ascended into heaven and sits at the right hand of God; from thence He shall come to judge the living and the dead." He will come to judge both, and that judgment awaits His return to this earth. What powerful truths are here! Peter knew his theology!

His Proclamation

All that is fairly clear...now the tough part. First of all, let's address the subject of Jesus' descent, as the creed calls it, "into hell." Referring to the Lord Jesus Christ, Peter tracks His itinerary following His crucifixion.

> ...in which also He went and made proclamation to the spirits now in prison, who once were disobedient, when the patience of God kept waiting in the days of Noah, during the construction of the ark, in which a few, that is, eight persons, were brought safely through the water. (1 Pet. 3:19–20)

What in the world does that mean? When exactly did this occur? Who were these spirits that He visited? And what is the "proclamation" that He made? Good questions.

Let me draw upon your knowledge of the Scriptures and ask you to remember a scene back in the days before the Flood. It's recorded in the sixth chapter of Genesis. (When you have time, you may want to go back and read it.) We are told that during this period the depravity of men and women reached an all-time high. Their wickedness was so severe that it grieved the heart of God—He was sorry He had even created humanity!

> Then the LORD saw that the wickedness of man was great on the earth, and that every intent of the thoughts of his heart was only evil continually. And the LORD was sorry that He had made man on the earth, and he was grieved in His heart. (Gen. 6:5–6)

If you read this in the context of the first four verses of Genesis 6, you learn of an amazing and seldom-mentioned series of events that had happened. There was sexual cohabitation at that time between spirit beings and women on this earth. It is believed that during the antediluvian era—the time prior to the Flood—these spirits came in bodily form and somehow had intercourse with human women. As a result, a generation of supernatural beings were born—admittedly a strange phenomenon rarely mentioned by preachers and therefore seldom taught to Christians.

When the Flood came, it put an end to that heinous lifestyle and that freakish generation. Also, God's judgment fell upon those spirits who cohabited with women, and He placed them in a location called, in the original, *Tartarus*. It was a special place, described here as "a prison." It was there Jesus made His victorious proclamation.

What was this proclamation? I find it helpful to know that this is not the word used for proclaiming the gospel. Rather, it is a word, *kerusso*, used to describe someone "heralding" a statement. It denotes one who proclaims that the king has made a decision or that someone is declaring a certain edict—actually, it can refer to a proclamation of any kind. Jesus openly and forthrightly proclaimed that He had fulfilled His mission. He had died for the sins of the world. The work of salvation was accomplished.

When I put all of this together, I come to the following conclusion. I believe verses 19 and 20 describe the time immediately after Jesus died. His body was taken down from the cross and placed in a grave, but His inner being, His soul and spirit, descended into the shadowy depths of the earth, into the place of Tartarus (the creed calls it "hell"), where the antediluvian wicked spirits were imprisoned. Once there, He proclaimed to them His victorious death over sin and His power over the enemy, Satan himself. It was this proclamation that caused them to realize their work of attempting to corrupt and confuse the human race had been in vain. All of their attempts to sabotage the cross, to keep it from happening, were null and void. He went to that place to proclaim His victory at Calvary.

Our Faith

That brings us to the second question raised by verse 21, where we read: "Baptism now saves you." What does this mean?

Again, we can't ignore the context. First, we must understand that the Flood is in Peter's mind. He has just said so (verse 20). It was the Flood that brought death and destruction to those who didn't believe. It was also the water that brought deliverance to those who did—eight of them. Imagine that. Though there were multiple millions of people, only eight got in the ark. Along with the animals, only eight human beings believed and lived!

It was the ark floating on the water that got them through the Flood, which became a beautiful picture to the early church. In fact, the ark was frequently used to describe salvation. Today, we see the cross as our ark. It is our way to life. It is the way we get through the death-like world about us. Thus, baptism became another beautiful expression or picture of just such a deliverance from death—through the water.

Baptism symbolizes deliverance, just as the ark did. In fact, look at the words in parentheses, which in my Bible, the New American Standard version, are placed between dashes:

And corresponding to that, baptism now saves you—not the removal of dirt from the flesh, but an appeal to God for a good conscience—through the resurrection of Jesus Christ. (1 Pet. 3:21, italics added)

Baptism doesn't cleanse anyone, either literally or symbolically. It does not cleanse us externally, as a bath does; nor does it cleanse us within. But, indeed, it is our appeal to God for a good conscience. That which saves us is faith in the Lord Jesus Christ, and this is what is illustrated beautifully in baptism as we come out of the water. The Living Bible, in 1 Peter 3:21, offers a fine paraphrase of this parenthetical section.

(That, by the way, is what baptism pictures for us: In baptism we show that we have been saved from death and doom by the resurrection of Christ; not because our bodies are washed clean by the water, but because in being baptized we are turning to God and asking Him to cleanse our *hearts* from sin.)

Now you understand why in a baptismal service each candidate testifies personally to his or her faith in Jesus Christ. Nothing in the waters of baptism cleanses the flesh or the soul, but the water does illustrate what has already happened in the life of the redeemed.

Practical Principles

As we wrap up our thoughts here, let me mention a couple of very practical principles we can draw from this section of Peter's letter. *First, when unjust suffering seems unbearable, remember the crucifixion.* I know you've heard that before, but it is something we cannot be reminded of too often. It can be a wonderful comfort. It is remarkable how focusing on the Lord Jesus Christ's body hanging on the cross as a payment for sin really does help alleviate the pain in my life. About the time I start thinking my suffering is terribly unjust I turn my attention to what He endured; that does a lot to ease or even erase any sense of bitterness or resentment within me. And so, when unjust suffering seems unbearable, remember the crucifixion. *Second, when the fear of death steals your peace, remember the resurrection.* There is nothing quite like the hope we derive from our Lord's resurrection. Every Easter we celebrate it. In fact, every Lord's Day we're to be reminded of it. Certainly the Apostles' Creed reinforces it. Which brings us back to where we began.

I believe in God the Father Almighty, maker of heaven and earth;
And in Jesus Christ, His only begotten Son, our Lord, who was conceived by the Holy Spirit, born of the Virgin Mary, suffered under Pontius Pilate, was crucified, dead and buried; He descended into hell; the third day He rose again from the dead; He ascended into heaven, and sits at the right hand of God the Father Almighty; from thence He shall come to judge the living and the dead.
I believe in the Holy Spirit. . . .

Despite the all-encompassing truths contained in these concise words, the most personal and crucial part of the creed is the first two words, "I believe." Without them, it's just a statement someone originated—a statement many worshipers recite every week without ever having any kind of personal relationship with Christ. A body of bright, godly, religious-minded men honed that statement to put in simple form the salient features of our faith. But without our faith, it's still just a creed—a statement of *their* faith. What we need most is a firm hope beyond any creed we may recite.

The question is, do I *believe* the truth of that statement? Do you *believe* it? If you do, there is hope for you beyond it or any other creed. And that hope is a heavenly home reserved for you.

A Prayer for Hope Beyond the Creeds

Father, thank You for the truth of Your Word, for its clarity and its simplicity. And, Lord, because it is so exact, there isn't any reason to doubt. We do believe. Freely and willingly and gratefully, we believe.

But our belief goes beyond any creed . . . far beyond any statement originated by humans, no matter how godly or sincere. With great faith, our Father, we believe in the Lord Jesus Christ who died for us. We believe He suffered unjustly. We believe His payment was sufficient to wash away sins. Our sins. And now that He has been raised and ascended, our Father, we believe that He is alive, interceding for us, and is coming again.

Because of Christ's crucifixion, proclamation, resurrection, and exaltation, give us a sense of peace when we face death. Give us a sense of hope when we suffer unjustly. Remind us that heaven is our ultimate hope. I pray in His matchless name, with great anticipation.

AMEN

11

Hope Beyond the Culture

How to Shock the Pagan Crowd

STEPPING ONTO FOREIGN soil and into the midst of another language and culture for the first time in one's life can be an uneasy experience.

It happened to me while I served in the Marine Corps in the late 1950s. Our troopship had carried us across the Pacific, and my comrades and I were about to step onto Japanese soil. We eagerly anticipated being on land after such a long time at sea. For many of us, it was our first visit to a foreign country. We were surging with excitement, imagination, and every other emotion you could think of due to those seventeen days on the same ship. We were ready!

Before we left the ship, however, our company commander called all of us together. He stood in front of us, looked around at the group, and then, staring deeply into our eyes, he said loudly and sternly, "I want all of you men to remember that for the first time in your lives, *you are the foreigners*. This is not your country or your culture. Now you are the minority. These are not your fellow citizens. They do not speak your language. They know nothing of your homeland except what they see in you."

It was one of those "behave yourself" pep talks, but it went beyond that. Our commander was also saying, "You, as individuals, are representing the entire United States. Don't blow it! Don't become another example of 'the ugly American.' Act in such a way that the Japanese people will gain a good impression of your country and what America must be like. Make us proud, not ashamed." Those words rang in my ears for many days.

As Christians, we face a similar situation. Since our citizenship is in heaven, planet Earth is really not our home. For us, it is foreign soil. We are citizens of another realm. We belong to the kingdom of God. Consequently, we need to be on our best behavior; otherwise, people will get a distorted perception of what our homeland is like. As a result of our behavior, they will either be attracted to or repelled by heaven, the place we call home.

The old gospel song is still right on target.

> This world is not my home.
> I'm just a passin' through.
> My treasures are laid up
> Somewhere beyond the blue.[1]

It's true! But it's easy to forget. Maybe this is a good time to be reminded... we live in a pagan culture, surrounded by people who embrace a pagan philosophy and a pagan way of life.

Just consider the latest Broadway fare being ecstatically hailed as "the breakthrough musical of the nineties" ... "the most exuberant and original American musical to come along this decade." The play, *Rent*, is set "among the artists, addicts, prostitutes, and street people of New York City's East Village." The leading characters are "a drug-addicted dancer in an S&M club who is suffering from AIDS" and a rock singer who is HIV positive. "AIDS is the shadow hovering over all the people in *Rent*, but the musical doesn't dwell on illness or turn preachy; it is too busy celebrating life and chronicling its characters' effort to squeeze out every last drop of it."

Those characters are a gay teacher, a transvestite, and a lesbian attorney, among others.[2]

A friend of mine would call that "being mugged by reality," but that's the world we live in. Our earthly culture is pagan to the core. Let's not forget that God has left us here on purpose. We're here to demonstrate what it is like to be a member of another country, to have a citizenship in another land, so that we might create a desire for others to emigrate. Our mission is to create a thirst and an interest in that land "beyond the blue."

In 1 Peter 4:1–6, the apostle gives some marching orders to Christian soldiers who are stationed on this foreign soil. He opens the subject by addressing a Christian's behavior before a watching world with the connective word, *therefore*.

> Therefore, since Christ has suffered in the flesh, arm yourselves also with the same purpose. (1 Pet. 4:1a)

Careful students of the Scriptures pay close attention to words, especially words that connect main thoughts. The word *therefore* is a word of summary that connects what the author is about to write with what he has just written. And what has he just written? Look back at 3:18 and 22.

> For Christ also died for sins once for all, the just for the unjust, in order that He might bring us to God, having been put to death in the flesh, but made alive in the spirit.... who is at the right hand of God, having gone into heaven, after angels and authorities and powers had been subjected to Him. (1 Pet. 3:18, 22)

Christ has suffered and died on our behalf, the just for the unjust. *Therefore*...Do you see how it all ties together? Since Christ has died for our sins, the just for the unjust, and since He has been seated at the right hand of God, and since all authorities have been subjected to Him, and since He has suffered in the flesh, *therefore*, we should arm ourselves with the same purpose He had when He was on this earth.

I like the way one scholar amplifies what was meant by "arm yourselves."

> [Peter] exhorts the saints to arm themselves with the same mind that Christ had regarding unjust punishment.... The Greek word translated "arm yourselves" was used of a Greek soldier putting on his armor and taking his weapons. The noun of the same root was used of a heavy-armed footsoldier who carried a pike and a large shield.... The Christian needs the heaviest armor he can get to withstand the attacks of the enemy of his soul.[3]

This word picture offers a blunt reminder that we Christians are not living on this earth as carefree tourists. We are not vacationing our way to heaven. We are soldiers on raw, pagan soil. Everywhere around us the battle rages. The danger is real, and the enemy is formidable. Christ died not only to gain victory over sin's dominion but to equip us for that fight—to give us the inner strength we need to stand against it. Therefore . . . we are to arm ourselves with the strength that Christ gives because our purpose in life is the same as His.

Martyn Lloyd-Jones's warning bears repeating:

> Not to realize that you are in a conflict means one thing only, and it is that you are so hopelessly defeated . . . you do not even know it—you are unconscious! It means that you are completely defeated by the devil. Anyone who is not aware of a fight and a conflict in a spiritual sense is in a drugged and hazardous condition.[4]

Transformation: Remarkable Difference in the Christian Life

Several years ago when I was preaching on First Peter, a man called me and said, "I just want to let you know, Chuck, that the message of First Peter is happening in my life." When I asked what he meant, he went on to describe some difficulties he'd been going through. As he did, he said, "The things you've been talking about recently came back to my mind."

He said he had felt a heaviness in his spirit... he called it "a dark oppression." We prayed together about his situation. A few days later when I saw him after the Sunday morning service, he said, "I just want you to know the cloud has lifted." He had sensed the beginning of deliverance from his private war in the realm of darkness.

Many of you live in the competitive jungle of the business world, and some of you may work for a boss who asks you to compromise your ethics and integrity. Pressured by the tension between pleasing your boss, who can fire you or demote you or just make your life difficult, and your commitment to Christ, you need the inner resources to stand firm. "Arm yourselves with the same purpose" is certainly applicable for you. The good news is this: you have it! The provision Christ gives will be sufficient for such a stress test.

> Therefore, since Christ has suffered in the flesh, arm yourselves also with the same purpose, because he who has suffered in the flesh has ceased from sin, so as to live the rest of the time in the flesh no longer for the lusts of men, but for the will of God. For the time already past is sufficient for you to have carried out the desire of the Gentiles, having pursued a course of sensuality, lusts, drunkenness, carousals, drinking parties and abominable idolatries. (1 Pet. 4:1–3)

Fortunately those who are "in Christ" have been transformed. This transformation brings with it at least four benefits that Peter mentions. We no longer serve sin as our master (verse 1b); we don't spend our days overcome by desires as we once did (verse 2b); we now live for the will of God (verse 2b); we have closed the book on godless living (verse 3).

We've sowed our wild oats. Most have had enough time to see the end result of this lifestyle of loose living. Peter calls that lifestyle "the desire of the Gentiles."

Before Christ entered our lives, we had no power to withstand sin. When temptation came along, we yielded. We were unable to do otherwise. When the weakness of the flesh appeared, we fell into its trap. Though we may have looked strong on the outside, we had no inner stability. But when Christ took up residence in our lives, He gave us strength so that we could cease serving sin as a master. (Romans 6 is a wonderful section of scripture on this subject.) Because Christ now lives within us, we have been released from sin's control. We are no longer enslaved to sin. We've been freed!

Observe how "the will of God" (verse 2) is contrasted with "the desire of the Gentiles" (verse 3). Notice, too, how "the desire of the Gentiles"—the old habits, practices, associations, places of amusement, evil motives, and wicked pastimes—are all scenes from the past. The list sounds like your average *Animal House* on some college campus:

- sensuality
- lusts
- drunkenness, carousals, and drinking parties.

The original terms are vivid. *Sensuality* refers to actions that disgust and shock public decency. *Lusts* go beyond sexual promiscuity and involve sinful desires of every kind, including the lust for revenge and the lust for money (greed). *Drunkenness, carousals, and drinking parties* describe a whole miserable spectrum of pleasure-seeking consumption, from wanton substance abuse to wild sexual orgies. And we thought these things represented twentieth-century wildness! When it comes to a shameless, pagan lifestyle, nothing is new.

What is so liberating about our relationship with Christ is that He fills the void in our lives that we once tried to fill with all that garbage. With the void filled, the gnawing emptiness that accompanied it is gone too. And with the emptiness gone, we no longer crave the things we used to crave.

That's where Christians are different from the world. That's where we stand out. That's where the light shines in the darkness. And invariably the darkness reacts to such a light.

★

Reaction: Angry Astonishment from the Unsaved World

While we may live in this foreign land, far from our ultimate home, we live for the will of God. As a result, there is a marked contrast between our lifestyle and the lifestyle of the pagans—people who do not know the Lord—around us. And when we don't partake of that lifestyle, we are considered "weird."

Make no mistake about it. If we don't participate in that lifestyle, you and I are weird. *We are really weird!* And they notice it. Again, Peter's words are as relevant as this morning's newspaper. Look how he describes the reaction of the unsaved world.

> And in all this, they are surprised that you do not run with them into the same excess of dissipation, and they malign you. (1 Pet. 4:4)

Talk about the relevance of Scripture! Peter sounds like he is alive today! Any lifestyle of restraint, no matter how tactful we try to be, makes unbelievers uncomfortable. Sometimes it makes them defensive and angry, causing them to lash out at us as though in living our lifestyle we were judging theirs. I experienced this among fellow marines on numerous occasions—those who spent their lives in a realm of lustful drives and carousals and one drinking party after another. We see the same thing today in the after-hours of the corporate world. It's all part of the so-called "happy hour."

Beyond their discomfort and defensiveness, of course, is the inner emptiness they live with, day in and day out, the natural result of a life of lust and debauchery. What emptiness there is when the party's over and everybody goes home! They're left with the horrors of the sunrise and a head-splitting hangover, the guilt and even some shame as they crawl out of somebody else's bed, wondering what disease they might have gotten this time. And there's always that dark-brown taste in their mouth.

It's a horrible lifestyle! I don't care how beautiful the commercials look, it stinks! It doesn't last an hour, and it's anything but "happy!" But if they haven't any power to overcome it, the only thing they have to look forward to is the next "happy hour." And if they play the music loud enough and if there's enough booze and drugs, they think they can drown their troubles. Another lie of the Enemy. He's got a thousand of them.

Do you get the picture? The time already past is sufficient for you to have had your fill of "the desire of the Gentiles." You've tasted it. You've known it firsthand. But when Christ transformed your life, He filled the void and took away a lot of that drive. It's borderline miraculous, in fact, especially if He's enabled you to quick-kick an addiction.

But when that happens, you stand out like a sore thumb in your neighborhood... in your university dorm... at the office party. You're noticed. Even without saying a word, you're noticed. Even if you very quietly and graciously request a 7-Up instead of a cocktail, the word gets out.

Why? Because you've been transformed. You're no longer a helpless slave to sin. You're not overcome by your glandular drives. You are now interested in God's will; you have closed the door on godless living. And the pagan sits up like a doberman, eyes open, ears perked. "What in the world is wrong with Sam? Remember when we used to run around together? Now he's got religion." Or, "Suzy's gotten really weird... became a Bible-thumper. She was once a ton o' fun. Now she's Miss Goody Two Shoes. Next thing we know she'll become a televangelist!"

Brace yourself for such reactions if you're getting serious about Jesus and you've just broken off from a wild bunch of friends. The fact is, He is transforming you. Your old friends will not only be surprised, even shocked, at your new lifestyle, they might also actively ridicule and unjustly judge you for it as well. Expect it... it'll keep you from being "mugged by reality." You've just begun to experience hope beyond the culture.

Sometimes I wonder if they are really saying, "Look, misery loves company. If I'm gonna be this miserable, then you need to be miserable with me—like you used to. I don't want to do this alone."

The terrible irony of our unsaved friends' judgment is that they will themselves face the ultimate judgment...but that's the *last* thing they want to hear. Nevertheless,

...they shall give account to Him who is ready to judge the living and the dead. (1 Pet. 4:5)

Some of you have discovered that your close friends have changed now that you're in Christ. Regarding that, let me first warn you, and then I want to commend you.

First, I want to warn you about spending all of your time with Christians. If your entire circle of friends and acquaintances is nothing but Christian people, you will really get idealistic and unrealistic about the world. You really will get weird! Furthermore, how are the lost going to hear the gospel if all the saved stay clustered, sipping their 7-Ups and reviewing Bible verses together? We need to guard against our tendency to be with believers exclusively. The lost, deep down, are curious...and we need to be nearby when they start asking questions.

Second, I commend you for changing your circle of close friends. Some of your former friends do you no good, especially if you cannot withstand the lifestyle temptations they bring your way. Most people who fall into gross sensuality do not do it alone. They're usually prompted or encouraged by other people. You need to be wise and tactful about it...but before long, your change in lifestyle needs to be communicated.

There's a line in a country-western song sung by Alabama, "I'm Not That Way Anymore," that says it well: "Time has closed yesterday's door."

That's the way it is with Christians. You're not like that anymore. The fact is, my friend, Christ has closed yesterday's door. The way you are is different from the way you *were*. You won't be able to hide it...nor should you want to. Hopefully, however, you'll become a magnet of understanding, drawing others to the Savior rather than an offensive porcupine, driving them away.

Ideally, we want to be a fragrant aroma of Christ, winsomely attracting the unsaved to Jesus, the Savior. But Scripture, as well as our own experience, teaches us that what is fragrant to some is occasionally fetid to others.

Live an Authentic Lifestyle

The point of all of this? Once again we're back to the theme of Peter's letter: finding hope beyond unjust suffering. Enduring hardship. Seeing the reasons behind unfairness. Simply because you desire to live for Christ you will have people who once really enjoyed your company now talking about you behind your back, wondering if you've lost it . . . gone over the deep end. That is tough to take, because you know they aren't representing you fairly. But it's to be expected, looking at life strictly from their pagan perspective.

In fact, the longer I live, the more I see the value of having a thick skin but a tender heart. If you do, their cutting comments won't get to you. Furthermore, you won't feel the need to "set the record straight." Those maligning and ugly words kind of glance off, freeing you from an attack-back reaction.

Let me tell you what's happening. The pagan crowd will never tell you this, but down deep inside, many of them envy you. They wonder, *How does she do that? . . . How can he no longer do these things? . . . I'm not able to stop. . . . What in the world has made the difference?* And when you get them alone, it's remarkable how many of them will really listen as you tactfully and graciously tell them what has transformed your life. That's the joy of being left on foreign soil. You get to acquaint them with a life that is now yours and can be theirs, if only they'll genuinely and completely turn their lives over to Christ.

But let me warn you: Don't beat them up for their lifestyle. Nobody ever got saved because he was rebuked for his drinking or shamed for taking drugs or sleeping around. To tell you the truth, I'm surprised more in the pagan world don't do more of that to fill the void. So don't make an issue of their lifestyle. They can't help it.

They have no power to stop. Let grace and mercy flow. Relax...and leave the rebuking to the Lord.

Admittedly, there will be times that it will get to you...and you'll find yourself reaching the end of your tether.

One of the Bible teachers who used to lecture at Dallas Seminary when I was a student on campus was as tough as nails yet pure in heart. On one occasion while he was in the city to deliver a series of lectures, he went to a local barbershop to get a haircut. (A friend of mine happened to work there and overheard this conversation.) The barber, who didn't have the faintest idea who the man was, began talking about various issues of the day, giving his opinion, as barbers usually do. He peppered every phrase with an oath or a four-letter word. The teacher bit his lip as long as he could. Finally, he grabbed the barber's arm, pulled him around to the side of the chair, and looked the man right in the eye. Quietly but firmly he pulled on his own earlobe and said to the barber, "Does that look like a sewer?" The rest of the haircut was done in absolute silence.

I realize that such a reaction may not win many friends...but I understand the frustration.

Sometimes I just get my fill of it, too, don't you? Especially something as prevalent as blasphemous profanity. Throughout my months in the marines, I listened to that stuff till I thought I'd scream, so it's not that I haven't heard it before or that I can't handle it. I just occasionally reach the place where I have to say something. If it's handled right, even *that* can result in an opportunity to witness.

But in the final analysis, you cannot clean up anybody's lips until you've cleaned up his or her heart. And, ultimately, that's Christ's job. He's a master at it. So you stand it as best you can, realizing these are all simply signs of being lost. Such habits make the inhabitants of this pagan culture appear rough and rugged, but down inside they're often frightened little children. And they're scared to DEATH of death and what it might mean—whether they believe that to be nothingness or judgment.

Thankfully, the believer doesn't have to fear any of that. Our judgment is behind us...but their judgment is in front of them. Christ took our judgment, and He bore it on a cross. And He's given us the power He had now that we're in Christ. Remember the words of Isaac Watts?

> Am I a soldier of the cross?
> A follower of the Lamb?
> And shall I fear to own His cause
> Or blush to speak His name?
>
> Sure I must fight if I would reign:—
> Increase my courage, Lord!
> I'll bear the toil, endure the pain,
> Supported by Thy Word.

It's a great hymn. Even though it is almost 275 years old it is really up to date! It applies to businessmen and women who are facing verbal from their fellow employees. It applies to athletes today who refuse to live the lifestyle of the others on the team. It applies to those in the military service who love Christ but serve alongside those who don't. You're a soldier of the cross. What more can you expect? You're not a martyr. You're just taking a few verbal punches. It's good for you and me to be talked about like that. It drives us back to our knees before Christ and reminds us of our dependence on Him.

All believers owe it to themselves to read at least a portion of *Foxe's Book of Martyrs*, which traces the martyrdom of Christians throughout the centuries and demonstrates how viciously the world can act in its attempt to extinguish the light of Christlike character. There are some scenes that will make you shake your head. Talk about paying a price for one's faith!

Do you, like the brave saints of old, want to stand out like a bright light against the darkness of your world? Do you want to shock the pagan crowd? You don't need flamboyance or fanaticism. You don't need to fly a giant JESUS SAVES flag over your house or to wag your finger and rail against others' lifestyles. You don't need put-down bumper stickers or T-shirts with big, bold messages. You certainly don't need to rely on sermons or shame. What you do need to do is live differently. And you need to be aware of the consequences of Christlike living. For some it may mean persecution; for others, it could mean death... as it did for John Hus, a Bohemian Reformer accused of heresy.

Prior to his appearance before the Council of Constance in 1414, Hus wrote to one of his friends,

> I shall not be led astray by them to the side of evil, though I suffer at His will temptations, revilings, imprisonments, and deaths—as indeed He too suffered, and hath subjected His loved servants to the same trials, leaving us an example that we may suffer for His sake and our salvation. If He suffered, being what He was, why should not we?[5]

I love that last sentence: "If He [Christ] suffered, being what He was [perfect, the ideal model], why should not we?"

You want to know how to really shock the pagan crowd? *Live an authentic Christian life.* No fanfare, of course. No need to wave John 3:16 signs at a ball game... or embarrass your colleagues by loudly spouting Bible verses to your unsaved friends at work. That's offensive, not winsome. They're lost, but they're not ignorant or beyond feelings. Just keep three things in mind—three simple but workable suggestions, not at all complicated.

First, continue living for Christ. That means being different on purpose. Let your integrity speak for itself. When opportunities occur for you to speak of your faith, do so graciously and kindly.

Second, expect to be misunderstood. Don't be surprised when ugly things are said or false accusations are made or twisted statements are passed along about your life. Your life will prove that they're wrong. Relax... and let the Lord defend you.

Third, keep your eyes fixed on Christ. Stay on a steady course. Keep on being different. Live an authentic godly life, and you'll blow the world away. This is especially true if you keep a healthy sense of humor! They will not be able to stay quiet about the difference between your life and theirs.

Never forget, this world is not your home . . . you're just passin'
through.

A Prayer for Hope Beyond the Culture

*Lord God, Your Son has closed yesterday's door, and we don't
live like that anymore. Not because we've been strong and good
and noble but because You have transformed our lives, Lord.
You've changed our course of direction. Even though You've
left us on foreign soil, we have a home in the skies. And
sometimes we get pretty homesick!*

*Hear the prayers of Your people as we call out to You. Give
us self-control on those occasions when we're tempted to
moralize and put people down. Make us aware that a godly
life, alone, preaches the most unforgettable message the
unsaved can be exposed to. Help us remember that we're
soldiers away from home, living in a culture that's lost its way
and is in desperate need of Jesus Christ. Keep us easy to live
with, strong in faith, unbending in our convictions, yet full of
grace toward those who are bound by sin and captured by
habits they cannot break. Enable us to shock this pagan culture
with lives that are real, that still have fun, and that ultimately
glorify You, O God . . . as Jesus did. In His name
I pray.*

AMEN

12

Hope Beyond Extremism

Marching Orders for Soldiers of the Cross

WHEN TIME IS short, things get urgent. And simplified. Something about the brevity of time introduces both urgency and simplicity to the equation of life.

When a friend or family member tells you he or she hasn't long to live, your time together becomes more urgent and your discussions return to the basics. When a hurricane is blowing in or the black funnel of a tornado looms on the horizon, you don't pull out a Monopoly game or begin preparing a gourmet meal. It's all about survival, and survival calls for simplicity. If you're driving to church and you see an accident happen and you are the only one there to assist, you don't worry about being late or about getting your Sunday clothes dirty or bloody. The situation is urgent. The mission is simple.

Jesus Himself modeled this for us. As long as there was time, He took time—to eat with His disciples, to train His disciples, to minister to individuals whenever and whatever their need. He would linger over a meal with friends. He would sit back and enjoy relaxed moments with close friends like Mary and Martha and Lazarus. But when the hour of the cross drew near, urgency gripped His voice and His attention focused on those few priorities that were in front of Him.

> From that time Jesus Christ began to show His disciples that He must go to Jerusalem, and suffer many things from the elders and chief priests and scribes, and be killed, and be raised up on the third day. (Matt. 16:21)

At that point, Peter—the same disciple who had just given a wonderful statement of faith—rebuked Jesus, saying, "God forbid it, Lord!" (v. 22), telling Him not to talk like that—that such things should never happen to Him.

Such audacity! Peter was planning on a kingdom. He was not planning on a cross.

But Jesus turned and said to Peter,

> Get behind Me, Satan! You are a stumbling block to Me; for you are not setting your mind on God's interests, but man's. (Matt. 16:23)

And then Jesus said to His disciples, in effect, "Let's get down to basics. Let's get down to the essentials, the simple requirements of discipleship."

> If anyone wishes to come after Me, let him deny himself, and take up His cross, and follow Me. (Matt. 16:24)

He was down to urgent, simple demands. Why? Because the hour was short.

During World War II, Winston Churchill encouraged and supported the people of Britain through endless dark hours. He made many memorable statements and speeches, but one rings particularly apt here. He was speaking to Parliament just after London had been bombed to smithereens, and he sensed the people were losing heart. It seemed as though Churchill never did. He must have had low moments, but his speeches don't reveal it. So he said to those people in Parliament, who were probably quaking in their spirits, "This is not the end. This is not even the beginning of the end. But it is, perhaps, the end of the beginning."

Jesus said the same sort of thing to His disciples, telling them, in essence, "When you see these things occurring, it isn't the end."

> And you will be hearing of wars and rumors of wars; see that you are not frightened, for those things must take place, but that is not yet the end. (Matt. 24:6)

If you live in the light of Christ's return each day of your life, it does wonders for your perspective. If you realize that you must give account for every idle word and action when you stand before the Lord Jesus, it does amazing things to your conduct. It also makes you recognize how many needless activities we get involved in on this earth. Sort of like rearranging the deck chairs on the *Titanic*. Don't bother! Don't get lost in insignificant details! He's coming soon! Recognize the urgency and the simplicity of the hour!

Peter seems to have gotten the message. He was a practical man. Prior to following Christ, his life consisted of very tangible, practical things: boats, nets, fish, supporting a family, hard work. And then he met the hard realities of the Master. Consequently, we should not be surprised that his personality and his prose followed suit.

Being neither scholarly nor sophisticated, Peter had little interest in theoretical discussions. Life was not meant to be talked about but lived out. If an urgent situation demanded action, Peter wasn't one to call for a committee to study the alternatives. He cut through the bureaucratic red tape and got down to business.

So when the big fisherman took up his pen to write about suffering saints, he cut to the chase. And when he addressed the reality of the end times, he summed up a game plan in a one-two-three fashion rather than waxing eloquent on the options. Pragmatic Peter at his best offers four commands and one goal to those of us who live nearer than ever to Jesus Christ's return. Simple. Direct. No beating around the bush.

Marching Orders for Soldiers of the Cross

Now remember, Peter is dealing with suffering saints, men and women who are being taken advantage of, men and women who can see no relief in sight. During days of suffering we often become even more intensely aware of the end—the final outcome, whatever that may be. And in writing to his brothers and sisters suffering in the trenches of persecution, Peter himself intensified his focus as he deployed the troops and briefed them for battle.

Observe the urgency and the simplicity in the words that follow.

> The end of all things is at hand; therefore, be of sound judgment and sober spirit for the purpose of prayer. Above all, keep fervent in your love for one another, because love covers a multitude of sins. Be hospitable to one another without complaint. As each one has received a special gift, employ it in serving one another, as good stewards of the manifold grace of God. Whoever speaks, let him speak, as it were, the utterances of God; and whoever serves, let him do so as by the strength which God supplies; so that in all things God may be glorified through Jesus Christ, to whom belongs the glory and dominion forever and ever. Amen. (1 Pet. 4:7–11)

Suddenly, with no relief in sight, Peter introduces the one thought that always helps people hope again: *the end of all things*. In doing so, he not only adds urgency to the moment, he also simplifies the game plan. He leaves his reader with four direct commands to obey and one clear goal to pursue in the midst of it all.

Four Commands to Obey

First, he says: *Use good judgment and stay calm in a spirit of prayer.*

> The end of all things is at hand; therefore, be of sound judgment and sober spirit for the purpose of prayer. (1 Pet. 4:7)

Be of sound judgment. Be of sober spirit. Be calm. Today we might say: Stay cool. Don't be filled with anxiety. Don't panic. Face life realistically. Realize God is in control.

Sober does not mean the opposite of *intoxication*. It means the opposite of living in a frenzy, in a maddening kind of extremism. For example, don't try to set dates regarding Christ's coming. That's an extreme reaction to prophecy. Here's another. Don't panic, as if things were out of control. And another. Don't be filled with anxiety. Don't quit your job, put on a white robe, and sit on some rooftop waiting for Christ to come back. That's extremism. And don't think you have to know every detail of the end times in order to feel secure, as Warren Wiersbe, in his book *Be Hopeful*, rightly notes.

Early in my ministry, I gave a message on prophecy that sought to explain everything. I have since filed away that outline and will probably never look at it (except when I need to be humbled). A pastor friend who suffered through my message said to me after the service, "Brother, you must be on the planning committee for the return of Christ!" I got his point, but he made it even more pertinent when he said quietly, "I've moved from the program committee to the welcoming committee."

I am not suggesting that we not study prophecy, or that we become timid about sharing our interpretations. What I am suggesting is that we not allow ourselves to get out of balance because of an abuse of prophecy. There is a practical application to the prophetic Scriptures. Peter's emphasis on hope and the glory of God ought to encourage us to be faithful today in whatever work God has given us to do (see Luke 12:31–48).[1]

The secret of maintaining the balance and calmness that my friend writes about is prayer. We don't need to parade through the neighborhood wearing a big signboard that says REPENT! THE END IS NEAR! Instead, Peter says, "Be calm, use sound judgment, and do it in a spirit of prayer." Such wise, reasonable counsel from a man who once was neither. Before, Peter would panic so easily. Now . . . he urges prayer.

We don't dream our way into eternity. We pray and watch. In fact, there is nothing quite like prayer to sharpen our awareness, to keep us alert, to make us more discerning, and yet to remind us who has the controls.

When I see a person who is all out of sorts, full of anxiety, on the ragged edge of extremism, I'm looking at a person who isn't spending enough time in prayer. Prayer calms your spirit, yet it doesn't make you indifferent. On the contrary, it reminds you: He has everything in control. Use sound judgment. Stay calm.

Let me go back, again, to yesteryear . . . a dark night in a garden near the edge of Jerusalem. Peter was one of the disciples who was told by the Lord in the Garden of Gethsemane to "Wait here and pray, while I go over there to pray." But when the Lord returned to them, he found Peter asleep. Sound asleep. And He said to Peter and the others, "Couldn't you have waited with Me for this hour?" That must have stung, especially since Peter was the disciple who, a few hours earlier, had bragged about his loyalty and commitment. You think Peter doesn't write with a sense of urgency and understanding here? You think he doesn't remember that rebuke? "I left you to pray, and you fell asleep." That's why Peter could add those words to his letter with a real sense of understanding.

Prayer was what allowed Jesus to submit to His arrest, and the lack of it was what made Peter resist.

The second command is: *Stay fervent in love for one another.*

Above all, keep fervent in your love for one another, because love covers a multitude of sins. (1 Pet. 4:8)

"Fervent" speaks of intensity and determination. It comes from the Greek word *ektene*, which literally means "strained." It's used to describe athletes straining to reach the tape at the finish line or stretching high enough to clear the bar.

When lean sprinters race around that last turn and are pressing for the tape, they'll get right to the end and then they'll deliberately lean forward. I've even seen runners fall on the track because they're pushing so hard to reach the tape before their competitors. That's "being fervent." It's the idea of stretching yourself. Those who do the long jump leap into the air and throw their feet forward as they stretch every muscle of their body to reach as far as they can. The same is true with the high jump or the pole vault. Athletes stretch to the utmost to reach the limit. All those actions describe "fervent." But here Peter applies it to love, not athletic events. He tells us to have fervency in our love for one another.

If there was ever a time when we needed to stay close, it is today. Don't play into the hands of the Enemy. This is the time to stick together. Don't waste precious time criticizing other Christians. Don't waste time criticizing another church or some pastor. Spend your time building up one another, staying fervent in love.

Look at how the verse begins: "Above all"—more than anything else. And then Peter gives them a compliment. He says, "Keep fervent." This implies that they already were fervent. Keep at it, he says. You're doing it already, so stay at it.

Because my schedule is already so full of regular responsibilities connected to both Dallas Seminary and our radio ministry, Insight for Living, I rarely accept invitations to minister elsewhere. But Cynthia and I have made an exception to this when it comes to the Christian Embassy in Washington, D.C., and a retreat they sponsor for many of the flag officers in the Pentagon and various members of Congress who serve on Capitol Hill.

On several occasions we have returned to this significant group of men and women to minister to them and spend some time getting to know their world better. Most of these generals and admirals are academy graduates who have spent many years in military leadership, some of which were during wars on land and at sea. The politicians are also seasoned veterans who have invested their time and effort serving the people of their states, standing for what is right and representing causes worth fighting for. Most who attend the retreat are Christians. They operate their lives on the cutting edge of our times. What amazing, admirable people they are!

As a result of our annual reunions, my wife and I have been able to see how these men and women have grown spiritually in their Christian walk (yes, there are *many* Christians in high places!). What stands out most eloquently to the two of us is their love for the Lord and their love for one another . . . as well as for us. Rather than being sophisticated and distant, these dear folks *fervently* express their love and *fervently* demonstrate compassion.

Peter would have been proud of them. They "keep fervent"—they stay at it, year after year.

If there's ever a time to stretch our love for one another to the limit, it's during the end times—*it's now*. And what is it that reveals this love? Forgiveness.

When Peter says that "love covers a multitude of sins," he's alluding to the principle in Proverbs 10:12:

> Hatred stirs up strife,
> But love covers all transgressions.

Nothing is a more compelling witness than the love and unity that Christians exhibit toward each other, and nothing is more disturbing or disruptive to the unity of the body than Christians who are stirred up against each other and experiencing strife. Nothing is a poorer witness.

Don't think the unsaved aren't watching when we bash our brothers and smash our sisters! They *love* it when we can't get along with each other. It makes news. They love to quote one Christian who is after another Christian. It's as if the journalist or pundit leans back and says, "Aha! Gotcha!"

Mahatma Gandhi, the Indian nationalist leader, once said, "I like your Christ but I don't like your Christians. . . . They are so unlike your Christ."[2]

What a rebuke. I deeply regret that his words are so often true!

And what is Christ like? He is characterized by love and forgiveness. An insightful person once said, "We are most like beasts when we kill. We are most like men when we judge. We are most like God when we forgive."

Let me repeat something I said earlier: I have never met a person who didn't have a reason to blame someone else. Every one of us can blame somebody for something that has happened in our lives. But don't waste your time. What we need most is a steady stream of love flowing among us. Love that quickly forgives and willingly overlooks and refuses to take offense.

Moffatt states that this passage "is a warning against loving others by fits and starts. It is a plea for steady affection, persisting through the irritations and the antagonisms of common life in a society recruited from various classes of people."

Some people are so easy to love that you just naturally fall into their arms. But others are so hard to love, you have to work overtime at it. There's something about their natures that's abrasive and irritating. Some are the opposite of magnets. They repel. Yet even they need our love, perhaps more than the others. How very important that we "stretch fervently" to love each other!

The third command Peter gives is: *Be hospitable toward one another.*

Be hospitable to one another without complaint. (1 Pet. 4:9)

Underscore the words "one another." It is the same phrase Peter uses in verses 8 and 10, and it doesn't refer just to those who are lovable or friendly or fun to be with. It refers to all who are in the body of Christ, even the unlovely and unfriendly.

Another little phrase tacked onto the end of verse 9 is a crucial one when it comes to showing hospitality—"without complaint."

What do you complain about when it comes to hospitality? About the time and trouble it takes? The energy it requires to invite someone into your home and entertain them? The expense? The mess? The clean-up? It's true that hospitality takes effort and planning, and it interrupts your privacy. But hospitality is never a problem when our priorities are in place, when love opens the door.

"True love is a splendid host," said the famous English preacher John Henry Jowett. In his excellent volume on the epistles of Peter, he writes with eloquence:

> There is love whose measure is that of an umbrella. There is love whose inclusiveness is that of a great marquee. And there is love whose comprehension is that of the immeasurable sky. The aim of the New Testament is the conversion of the umbrella into a tent and the

merging of the tent into the glorious canopy of the all-enfolding heavens. . . . Push back the walls of family love until they include the neighbor;
again push back the walls until they include the stranger; again push
back the walls until they comprehend the foe.[3]

When was the last time you entertained someone who was
once your enemy? There is something about hospitality that dis-
arms a foe.

Since the former head coach of the Dallas Cowboys, Tom Landry,
has served on our Dallas Seminary board for many years, I have had
the opportunity to get to know the man. My respect for him has
grown, not lessened, as time and our mutual roles have linked us
together.

I was told a wonderful story about Coach Landry that illustrates the
level of his Christian love for others. Years ago, the late Ohio State
coach, Woody Hayes, was fired for striking an opposing player on the
sidelines during a football game. The press had a field day with the
firing and really tarred and feathered the former Buckeye coach. Few
people in America could have felt lower than he at that time; he not
only lost control in a game and did a foolish thing, but he also lost his
job and much of the respect others had for him.

At the end of that season, a large, prestigious banquet was held
for professional athletes. Tom Landry, of course, was invited. Guess
who he took with him as his guest? Woody Hayes . . . the man
everyone was being encouraged to hate and criticize.

The quality of our love is determined by its inclusiveness. At the one
extreme there is self-love; but at the other extreme there is philanthropy!
What is the "tense," the stretch, of my love? What is its covering power? . . . "Love covereth a multitude of sins." Not the sins of the lover, but the
sins of the loved! Love is willing to forget as well as to forgive! Love does
not keep hinting at past failures and past revolts. Love is willing to hide
them in a nameless grave. When a man, whose life has been stained and
blackened by "a multitude of sins," turns over a new leaf, love will
never hint at the old leaf, but will rather seek to cover it in deep and
healing oblivion. Love is so busy unveiling the promises and allurements

of the morrow, that she has little time and still less desire to stir up the choking dust on the blasted and desolate fields of yesterday.[4]

Are you hospitable . . . I mean *really* hospitable? Do you make room in your life to be interrupted? Do you allow people to be drawn by the magnet of your love because of Christ's presence? One more question: Would you have done what Tom Landry did?

There's something about sitting down with someone over a cup of coffee or a sandwich. Something about taking time . . . making time. I am fully aware that there are times when we need to be alone. *But not all the time.*

Have you ever opened your home for a traveling college choir or other strangers who need lodging? Remember how Jesus and His disciples always stayed in private homes when they traveled and preached? Is your home open to those in need?

I can't tell you how many times people have told me what a blessing it has been to open their homes. Many of these were folks who felt a little uneasiness or apprehension at first, letting strangers invade their most private domain. But there's an unforgettable job connected with hospitality. Folks never forget the warmth of a home . . . the joy of kids around the table . . . the pleasure of meaningful conversation. A friend of mine traveled with a musical group during her college days, over thirty years ago, and she says she can still remember homes she stayed in and Christian hospitality demonstrated on her behalf. Such expressions of hospitable love gave her numerous opportunities to hope again during the three decades that followed.

From the perspective of the guest, however, hospitality is not something we should ever abuse. Apparently this was happening in the first century, largely by people who were living unbalanced lives in response to prophetic teaching. They reasoned, "Since Christ is coming soon, why bother working? Why not liquidate all assets and live off others?" The apostle Paul speaks directly to this heretical reasoning in 2 Thessalonians 3:6–15. Peter speaks to it more indirectly in the next two verses by promoting involvement in the local church and the exercise of spiritual gifts.

In fact, verses 10–11 contain his fourth command: *Keep serving one another.*

As each one has received a special gift, employ it in serving one another, as good stewards of the manifold grace of God. Whoever speaks, let him speak, as it were, the utterances of God; whoever serves, let him do so as by the strength which God supplies. (1 Pet. 4:10–11a)

Do you know, fellow Christian, that you have at least one—perhaps more than one—spiritual gift? Several sections of the New Testament talk about these gifts—special abilities God has given the body of Christ with which we minister until He returns. Each gift we have needs to be used in serving one another. That is how we become good stewards of our gifts.

Here's a list of some of the places where spiritual gifts are listed. Look them up and examine your own life in the light of them.

- Ephesians 4:11–12
- 1 Corinthians 12:28–30
- Romans 12:6–8

Make a list of these gifts and then ask yourself, where do I best fit in this list? You might approach it the way you would approach applying for a job. If you don't find your spot right away, keep pursuing it. Keep thinking about it. Ask other Christians—those who know you and have been around you during various experiences—what they think your gifts are. Then try them out. Put them into action as you serve others. You'll discover what you do well . . . then do that throughout the balance of your life.

But note the warning in verse 11 that goes along with exercising our gifts.

Whoever speaks, let him speak, as it were, the utterances of God; whoever serves, let him do so by the strength which God supplies. (1 Pet. 4:11)

When we speak, we shouldn't be voicing our own opinions and

philosophies about life; we should be speaking "the utterances of God." And when we serve, we shouldn't be doing so in our own strength but "by the strength which God supplies."

When you speak for Christ, base your words on the Scriptures, not on your own opinions. You will be forever relevant if you do. And you'll never lack for a message! When you serve, serve in His strength, not your own. That way, He gets the glory.

Many of you have the gift of teaching. You can teach children, teenagers, or adults. You can lead a Bible study at work or in your neighborhood.

Many gifted people also serve behind the scenes, doing vital but perhaps not-so-visible jobs. You help, encourage, and pray. The body would be crippled without the many parts that are able to serve, to help, to encourage.

Others have the gift of showing mercy, of ministering to those who are laid aside or suffering. You visit hospitals and nursing homes. You spend hours listening, caring.

Still others have the gift of evangelism. With ease they communicate the gospel and lead people to Christ. It's a natural part of their lives. God uses them again and again as He harvests souls for His kingdom.

But all of these gifts—there are many others—have one thing in common. They come alive in serving other people. So get out of your own tiny radius. It will do wonders for your depression, for your pity parties, for those times when you sit alone and want to sing, "Woe is me. Woe is me. Woe is me." (That's a very dull song.)

Think of it this way: When we employ our spiritual gift(s), others benefit. Others are encouraged. Others gain fresh hope. Interestingly, so do we!

A Goal to Pursue

Verse 11 ends with a purpose clause that reveals the logical reason we should obey these four commands. Why stay calm and pray? Why be fervent in love? Why demonstrate hospitality? Why serve one another?

...so that in all things God may be glorified through Jesus Christ, to whom belongs the glory and dominion forever and ever. Amen.

In everything, God gets the glory. How many church conflicts could be resolved if God's glory were everybody's goal? How many egos would be put in their place if God's glory—not human glory—were at stake? How much extremism would be avoided if we did all for the greater glory of God?

"But that's so basic," you may say. "Why even spend time on it?" Because without that, your teaching becomes drudgery, your helping leads to burnout, your evangelism becomes either frenetic or self-glorifying.

When we keep His glory uppermost in our minds, it's amazing how much else falls into place. Since He gets the glory, we're more comfortable leaving the results with Him in His time. Since He gets the glory, our umbrella of love expands to cover others. Since He gets the glory, it's easier for us to show hospitality to others, for we're ultimately serving Him. Since He gets the glory, exercising our gifts is not a pain but a privilege. The benefits are endless when the glory goes to God!

A Concluding Thought

Let me bring this to a close by returning to a comment I made at the beginning of the chapter: Time is short. You and I don't have forever to put these things into action. Whatever needs to be simplified, *let's simplify!* Whatever it takes to remind us of the urgency of the hour, *let's do it!* Time is short. That means we need to move the words off the pages and slide them into our lives—*now.*

Need a little boost? One of the most encouraging promises in all the New Testament comes to mind:

> For God is not unjust so as to forget your work and the love which you have shown toward His name, in having ministered and in still ministering to the saints. (Heb. 6:10)

Read that again, only this time *with feeling.*
Your effort is not in vain. Your love will not be overlooked. Your ministry—whatever it includes—will be rewarded. You will maintain a wonderful balance in the process. Keep your eyes on the Shepherd as you open your heart to His flock. And remember, He gets all the glory!

> The Bride eyes not her garment,
>   But her dear Bridegroom's face;
> I will not gaze at glory
>   But on my King of grace.
> Not at the crown He giveth
>   But on His pierced hand,
> The Lamb is all the glory
>   Of Immanuel's land.[5]

A Prayer for Hope Beyond Extremism

Our Father, keep us calm and cool in a spirit of prayer. Give us a fervency in our love for one another that has a way of covering a multitude of sins. Find us to be hospitable people who take time, who are accessible, available, and caring. And, Lord, as we put our gifts into action, use us to give a hope transplant to someone really in need. And may we do it all for Your glory.

May these words make a difference in the way we live, and may the difference be so significant that it is noticed, so that others have cause to give You praise . . . for You, alone, deserve all the praise and all the glory. I pray in Jesus' wonderful name.

AMEN

13

Hope Beyond Our Trials

"When through Fiery Trials..."

I am progressing along the path of life in my ordinary, contentedly fallen and godless condition, absorbed in a merry meeting with my friends for the morrow or a bit of work that tickles my vanity to-day, a holiday or a new book, when suddenly a stab of abdominal pain that threatens serious disease, or a headline in the newspapers that threatens us all with destruction, sends this whole pack of cards tumbling down.

At first I am overwhelmed, and all my little happinesses look like broken toys. Then, slowly and reluctantly, bit by bit, I try to bring myself into the frame of mind that I should be in at all times. I remind myself that all these toys were never intended to possess my heart, that my true good is in another world and my only real treasure is Christ. And perhaps, by God's grace, I succeed, and for a day or two become a creature consciously dependent on God and drawing its strength from the right sources. But the moment the threat is withdrawn, my whole nature leaps back to the toys.[1]

HOW ELOQUENTLY C. S. LEWIS'S words from his penetrating book, *The Problem of Pain*, describe the role of trials in our lives. Such is human nature, and such is the nature of trials and tribulations.

Remember the words from the old hymn: "When through fiery trials my pathway shall lie, Thy grace all sufficient shall be my supply"? Well, fiery trials and painful ordeals aptly describe what most of us must pass through at one time or another in life...some, more frequently than that.

Peter addresses Christians who are going through just such desperate circumstances.

> Beloved, do not be surprised at the fiery ordeal among you, which comes upon you for your testing, as though some strange thing were happening to you. (1 Pet. 4:12)

Ever had anything like that in your life? Not simply trials, but what Peter calls "fiery ordeals"? If so, ever heard this kind of advice on how to handle such trials?

> ...but to the degree that you share the sufferings of Christ, keep on rejoicing; so that also at the revelation of His glory, you may rejoice with exultation. (1 Pet. 4:12–13)

Probably not!

Practical Truths about Trials

Peter was not the only apostle who wrote to Christians who were strangers and aliens in a foreign land. James addressed his letter to those who were "dispersed abroad"—another group of people far away from home, and not by choice. This also applies to those of us who are strangers in this world below and those of us forced to live in the midst of circumstances that are not our choice. To all these, James wrote:

> Consider it all joy, my brethren, when you encounter various trials, knowing that the testing of your faith produces endurance. And let

endurance have its perfect result, that you may be perfect and complete, lacking in nothing. (James 1:2–4)

From these three verses we learn a great deal about trials. Four specifics stand out.

First, trials are common for Christians to encounter.

Don't ever let anybody tell you (and don't you dare tell anybody else!) that when you become a Christian your trials are over, from then on, "you can just trust Christ and fly away like birds toward the heavens." Get real! Notice that James says *"when* you encounter," not "if."

If you're experiencing trials, you're the rule, not the exception. If you have just gotten through one, take heart; there are more around the corner! Going through a trial is one thing that pulls us together. We've got that in common.

Second, trials come in various categories.

They may be physical, emotional, financial, relational, or spiritual. They may slip in unexpectedly and knock on the door of your business, your church, or your home. They may arrive at any time or at any season. They may come suddenly, like a car accident or a natural catastrophe. They may be prolonged, like a drawn-out court case or a lingering, nagging illness. Trials can be public in nature or very private. They can be directly related to our own sin, the sin of others, or not related to sin at all.

A trial can be like a rock hitting the water. You don't cause the jolt, but you're impacted by it. You're just standing there, and suddenly the smooth lake of your life surges into giant waves and almost drowns you.

Frankly, some trials seem to blow in absolutely without reason. My brother, Orville, encountered something like that when a hurricane named Andrew blew through the community where he lived in south Florida a few years ago. It tore and ripped and screamed its way through, tearing his house apart. He had a great attitude, though. He called and said, "What an experience! It really did a lot of damage. But the good news is it tore down everyone's fences, so now we'll get to meet our neighbors."

Third, trials put our faith to the test.

No matter what its source or intensity, there's something about suffering that simplifies life and draws us back to the basics. Invariably, especially during a time of intense trial, I go back to my theological roots. I go back to what I really believe. I return to the elementals such as prayer and dependence, like getting quiet and waiting on God. I remind myself, God is sovereign . . . this is no accident. He has a plan and a purpose. Those thoughts give us hope beyond our trials.

Trials put our faith to the test as well as stretch our confidence in Him. They force us back to the bedrock of faith upon which our foundation rests, and this becomes a refining and necessary process.

Fourth, without trials, there could not be maturity.

James says we experience trials so that we may be become "perfect and complete" (verse 4), like a plant that has matured to its maximum growth and fruitfulness. That, he says, is the "perfect result" of "endurance."

Most often, because of the discomfort, the pain, or the hardship, we try to cut our trials short—to put an end to them. Before long, we're resenting them to such an extreme that we'll try anything to escape, to run from them. Instead, James says, *endure* the trial; let it come to completion. When it does, you'll be a better person for it.

Remember the words of song writer Andrae Crouch? "If I'd never had a problem, I'd never know that He could solve them. I'd never know what faith in God could do."[2]

Few feelings compare with the joy of watching God step in and solve a problem that seems impossible.

Some trials are slight, brief, and soon forgotten. Others hang on and weigh heavily upon us. They leave us exhausted and sometimes bench us on the sidelines. The latter category is what Peter is talking about when he writes of "the fiery ordeal." This is no slight struggle Peter has in mind. It's an "ordeal" . . . one from which we cannot find relief.

Biblical Strength for Fiery Ordeals

What do you do when the rug is jerked out from under you? Do you panic? Do you doubt the Lord's love? Do you trust in God to get you through the tough times? Perhaps this is a good time to go back to God's truth and read His counsel written by Christ's closest companion while He was on earth.

We can learn a lot from Peter, a man who spent over three years with Christ and who, as we have seen, both pleased Him and failed Him. In fact, most of us should be able to identify with Peter. He'd been an eager disciple, defending his Master against all comers. He'd also been a failure, denying his Lord in the pinch...not once, but three times, back to back. Through all this, God reshaped him into a powerfully effective man of God. The vacillating, impulsive, overly zealous Simon was changed and broken, emerging as "Peter, the rock." Now, he writes out of his maturity and seasoned wisdom, under the guidance of the Holy Spirit. These are not theoretical terms the old fisherman tosses around but words shaped in the blast furnace of his own afflictions and pain. Read them again with that in mind:

> Beloved, do not be surprised at the fiery ordeal among you, which comes upon you for your testing, as though some strange thing were happening to you; but to the degree that you share the sufferings of Christ, keep on rejoicing; so that also at the revelation of His glory, you may rejoice with exultation. (1 Pet. 4:12–13)

He begins this section by addressing his letter to the "Beloved." This is truth directed to the beloved of God...in other words, truth for the believer only. This is information just for the Lord's people. It's got your name on it. Think of your name here in place of unnamed folks who were "beloved" to Peter.

He then goes on to tell us how to react to this more intense form of suffering.

How to React

Interestingly, our first response to an ordeal is usually surprise—"I can't believe this is happening." But Peter says, *"Don't be surprised."* The lack of surprise will enable us to remain calm.

Life is a schoolroom. In it, we encounter pop quizzes and periodic examinations. You can't have a schoolroom without tests—at least I've never seen one. I've never seen anyone earn a high school diploma or college degree without taking exams. The same is true in graduate school. Throughout the educational process our knowledge is assessed on the basis of examinations. The curriculum of Christlikeness is much the same. Our Christian maturity is measured by our ability to withstand the tests that come our way without having them shake our foundation or throw us into an emotional or spiritual tailspin.

The wonderful thing about God's schoolroom, however, is that we get to grade our own papers. You see, He doesn't test us so He can learn how well we're doing. He tests us so *we* can discover how well we're doing. So we can put our own benchmarks on our level of maturity.

Back in 1984, when you were tested, perhaps you didn't do too well. Maybe others didn't know that, but you did. In 1989, you did better. In 1993 an even tougher test confronted you, and you did rather well. As you grade your own paper, you can see the improvement. The testing of your faith reveals your increasing level of maturity.

Many years ago a good friend of mine, Dr. Robert Lightner, who is a long-time member of the theology department faculty at Dallas Seminary, was involved in a terrible plane crash. He was in a single-engine plane that flipped over during takeoff. He was badly injured and bruised beyond recognition. His wife, Pearl, said that when she first saw him at the hospital, "I looked at this black mass of flesh, and I didn't even know who he was." Thankfully, he did recover, and today he is a living testimony of the grace of God through that ordeal. "I learned things I didn't know I needed to learn," I heard him say on one occasion. Isn't that the way it usually is? What hope this should give us!

Don't be surprised when a test comes. Even though you don't know you need to learn certain things, God knows, and He sovereignly determines, "Now's the time." God is molding you into the image of His Son, and that requires trials. So, first off, don't be surprised.

But the second reaction Peter says we are to have is even more amazing: "*Keep on rejoicing.*"

I hear some of you saying right now, "What! Are you kidding me? We're talking trials, right?" Right. "We're talking fiery ordeals, correct?" Correct. "And you're telling me to keep on rejoicing?" Wrong! I am not telling you this—*God* is telling you to keep on rejoicing. "To the degree that you share the sufferings of Christ, keep on rejoicing."

James put it another way: "Consider it all joy" (1:2). Why? Because trials enable us to enter into a more intimate partnership with Christ, and if we endure them faithfully, we will receive a future reward (see Phil. 3:10 and James 1:12). Along with that, our trials here give us at least a glimpse into the magnitude of Christ's suffering for us.

Trials, therefore, become a means to a greater end: a deeper relationship with Christ on earth and a richer reward from Him in heaven.

You and I would never know such fellowship were we not put to the test. Some of you are going through trials right now that have dropped you on your knees. At the same time those trials are pulling you closer to the Lord than you've ever been in your life. That ought to bring rejoicing. You'll be more closely linked to Him. Some of the mysterious themes threaded through His Word will become clearer because you have been leveled by some unexpected affliction or enduring persecution or facing misunderstanding.

Furthermore, you can rejoice because you will receive a future reward.

As I write these words, it happens to be getting close to graduation time, those days when diplomas, honors, and special awards are granted. Each year at Dallas Seminary we have a special chapel service near spring graduation during which we distribute special awards to those who have earned them. Our "Awards Chapel" is one of the highlights in our academic year.

Did you know that in the future when we stand before Christ our Lord, there will be special awards distributed by Christ Himself? They are called crowns. And did you know that there is a unique crown given to those who endure suffering? Read James 1:12:

> Blessed is a man who perseveres under trial; for once he has been approved, he will receive the crown of life, which the Lord has promised to those who love Him.

God has a crown reserved for those who endure the fiery ordeal. My brother, Orville, will have one. Bob Lightner will have one. My wife deserves one for living with me for over forty years! And many of you will have earned that crown as well.

In case you still are not convinced that trials can bring rejoicing, I want you to look at a classic case in point, recorded at the end of Acts 5. There we find that the apostles, including Peter, had just been flogged and ordered to stop preaching about Jesus. (Pause and imagine that bloody, brutal scene.) Look at what they did while they were still bleeding from the beating.

> So they went on their way from the presence of the Council, *rejoicing* that they had been considered worthy to suffer shame for His name. And every day, in the temple, from house to house, they kept right on teaching and preaching Jesus as the Christ. (Acts 5:41–42, italics added)

These men were people just like us . . . not super saints, but real-life folks. Only difference—they refused to let their "fiery ordeal" steal their joy or deter their objective. An attitude of joyful gratitude opens our minds to glean lessons from suffering we would not otherwise learn.

So much for how to react. Now let's focus on what to remember.

What to Remember

First: *Trials provide an opportunity to draw upon maximum power.*

> If you are reviled for the name of Christ, you are blessed, because the Spirit of glory and of God rests upon you. (1 Pet. 4:14)

We must remember that we are never closer to Him, never more a recipient of His strength, than when trials come upon us. This is especially true when we are reviled for the name of Christ. One of the highest privileges on earth is to suffer for His sake. At those times the Holy Spirit draws near, administers strength, and provides an abiding presence of God's glory. If you recall the account of Stephen's martyrdom in Acts 7:54–60, which we read earlier, you'll see that's exactly what happened to him.

The second thing to remember is: *Sometimes our suffering is deserved.*

By no means let any of you suffer as a murderer, or thief, or evildoer, or a troublesome meddler. (1 Pet. 4:15)

If our "fiery ordeal" comes as a result of our own sinful behavior, then we're not suffering for the glory of God; we're merely reaping the consequences of wrongdoing we have sown. As the prophet put it, when we "sow the wind" we "reap the whirlwind" (Hos. 8:7).

Sometimes we deserve the treatment we're getting. We deserve the punishment or the loneliness, the brokenness and pain. And notice that "troublesome meddlers" are listed right along with such reprehensible sinners as murderers, thieves, and other evildoers. That ought to get our attention! The term that is translated here as "troublesome meddler" literally means "one who oversees others' affairs." In other words, a busybody. Ouch! Suffering the consequence of being a busybody brings no one applause or affirmation, only a whirlwind of anguish.

The third thing Peter wants us to remember is: *Most suffering should in no way cause us to feel shame.*

But if anyone suffers as a Christian, let him not feel ashamed, but in that name let him glorify God. (1 Pet. 4:16)

I have met folks who are ashamed that they are going through trials. Many apologize for their tears, almost as if they are embarrassed to weep. I've even known people who felt they needed to apologize because they had sought help from a professional to get through a very personal "fiery trial." Others feel ashamed because their walk of faith has caused a negative reaction. No need!

Instead of shame, we should feel honored when we suffer for our Lord. It is a privilege to bear wounds for the One who was "pierced through for our transgressions" and "crushed for our iniquities" (Isa. 53:5). That's the way Peter and the other apostles must have felt when they left the Sanhedrin, bloody but unbowed.

Self-imposed guilt and shame can be terrible taskmasters in our souls, whipping us down and keeping our spirits from soaring. Such guilt and shame have no place in our lives!

The fourth thing we need to remember is: *Suffering is usually timely and needed.*

> For it is time for judgment to begin with the household of God.
> (1 Pet. 4:17a)

One of the most difficult things to keep in mind is that we need to be purged and purified. After the fact we usually look back on the test or trial and say, "I really needed that," or, "The benefits that came from that are incredible," and we can name three or four insights we would not have gained had we not gone through the valley. Such perspective enables us to hope again.

Purging is not only needed among individuals in the household of God, but also in the church as a whole—locally, denominationally, or otherwise. Sometimes the "house of God" needs not only daily dusting but a thorough spring cleaning. Remember this the next time a scandal surfaces in the church. Don't get disillusioned. It's just God refusing to let us sweep the dirt in His house under the rug.

Sometimes we're rolling along happily, meeting our budgets, running our programs, yet there is no sense of zeal or revival among God's people. It's sort of sit, soak, and sour time for the flock. Congregations can get spoiled. With a smug shrug, they can be saved, sanctified, galvanized, and petrified. Church attendance becomes business as usual. What a miserable existence! About then God comes in and sweeps things clean as He works *through* the church in a timely and needed way.

Now look at the perspective Peter adds:

> If it begins with us first, what will be the outcome for those who do not obey the gospel of God? And if it is with difficulty that the righteous is saved, what will become of the godless man and the sinner? (1 Pet. 4:17b–18)

The latter part of that verse is a quotation from Proverbs, which the New International Version renders this way:

> If the righteous receive their due on earth,
>   how much more the ungodly and the sinner! (Prov.11:31)

In other words, if you think your testing is tough, imagine how tough it is for the person going through trials *without* the Lord. I'll be candid with you: I am absolutely at a loss to know how the lost person makes it when the bottom drops out of his or her life. This person has no Savior. No foundation. No borders. No absolutes. No reason to go on. Nothing to hold on to . . . no one to turn to . . . no way to calm his or her fears . . . no purpose for living . . . no peace in dying. Can you imagine that kind of hopelessness? If you can't, just look at what's happening in the world around you.

Imagine being without the Lord and hearing the worst kind of news from your physician or from the policeman who knocks on your door late at night. Though we, too, are rocked back on our heels by such things, as Christians we immediately turn to our sovereign absolute, our firm foundation, and we lean hard on Him. And if these earthly trials are hard for the lost to bear, imagine their having to face *eternal* judgment!

Which brings me to the fifth thing to remember: *There is no comparison between what we suffer now and what the unrighteous will suffer later.*

If we who are justified by faith have "fiery ordeals" in our walk now, imagine the inferno the lost will face in the literal fiery future that awaits them. Turn to Revelation 20:10–15 and take a few minutes to read and then imagine the horror. Talk about fiery ordeals. Talk about a reason to give your life to Christ.

Thus far, Peter has told us how to react and what to remember when we are going through fiery trials. Now he encourages us by telling us *on whom we are to rely.*

> Therefore, let those also who suffer according to the will of God entrust their souls to a faithful Creator in doing what is right. (1 Pet. 4:19)

Entrust. What a wonderful word! It is a banking term in the original text, meaning "to deposit." One commentator has said, "The idea is that of depositing treasure into safe and trustworthy hands."[3] When it comes to trials, we deposit ourselves into God's safekeeping, and that deposit yields eternal dividends.

When you deposit money in the bank, there's a limit on how much the FDIC will insure under one account ownership; usually it's about $100,000. But our infinite God has no limits. Millions upon multimillions of Christians can deposit themselves in His care, and He will make every one of them good. He will hold every one of us securely. No one can declare Him bankrupt of compassion or care. God will never say to anyone, "Sorry. We're full up. That's the limit. We can't guarantee more." You can entrust your soul to this "faithful Creator."

Interestingly, the Greek word that is translated "entrust" here is the same one used by Jesus on the cross when He said, "Father, into Thy hands I *commit* My Spirit" (Luke 23:46, italics added). When we entrust our souls to God during our trials, we are following Jesus' example on the cross when He deposited His soul into the care of the Father. Again, I remind you, those without faith in Christ have no one in whom they can "entrust" their souls.

Personal Growth Through All the Heat

Tests are never wasted. God never says, "Oops, made a mistake on that one. I shouldn't have given you that. I meant that for Frank.

Sorry, Bob." It's as if the Lord has our name on specific trials. They are specifically designed for us, arranged with our weaknesses and our immaturity in mind. He bears down and doesn't let up. And we groan and we hurt and we weep and we pray and we grow and we learn. Through it all we learn to depend upon His Word. You see, there really is hope beyond our trials.

The furnace of suffering provides not only light by which to examine our lives but heat to melt away the dross. Just as famine and financial ruin brought the prodigal son to his senses, so our trials bring us to our senses and draw us into the embrace of our Father. The common response to trials is resistance, if not outright resentment. How much better that we open the doors of our hearts and welcome the God-ordained trials as honored guests for the good they do in our lives.

> Thus the terrible necessity of tribulation is only too clear. God has had me for but forty-eight hours and then only by dint of taking everything else away from me. Let Him but sheathe that sword for a moment and I behave like a puppy when the hated bath is over—I shake myself as dry as I can and race off to reacquire my comfortable dirtiness, if not in the nearest manure heap, at least in the nearest flower bed. And that is why tribulations cannot cease until God either sees us remade or sees that our remaking is now hopeless.[4]

As C. S. Lewis implies here, trials are not an elective in the Christian-life curriculum; they are a required course. Trials 101 is a prerequisite to Christlikeness. But sometimes the tests are so gruelingly comprehensive that our tendency is to drop the course entirely. Especially if we feel abandoned by God.

If that's how you're feeling in the test you are going through now, you need to consult the course syllabus for a few guiding principles. First, when trials come, it's important to remember that God is faithful and that you can rely on Him. Second, when trials stay, it's important to remember to do the right thing and to take refuge in Him. Rest in Him.

When the X-ray comes back and it doesn't look good, remember,

God is still faithful. When you read that heartbreaking note from your mate, remember, God is still faithful. When you hear the worst kind of news about one of your children, remember, God is still faithful. He has not abandoned you, though you're tempted to think He has.

At the height of one of his own personal tests, Hudson Taylor expressed his response in these words: "It doesn't matter how great the pressure is. What really matters is where the pressure lies, whether it comes between me and God or whether it presses me nearer His heart."

When we are pressed near the heart of God, He is faithful and He will hold us. He will hug us through it. We can entrust our souls "to a faithful Creator in doing what is right." But that doesn't mean things will calm down and start making better sense. Not necessarily! Our Lord's agenda for us is full of surprises, unexpected twists, and abrupt turns.

I like the way one fellow pastor put it:

> One of the most frustrating things about Jesus is that He just won't settle down. He is constantly moving us away from the places where we would prefer to stay . . . And moving us closer to . . . where we do not want to go.[5]

When you are tested, you will be tempted to resist such redirection, go your own way, fight in your own strength, and do what is wrong because it just comes naturally. It's called being streetwise (another word for *carnal*). You've fought your way thus far through life; you can fight your way through this test too.

But wait! Is that what God wants you to do? When trials linger on and you begin to wear down, the Enemy will be whispering all kinds of new carnal ideas. He'll even give you evidence that other people did those trials and got away with them. How much better to remember when trials *come* that God is faithful, still faithful. When trials *stay*, remind yourself to do what is right and take refuge in Him. Find your hiding place in Him.

"Suffering" and "glory" are twin truths that are woven into the fabric of Peter's letter. The world believes that the *absence* of suffering means glory, but a Christian's outlook is different. The trial of our faith today is the assurance of glory when Jesus returns.... This was the experience of our Lord...and it shall be our experience.

But it is necessary to understand that God is not going to *replace* suffering with glory; rather He will *transform* suffering into glory.[6]

When you and I take the long view, we should be grateful that Jesus just won't settle down. He's busy shaping us into His image...and for some of us, He's got a long way to go.

A Prayer for Hope Beyond Our Trials

Father, I pray today especially for those who find themselves in a dark place, who see no light on the horizon, who feel the hot blast from the fiery trials, with no relief in sight. Change this painful place into their hiding place where You are near, where You are real. Use this particular chapter to minister in a very special way to those chosen ones whom You are testing to prove their faith. Calm their fears. Quiet their spirits. Remind them that trials are essential if we hope to become Christlike.

This I pray through Jesus, who was, Himself, a Man of Sorrows, acquainted with grief ... and who, though Your Son, learned obedience from the things which He suffered.

AMEN

14

Hope Beyond Religion

A Job Description
for Shepherds

OF ALL THE PREACHERS who ever lived, Charles Haddon Spurgeon was among the most colorful. He was also among the most prolific... and among the most controversial... and among the most eloquent... and on and on I could go. Spurgeon was one of a kind—if not the greatest preacher in the history of the church, certainly among the top ten, in my opinion. Any time the subject of preaching arises either in a classroom or among a group of pastors, the name Spurgeon will soon surface.

His works are both helpful and insightful. That is all the more remarkable because he lived over one hundred years ago, from 1834 to 1892. At the age of twenty, Spurgeon was called to the New Park Street Baptist Chapel in London, where he served his Lord until he preached his last sermon on June 7, 1891. He died the following January. During his years there, it was not uncommon for his congregation to number as many as 6,000. One biographer states that people would stand in the snow in the dead of winter waiting for the doors to open to assure themselves of a seat to hear this prince of the pulpit preach. During his thirty-eight years at the Metropolitan Tabernacle (five years after Spurgeon began his ministry there, they had to build a new building, which they renamed the Metropolitan Tabernacle), he was responsible for the swelling of the membership of the church to approximately 14,500. Remarkable, remarkable man. Although a Baptist, he was an evangelical Calvinist. Most of all, he was a man made for the pulpit. As one biographer put it:

> Preeminently he was a preacher. His clear voice, his mastery of Anglo-Saxon, and his keen sense of humor, allied to a sure grasp of Scripture and a deep love for Christ, produced some of the noblest preaching of any age.[1]

Despite all his strengths and noble accomplishments, however, a great deal of criticism was leveled against Spurgeon in his day. Like Martin Luther, he seemed to thrive in the storm. He was a man I would call *unflappable*. While he was criticized for a number of things in his preaching, the two things he was criticized for in his private life are curious.

First, he loved a good cigar. One of my favorite stories goes back to an occasion when a man called on him and criticized his cigar smoking. Spurgeon's response was classic: "When I take this to an extreme, then I will stop." When the man asked, "What is an extreme?" Spurgeon replied with a twinkle in his eye, "Two cigars at one time."

The other private criticism was leveled against him and his wife because, out of their own funds, they purchased and enjoyed an extremely large home on a sizable acreage. Predictably, the American press arrived on the scene and exaggerated the report of the home. This *infuriated* Spurgeon. But he pressed on, refusing to allow petty minds and exaggerated comments to deter him from his objectives. While many around him were "religious" and tried very hard to squeeze him into their proper religious mold, Spurgeon remained a maverick at heart, fiercely independent yet Christian to the core, thoroughly committed to Christ and His Word but unmoved by the pressure in Victorian England to fall in line and blend in with his peers.

The longer I live, the greater my admiration grows for this unique vessel so mightily used of God yet so vehemently criticized by others—especially other Christians. Though dead, he still speaks. His volumes continue to stimulate and instruct those of us in vocational Christian service. Anyone who enters the ministry owes it to himself or herself to read Spurgeon and to do so at least once a month. I especially recommend his book, *Lectures to My Students*. In it he writes:

> Every workman knows the necessity of keeping his tools in a good state of repair.... If the workman lose the edge...he knows that there will be a greater draught upon his energies, or his work will be badly done....
>
> ...It will be in vain for me to stock my library, or organize societies, or project schemes, if I neglect the culture of myself; for books, and agencies, and systems, are only remotely the instruments of my holy calling; my own spirit, soul, and body are my nearest machinery for sacred service; my spiritual faculties, and my inner life, are my battle axe and weapons for war....
>
> [Then, quoting from a letter of the great Scottish minister, Robert Murray McCheyne, he concludes,] "Remember, you are God's sword, His instrument—I trust a chosen vessel unto Him to bear His name. In great measure, according to the purity and perfection of the instrument, will be the success. It is not great talent God blesses so much as likeness to Jesus. A holy minister is an awful weapon in the hand of God."[2]

There is every temptation for God's people (especially God's *ministers!*) to fall in line, get in step, and follow the cadence of our times...and in so doing, we will become unauthentic, boring, predictable, and, well, "religious." We need to be warned against that! While we cannot be Spurgeons (one was enough), there is much we can learn much from this model of clear thinking, passionate preaching, creative writing, and unbending determination. It is nothing short of amazing that a man of his stature and gifts remained at the same church almost four decades...especially since he was such a lightning rod, drawing criticism for so long from so many people.

One Practical Guideline for All to Remember

Let me begin with a few practical words of exhortation about sustaining a long-term ministry. My comments here have to do with unrealistic expectations—and they occur on both sides of the pulpit. A young minister comes to a church and has expectations of the flock. On the other side, the flock contacts and calls a man to pastor the church, and they also have their expectations. Both sets of expectations are so idealistic they're usually off the graph. This has the makings of early madness in any ministry.

One of the secrets of a long-term pastorate is clear-thinking realism on the part of both the pastor and the congregation. Let's understand, most churches will never be anything like a Metropolitan Tabernacle...and none of us in ministry will ever be a Spurgeon. My opening illustrations in this chapter are examples of the extreme. But the fact is, most of us are far down the scale from that, and we must learn to live with that, accept it, and be content with where and who we are.

The irony is, I think if Charles Haddon Spurgeon lived today, most churches would never even consider extending a call to him. They couldn't get over his style. And if they knew in-depth the whole story behind the Tabernacle, most pastors today would not want to serve in that place. (It's amazing what a hundred years' history will do to enhance our vision of a church or a man.)

The importance of two-way tolerance is extremely significant. A pastor needs to be very tolerant of the people he is serving. And the people who are being served by the minister need to be very tolerant of him. We need to give each other a lot of wobble room. Congregations need to give each other—and their pastors—room to be themselves. Religion, by the way, resists such freedom.

Please understand, I'm not saying anyone should live a lie; nor am

I promoting an unaccountable, sinful lifestyle. I'm simply encouraging grace here...giving room for others to be who they really are. All of us have quirks. All of us are unique in our own way. It's important that we adapt to a broad spectrum of personality types.

I smiled when I read this little sign recently:

Welcome to the Psychiatric Hotline!

IF YOU ARE OBSESSIVE-COMPULSIVE: Please press 1 repeatedly.

IF YOU ARE CO-DEPENDENT: Please ask someone to press 2.

IF YOU HAVE MULTIPLE PERSONALITIES: Please press 3, 4, 5, and 6.

IF YOU ARE PARANOID-DELUSIONAL: We know who you are and what you want. Just stay on the line so we can trace the call.

IF YOU ARE SCHIZOPHRENIC: Listen carefully—a little voice will tell you which number to press.

IF YOU ARE MANIC-DEPRESSIVE: It doesn't matter which number you press. No one will answer.[3]

If we're going to live together comfortably over a long period of time, we have to accept one another's idiosyncrasies and styles. This is an appropriate time for me to repeat something I wrote earlier: A good sense of humor is essential, especially if you hope to survive many years in church and/or the ministry.

Two Biblical Principles Regarding Ministry

I've expressed my concern about all this because we have come to a section in Peter's letter that sort of stands on its own as it deals with the pastor and the flock among whom he ministers. It's helpful because Peter's counsel doesn't have a religious ring to it. It's refreshingly insightful. The opening lines of the chapter offer a couple of effective and important principles worth mentioning.

> Therefore, I exhort the elders among you, as your fellow elder and witness of the sufferings of Christ, and a partaker also of the glory that is to be revealed, shepherd the flock of God among you.... (1 Pet. 5:1–2a)

The first principle is this: *The pride of position must be absent.* Remember who wrote these words: Peter the apostle, the spokesman for the early church, the one who saw Jesus with his own eyes, who literally walked with the Messiah for more than three years. What honor had been his... what privileges, and yet he never hints at his own position of authority. Any sense of pride of position is absent from Peter's opening remarks. He simply calls himself, "a fellow elder, a witness of the sufferings of Christ, and a partaker of the glory that is to be revealed."

I consider these very humble words. He says nothing about his authoritative apostleship. Nothing about the importance of the recipients of his letter being obedient to his advice. He simply identifies with the elders as a "fellow elder." And if you want to make the word "partaker" a little bit more understandable, think of the word *partner.* "I'm a partner with you in the same glory that's going to be revealed hereafter." He saw himself on the same level as the other elders.

A religious ministry is an easy place to secretly construct a proud life. Unfortunately, pride can consume a person in ministry. It not only can, it *has* for some.

Stop and think about why. We speak for God. We stand before large groups of people regularly. Most ministers address more people more often (without being interrupted) than most executives of large corporations do in their work. Those in ministry can live virtually unaccountable. We are respected and trusted by most. And throughout our careers, only rarely are we questioned. When we are, our answers are seldom challenged. We do our preparation away from the public eye as we work alone in our studies. All of that is fine... but it's like a mine field of perils and dangers. Because before you know it, we can begin to fall into the trap of believing only what we say and seeing only what we discover. This is especially true if your ministry grows and your fame spreads. When that happens, your head can swell and your ears can become dull of hearing.

If Peter, one of the original Twelve, the earliest spokesman for the church, an anointed servant of God, would not mention his role of importance, I think we can learn a lesson about humility. Mark it down. Don't forget it. The pride of position must be absent.

There is a second principle, equally significant: *The heart of a shepherd must be present.* Remember his opening imperative? "Shepherd the flock of God which is among you." The original root word means "to act as a shepherd, to tend a flock." And don't miss the flip side of the coin: He calls the people "the flock of God."

That is why I have never cultivated the habit of referring to any congregation I serve as "my people." The flock isn't owned or controlled by the under-shepherd; they are God's people! They must ultimately answer to Him. They live their lives before Him. They are to obey *Him.* It is His Word that guides us all, shepherd and flock alike.

I like this description: "By definition, the true elder is the shepherd of the flock in which God has placed him . . . who bears them on his heart, seeks them when they stray, defends them from harm, comforts them in their pain, and feeds them with the truth."

This is a good time to add that unless you have the heart of a shepherd, you really ought not to be in a pastorate. You might wish to teach. You might choose to be involved in some other realm of ministry, and there are dozens of possibilities. But if you lack the heart of a shepherd, my advice is simple: don't go into the pastorate. It soon becomes a mismatch, frustrating both pastor and flock.

This saying used to hang in the office of my good friend and former minister of worship, Dr. Howie Stevenson. "Never try to teach a pig to sing. It wastes your time, and it annoys the pig!"

I've heard some people say, "Well, I'll just learn how to be a shepherd." Sorry. There is more to it than that. Shepherding has to be in your heart. There isn't a textbook, there isn't a course, there isn't some relationship that will turn you into a shepherd. It is a calling.

It's a matter of gifting by God, as we saw in the previous chapter. You are not educated into becoming a shepherd. Seminary may help, for during their years in seminary, most students discover whether or not they have a shepherd's heart. If they do not, I repeat, they should not pursue the pastorate.

I've seen evangelists filling pulpits, and the church is evangelized. But it isn't shepherded. I've seen teachers, bright and capable teachers, filling the pulpit, and the church is carefully instructed and biblically educated. But it isn't shepherded. A shepherd's heart certainly includes evangelism, teaching and exhortation, but it must also include love and tolerance, servant-hearted patience and understanding, and a lot of room for those lambs and sheep who don't quite measure up. Pastoring a church isn't a religious profession, not really. It isn't a business decision but rather a call of God that links certain shepherds with certain flocks.

Religion speaks in terms of hiring qualified professionals to fulfill certain responsibilities. The result is "hirelings," as Jesus called them (John 10:11–15). But in God's flock, shepherds are gifted; they are called to serve and to give themselves, to love and to encourage, to model the Savior's style. When this occurs churches are blessed and they enjoy hope beyond religion.

Three Essential Attitudes for Non-Religious Shepherds

Shepherd the flock of God among you, exercising oversight not under compulsion, but voluntarily, according to the will of God; and not for sordid gain, but with eagerness; nor yet as lording it over those allotted to your charge, but proving to be examples to the flock. (1 Pet. 5:2–3)

I find at least three vital attitudes set forth in the verses you just read. Each attitude begins with a negative, followed by the positive side.

1. Not under compulsion...
   but voluntarily, according to the will of God

2. Not for gain...
   but with eagerness
3. Nor yet as lording it over those allotted to your charge...
   but proving to be examples to the flock.

Attitude number one is *an attitude of willingness*. "Not under compulsion, but voluntarily." *Compulsion* means "to be compelled by force." Like getting your teenager out of bed early in the morning to go to school. That is compulsion. Peter, however, isn't referring to a teenager at school but a shepherd with his flock.

This reminds me of a story I heard several years ago. A young man was sleeping soundly one Sunday morning when his mother came in, shook him, and said, "Wake up, son. You've got to get up... you've got to get out of bed." He groaned and complained. "Give me three good reasons why I have to get up this morning." Without hesitation his mother said, "Well, first of all, it's Sunday morning, and it's only right that we be in church. Second, because it's only forty minutes until church starts, so we don't have much time. And third, *you're the pastor!*"

Paul writes in his swan song that God's messengers are to "be ready in season and out of season" (2 Tim. 4:2). Faithful shepherds are to be willing "in season and out of season." ... when we feel like it, when we don't... when the church is growing as well as when it's not.

One of the things that intensifies burnout in ministry is a lack of willingness. And willingness depends on resting when we should so we can give it our all when we must. That's why, each time I speak to them, I encourage ministers to take a day off every week—when possible, a day and a half or two days. Why? To replenish the soul, to refresh the spirit. Furthermore, it is also imperative to take sufficient vacation time, to get away. I encourage "mini-vacations" as well—to get away with your mate, to spend time in refreshment and romance and simply the enjoyment of one another. By doing so, we are better able to do our work willingly and "not under compulsion."

I see many a frowning face and weary body when I go to pastors' conferences. Candidly, of all the groups that I minister to, few are more depressed and exhausted than a group of pastors. They are overworked, usually underpaid, and almost without exception underappreciated, though most of them are doing a remarkable piece of work.

Mild depressions can come upon us unexpectedly that erode our willingness. Often we can't explain such depressions at the time. Later, perhaps, but not when they occur.

I was reading to Cynthia the other day from the book I mentioned earlier in the chapter, Spurgeon's *Lectures to My Students*. She was in the kitchen working, and I walked over and said, "You've got to hear this." Then I read her about three pages! (Talk about a willing spirit!) Though writing more than one hundred years ago, Spurgeon described exactly some of the reasons we suffer from "burn out" in ministry today. He even admitted to depression in his own life, often before a great success, sometimes after a great success, and usually because of something he couldn't explain. He called this chapter "The Minister's Fainting Fits" (great title!). Listen to his candid remarks.

> Fits of depression come over most of us. Usually cheerful as we may be, we must at intervals be cast down. The strong are not always vigorous, the wise not always ready, the brave not always courageous, and the joyous not always happy. There may be here and there men of iron ... but surely the rust frets even these.[4]

Let me add one final comment here ... for the flock of God. Be tolerant with your pastor. A better word is *patient*. Try your best not to be too demanding or set your expectations too high. Multiply your own requests by however many there are in your church, and you'll have some idea of what the shepherd of the flock must live with. Be very understanding. Remember, if you write a letter that will bring his spirit down, it could wound him for weeks. Sometimes a confrontation is necessary. But even then, be kind. Be tactful. Pray for him! Encourage him! When you do, you'll find him all the more willing to serve his Lord among you.

Now, look at the second attitude: *an attitude of eagerness.* This next phrase describes not just willingness but an attitude of enthusiastic eagerness. Look how Peter expresses this: "Not for sordid gain, but with eagerness." The old King James Bible called sordid gain (money) "filthy lucre." Make certain your ministry is not motivated by the monetary, external perks. Religious circles emphasize, think about, and make a big thing of money. Guard against that.

I challenge preachers—and I have done it myself through the years—not to do a wedding just because they may get fifty dollars (or whatever) to do that wedding. Be eager to serve, not greedy! And if you're invited to participate in a week-long conference, do it because you really want to, not because you'll get an honorarium. Money is not a healthy motivation, so watch your motives.

When I was in seminary, my sister made me a small black-and-white sign that I hung on the wall in front of my desk where I studied. It read simply, *"What's your motive?"* What a searching question. I looked at it, off and on, for four years. It's a question every shepherd needs to ask on a weekly basis. Motives must forever be examined.

There is nothing quite as exciting or delightful as a shepherd who emits enthusiasm. Such zeal is *contagious!* His love for the Scriptures becomes the flock's love for the Scriptures. His zest for life becomes the congregation's zest for life. His commitment to leisure and enjoyment of life becomes their commitment to leisure and enjoyment of life. His joyful commitment to obeying God becomes theirs. No wonder Peter emphasizes eagerness. His passion for the unsaved becomes their passion. How refreshing it is to be around shepherds who are getting up in years but still eager and enthusiastic!

There's a third attitude Peter highlights: *an attitude of meekness.* I think it was with an extra boost of passion that he wrote:

> ...nor yet as lording it over those allotted to your charge, but proving to be examples to the flock. (1 Pet. 5:3)

I like the way Eugene Peterson paraphrases this:

Not bossily telling others what to do, but tenderly showing them the way. (MSG)

What concerns the old apostle here is a shepherd's exercising undue authority over others. We as shepherds must learn to hold our congregations loosely. We must watch our tendency to try and gain dominion over them, thinking of them as underlings. To avoid this, we must think of ourselves as servants, not sovereigns. Give the flock room to disagree. Assure them that they are to think on their own. But make no mistake. A shepherd who is "meek" is not weak. It takes great inner strength and security to demonstrate grace. He's willing to serve rather than demand. How beautiful, how marvelous it is, to witness one who is gifted and strong of heart, yet secure enough to let God's people grow and learn without having to fall in line with him at every point and march in lockstep to his drumbeat. The best shepherds are those who do their work unto the Lord, expecting no one to bow down before them.

While reading a recent issue of *Sports Illustrated*, I came across an article about Al Davis, owner of the Oakland Raiders football team. If you're a sports fan, you know that Davis is considered by many as one of the most greedy and proud of all owners in the business. He goes through more coaches in a decade than some owners do in a lifetime. This article reports that . . .

Davis's abuses of power have become increasingly visible. For example, after practice it is customary for him to enter the equipment room, drop a towel on the floor and wait for an employee to clean his shoes. "I saw him make someone wipe his shoes in front of 75 people," says Denver Broncos coach Mike Shanahan, who coached the Raiders in 1988.[5]

When I read that, I thought—here's the *opposite* of servant-hearted leadership. Yet I've witnessed leaders in ministry positions who have abused their positions almost as blatantly.

I've just finished listening to a cassette tape. It's the voice of a man who has been in ministry for years, and it was as if I were listening to another Jim Jones as he preached. My heart ached for that flock who sat and endured his self-serving style. Here was a man who had gained the mastery; verbal abuse was commonly practiced. He snapped his fingers... they jumped. He cracked his whip... they bowed down. Friend, that is not "proving to be an example to the flock." That is religious abuse... the manipulation of a congregation... legalistic religion at its worst.

The pastorate brings an enormous amount of authority. Not even a board of elders or deacons, as powerful as they may be, can take the shepherd's place in the pulpit on Sunday. It is a place where he can wield incredible authority and, if he chooses to do so, pull rank. All the more reason not to abuse it. The shepherd is not a stand-in for the Lord!

What God's people need most in their minister is a model of the life of Jesus Christ. There is something convincing about a model. That's Peter's point here. The very best thing for the minister to do is live a life of authenticity, accountability, and humility. Few things win the hearts of sheep like a tender shepherd!

You may remember that Moses, toward the end of his life, was said to have been "very humble, more than any man who was on the face of the earth" (Num. 12:3). Here was a man who "pastored" millions of people, but he refused to pander to his fame. He cared nothing for the applause of the public. He would not manipulate the people. In fact, brokenhearted before God, he even said, "Just take me out of the way." This wonderful section of Scripture is a good reminder that as important as it is to be a decisive leader with strong convictions, accepting the responsibilities of the position, it is never appropriate for the shepherd to "lord it over" those in his care.

No extra charge for this little comment, but I want to underscore an earlier observation that taking control of others is a mark of insecurity. Those who must have absolute agreement from everyone are terribly insecure people. Isn't it interesting that Christ Jesus never demanded that His disciples write anything down, never once exhorted them to memorize things He said? What He told them most of all was, "Do not be afraid." That was His most frequent command. "Do not be afraid." And the other was given by implication, "Watch Me and follow My model." No one has ever had the authority over a flock like Christ, but only on the rarest of occasions did He even raise His voice ... or rebuke His followers. Sheep do best when they are led, not driven ... when they are released, not controlled ... when they know they are loved, not shamed.

An Eternal Reward to Be Claimed

And when the Chief Shepherd appears, you will receive the unfading crown of glory. (1 Pet. 5:4)

I've mentioned crowns before in this book, but I've not mentioned *this* crown. Unlike the others, this is an exclusive crown. It is reserved for those who faithfully shepherd God's flock God's way. Only those who serve in this capacity will be able to receive the "unfading crown of glory." Notice, as a result of fulfilling these two principles and these three attitudes, the "crown of glory" will be awarded by "the Chief Shepherd" Himself.

Count on it, fellow shepherds. We have this to anticipate when we meet our Lord face to face.

Personal Suggestions for Both Sides of Ministry

To summarize, let me first address you who lead by saying, *keep a healthy balance*. If you teach, also be teachable. Read. Listen. Learn. Observe. Be ready to change. Then change! Admit wrong where you were wrong. Stand firm where you know you are right. You cannot win them all. And keep in mind, you're a servant of God, not a slave of the flock.

Since you are called to be a leader, when it's necessary, be a good follower—which takes us back to servanthood. When you lead, put yourself in the followers' shoes; think about what it would be like if you were sitting there listening to those things you are saying.

Neither underestimate your importance nor exaggerate your role. You are, admittedly, called of God. You represent Him, His message, His vision. You can become whipped by a congregation. (It happened to me once. It will never, by the grace of God, happen to me again.) Something tragic happens to a leader who has lost his drive and his determination. But you cannot do it all, so delegate. It's a big job to do, so invite others to help you do it. And when they do it well, give them credit.

Stay balanced. You are engaged in serious work, but (I repeat) keep a good sense of humor. Laugh often and loudly! And don't be afraid to laugh at yourself. My fellow laborers at Insight for Living make sure I do! On several occasions they have presented me with a tape containing all the "outtakes"—things they cut out of my taped messages during the year. Sort of my own private "bloopers." Some have even had the audacity to play this tape at a Christmas party for hundreds to hear and enjoy! As I listen, I cannot believe the dumb things I have said in any given year. It's enough to reduce even a strong-hearted shepherd to the size of a nit-pickin' termite!

Take God seriously, but don't take yourself too seriously.

Now, finally, to those of you being led, may I suggest that you be *a reason for rejoicing*. What a wonderful assignment!

Read the following slowly . . .

Obey your leaders, and submit to them; for they keep watch over your souls, as those who will give an account. Let them do this with joy and not with grief, for this would be unprofitable for you. (Heb. 13:17)

Think of ways to encourage your minister or leader. Pray often for him. Model gratitude and love. Demonstrate your affection with acts of generosity. Defend the shepherd whenever possible. And when you can't, tell him face to face, and tell no one else. Do it briefly, graciously, then forgive quickly. Try to imagine being in the shoes of the one who lives with the burden of the whole flock and is never free of that. And one more thought . . . think of how it would be if everyone else in the flock were *just like you*. C'mon, have a heart! The guy's not Spurgeon...and even if he were, you wouldn't agree with him either.

If you will do these things for your shepherd-leader, not only will you be rewarded, you will give him and yourself new hope...hope to press on, hope for the second mile, and everyone in the flock will enjoy hope beyond religion.

A Prayer for Hope Beyond Religion

Father, we consider it a priceless privilege to serve You, the living God. You've made all of us with different personalities, given us different gifts and responsibilities, and yet chosen to mingle us together in the same body, over which Christ is head. There are great temptations we face as shepherds and as sheep...to be in charge, to force others to get in line, to make things more uniform and rigid, to get narrow and demanding, to set our expectations too high...to handle ministry as if it were a secular enterprise. God, we need You to keep things fresh and unpredictable and especially to keep us authentic, servant-hearted people, and easy to live with.

So give us new hope...hope beyond religion, hope that motivates us to press on, serving You with pure motives and eager hearts. Thank You for Your grace, our only hope, dear Savior...in Your name.

AMEN

15

Hope Beyond Dissatisfaction

A Formula That Brings Relief

OUR SOCIETY HAS gorged itself on the sweet taste of success. We've filled our plates from a buffet of books that range from dressing for success to investing for success. We've passed the newsstands and piled our plates higher with everything from *Gentleman's Quarterly* and *Vogue*, to the *Wall Street Journal* and *Time*. When we've devoured these, we have turned our ravenous appetites toward expensive, success-oriented seminars. We've gobbled down stacks of notebooks, cassette albums, and video tapes in our hunger for greater success.

The irony of all this is that "there is never enough success in anybody's life to make one feel completely satisfied."[1] Instead of fulfillment, we experience the bloated sensation of being full of ourselves—*our* dreams, *our* goals, *our* plans, *our* projects, *our* accomplishments. The result of this all-you-can-eat appetite is not contentment. It's nausea. How terribly dissatisfying!

"The trouble with success is that the formula is the same as the one for a nervous breakdown," says *The Executive's Digest*. If you find yourself a little queasy after just such a steady diet, you don't need a second helping of success. You need a healthy dose of relief.

Interestingly, very few address that which most folks want but seldom find in their pursuit of success, and that is contentment, fulfillment, satisfaction. Rarely, if ever, are we offered boundaries and encouraged to say, "Enough is enough." And so we work harder and harder, make more and more, yet enjoy all of it less and less.

If we're hung up on any one subject in America today, we are hung up on the pursuit of success. Yet I don't know of another pursuit that is more deceptive—filled with fantasy dreams, phantoms, mirages, empty promises, and depressing disappointments.

Johnny Cash wasn't far off when he groaned, "If you don't have any time for yourself, any time to hunt or fish—that's success."

Today's Major Messages, Promising "Success"

The ad campaigns that come out of Madison Avenue promise much more than they can deliver. Their titillating messages fall into four categories: fortune and fame, power and pleasure.

Fortune says that to be successful you need to make the big bucks. Why else would the Fortune 500 list make such headlines every year? Anyone who is held up as successful must have more money than the average person.

Understand, there is nothing wrong with money earned honestly. Certainly there is nothing wrong in investing or giving or even spending money if the motive is right, if the heart is pure. But I have yet to discover anyone who has found true happiness simply in the gathering of more money. Although money is not sinful or suspect in itself, it is not what brings lasting contentment, fulfillment, or satisfaction.

Fame says that to be successful you need to be known in the public arena. You need to be a celebrity, a social somebody. Fame equates popularity with significance.

Power says that to be successful you need to wield a lot of authority, flex your muscles, take charge, be in control, carry a lot of weight. Push yourself to the front. Expect and demand respect.

Pleasure implies that to be successful you need to be able to do whatever feels good. This philosophy operates on the principle: "If it feels good, do it." It's just a modern version of the ancient epicurean philosophy, "Eat, drink, and be merry, for tomorrow you may die."

Fortune. Fame. Power. Pleasure. The messages bombard us from every direction. But what's missing in all this? Stop and ask yourself that question. Isn't something very significant absent here?

You bet. A *vertical* dimension. There's not even a hint of God's will or what pleases Him in the hard-core pursuit of success. Note also that nothing in that horizontal list guarantees satisfaction or brings relief deep within the heart. And in the final analysis, what most people really want in life is contentment, fulfillment, and satisfaction.

My sister, Luci, told me about the time she visited with a famous opera singer in Italy. This woman owned a substantial amount of Italian real estate, a lovely home, and a yacht floating on the beautiful Mediterranean in a harbor below her villa. At one point, Luci asked the singer if she considered all this the epitome of success.

"Why, no!" said the woman, sounding a bit shocked.

"What is success then?" asked Luci.

"When I stand to perform, to sing my music, and I look out upon a public that draws a sense of fulfillment, satisfaction, and pleasure from my expression of this art, at that moment I know I have contributed to someone else's need. That to me describes success."

Not a gathering of expensive possessions but a deliberate investment in the lives of others seems to be a crucial factor in finding fulfillment and contentment. Service. Help. Assistance. Compassion for others. Therein lies so much of what brings a sense of peace and true success.

In light of that, it seems, success is not a pursuit as much as it is a surprising discovery in an individual's life. All this brings us back to Peter's letter—old, but as we're discovering, ever relevant.

God's Ancient Plan: The Three A's

You younger men, likewise, be subject to your elders; and all of you, clothe yourselves with humility toward one another, for God is opposed to the proud, but gives grace to the humble.

Humble yourselves, therefore, under the mighty hand of God, that He may exalt you at the proper time, casting all your anxiety upon Him, because He cares for you. (1 Pet. 5:5–7)

The world's strategy to climb the ladder of success is simple: Work hard, get ahead, then climb higher—even if you have to claw and step on and climb over the next guy; don't let anything get in your way as you promote yourself. The goal is to make it to the top. It doesn't matter how many or who you push aside along the way, and it doesn't matter who you leave behind, even if it's your family or your friends or your conscience. It's a dog-eat-dog world, friends and neighbors, and the weak puppies don't make it. To survive, you have to hold on to the ladder for dear life. To succeed, you have to fight your way to the top . . . and never stop climbing.

I shook my head in disappointment when I read of Jimmy Johnson's decision to walk away from his wife and family several years ago when he became head coach of the Dallas Cowboys. He didn't deny it or hide it or apologize for his decision. He saw this major career promotion from the University of Miami to the Cowboys organization as his opportunity to make it to the top, big time. There was no way he would let anyone or anything get in his way; this was his moment to succeed, to move into big money. And things like home and family and kids (and grandkids!) were not going to stop him. He dropped all those responsibilities like a bad habit and split for Dallas like a hungry leopard searching for food.

In the world's eyes, he's now reached the pinnacle. A winning record, two Super Bowl rings, enormous amounts of money, fame, a yacht, several private enterprises, and now the Miami Dolphins with even greater hopes for more and more and more. As the public watches and reads of Johnson's accomplishments, most salivate. "The man's got it made!" would be the general opinion of athletes and sports fans and entrepreneurs and executives around the country. That, to them, represents success at its best.

God's plan, His ancient plan, is much different. We see it spelled out for us here in Peter's strategy for the right kind of success. In the three verses above, we see a series of contrasts to the kind of thinking I just illustrated. To keep everything simple, I call them the three A's: authority, attitude, and anxiety.

Authority

Peter's first piece of counsel advises us to submit ourselves to those who are wise and to "clothe" ourselves with humility.

> You younger men, likewise, be subject to your elders; and all of you, clothe yourselves with humility toward one another, for God is opposed to the proud, but gives grace to the humble. (1 Pet. 5:5)

The "clothe yourself" metaphor comes from a rare word that pictures a servant putting on an apron before serving those in the house. Perhaps Peter was recalling that meal in the upper room when Jesus wrapped Himself with a towel and washed the disciples' dirty feet (see John 13). Reclining at the table for their last meal with the Master, Peter and the other disciples had come to the table with dirty feet. The Savior, humbling Himself to the role of a servant, "clothed Himself" with a towel and, carrying a basin of water, washed their feet. I really believe the old fisherman was remembering that act of humility as he wrote these words in verse 5.

"Be subject to," he says—it's in the present tense here, "Keep on being subject to..." In other words, submission is to be an ongoing way of life, a lifestyle. We are to listen to the counsel of our elders in the faith, to be open to their reproofs, watch their lives, follow the examples they set, respect their decisions, and honor their years of seasoned wisdom. We must always remember that we need others. Their advice and model, their warnings and wisdom, are of inestimable value, no matter how far along in life we are.

I remember Dr. Howard Hendricks telling me years ago, "Experience is not the best teacher. *Guided* experience is the best teacher." The secret lies in the "guide"!

Bricklaying is a good illustration of this. As a novice, you can lay brick from morning to night, day in and day out, gaining several weeks of experience on your own, and you'll probably have a miserable-looking wall when you're finished. But if you work from the start with a journeyman bricklayer who knows how to lay a course of brick, one after the other, your guided experience can create a wall that is an object of beauty.

Proud independence results in a backlash of consequences, the main one being the opposition of God (see James 4:6). The original idea of God's opposing the proud is found in Proverbs 3.

> Do not envy a man of violence,
> And do not choose any of his ways.
> For the crooked man is an abomination to the LORD;
> But He is intimate with the upright.
> The curse of the LORD is on the house of the wicked,
> But He blesses the dwelling of the righteous.
> Though He scoffs at the scoffers,
> Yet He gives grace to the afflicted.
> The wise will inherit honor,
> But fools display dishonor. (Prov. 3:31–35)

In contrast to the humble, those who are proud in their hearts *scoff* at the Lord. This term expresses scorn and contempt. But God, not the proud, has the last scoff! As Solomon put it, "He scoffs at the scoffers."

When you submit yourself to those who are wise, instead of flaunting your own authority, you will have a greater measure of grace.

> But He gives a greater grace. Therefore it says, "God is opposed to the proud, but gives grace to the humble." (James 4:6)

And that is certainly what today's models of success could use a lot more of—a greater measure of grace. Isn't it noteworthy how rarely those who are on an aggressive, self-promoting fast track to the top even use the word *grace*. Grace, says Peter, is given by God to the humble, not to the proud.

Attitude

Peter's second strategy for success has to do with attitude. We must, he says, humble ourselves under God's mighty hand.

Humble yourselves, therefore, under the mighty hand of God, that He may exalt you at the proper time. (1 Pet. 5:6)

In the Old Testament, God's hand symbolizes two things. The first is discipline (see Exod. 3:20, Job 30:21, and Ps. 32:4). The second is deliverance (see Deut. 9:26 and Ezek. 20:34). When we humble ourselves under the mighty hand of God, we willingly accept His discipline as being for our good and for His glory. Then we gratefully acknowledge His deliverance, which always comes in His time and in His way.

In other words, as we saw in the previous chapter, we don't manipulate people or events. We refuse to hurry His timing. We let Him set the pace. And we humbly place ourselves under His firm, steadying hand. As a result of this attitude—don't miss it!—"He may exalt you at the proper time."

I must confess there are times when God's timing seems awfully slow. I find myself impatiently praying, "Lord, hurry up!" Is that true for you too?

In today's dog-eat-dog society, if something isn't happening as quickly as we want it to, there are ways to get the ball rolling, and I mean *fast*. There are people to call, strings to pull, and strong-arm strategies that make things happen. They are usually effective and always impressive . . . but in the long run, when we adopt these methods, we regret it. We find ourselves feeling dissatisfied and guilty. God didn't do it—we did!

When I was led by God to step away from almost twenty-three marvelous years at the First Evangelical Free Church in Fullerton, California, and step into the presidency of Dallas Theological Seminary, Cynthia and I immediately faced a challenge . . . in many ways, the greatest challenge of our lives and ministry. What about our radio ministry, Insight for Living?

The seminary is in Dallas, Texas; IFL is in Anaheim, California. In order for Cynthia to remain in leadership at IFL and provide the vision that ministry needs, she has to be in touch with and available to our radio ministry, and she and I, both, need to be engaged in some of the day-to-day operations of IFL. Meanwhile my work at the seminary requires my presence and availability on many occasions. If I hope to be more than a figurehead, and I certainly do, then my presence on and around that campus is vital. But it's hard to be two places at once. I tried that several years ago, and it hurt!

Obviously, then, it makes sense for IFL to move to Dallas. But moving an organization that size (with around 140 employees) is a costly and complicated process. We have a continuing lease on our building in Anaheim, no property or building as of yet in Dallas ... but she and I cannot continue to commute indefinitely. We have been doing that for well over two years—long enough to know we don't want to do that much longer! On top of all that, there's no money to move us.

So ... we have two options, humanly speaking. We can run ahead, make things happen, manipulate the money needs, and get the move behind us ... or we can "humble ourselves under the mighty hand of God" and pray and wait and watch Him work, counting on Him to "exalt us at the proper time" (answer our prayers, provide the funds, help us find a place in Dallas for relocating IFL, and end our commuting). And so we wait. We make the need known ... and we wait.

We're still waiting. We're still praying. We *refuse* to rush ahead and "make things happen." Admittedly, we get a little impatient and anxious at times, but we're convinced He is able to meet our needs and He will make it happen! Meanwhile we must be content to humble ourselves under God's mighty hand.

What does it mean to humble *yourself* under the mighty hand of God in *your* job, vocation, or profession? What if you're not getting the raise or the promotion you deserve? What if you are in a situation where you could make things happen ... but you really want God to do that?

Think of David, the young musician, tending his father's sheep back on the hills of Judea many centuries ago. He was a self-taught, gifted musician. He didn't go on tour, trying to make a name for himself. Instead, he sang to the sheep. He had no idea that someday his lyrics would find their way into the psalter or would be the very songs that have inspired and comforted millions of people through long and dark nights.

David didn't seek success; he simply humbled himself under the mighty hand of God, staying close to the Lord and submitting himself to Him. And God exalted David to the highest position in the land. He became the shepherd of the entire nation!

You don't have to promote yourself if you've got the stuff. If you're good, if you are to be used of Him, they'll find you. God will promote you. I don't care what the world system says. I urge you to let *God* do the promoting! Let *God* do the exalting! In the meantime, sit quietly under His hand. That's not popular counsel, I realize, but it sure works. Furthermore, you will never have to wonder in the future if it was you or the Lord who made things happen. And if He chooses to use you in a mighty way, really "exalt" you, you won't have any reason to get conceited. He did it all!

How refreshing it is to come across a few extremely gifted and talented individuals who do not promote themselves ... who genuinely let God lead ... who refuse to get slick and make a name for themselves! May their tribe increase.

Anxiety

Peter's third strategy for success tells us to cast all our anxiety upon God.

Humble yourselves ... casting all your anxiety upon Him, because He cares for you. (1 Pet. 5:6–7)

The original meaning of the term *cast* literally is "to throw upon." We throw ourselves fully and completely on the mercy and care of God. This requires a decisive action on our part. There is nothing passive or partial about it.

When those anxieties that accompany growth and true success emerge and begin to weigh you down (and they will), throw yourself on the mercy and care of God. Sometimes the anxiety comes in the form of people, sometimes it comes in the form of the media, sometimes it comes in the form of money and possessions, or a dozen other sources I could mention. The worries multiply, the anxieties intensify. Just heave those things upon the Lord. Throw them back on the One who gave them.

I love David's advice:

> Cast your burden upon the LORD, and He will sustain you;
> He will never allow the righteous to be shaken. (Ps. 55:22)

I have a feeling David wrote that one after he'd "made it," don't you?

If you've ever carried a heavily loaded pack while hiking, mountain climbing, or marching in the military, you know there is nothing quite like the wonderful words from the leader, "Let's stop here for a while." Everybody lets out a sign of relief and *thump, thump, thump, thump*, all those packs start hitting the ground. That's the word picture here. Release your burden. Just drop it. Let it fall off your back. Reminds me of John Bunyan's pilgrim when he came to the place of the sepulcher and the cross; the burden of sin fell off his back.

So here's the simple formula that will enable you to handle whatever success God may bring your way and will provide you with the relief you need while waiting:

SUBMISSION + HUMILITY − WORRY = RELIEF

Submission to others plus humility before God minus the worries of the world equals genuine relief. It will also provide hope and contentment without the pain of dissatisfaction.

Our Great Need: Effecting Change

Now I wish all this were as simple as just reading it and saying, "That's it. I'm changed. It's gonna happen." Believe me, it doesn't work that way. So let me suggest some things we need in our lives to effect these changes.

To grasp what true success really is and how to obtain it, we need to tune out the seductive messages from the world and tune in to the instructive messages from the Word. How? It occurs to me we need at least three things to make this happen.

First, we need direction so we can know to whom we should submit.

Let's understand . . . start trying to please everybody, and you're assured of instant failure and long-term frustration. We need God to direct us to those to whom we should submit.

Who are the people I should follow? Who are the folks I should watch? Whose writings should I read? Whose songs should I sing? Whose ministry should I support financially? Whose model should I emulate?

We need direction from God. So begin to pray, "Lord, direct me to the right ones to whom I should submit." Count on Him for direction.

Second, we need discipline to restrain our hellish pride.

Pride will keep rearing its ugly head. The more successful we get, the stronger the temptation to rely on the flesh. We've thought about that already in previous chapters. I use the words "hellish pride" because it is just that. Pride will whisper ways to promote ourselves (but look very humble and pious). Pride will tell us how and when to manipulate or intimidate others. We need discipline to keep ourselves from being our own deliverers. We need discipline to stay *under* the hand of God. Remember that—*under* His mighty hand. But pride hates being *under* anything or anyone. So ask God for discipline here.

Third, we need discernment so we can detect the beginning of anxiety.

Ever have something begin to kind of nag you? You can't put your finger on it. It's fuzzy. Sort of a slimy ooze. It's just growing in the corners, nagging you, getting you down. That is the beginning of a heavy anxiety. We need discernment to detect it, identify it, and get to its root so we can deal with it. When we see the beginning of anxiety for what it is, that's the precise moment to cast it on God, to roll that pack on Him. At that moment we say, "I can't handle it, Lord. You take over."

And how are these needs met? Through the Word of God. The principles and precepts of Scripture give us direction, discipline, and discernment.

Do you find yourself caught up in the success syndrome? Are you still convinced that the world's formula is best? Do you find yourself manipulating people and pulling strings to get ahead? Are you, at this moment, in the midst of a success syndrome you started, not God? No wonder you feel dissatisfied! That type of success *never* satisfies. Only God-directed success offers the formula that brings contentment, fulfillment, satisfaction, and relief.

God's success is never contrived. It is never forced. It is never the working of human flesh. It is usually unexpected—and its benefits are always surprising.

The hand of God holds you firmly in His control. The hand of God casts a shadow of the cross across your life. Sit down at the foot of that cross and deliberately submit your soul to His mighty hand. Accept His discipline. Acknowledge His deliverance. Ask for His discernment.

Then be quiet. Be still. Wait. And move over so I can sit beside you. I'm waiting too.

A Prayer for Hope Beyond Dissatisfaction

*We are so grateful, Father, for the truth of Your Word—for the
Old and New Testaments alike . . . the teachings of Jesus, the*

writings of Peter, the profound songs of David, the law of Moses. All of it blends together in a harmony, a symphony of theological and practical significance. You have us under Your hand, and in our more lucid moments we really want to be there. In times of impatience and wildness we want to squirm free and run ahead. Thank You for holding us, for forgiving us, for cleaning us up, for accepting us, for reshaping us, for not giving up on us. And at this moment, we give You the full right to discipline, to direct, to deliver in Your way and in Your time. Give us great patience as we wait. Humbly, I pray and submit to You in Jesus' name.

AMEN

16

Hope Beyond the Battle

Standing
Nose-to-Nose
with the Adversary

AS YOU LOOK back over your life, at what places did you grow the most?"

Whenever I ask this question, almost without exception the person will mention a time of pain, a time of loss, a time of deep and unexplained suffering in his or her life. Yet when suffering rains down upon us, our tendency is to think that God has withdrawn His umbrella of protection and abandoned us in the storm. Our confusion during those inclement times stems from our lack of understanding about the role of pain in our lives. Philip Yancey is correct in his analysis.

> Christians don't really know how to interpret pain. If you pinned them against the wall, in a dark, secret moment, many Christians would probably admit that pain was God's one mistake. He really should have worked a little harder and invented a better way of coping with the world's dangers.[1]

Nevertheless, the pain rages on. With relentless regularity, we encounter hardship and heartache. We give ourselves to a friendship, only to lose that person in death. We grieve the loss and determine not to give ourselves so completely again . . . so loneliness comes to haunt us. Is there no hope beyond this? We find the answer to that age-old question, according to Peter, is a resounding YES!

Interestingly, the apostle never once laments the fact that the people he was writing to were suffering pain and persecution, nor does he offer advice on how to escape it. Instead, he faces suffering squarely, tells them (and us) not to be surprised by it, and promises that God provides benefits for enduring life's hurts. Even when life is dreary and overcast, rays of hope pierce through the clouds to stimulate our growth. In fact, without pain there would be little growth at all, for we would remain sheltered, delicate, naive, irresponsible, and immature.

Let's get something straight. Our real enemy is not our suffering itself. The real culprit is our adversary the Devil, the one responsible for much of the world's pain and danger. Although God is at work in the trials of life, so is Satan. While God uses our trials to draw us closer to Him, Satan tries to use them as levers to pry us away from Him. That tug-o'-war only intensifies the battle! Not surprisingly, Peter gives us some crucial advice on how to do battle with the Devil and how to keep him from gaining victory over our lives.

Battle Tactics

In his book *Your Adversary the Devil*, Dwight Pentecost compares the tactics of a physical battle to those of a spiritual one.

> No military commander could expect to be victorious in battle unless he understood his enemy. Should he prepare for an attack by land and ignore the possibility that the enemy might approach by air or by sea, he would open the way to defeat. Or should he prepare for a land and sea attack and ignore the possibility of an attack through the air, he would certainly jeopardize the campaign.
>
> No individual can be victorious against the adversary of our souls unless he understands that adversary; unless he understands

his philosophy, his methods of operation, his methods of temptation.[2]

This being the case, it should not surprise us that Peter begins by identifying the enemy and his general modus operandi. Whoever denies the fact that there is a literal enemy of our souls chooses to live in a dream world, revealing not only a lack of understanding but also a lack of reality. Throughout the Old Testament and the New we find ample evidence of a literal Devil, an actual Satan—a very real "adversary," to use Peter's word.

His Identity, Style, and Purpose

> Be of sober spirit, be on the alert. Your adversary, the devil, prowls about like a roaring lion, seeking someone to devour. But resist him, firm in your faith, knowing that the same experiences of suffering are being accompanied by your brethren who are in the world. (1 Pet. 5:8–9)

The original term translated *adversary* refers to an opponent in a lawsuit. This individual is a person on the other side. An adversary is neither a friend nor a playmate. An adversary is no one to mess around with—and no one to joke about.

Satan's constant relationship with the child of God is an adversarial relationship. Make no mistake about it; he despises us. He hates what we represent. He is our unconscionable and relentless adversary, our opponent in the battle between good and evil, between truth and falsehood, between the light of God and the darkness of sin.

"Your adversary, the devil," puts it well. That's the way Peter identifies the Enemy—boldly, without equivocation. "The devil" comes from the word *diabolos*, which means "slanderer" or "accuser." Revelation 12:10 states that the enemy of our souls is "the accuser of our brethren." He accuses us "day and night," according to that verse. Not only does he accuse us to God, he also accuses us to ourselves. Many of our self-defeating thoughts come from the demonic realm. He is constantly accusing, constantly building guilt, constantly prompting shame, constantly coming against us with hopes of destroying us.

Did you notice his style? "He prowls about." The Devil is a prowler.

Think about that. He comes by stealth, and he works in secret. His plans are shadowy. He never calls attention to his approach or to his attack. Furthermore, he is "like a roaring lion." He is a beast, howling and growling with hunger, "seeking someone to devour"! To personalize this, substitute your name for "someone." When you do, it makes that verse all the more powerful. "Your adversary, the devil, prowls about like a roaring lion, seeking to devour _____ ." I find that has a chilling effect on my nervous system.

He isn't simply out to tantalize or to tease us. He's not playing around. He has a devouring, voracious appetite. And he dances with glee when he destroys lives, especially the lives of Christians.

A. T. Robertson wrote, "The devil's purpose is the ruin of mankind. Satan wants all of us." It's wise for us to remember that when we travel. It's wise for us to remember that when we don't gather for worship on a Sunday and we're really out on our own. It's wise to remember that when we find ourselves alone for extended periods of time, especially during our more vulnerable moments. He prowls about, stalking our every step, waiting for a strategic moment to catch us off guard. His goal? To devour us...to consume us...to eat us alive.

I hope you've gotten a true picture of your enemy. He's no sly-looking imp with horns, a red epidermis, and a pitchfork. He is the godless, relentless, brutal, yet brilliant adversary of our souls who lives to bring us down...to watch us fall.

Our Response

Peter's opening command alerts us to our necessary response: "Be of sober spirit, be on the alert."

Satan doesn't like chapters like this. He hates exposure. He hates being talked about. He certainly hates it when truth replaces fantasy and people are correctly informed. He especially hates having all of his ugly and filthy plans and destructive ways identified.

> *Be Alert.* As his possible prey, however, our primary response should be to keep on the lookout for the predator.

Satan is a dangerous enemy. He is a serpent who can bite us when we least expect it. He is a destroyer...and an accuser.... He has great power and intelligence, and a host of demons who assist him in his attacks against God's people.... He is a formidable enemy; we must never joke about him, ignore him, or underestimate his ability. We must "be sober" and have our minds under control when it comes to our conflict with Satan.[3]

The Devil's great hope is that he will be ignored, written off as a childhood fairy tale, or dismissed from the mind of the educated adult. Like a prowler breaking into a home, Satan doesn't want to call attention to himself. He wants to work incognito, undetected, in the shadows. The thing he fears most is the searchlight of the Scriptures turned in his direction, revealing precisely who he really is and what comprises his battle plan.

> *Respect Him.* To defeat the Devil we must first be alert to his presence...respect him—not fear or revere him, but respect him, like an electrician respects the killing power of electricity.

One caution here, however.

A part of this soberness includes not blaming everything on the devil. Some people see a demon behind every bush and blame Satan for their headaches, flat tires, and high rent. While it is true that Satan can inflict physical sickness and pain (see Luke 13:16 and the Book of Job), we have no biblical authority for casting out demons of headache or demons of backache. One lady phoned me long-distance to inform me that Satan had caused her to shrink seven and a half inches. While I have great respect for the wiles and powers of the devil, I still feel we must get our information about him from the Bible and not from our own interpretation of experiences.[4]

Please be careful that you don't identify every ache and pain or every significant problem you encounter as being satanic in origin. My brother mentioned to me that he once counseled a woman who said she had "the demon of nail-biting." I've met a few who said they fought against "the demon of gluttony." (From their appearance, they were losing the war.) That is not a sign of maturity. I get real concerned about folks who blame the Devil every time something happens that makes life a little bit difficult for them. In fact, it can even become an excuse for not taking responsibility for your own life and your own decisions and choices.

So be alert and be sober. Be calm and watchful. Or, as Moffatt renders it, "Keep cool. Keep awake." We use that word *cool* very lightly today, but here it means a calm coolness. Like professionals in an athletic contest. The best in the game stay cool, calm, collected, and clear-headed, even in the last two minutes as they drive hard for the win, the ultimate prize. So be calm, but be on the alert. Satan's prowling around. This is no time for a snooze in the backyard hammock. He's silently maneuvering a brilliant strategy with plans to destroy us. This is serious stuff!

By the way, I've never seen a prowler who wore a beeper. I've never heard of a prowler who came honking his way down the street with a loudspeaker, saying, "I'm gonna slip in through the sliding door of that home at 7147 Elm at two o'clock in the morning." No, you know a prowler doesn't do that. He comes with stealth. He silently slides his way in. And you never even know he's in your house until he's robbed you blind.

Last fall Cynthia and I had the scare of our lives—literally. I was ministering at a hotel in Cancun—a nice, safe, well-equipped hotel. We turned in for the night around 11:30 or so and were soon in Dreamland. Shortly before 1:00 A.M. Cynthia's loud, shrill scream startled me awake. "There's a man in our room!!"

I looked toward the sliding-glass door that opened onto the patio ... and there he stood, silent and staring into our room. A chill raced down my spine. The door had been slid open, and the curtains were blowing like sails into the room from the wind off the gulf waters. In fact, it was the surge of the surf that had awakened Cynthia, not the intruder. He had not made a sound ... nor was he easily visible, since he was dressed in dark clothing.

I jumped out of bed and stood nose-to-nose with him ... and yelled at the top of my lungs, hoping to frighten him away. For all I knew he had a gun or a knife, but this was no time to close my eyes and pray and lie there like a wimp. Slowly, he backed out of the room, jumped off the seawall, and quickly escaped. Hotel security never found a trace of him, except for a few footprints in the sand. He was a prowler who came, most likely, to steal from our room. Talk about a lasting memory!

Our adversary is a prowler. He comes without announcement, and to make matters worse, he comes in counterfeit garb. He is brilliant, and you and I had better *respect* that brilliance.

I've heard young Christians say things like, "This Christian life is thrilling. I'm ready to take on the Devil." When I can, I pull them aside and say, "Don't say that. It's a stupid comment! You're dealing with the invisible realm. You're dealing with a power you cannot withstand in yourself and a presence you have no knowledge of when you say something like that. Get serious. Be on the alert." Usually that's enough to wake 'em up. Every once in a while it's helpful to be knocked down a notch or two, especially when we're starting to feel a little big for our britches.

I heard a funny but true story recently about Muhammad Ali. It took place in the heyday of his reign as heavyweight champion of the world. He had taken his seat on a plane and the giant 747 was starting to taxi toward the runway when the flight attendant walked by and noticed Ali had not fastened his seat belt.

"Please fasten your seat belt, sir," she requested.

He looked up proudly and snapped, "Superman don't need no seat belt, lady!"

Without hesitation she stared at him and said, "Superman don't need no plane ... so buckle up."

Don't be fooled by your own pride or softened by some medieval caricature of an "impish" little devil. Our adversary is a murderer, and except for the Lord Himself, he's never met his match. We may hate him ... but, like any deadly enemy, we had better respect him and keep our distance. There's a war on!

Resist Him. After we are alert to him and respect him, we must resist him. Don't run scared of the enemy. Don't invite him in; don't play with him. But don't be afraid of him either. Resist him. Through the power of the Lord Jesus Christ, firmly resist him.

"But resist him, firm in your faith," writes Peter. Kenneth Wuest has a wise word of counsel on this.

> The Greek word translated "resist" means "to withstand, to be firm against someone else's onset" rather than "to strive against that one." The Christian would do well to remember that he cannot fight the devil. The latter was originally the most powerful and wise angel God created. He still retains much of that power and wisdom as a glance down the pages of history and a look about one today will easily show. While the Christian cannot take the offensive against Satan, yet he can stand his ground in the face of his attacks. Cowardice never wins against Satan, only courage.[5]

I like that closing line.

Once we have enough respect for Satan's insidious ways to stay alert and ready for his attacks, the best method for handling him is strong resistance. That resistance is not done in our own strength, however, but comes from being "firm in faith." An example of this can be seen in the wilderness temptations of Christ when He resisted Satan with the Word of God (see Matt. 4:1–11).

You know what helps me when I sense I'm in the presence of the enemy? Nothing works better for me in resisting the Devil than the actual quoting of Scripture. I usually quote God's Word in such situations. One of the most important reasons for maintaining the discipline of Scripture memory is to have it ready on our lips when the enemy comes near and attacks. And you'll know it when he does. I don't know how to describe it, but the longer you walk with God, the more you will be able to sense the enemy's presence.

And when you do, you need those verses of victory ready to come to the rescue. The Word of God is marvelously strong. It is alive and active and "sharper than a two-edged sword." And its truths can slice their way into the invisible, insidious ranks of the demonic hosts.

Although our own strength is insufficient to fend him off, when we draw on the limitless resources of faith, we can stand against him nose-to-nose, much like I did with that intruder at Cancun. And such faith is nurtured and strengthened by a steady intake of the Scriptures.

Furthermore, the strength that comes from faith is supplemented by the knowledge of that company of saints stretching down through history, as well as present-day believers joining hands in prayer across the globe. There is something wonderfully comforting about knowing that we are not alone in the battle against the adversary.

In spite of faith and in spite of friends, however, the battle is *exhausting*. I don't know of anything that leaves you more wrung out, more weary. Nothing is more demanding, nothing more emotionally draining, nothing more personally painful than encountering and resisting our archenemy.

The devil always has a strategy, and he is an excellent strategist. He's been at it since he deceived Eve in the Garden. He knows our every weakness. He knows our hardest times in life. He knows our besetting sins. He knows the areas where we tend to give in the quickest. He also knows the moment to attack. He is a master of timing . . . and he knows the ideal place.

But I have good news for you. Better still, Scripture has good news for you. When you resist through the power and in the name of the Lord Jesus Christ, the Devil will ultimately retreat. He will back down. He won't stay away; he'll back away. He will retreat as you resist him, firm in your faith.

Remember Ephesians 6:10–11: "Be strong in the Lord, and in the strength of His might. Put on the full armor of God, that you may be able to stand firm against the schemes of the devil."

This is where the Christian has the jump on every unbeliever who tries to do battle against the enemy. Those without the Lord Jesus have no power to combat or withstand those supernatural forces.

No chance! They are facing the enemy without weapons to defend themselves. But when the Christian is fully armed with the armor God provides, he or she is invincible. Isn't that a great word? Invincible! That gives us hope beyond the battle.

It's a mockery to say to those who are not Christians, "Just stand strong against the enemy." They can't. They have no equipment. They have no weapons. A person must have the Lord Jesus reigning within to be able to stand strong in His might.

Our Rewards

Will there be suffering in resisting Satan? Yes. Will it be painful? Without a doubt. I have found that there are times we emerge from the battle a little shell-shocked. But after the dust settles, our Commander-in-Chief will pin medals of honor on our lapels. And what are they? Peter tells us.

> And after you have suffered for a little while, the God of all grace, who called you to His eternal glory in Christ, will Himself perfect, confirm, strengthen and establish you. (1 Pet. 5:10)

He will "perfect, confirm, strengthen and establish" us. Talk about hope beyond the battle! Here is the biblical portrait of a decorated war hero, a seasoned veteran from the ranks of the righteous whose muscles of faith have been hardened by battle. It is the portrait of a well-grounded, stable, mature Christian. Christ will make sure the portrait of our lives looks like that, for He himself will hold the brush. And His hand is vastly more powerful than our enemy's.

I remember one night when I was taking care of a couple of our grandchildren. It was late in the evening, but since grandfathers usually let their grandchildren stay up longer than they should, they were still awake. We were laughing, messing around, and having a great time together when we suddenly heard a knock at the door. Not the doorbell, but a mysterious knocking. Immediately one of my grandsons grabbed hold of my arm. "It's OK," I said. The knock came again, and I started to the door. My grandson followed me, but he hung onto my left leg and hid behind me as I opened the door. It was one of my son's friends who had dropped by unexpectedly. After the person had left and I'd closed the door, my grandson, still holding on to my leg, said in a strong voice. "Bubba, we don't have anything to worry about, do we?" And I said, "No, we don't have anything to worry about. Everything's fine." You know why he was strong? Because he was hanging on to protection. As long as he was clinging to his grandfather's leg, he didn't have to worry about a thing.

That happens to us when we face the enemy. When he knocks at the door or when he prowls around back or when he looks for the chink in your armor, you hang on to Christ. You stand firm in faith. You put on the "armor of God" (Eph. 6:11–20—please read it!). You have nothing to worry about. *Nothing*. For, as Peter reminds us, our Lord has "dominion forever and ever. Amen" (1 Pet. 5:11). He is the one *ultimately* in control, and that is something in which every believer can find strength to hope again.

Necessary Reminders

Now, I want to tie a couple of strings around your finger as reminders as we bring these thoughts to a close. This advice has helped me throughout my Christian life, and I think you may find it useful.

First, never confuse confidence in Christ with cockiness in the flesh.

Confidence and cockiness are two different things. When you're facing the enemy, there's no place for cockiness. There is a place for confidence, however, and it's all confidence in Christ. You tell Him your weakness. You tell Him your fears. You ask Him to assist you as you equip yourself with His armor. You ask Him to think through you and to act beyond your own strength and to give you assurance. He'll do it. I repeat, it's all confidence in Christ. It's not some sense of cockiness in the flesh. You're a Christian, remember, not Superman or Wonder Woman.

Second, always remember that suffering is temporal but its rewards are eternal. Paul's wonderful words come to mind:

> Therefore we do not lose heart, but though our outer man is decaying, yet our inner man is being renewed day by day. For momentary, light affliction is producing for us an eternal weight of glory far beyond all comparison, while we look not at the things which are seen, but at the things which are not seen; for the things which are seen are temporal, but the things which are not seen are eternal. (2 Cor. 4:16–18)

Our Lord set the example for us, "who for the joy set before Him endured the cross" (Heb. 12:2). We have all read the Gospel accounts that chronicle Christ's suffering on the cross. We have all heard the Good Friday sermons that recount the horrors of crucifixion. As we look up at Him there on the cross, we can sense His shame and feel the anguish of His heart as we stand at arm's length from His torn and feverish flesh. What we can't see is the joy that awaited Him when He surrendered His spirit to His Father. But He saw it. He knew.

Imagine for a minute how horrible that nightmare of the cross really was. Then imagine, if you can, how wonderful the joy awaiting Jesus must have been for Him to have willingly endured that degree of suffering and injustice. That same joy awaits us. But we have to stoop through the low archway of suffering to enter into it. And part of that suffering includes doing battle with the adversary.

There is probably no book, other than the Bible, that is as insightful or creatively written concerning the strategies of Satan than C. S. Lewis's *The Screwtape Letters*. Here is a sampling of Satan's strategy as articulated by the imaginary Screwtape, a senior devil, who corresponds with his eager nephew to educate the fledgling devil for warfare against the forces of "the Enemy"—that is, God.

> Like all young tempters, you are anxious to be able to report spectacular wickedness. But do remember, the only thing that matters is the extent to which you separate the man from the Enemy. It does not matter how

small the sins are, provided that their cumulative effect is to edge the man away from the Light and out into the Nothing. Murder is no better than cards if cards can do the trick. Indeed, the safest road to Hell is the gradual one—the gentle slope, soft underfoot, without sudden turnings, without milestones, without signposts.[6]

A Prayer for Hope Beyond the Battle

Almighty God, You are our all-powerful and invincible Lord. How we need You, especially when the battle rages! Thank You for standing by our side, for being our strong shield and defender. We have no strength in ourselves. We are facing an adversary far more powerful, more brilliant, and more experienced than we. And so, with confidence, we want to put on and wear the whole armor of God . . . and, in Your strength alone, resist the wicked forces that are designed to bring us down.

Give new hope, Lord—hope beyond the battle. Encourage us with the thought that, in Christ, we triumph! In His great name I pray.

AMEN

17

Hope Beyond Misery

Lasting
Lessons

I HAVE BEEN encouraged by the fact that in his writings Peter gets us beyond the misery part of suffering.

You have noticed, haven't you, how we all throw pity parties for ourselves when suffering comes? It's almost as though we capitalize on the downside rather than focus on the benefits that come from the hard times. How easily we forget that growth occurs when life is hard, not when it's easy. However, it is not until we move beyond the misery stage that we're able to find the magnificent lessons to be learned. The problem is, we almost delight in our own misery.

In keeping with that, Dan Greenburg has written a very funny book, *How to Make Yourself Miserable*, in which he says:

> Too long have you...gone about the important task of punishing yourself...by devious or ineffective means. Too long have you had to settle for poorly formulated anxieties...simply because this vital field has always been shrouded in ignorance—a folk art rather than a science. Here at last is the frank report you have been waiting for....It is our humble but earnest desire that through these pages you will be able to

find for yourself the inspiration and the tools for a truly painful, meaningless, miserable life.[1]

The truth is, of course, that we don't need any help in this area. We have perfected the art of misery all by ourselves. We know very well how to capitalize on misery, how to multiply our troubles rather than learn—through the sometimes torturous and yes, humiliating experiences of life—the vital lessons that bring about true joy, true meaning, and true significance in life.

I think it was Charlie "Tremendous" Jones who said, "There is something wrong with everything." Have you found that true? No matter where you go or what you do, is there something wrong with it? Murphy's Law says, "If something can go wrong, it will." Another of Murphy's Laws says, "That's not a light at the end of the tunnel. That's an oncoming train." And then one wag adds, "Murphy was an optimist."

The problem is, when we're all alone, when we are feeling the brunt of the experience, when we are in the midst of the swirl, when we can't see any light at the end of any tunnel, it isn't funny.

As the apostle Peter so masterfully presents in his letter, however, suffering is not the end; it's a means to the end. Best of all, God's end for us is maturity. It is growth. It is a reason for living and going on.

Five Observations and a Set of Bookends

As we look back at the things we've seen in this book, a few broad-stroked observations stand out in sharp relief. Perhaps by reviewing where we've been, we'll be able to sharpen our perspective to an even keener edge.

First, Peter wrote the letter. Though it may seem simplistically obvious, this fact offers us a unique encouragement. Along with James and John, Peter was one of the inner circle of three confidants to whom Jesus revealed himself most fully. Of the twelve disciples, Peter was regarded as the spokesman. Never one to teeter on the fence of indecision, Peter was impulsive, impetuous, and outspoken. He often put his foot in his mouth. He knew the heights of ecstasy on the Mount of Transfiguration and the depths of misery and shame on the night of his denials. And yet, in spite of his flaws and his failures, he is called an apostle of Jesus Christ. What grace!

This is tremendous encouragement for all who fear that their flaws are too numerous or their failures too enormous to be given another chance.

I'm sure Peter looked back on many occasions and thought, *I wish I hadn't said that.* (Haven't we all?) But I'll tell you something else about Peter; he wasn't afraid to step forward—to put it all on the line.

Are you one of those people who never goes anywhere without a thermometer, a raincoat, an aspirin, or a parachute? Not Peter. He went full-bore into whatever he believed in. No lack of passion in Peter! What he lacked in forethought he made up for in zeal and enthusiasm.

Admittedly, that kind of lifestyle is a bit risky and unpredictable.

Do you ever envy some of the experiences of Peter kind of people—folks who are willing to say what they think or admit how they feel, even though they may be wrong? How much more fun it is to be around people like that than around those who are so careful and so closed-in and so protected you never know what they really feel or where they really stand. They're very, very cautious, ultra-conservative thinkers who wouldn't even consider taking a risk. And they get very little done for the kingdom because they are so busy guarding everything they do and say.

Not Peter. Peter says, in effect, "I wrote this. Yes, I'm the Disciple who blew it. I failed Him when He was under arrest. I spoke when I shouldn't have. But I write now as one who has learned many things the hard way, things about pain and suffering. I don't write out of theory; I write from experience."

Second, hurting people received the letter. They are not named, but their locations are stated in the first verse of the letter. Peter wrote "to those who reside as aliens, scattered throughout Pontus, Galatia, Cappadocia, Asia, and Bithynia."

These hurting people, scattered outside their homeland, were lonely and frightened aliens, unsure of their future. But though they were homeless, they were not abandoned; though they were frightened, they were not forgotten. Peter reminds them of that. They were chosen by God and sanctified by His Spirit, and His grace and peace would be with them "in fullest measure."

Whenever you find yourself away from home, whenever you find yourself feeling abandoned and frightened, overlooked and forgotten, Peter's first letter is magnificent therapy. I suggest you read it in several versions. The Living Bible, the New International Version, J. B. Phillips's paraphrase, and Eugene Peterson's paraphrase, *The Message*, will give you a good start. Read through without a break, if possible. Read it through sitting there in that hotel room or alone in your cell or apartment or home. It is excellent counsel for those who are hurting. It will assure you of your calling and reassure you that grace and peace are yours to claim in fullest measure.

Third, this letter came through Silas. The person to whom Peter dictated his words was Silas, one of the leaders in the early church (referred to in 1 Peter 5:12 as Silvanus).

Silas was a cultured Roman citizen, well educated and well traveled. Peter was a rugged fisherman, a blue-collar Galilean with little or no schooling, but apparently (beginning with 5:12) he took the pen in his own hand and wrote the final lines of the letter. We know that, not only because of the substance of verses 12–14, but because of the style. The grammar, syntax, and vocabulary become simpler in the Greek text.

The rest of the letter, however, came *through* Silas. If you're like most people, you don't know enough about Silas to fill a three-by-five card. Some people know him only as the guy who carried Paul's bags on long trips. Paul gets all the attention, yet it was Paul *and* Silas who carried the gospel. Silas was Barnabas's replacement on Paul's missionary journeys. Paul *and* Silas were the ones who sang in the jail there in Philippi at midnight. And Silas was the one alongside Paul when the man was stoned. Silas was one who really understood the hearts of Paul and Peter.

Look at Acts 15:22 in case your respect for Silas needs a little bolstering.

Then it seemed good to the apostles and the elders, with the whole church, to choose men from among them to send to Antioch with Paul and Barnabas—Judas called Barsabbas, and Silas, leading men among the brethren.

Here is a man who was one of the "leading men" of the church in the first century, and at the writing of this letter, he remained alongside Peter. In fact, Peter calls him "our faithful brother (for so I regard him)" (1 Pet. 5:12).

God gives Peter the message, Silas writes it down, and the Spirit of God ignites it. There may have been times when Silas was the wind beneath Peter's wings. We all need a Silas... someone willing to stand alongside us.

Fourth, the letter concludes with a greeting from a woman.

She who is in Babylon, chosen together with you, sends you greetings, and so does my son, Mark. (1 Pet. 5:13)

Now, obviously, everybody wonders who "she" is; who is the woman "who is in Babylon"? Most interpretations fall into two categories: Peter could either be referring to "woman" in the figurative sense, as the bride of Christ, or he could be using the word literally. If the latter is correct, the woman referred to may possibly be Peter's wife. We know Peter had a wife because Jesus healed Peter's mother-in-law. Then, in 1 Corinthians 9:5, Paul makes note of the other apostles' wives, which likely included Peter's wife. Clement of Alexandria states that she died as a martyr for the faith, so she may have been well-known among the early Christians. No doubt those who first received this letter knew who the woman was whether or not we do.

Fifth, the letter's final command is one of intimate affection. This old fisherman still has a lot of love left in him. He has not become jaded. Look how he expresses himself.

Greet one another with a kiss of love.
Peace [*Shalom*] be to you all who are in Christ. (1 Pet. 5:14)

The kiss of the Christian was called "the shalom," or "the peace." With the passing of time, the practice of the kiss of peace has disappeared from the church. It is fascinating to trace through church history how the kiss shared between people of the faith became less and less intimate. In fact, if you are a romantic-type person given to warm affection, it's enough to completely deplete all wind from your sails! In the first century, a kiss was placed on the cheek of believers as they arrived and as they left the fellowship of the saints. As time passed, people began kissing the precious documents rather than each other. And before long, a wooden board was passed among the people and everyone kissed that plank of wood. (That sounds exciting, doesn't it? "Let's go to church tonight. We'll get to kiss the board.") Anyway, through it all, the church lost the sense of affection and intimacy along with the embrace of peace.

Originally, as they kissed each other's cheeks, they would say to one another, "Peace be with you," or simply *Shalom*. And that's exactly what Peter does here. "Greet one another with the kiss of peace."

Augustine said that when Christians were about to communicate, "they demonstrated their inward peace by the outward kiss."

The formal kiss was the sign of peace among early Christians, demonstrating their love and unity. This outward sign reflected an inward peace between believers, a sign that all injuries and wrongdoing were forgiven and forgotten. Some traditions should be reinstated!

Personal Applications

Well, so much for the bookends that open and close Peter's letter. Now let's take a last look at the contents and how they can speak to us in our personal situations.

Three times in the letter Peter refers to the reader, which gives us a clue to the letter's structure. In fact, the letter falls neatly into three distinct sections, each one detailing the "how" of an important truth: a living hope and how to claim it (1:1–2:10), a pilgrim life and how to live it (2:11–4:11), and a fiery trial and how to endure it (4:12–5:11). An application of these three major messages should give us hope beyond our misery.

A Living Hope and How to Claim It

> Blessed be the God and Father of our Lord Jesus Christ, who according to His great mercy has caused us to be born again to a living hope through the resurrection of Jesus Christ from the dead. (1 Pet. 1:3)

The idea of "living hope" occupies Peter's mind throughout this section of the letter. And how do we claim that living hope? By focusing on the Lord Jesus Christ and by trusting in "the living and abiding word of God." Living hope requires faith in the living Lord and His Word.

The grass withers and dies, flowers bloom and die, but the Word of God "abides forever."

That's a great image, isn't it? Especially in a culture like ours where people are so grass conscious. Just look at the commercials that start appearing on television in late winter, and the countless "garden centers" devoted to our yards and gardens that you can find across the country. We know what happens when we neglect our grass or our gardens—but the truth is, they will eventually wither and die anyway.

There is nothing tangible on this earth that is inspired but the Word of God, this book that holds God's counsel. It doesn't tell us about the truth; it *is* truth. It doesn't merely contain words about God; it *is* the Word of God. We don't have to try real hard to make it relevant; it *is* relevant. Don't neglect it. You can neglect your grass. You can neglect your garden. But you dare not neglect the Word of God! It is the foundation of a stable life. It feeds faith. It's like fuel in the tank. Don't wait till Sunday to see what the Scripture teaches.

We have a living hope, and Peter's words in this section tell us how to claim it—by faith in our Lord Himself and by faith in what He has written, His Word.

The Pilgrim Life and How to Live It

As Christians we live in a world that is not our home. We looked at this, in depth, in chapter 11. We live as pilgrims on a journey in another land. If you want to know how to live the life of an alien, a stranger, a pilgrim, Peter's letter will help.

We claim our living hope through faith, and we live the pilgrim life by submission. In fact, if there is one theme that stretches through this central section of Peter's letter, it is submission. We need to be reminded of it again and again and again because we are an independent lot. Especially here in America, we are so ornery and stubborn. It's come to be known as "the American way." It's the reason many sailed the Atlantic and later came west. It's built into our independent spirit to make it on our own, to decide for ourselves, to prove, if only to ourselves, we can do it! That may be the explorer's life or the pioneer's life . . . but it's not the pilgrim life. The pilgrim life is a life of submission, which works directly against our nature.

But where? When? To whom do we submit? As we saw earlier, Peter spells it out.

In government and civilian affairs. "Submit yourselves for the Lord's sake to every human institution, whether to a king . . . or to governors . . ." (1 Pet. 2:13–14). If you have a president, submit to the president. In Peter's case, they had an emperor. And what a monster he was. Nero. Yet Peter said, "Don't fight the system. Submit."

At work. "Servants, be submissive to your masters" (1 Pet. 2:18). My, that cuts cross-grain in our day of unions and strikes and lawsuits and stubborn determination to have it our own way. Peter says, in effect, "Submit to your boss or quit!"

Submit! Make the thing work or get out. Submit.

At home. "In the same way, you wives, be submissive to your own husbands." And in order for that to work, "You husbands likewise, live with your wives in an understanding way" (1 Pet. 3:1, 7). "Likewise" is a rope-like word that wraps itself around this chapter and part of the previous one, sustaining the thought of submission.

I remember talking with a young couple a few years ago when I observed a sterling example of this. He was a dentist in his mid- to late thirties, and he and his wife had come to a meeting where they found themselves rethinking their life plans for the future. Afterward, he said to me, "I'm thinking seriously about going into the ministry."

I said, "Really? Have you had any training at all?"

He said, "No, not formally. I'd have to go back to school. I'd like to have your suggestion about seminary and what you think would be best for me."

So we talked for a few minutes, and I concluded with this counsel. "If you are happy doing what you're doing, don't just jump into ministry because it seems fascinating or appealing to you."

The next day he came to me and said, "Your words really made me think throughout the night. To tell you the truth, I am very fulfilled in dentistry, and I find a lot of satisfaction in it."

His wife was standing beside him, and I turned to her and said, "And how do you feel about this?" She had a terrific answer. She said, "You know, Chuck, when I married this man I really gave myself to this marriage. And I determined that this man who is walking with God was worth working alongside of, no matter what and no matter where. However God leads him, I'm a part of that plan."

"How do you feel about going into ministry?" I asked.

"If he's convinced, I'm convinced," she said.

Now I know this woman. She's no dummy. She's no vanilla shadow, standing there sighing, "Whatever he wants is fine with me." She's not a beaten-down, doormat kind of wife. That's not the kind of woman she is, and that's not the kind of woman Peter is talking about here. There's vitality and zeal and strength of soul in her life. And she can say, "I am confident God is working in my husband. I wouldn't think of going some other direction." A harmonious blend of give and take is what Peter has in mind here.

In the church. "To sum up, let all be harmonious, sympathetic, brotherly, kindhearted, and humble in spirit; not returning evil for evil, or insult for insult, but giving a blessing instead; for you were called for the very purpose that you might inherit a blessing" (1 Pet. 3:8–9). Now isn't there a lot of submission at work there?

And a few verses later (3:22) we see that even the angels, the authorities, and the powers are subjected to Him. Just picture those magnificent angelic creatures bowing in submission to the risen Christ.

My suggestion on the heels of all this? Work on a submissive spirit. Don't wait for the media to encourage you to do this... it'll never happen. Ask God, if necessary, to break the sinews of your will so that you become a person who is cooperative, submissive, harmonious, sympathetic, brotherly or sisterly, kindhearted in every area of this pilgrim life.

Remember, ultimately we are not submitting to human authority but to divine authority. God will never mistreat us. Bowing before Him is the best position to take when we want to communicate obedience.

The Fiery Trial and How to Endure It

No matter how fiery the trial, the main thing is that you and I remember the temperature is ultimately regulated by God's sovereignty (see 1 Pet. 4:12–19). It's also important to understand that we don't suffer our trials in isolation; we are part of a flock that is lovingly tended by faithful shepherds (see 1 Pet. 5:1–5). Finally, we need to know that no matter how formidable our adversary, the power of God is available to help us endure (see 5:6–11).

And how do we endure the fiery trials that engulf us? By cooperation. We need to cooperate with God by trusting Him—with the leaders of the church by submitting to them, and with faith by standing firm and resisting the assault of the devil.

As you struggle with fiery trials, call to mind the sovereignty of God. Nothing touches you that hasn't come through the sovereign hand and the wise plan of God. It must all pass through His fingers before it reaches you. Ultimately He is in control.

As you endure the fiery trial, be in touch with and faithful to the flock of God.

And through it all, rely on the power of God. As we learned in the previous chapter, we must rely on that.

Four Lasting Lessons/Secrets of Life

We have finished his letter . . . but the ink from Peter's pen leaves an indelible impression on our lives. Along with everything else he tells and teaches us, I want to mention four lasting lessons, four secrets of life, that stand out in bold relief. All of these give us hope beyond our misery.

First, when our faith is weak, joy strengthens us.

In this you greatly rejoice, even though now for a little while, if necessary, you have been distressed by various trials, that the proof of your faith, being more precious than gold which is perishable, even though tested by fire, may be found to result in praise and glory and honor at the revelation of Jesus Christ; and though you have not seen Him, you love Him, and though you do not see Him now, but believe in Him, you greatly rejoice with joy inexpressible and full of glory. (1 Pet. 1:6–8)

Beloved, do not be surprised at the fiery ordeal among you, which comes upon you for your testing, as though some strange thing were happening to you; but to the degree that you share the sufferings of Christ, keep on rejoicing; so that also at the revelation of His glory, you may rejoice with exultation. (1 Pet. 4:12–13)

No matter how dark the clouds, the sun will eventually pierce the darkness and dispel it; no matter how heavy the rain, the sun will ultimately prevail to hang a rainbow in the sky. Joy will chase away the clouds hovering over our faith and prevail over the disheartening trials that drench our lives. In this regard I am often reminded of the promise from the Psalms.

Weeping may last for the night,
But a shout of joy comes in the morning. (Ps. 30:5)

Second, when our good is mistreated, endurance stabilizes us.

For this finds favor, if for the sake of conscience toward God a man bears up under sorrows when suffering unjustly. For what credit is there if, when you sin and are harshly treated, you endure it with patience? But if when you do what is right and suffer for it you patiently endure it, this finds favor with God. (1 Pet. 2:19–20)

The word *endure* in verse 20 means "to bear up under a load," as a donkey bears up under the load its owner has stacked high on its back. This patient bearing of life's cumbersome loads is made possible by love, made steadfast by hope, and made easier by example.

When we suffer, even though we have done what is right, there is something about endurance that stabilizes us. When our good is mistreated, endurance stabilizes us.

My hope for every one who reads these pages is that you will learn how to endure. Picture yourself as that little burro, abiding under the heavy load piled upon its back. Such quiet and confident endurance stabilizes us.

Third, when our confidence is shaken, love supports us.

Above all, keep fervent in your love for one another, because love covers a multitude of sins. (1 Pet. 4:8)

Love is the pillar of support when our world comes crumbling down around us. That's why, when warning about the end times, Peter puts love on the top of the survival checklist.

Fourth, when our adversary attacks, resistance shields us.

Be of sober spirit, be on the alert. Your adversary, the devil, prowls about like a roaring lion, seeking someone to devour. But resist him, firm in your faith, knowing that the same experiences of suffering are being accomplished by your brethren who are in the world. (1 Pet. 5:8–9)

When Satan stalks us like a roaring lion, we're not instructed to freeze, to hide, or to tuck tail and run. We're told to resist. And that

resistance forms a shield to protect us from our adversary's preda-
tory claws.

What Really Counts

And so we reach the end of Peter's letter that has endured the centuries . . . and the end of my book that may not endure to the end of
this century, less than five years from now. But that is as it should be.
God's Word will never fade away, though human works are quickly
erased by the sands of time.

My concern is not about how long these pages remain in print but
how soon you will put these principles to use in your life. That's
what really counts in the long run. That's the important issue. Frankly, that's why the old fisherman wrote his letter in the first place. To
help us hope again.

Hope to go on, even though we're scattered aliens.

Hope to grow up, even though we, like Peter, have failed and
fallen.

Hope to endure, even though life hurts.

Hope to believe, even though dreams fade.

A Prayer for Hope Beyond Misery

*Our Father, we thank You for sustaining us in Your grace
through times that absolutely defy explanation, times of
suffering and misery, times of mistreatment and
disappointment.*

*Thank You for being a Friend who is closer than a brother,
for meaning more to us than a mother or a father. Thank You
for Your mercy that takes us from week to week through a life
that isn't easy, dealing with people who aren't always loving*

and encountering battles that leave us exhausted. Thank You for strength that has come from a little letter written by an old fisherman who understood life in all its dimensions: failure and disappointment and victory and joy and intimacy. We commit to You, our Father, the truth of what we have read. Help us to find hope again as a result of putting these truths into practice. In the lovely and gracious name of Jesus Christ I pray.

AMEN

Notes

CHAPTER 1   HOPE BEYOND FAILURE

1   Eugene H. Peterson, *The Message: The New Testament in Contemporary English* (Colorado Springs, Colo.: Navpress, 1993), 486.

CHAPTER 2   HOPE BEYOND SUFFERING

1   Warren W. Wiersbe, *Be Hopeful* (Wheaton, Ill.: SP Publications, Victor Books, 1982), 11.
2   Julie Ackerman Link, "Fully Involved in the Flame," *Seasons: A Journal for the Women of Calvary Church*, Spring 1996, 1. © Calvary Church, Grand Rapids, Michigan. Used by permission.

CHAPTER 3   HOPE BEYOND TEMPTATION

1   Kenneth S. Wuest, *In These Last Days*, vol. 4 in *Wuest's Word Studies from the Greek New Testament* (Grand Rapids, Mich.: Eerdmans, 1966), 125–26.
2   Randy Alcorn, "Consequences of a Moral Tumble," *Leadership* magazine, Winter 1988, 46.
3   Stuart Briscoe, *Spiritual Stamina* (Portland, Oreg.: Multnomah Press, 1988), 133.

CHAPTER 4   HOPE BEYOND DIVISION

1 Kenneth S. Wuest, *First Peter: In the Greek New Testament* (Grand Rapids, Mich.: Eerdmans, 1956), 48.

2 Edward Gordon Selwyn, *The First Epistle of St. Peter*, 2d ed. (London, England: Macmillan Press, 1974), 153.

CHAPTER 5   HOPE BEYOND GUILT

1 Quoted in *Dear Lord*, comp. Bill Adler (Nashville: Thomas Nelson, 1982).

2 Quoted in *More Children's Letters to God*, comp. Eric Marshall and Stuart Hample (New York: Simon and Schuster, 1967).

3 Quoted in William Barclay, *The Letters of James and Peter*, rev. ed., The Daily Study Bible Series (Philadelphia, Pa.: Westminster Press, 1976), 203.

4 Wiersbe, *Be Hopeful*, 57.

CHAPTER 6   HOPE BEYOND UNFAIRNESS

1 Barclay, *The Letters of James and Peter*, 210–11.

2 J. H. Jowett, *The Epistles of St. Peter*, 2d ed. (London: Hodder and Stoughton, n.d.), 92.

CHAPTER 7   HOPE BEYOND "I DO"

1 Joseph C. Aldrich, *Secrets to Inner Beauty* (Santa Ana, Calif.: Vision House, 1977), 87–88.

2 Philip Yancey, *I Was Just Wondering* (Grand Rapids, Mich.: Eerdmans, 1989), 174–75.

3 Barclay, *The Letters of James and Peter*, 218.

4 Edwin A. Blum, "1 Peter" in *The Expositor's Bible Commentary*, vol. 12, ed. Frank E. Gaebelein (Grand Rapids, Mich.: Zondervan, 1981), 237.

5 *Los Angeles Times*, 23 June 1988.

6 Gary Smalley and John Trent, *The Gift of Honor* (Nashville: Thomas Nelson, 1987), 23, 25–26.

CHAPTER 8   HOPE BEYOND IMMATURITY

1   Robert A. Wilson, ed., *Character Above All* (New York: Simon and Schuster, 1995), 219–21.

2   Oswald Chambers, *My Utmost for His Highest*, special updated edition, ed. James Reimann (Grand Rapids, Mich.: Discovery House, 1995), November 16, n.p.

3   Alvin Goeser quoted in *Quote-Unquote*, comp. Lloyd Cory (Wheaton, Ill.: SP Publications, Victor Books, 1977), 200.

4   Cited in Jon Johnston, "Growing Me-ism and Materialism," *Christianity Today*, 17 January 1986, 16-I.

CHAPTER 9   HOPE BEYOND BITTERNESS

1   Retold from "Toads and Diamonds," *The Riverside Anthology of Children's Literature*, 6th ed. (Boston: Houghton Mifflin, 1985), 291–93.

2   Malcolm Muggeridge, *Twentieth-Century Testimony*, (Nashville: Thomas Nelson, 1988), 18–19.

3   Barclay, *The Letters of James and Peter*, 230–31.

CHAPTER 11   HOPE BEYOND THE CULTURE

1   J.R. Baxter, Jr., "This World Is Not My Home," © 1946. Stamps-Baxter Music. All rights reserved. Used by permission of Benson Music Group, Inc..

2   Quotes from Georgia Harbison, "Lower East Side Story," *Time*, 4 March 1996, 71.

3   Wuest, *First Peter: In the Greek New Testament*, 110.

4   D. Martyn Lloyd-Jones, *The Christian Warfare* (Grand Rapids, Mich.: Baker, 1976), 41.

5   John Hus, quoted in John Moffatt, *The General Epistles: James, Peter, and Judas* (London: Hodder and Stoughton, 1928), 147.

CHAPTER 12   HOPE BEYOND EXTREMISM

1   Wiersbe, *Be Hopeful*, 107.

2 Mahatma Gandhi quoted in Brennan Manning, *Lion and Lamb* (Old Tappan, N.J.: Revell, Chosen Books, 1986), 49.
3 Jowett, *The Epistles of St. Peter*, 166–67.
4 Ibid., 167.
5 Anne Ross Cousin, "The Sands of Time Are Sinking."

CHAPTER 13   HOPE BEYOND OUR TRIALS

1 C. S. Lewis, *The Problem of Pain* (New York: Macmillan, 1962), 106.
2 R. C. H. Lenski, *The Interpretation of the Epistles of St. Peter, St. John and St. Jude* (Columbus, Ohio: Wartburg Press, 1945), 213.
3 Andre Crouch, "Through It All," © 1971, by Manna Music Inc., 35255 Brooten Road, Pacific OR. 97135. International copyright secured. All rights reserved. Used by permission.
4 Lewis, *The Problem of Pain*, 107.
5 M. Craig Barnes, *When God Interrupts* (Downers Grove, Ill.: Inter-Varsity, 1996), 54.
6 Wiersbe, *Be Hopeful*, 115–16.

CHAPTER 14   HOPE BEYOND RELIGION

1 J. G. G. Norman, "Charles Haddon Spurgeon," in *The New International Dictionary of the Christian Church*, rev. ed., ed. J. D. Douglas (Grand Rapids, Mich.: Zondervan, 1978), 928.
2 C. H. Spurgeon, *Lectures to My Students* (Grand Rapids, Mich.: Zondervan, 1962), 7–8.
3 Source unknown.
4 Spurgeon, *Lectures*, 154.
5 Michael Silver, "White Tornado," *Sports Illustrated*, 3 June 1996, 71.

CHAPTER 15   HOPE BEYOND DISSATISFACTION

1 Jean Rosenbaum, quoted in *Quote-Unquote*, 315.

CHAPTER 16   HOPE BEYOND THE BATTLE

1 Philip Yancey, *Where Is God When It Hurts?* (Grand Rapids, Mich.: Zondervan, 1977), 22–23.

2   J. Dwight Pentecost, *Your Adversary the Devil* (Grand Rapids, Mich.: Zondervan, 1969), Introduction.

3   Wiersbe, *Be Hopeful*, 138.

4   Ibid.

5   Wuest, *First Peter: In the Greek New Testament*, 130.

6   C. S. Lewis, *The Screwtape Letters* (New York, N.Y.: Macmillan, 1961), 3.

CHAPTER 17   HOPE BEYOND MISERY

1   Dan Greenburg, *How to Make Yourself Miserable*, (New York: Random House, 1966), 1–2.

DR. CHARLES R. SWINDOLL is senior pastor of Stonebriar Community Church, chancellor of Dallas Theological Seminary, and the Bible teacher on the internationally syndicated radio program Insight for Living. He has written more than thirty best-selling books, such as *Strengthening Your Grip, Laugh Again, The Grace Awakening,* and the million-selling *Great Lives from God's Word* series. Chuck and his wife, Cynthia, live in Frisco, Texas.